THE STORY OF ALEXANDER GEORGE MILL
(1885–1969)

AND

ETHEL CLARA STARTE
(1880–1955)

D0875101

BANDOMBELE* AND MAMA BANDOMBELE OF THE BELGIAN CONGO:

THE STORY OF MY MISSIONARY UNCLE AND AUNT

To Nancy

With gratitude for your friendship over the years

In Christ,

10/31/14

John

BY
JOHN H. SINCLAIR
2014

(* "a tall, white man walking in the forest")

PREFACE

I have waited until my ninetieth year to finish and publish this biography of my revered aunt and uncle. Two decades have sped by since I wrote the basic text. I have now come to realize that in addition to the model of Christian service of my parents, my life and ministry have also been deeply affected by the life and work of this amazing missionary couple who gave their lives for the advancement of Christianity in Africa.

Across the past sixty years, I have been able to visit twenty countries on the African continent on three trips as a delegate to global church conferences which met there. On one of these memorable trips, Maxine and I were guests of a missionary nurse in the Cameroons, Ms. Maribel Taylor, and her African chofer, Eboko. We clocked over five hundred miles visiting mission hospitals and village clinics.

During our years in seminary, 1944–47, we had applied for overseas missionary service, indicating our preferred place of service as West Africa. As it turned out we were commissioned to serve in Venezuela. Five years of our work there was in a village among the descendants of slaves brought from West Africa in the 16th and 17th centuries. Yes, we can say that we have served in a certain sense "in Africa"!

Years later in 1977 I was able to visit the Lower Congo, but the political chaos in that period was such that I was never able to travel to the Upper Congo where Uncle Alex worked.

This book is written as a small down payment on the Church's immense debt of gratitude to God for the thousands of missionaries from many nations who have shared the Gospel by word and deed in the African continent across many centuries. I have placed in the Appendices a number of important articles, maps, charts, and bibliography which will help the reader understand some of the complexities in the history of colonialism and cultures which the early missionaries faced.

DEDICATORY

This book is dedicated to my beloved wife, Maxine, my partner and soul companion on our faith journey, and also to our five wonderful grandchildren: Charlotte, Ashley, Ian, Natalia and Gabriel, whose lives brighten our future.

TABLE OF CONTENTS

PART SIX

Included are some letters which reveal the concerns and struggles of her life as a child and young woman. The letter dated June, 1942 gives some indication that she may have been developing serious problems of mental health. This is the only letter which has survived from her adult years. I have attached her birth certificate from the Belgian Congo.

APPENDICES: ARTICLES, LETTERS, DOCUMENTS

A. The Baptist Missionary Society in the Belgian Congo. Some notes on early explorations and missionary endeavors; Leopold I and his exploitation of the native people; the first B.M.S. stations in the Lower and Upper Congo; the story of Salamu; and the atrocities in the Congo Free State.

B. "The Scramble for Africa": the historical context and legacy of colonialism, 1876–1907. A summary of this important book.

C. A statistical survey of the Christian community in Zaire, 1982

D. A genealogical chart of the Starte family by Michael Nurse (incomplete)

E. "Picture letters" written by Uncle Alec to the Sinclair nieces and nephew, 1927–1940.

F. Memorial resolution upon the death of Mrs. A. G. Mill,1956

G. Funeral message preached by Rev. John H. Sinclair at the memorial service for Rev. A. G. Mill, 1969

H. The Congo under King Leopold II and Joseph Mobuto: a brief summary of the book KING LEOPOLDO'S GHOST by Adam Horchschild; a list of BMS missionaries who served in the Congo, 1878–1926

I. Bibliography: books, journals, periodicals, magazines, pamphlets and correspondence

J. "Yalikina in the 1930s" and several articles by Rev. A.G. Mill and one by Ethel Mill

K. The Lingala New Testament: an appreciation by Rev. A. G. Mill; A page from a catechism in Lingala; two hymns in Lingala translated by Rev, Mill; A tribute to Pastor Abraham; Map of Upper Congo Areas, 1940; The tonal structure of the Kele language; African traditional literature,

L. An index of the photos and maps of the Upper Congo.

M. Application papers of Alexander George Mill for missionary service. (see also pp. 395–397)

N. Article "The Severed Hands"

O. Barbara Mary Mill (1920–1966)

P. Photos of Guy's Hospital, London

Q. "The Bard" by Rev. A. G. Mill

R. A historic letter from Rev. George Grenfell-1903

S. Government registration card of Rev. A. G. Mill, 1919

T. Government registration card of Rev. A. G. Mill, 1924

U. Article "Music for African worship" by Ephraim Amu

V. Letter from BMS and American Baptists asking clemency for "Prophet" Kimbangu

W. Song text by Ethel Mill; copy of will of A.G. Mill, 1939

THE MILL-STARTE FAMILY OF GLASGOW AND CAMBRIDGE

PART ONE

THE MILL-GOUDIE FAMILY OF GLASGOW: UNCLE ALEC'S SCOTTISH ROOTS

A. THE MILL-GOUDIE FAMILY OF GLASGOW
Uncle Alec's Scottish roots

A. The Mill Family and my Grandfather Frederick Stuart Mill

The home of the Mill family is in Clackmannshire, Scotland where the name is still common. They claimed to be related to the philosopher, John Stuart Mill, and more distantly to an early Protestant martyr, Walter Mill, of the XVI century Reformation.

James Mill and John Stuart Mill

"In the 1820s, British political thinker James Mill argued that women did not need the right to vote because others in their families—their fathers, brothers and husbands would look after their interests! But his son, John Stuart Mill, turned his father's argument on its head. This noted philosopher affirmed that asking men to represent women in their families is like asking industrialists to represent the financial interests of wage earners in their employ. Policymakers today who oppose the rights of women are the same benign daddies that were around in the time of James Mill. . ." (MINNEAPOLIS STAR-TRIBUNE, January 6, 1992)

My Grandfather Mill seemed to commune with the ideas of John Stuart Mill more than those of James Mill. Grandfather Frederick George Stuart Mill was a non-conformist, even a radical in his day. I do not know if there was any close family relationship between the philospher and my grandfather. I do know that my mother was nicknamed by her classmates at the Burnbank Training Home "Millie, the philosopher"! So much for the little we know about the Mill family before the birth of my grandfather in 1863.

My great-grandfather Alexander Mill was a hairdresser in Glasgow, having a high-class clientele on Buchanan Street. Of him we know little, for he had passed on before my mother and her brothers were born. Rumors have it that he was genteel to a fault and would dress and live above his income. . . that he spoke perfect English and even though he found it hard to make ends meet kept a 'good front'.

My grandfather Mill had three brothers: Lorimer, Gladstone and Alex and one sister Colina. Lorimer was the only son who survived to full maturity since the others died in early maturity with tuberculosis. Gladstone was a concert master in elocution and Alec a ship's captain. Lorimer became a successful businessman. The marriage certificate of Frederick Mill and Kate Goudie in 1883 listed my great-grandfather as a "perfume maker", not a hairdresser! My great-grandmother Mill died when my grandfather was two years old. Her name was Jane Laurie Valentine. Frederick George Stuart was reared by a housekeeper.

My grandfather, Frederick George Stuart Mill, was born in Glasgow on February 3, 1863 and died in Creston, British Columbia in February 14, 1923. He married my grandmother, Catherine Goudie, on May 1, 1883 in Glasgow. The marriage certificate states that Frederick Mill was an ironmonger's clerk and "Kate" Goudie was a domestic servant. He was 21 and Kate was 27, according to the marriage certificate, however according to their birth certificates, Frederick was only 20 and Kate was 29. Kate's father, John Goudie, was a block printer ("calico printer") married to Catherine Fairlie Goudie. The witnesses were William Ross and Barbara Goudie (her sister). The minister was Walter MacKenzie of Frederick Street United Presbyterian Church, Glasgow. The address of both Frederick and Kate was 138 West Graham Street, Glasgow at the time of marriage.

Their first child, Frederick Gladstone Stuart, was born on October 28, 1883 at 11 Palm Street, Glasgow; the second child, Alexander George, was born on July 22, 1885 at the same address; and Clara Anna, my mother, was born on June 7, 1887 at 26 Vernon Street, Maryhill, Glasgow.

GRANDFATHER MILL

My mother recalls in her TRANSPLANTED HEATHER (mss., 1949): "My father was handsome. . .six feet tall, slender, with dark eyes and a well-formed nose and coal-black hair when he was young. I fear my father's life was precarious and that he, like Topsy, just grew. Fortunately he followed the path of rectitude from his own volition. All his life he had to bolster his strength and only by good food and care did he escape serious chest troubles. When he was over forty he became a prey to active tuberculosis but he quite overcame it by rest and care.

"Father worked for over 30 years as bookkeeper and store manager in the firm of R. Murdoch and Company in Glasgow. No firm ever had a more faithful servant. But of worldly ambitions, father knew none. His tastes ran in reading and how he shared that with us! Our home was humble and our library small but father loved to gather us around him and read to us at nights. The Bible took first place and Pilgrim's Progress a close second and then the books which Mr. Dobie, a friend of the family, sent us for Christmas. It seems to me that there could be no joy like that. Even television seems pale before the unfolding of a good story on the pages of a good writer.

"Both my parents had a religious experience which caused them to start on a new life from which they never wavered. There was a revival in Glasgow led by Dr. Pentecost at St. George's Cross Tabernacle. Under God many people were lifted out of a mere formal religion into a vital experience with Christ. And as it happened, (shall I say?) that a neighbor, Mrs. McInnes by name a West Highland woman invited my parents to attend the meeting this night with her. Her own daughter kept care of me. That night the Lord met both father and mother and wrought a work of grace in their hearts. . .which issued in a new life for us too. My father never drank but on the way home that night he threw his pipe away never to see it again.

"The Bible became a living book to us. In later years he could use the Old as well as the New Testament with skill. I shall never forget once when I wouldn't go and fetch him his slippers (I was being good and listening to him read to us!). So one of brothers got the slippers. Father then said to me, quoting from 1st Samuel 15:22:

'To obey is better than sacrifice and to hearken than the fat of rams'.

Young as I was it stung me deeply. I seemed to sense its meaning.

"Father read widely too in both secular and religious history. I said of worldly ambitions he had none. This was a source of irritation between my business-like Mother and him. Father's ambitions were all in the realm of the spirit. He never saved a penny and his wages being very ordinary Mother found it hard to keep up the standard of living she sought for us.

"Father's natural refinement and intellectual tastes more or less separated him from others on his own social level. Of pride I think he had none. He was thoroughly democratic, hating all Kant and hypocrisy. Yet somehow he was happiest in his own company and lacked the ability to get close to the common person. He was endowed with little leadership ability. He was an extrovert and liked to argue. This desire arose, I think, from trying to enlist others in unpopular causes. He would deplore, for example, some of the unchristian practices between labor and capital. In those days the working man and his employer were worlds apart. Father saw the need for a social Gospel and for a clergy who would walk with the common man and for layman who lived the spirit of Christianity seven days in the week. Looking back now I see how right he was.

"In many ways Father was a lonely man partly his own fault. In his later years he broke from all organized church affiliation and for years spent his Sundays reading. But by and by he came back to regular church attendance and seemed to enjoy it more than ever. I think he regretted these years of absence. But he never became bitter towards life and was always generous and kind.

"He liked to sing hymns. After we were bedded he would come into the room and say 'Now children let's harmonize our thoughts'. This was done by singing and his favorite hymn was

'Heaven around is softer blue
Earth around is deeper green
Something lives in every hue
Christless eyes have never seen.
Birds with gladder songs oe'r flow
Earth with deeper beauties shine
Since I know as now I know
I am His and He is mine.'"

(From "Loved with Everlasting Love")

"How I thank God today for such a lullaby as that! Who will deny that this is much more healthful and happy way to bed children than to push them to bed after viewing 'a wild western' or something worse, without a thought of God.

"The Scottish Sabbath was generally accepted as a day of worship and rest. Labor was reduced to a minimum from the home to the factory. Great concerns employed just enough men to keep the furnaces going. The great industrial city of Glasgow in which we were reared was transformed over the weekend as the great smoke stacks ceased to billow out the black stuff.

"Our family attended at this time a little mission called the Faith Mission. We had to walk two miles to reach its doors (street car riding was taboo on Sunday for church people). So we all walked and what we would have missed if we hadn't. As we walked Father would say 'look back now' and there, in the far distance, we would see the Campsie Hills or Fells. These were only seen on Sundays and on a very clear Sunday we could see Ben Lomond. We three children always walked on in front and Father would always tell us how to walk healthfully.

"Our little mission furnished an outlet as well as an inlet for our spiritual lives. There was no minister but a businessman named George M. King, the moving spirit, and he was a Christian aristocrat. . .a true Christian gentleman of the first order. I remember also Miss Johnstone and others. A pale-faced lady sat behind the little harmonium which led us in singing and the text 'Behold the Lamb of God which taken away the sin of the world' was emblazoned on a red cloth in front of the instrument. It was a bethel to us.

"One of my earliest recollections was when I sat on Father's knee and he would give me 'beardy'. Also one day he asked me to put my hand into his pocket and lo and behold I felt a moving mass of fur: a live kitten!

"He loved to walk and often he would bring us home violets or primroses in his hat so he'd take off his hat and hand us the flowers. One day I told a lie about spilling ink. Then I confessed. Father, I remember, told me that all sins, including lies, were not wrong only because they hurt each other but that they were contrary to God's law for our happiness. So together he and I kneeled down for me to confess to God. This made a great and lasting impression on my heart and mind. Joy returned, and since then, many times I've had to confess but always the experience was the same . . . happiness and a freedom follows confession and forgiveness. This has always given me hope that little children can know themselves and God in a very real way.

"Visual education has not advanced far fifty years ago, but we occasionally saw stereopticon slides. We saw the Pilgrim's Progress and pictures from Africa. My brother Alex, who later become a missionary, said that that is where he got his first desire to be a missionary.

"One big family event was our annual 'holiday'. It consisted of two weeks at a country or coast town according to the conditions of the family pocketbook. The high spot was when the cab drove up to the door and we all ceremoniously filed out each carrying our respective boxes containing changes of clothing, etc. One of the boys got the privilege of sitting up beside the driver or 'cabby', who, with a crack of the whip started our steed on the direction of one of the large railroad terminals. There we boarded the train and sat back to enjoy what seemed an interminable ride of about 40 or 50 miles. Some years in true Scottish climate weather it would rain every day during the two weeks. Walking and gathering berries and fishing provided our diversions and father always enhanced the vicinity by telling us lore and traditions of which every vicinity in Scotland has it's share.

"Glasgow still had its horse-drawn trams. Alex and I ran home from school (1890's) beside these trams for a full month one Christmas season in order to surprise our parents with a small gift purchased from the savings on tram fares."

Clara, Alex and John

"Alex and my future husband, John Peat Sinclair, met each other when Alex was 14 and John was 12. Their friendship was always a close one, so it was not surprising that John fell in love with Alex's little sister!

"In those days most young people's schooling ended around twelve or thirteen years of age. Higher education was reserved for the few. Both Alex and John worked hard all day and attended evening classes. John began as a messenger boy of the Western Union when he was twelve years of age in 1899. One of the family souvenirs is John's identification card as a messenger during the Glasgow Exposition of 1899."

Alex worked as an apprentice to an architect for seven years and studied night classes. (1900–1907). The religious life of the Mill family developed further around 1898–1899 when the children began to attend the Kelvinside Baptist Church. Grandfather and Grandmother Mill were United Presbyterians but they felt it wise to allow the children to attend the church where they had become very attached. The congregation was served by Rev. A.W. Bean who later went to New Zealand and Rev. R. A. Anderton. Both pastor and a Miss Mathison took a great interest in the young people of the congregation. Mother continues her story,

"When only about 13 years of age my brother Alex and I would begin the day with an early morning prayer service and at least subsequent 'diets' later during each Sunday. Being so young we occasionally got the giggles. I can remember the remorse I felt when Miss Graham, the organist chided me afterwards.

"Deep and lasting were the impressions made upon during those adolescent years and the friendships formed in that little Kelvinside Baptist Church. The kindly, intelligent and strong faces of many of them are in-delibly imprinted in my mind. We remember the Saturday night open-air meetings and the tea meetings which followed. Fair weather or foul we three never missed and many a night took home drunkards whom we had managed to bring to the meeting. We did everything but sleep in the church especially on Sundays.

"My Brother Alex (whom I have always deeply loved) led the Christian Endeavor of youngsters once a week. Many a night he was pestered with hoodlums throwing rocks at the hall door and occasionally had to call the police. But he was never discouraged. During those formative years our minister, the Reverend Anderton and Miss Matteson poured into our hearts the needs of the unevangelized countries of the world. They were tireless in giving us missionary information and inspiration. The seed fell on good ground. Alex had always wanted to give his life to Africa after seeing pictures by Dr. Harry Guiness of the Congo Bololo Mission. So it was not strange that when he was twenty-one years old and after he had finished his apprenticeship as an architect he entered the well-known "Pastor's College" (Spurgeon's College) in London. Now I must go back. . ."

THE GOUDIE FAMILY

My mother recounts the sudden death of her mother in 1904:

"On June 24, 1904 my dear Mother died suddenly at the age of fifty. The death certificate reads "apoplexy" and that the attack lasted only six hours. We lived then at 27 Byres Road, Partick. I was seventeen, Alex was nineteen and Gladstone was twenty-one. Father was only forty-one years of age. My mother's death left a void in my life and caused a new seriousness to come upon me. Mother was buried in the Craigton Cemetery in Glasgow. At this time I left my job in a plumber's office and kept house for a few years for my Father, Gladstone and Alex. One year later Gladstone married Jean Young of Newton Mearns (near Glasgow) and it proved to be a most happy union. Then Brother Alex went to London to college in 1907. I took a position for several years, along with my housekeeping. By 1910 I was engaged to John and I wanted to take some nursing training before going out to Canada.

"It was a hard decision to make (in 1910) but I left Father and entered Burnbank Training Home in Glasgow for two years. Father was quite willing that I should and I could be with him each Saturday afternoon and would often meet him down city during his forenoon hour off. He was always so glad to see me and we always kissed on leaving (not too common a sight in Scotland). I had a neighbor keep the house clean and have the supper ready each night and then Gladstone and Jean lived quite near and kept an eye on his needs."

Burnbank Lady Missionary Training School

"No words could fully express all that these two years of residence meant to me. It was a small college with rather high tuition fees but Miss Forrester-Patton (of the thread and wool industries of Scotland) gave me, along with many others of her charitable deeds, a liberal scholarship. At Burnbank half of our studies were Bible and half were medical with emphasis on tropical diseases which the graduates might encounter in their missionary career. Names never to be forgotten for their character and influence were Miss Clara M. Williams, our Welsh superintendent, and Miss M. Maxwell, the housekeeper who still remains my ideal. Fast friendships and lasting impressions remain with me to this day as I remember dear 'Burnbank'. I was a fair student and loved the work."

Recently I researched the origins of the Ladies' Missionary Training Home which was founded by Miss Catherine Forrester-Paton, a member of a well-known cotton spinning family ("Patons and Baldwins" is still a well-known trade name in Britain). Miss Forrester-Paton belonged to Alloa and lived in a house called Mars' Hill. She was a member of the United Presbyterian Church and a great temperance worker. She actually bought a pub in Alloa to convert it into a teashop. She was zealous for many good works of essentially practical kinds. Mars' Hill also housed a kind of missionary museum. She opened this home for lady missionaries on furlough in 1890 on the grounds that single women had no families and no place to go on return from the mission field.

Burnbank Training School was the fruit of Miss Forrester-Paton's own initiative, supported by her energy and the resources of the family. The 1911–12 report which is in my possession indicates that the Burnbank Gardens property was maintained by her brother, the cotton spinner. He probably had purchased it to form the training home when it moved to Glasgow. According to my informants (the Reverend Colin Forrester-Paton of Peebles, a former missionary to Ghana, and Mrs. Isobel Lusk of Dunblane, the great-nephew and great-niece of Miss Catherine), the Home did not survive World War I. At least it closed before their childhood memories began.

Miss Catherine and her brother died in 1914 and 1915 (six months apart) according to a letter to my mother from a Burnbank classmate in year 1914. (The letter was sent from "The Dale, Bousall, Attn: Mr. Matlock," but the final page of the letter with the signature is missing). The informants neither remember the Home itself, but recalled that the last superintendent of the Home continued to live at Mars' Hill during their childhood as housekeeper for Miss Catherine's legatee.

"When I finished at Burnbank, I stayed home during the year 1912–13. John had promised me that I could come out in the summer of 1913 to be married in Winnipeg. He would get a summer charge in June, 1913 after his graduation and ordination that month. So I studied more piano without much success and gave much time to the churchwork at the Kelvinside Baptist Church. I also enjoyed many visits with dear Aunt Barbara and brother Gladstone and Jean and their two little children. A very tender affection existed between my Father and me. His kindness to me was very great and our fellowship was sweet. So, for both of us, it was a hard parting when I sailed from Glasgow's wharf on board the steamship 'Grampion' on June 20, 1913, en route to Canada.

GRANDFATHER MILL COMES TO CANADA

"However five years later, just before the close of World War I, my Father came out to Canada and stayed with us for sometime in Cranbrook, B.C. This was in the summer of 1918. He loved to take Martha out on her daily walk when she was tiny and I found a great help in having him stay with us.

"When we left for the States (Dad had already gone ahead), my Father came up from a little town to which he had moved and where he enjoyed keeping chickens, to help me move. Together Father and I and the four little girls traveled together on the train south to Yak, B.C., and I said goodbye to him there little thinking it would be the last time I would ever see him. This was in September, 1920. By the time we moved to New Mexico in 1922, my father had found a nice home in the lovely town of Creston, B.C., where he stayed until his death in February, 1923 at the age of sixty years and where he is buried. (My sister Clara and I have both tried to locate his grave in Creston, but have thus far been unsuccessful.)

"When the news came of Father's critical illness I was in bed sick and Edith was yet only one year old. So Father had died and was buried before I was up. For this I do not grieve for Father ever taught us that the body was of no value and he had no desire ever to visit grave yards. But my great consolation was to know that he was now beyond the reach of the ravages of time and had safely crossed to 'the other side' from whence no traveler would return. I was consoled when the banker of the little town wrote saying how respected and esteemed my father had been and said that if Father's passing was attended by so many as at his (my father's funeral) he would be very satisfied.

"My father would seek no eulogy. My tribute to his life, his guiding hand in spiritual things and his international mind is that among his closest friends was a Polish Jew (Simon Salonamer) and a Dane. Simon lived with Grandfather Mill and Clara for several years. Mother was irked at times because he did not get a job. She had to cook his meals and wash his clothes. When she complained to her father, he replied, 'Clara, we must be kind to the Jews.'"

Grandfather Mill had been encouraged to come to Canada from 1914–1918 since the correspondence between Alex and Clara indicate that he was very lonesome. John and Maggie Goudie wrote in 1914 that Grandfather Mill had a housekeeper to come in to tidy up the place, but it was not a happy arrangement. But he finally did travel to British Colombia in September, 1918. He crossed by ship to New York City, took the train to Winnipeg and on to Cranbrook, B.C. He evidently did manual labor picking fruit and keeping some chickens to support himself. He wrote to Clara on October 2 and again on October 22, 1922 about his life: "...I have been pretty busy of late but am keeping extra well ...We are having an unusual fall thro' the day and the sun is very hot and only the mornings are cold. We have had no snow but only rain. You seem to have got into a wonderful land. I will be glad to hear how your health takes it. I am keeping very well. This fine fall has given me a lot of work. We had a big crop of apples and potatoes, etc...As long as the weather keeps fine I have lots of jobs to do to keep busy. But if the frost comes this will set me idle as most of the work is on the soil ...I hope you will come to visit me next year as John said. If you had a servant girl you might bring all the children and meet Alex here. Of course if John could come all the better you would not need a servant!" (It seems that Grandfather Mill was eagerly looking forward to the visit of Alex, Ethel and Barbara in mid-1923. However he died on February 14, 1923 in Creston, B.C.) He had written to Alex on January 8, 1923: "You say I have not to put myself about your coming. I may tell you that everything I do this year is in view of your visit. I am keeping exceedingly well. The thought of your coming is lifting me out of myself...".

GRANDMOTHER "KATE" AND HER TWO SISTERS

My grandmother Catherine Goudie, known as "Kate", born in 1854, had two sisters: Barbara who never married (born 1842) and Margaret (born 1844). These three daughters were born to John Goudie and Margaret ("Maggie") Fairlie Goudie. According to the Goudie family Bible which I have in my possession, John Goudie was born in Glasgow in 1815, lived in Dumbartonshire (1838–40), Perth (1840–53) and Glasgow (1853–1900 ?). My great-grandmother Margaret Fairlie Goudie was born in 1820 and had passed away before 1904 the year my grandmother Mill died. They were members of the United Presbyterian Church. Their letter of transfer of member from the congregation in Perth to the congregation in Glasgow is attached to the inside cover of the Goudie family Bible. How I wish that I knew more about my Grandmother "Kate"!

The Kyle and Cruden Relatives

Margaret Goudie married John Kyle in 1863 (?) and had two sons: John Kyle (9-28-1864) and James Kyle (4-26-1867). These cousins of my mother were evidently not the best behaved young men. She referred to them as she was growing up in the 1890's as "unruly boys". My mother knew no other cousins, except "Cousin Lizzie" Cruden and much later in life a granddaughter of John Kyle (son), Audrey Chapman Turner who settled in Gloucester, England. Audrey is the daughter of Jeannie Kyle (born 1887).

Cousin Lizzie Cruden Boyle

John Kyle (the father) evidently died around 1867–68 and Margaret re-married John Cruden sometime in 1870. From that second union there was one daughter, Margaret Cruden, born August 22, 1871. "Cousin Lizzie", as we knew her, lived to a ripe age and died in Pawtucket, Rhode Island in 1955. She was a favorite cousin of my mother's. She married John Boyle and moved to the U.S.A. so my parents visited her several times. Her son, Colin, brought his mother to visit us in Pennsylvania in 1953.

Auntie Barbara Goudie

A word about Barbara Goudie, known to us by reference as "Auntie Barbara". She never married and was a devoted "Covenanter", a member of the original Secession Church which opposed, to death, the imposition of the Anglican rites on the Scottish Church. Mother told us that Auntie Barbara faithfully decorated the graves of the Covenanter martyrs. She also questioned her nephews, John and James, if they had gone to church and what the sermon was about. The story goes that one always had the same stock answer to the question about the sermon theme: "Peter and the Cock"! We do not have a record of when she died. It was probably around 1915 since Alex wrote to Clara on April 26, 1915: "As for Auntie, I understand that 'life' has really left her though she still keeps existing in a semi-intelligent senility." On May 19: "So Auntie is still in the land of the Living and getting her bread and water still. I wish she could get a little luxury besides. She deserves it ever for her kindness to us when children. . ."

Auntie Barbara was certainly one of the "role models" for Clara and Alex. She seemed to take the place of their mother whom they lost when they were 17 and 19 years of age.

The Mill-Goudie relatives of Glasgow were lower, middle class worker families, imbued with disciplined lives, religious commitment and egalitarian attitudes. They were typically "Glaswegians" of their day.

Note: In July, 2002 I was able to locate the grave of my grandmother, Catherine Goudie Mill, and her sister, Barbara Goudie, in the Craigton Cemetery in Glasgow. They are buried in an unmarked plot identified as Section U, Lair 95.

B. THE KELVINSIDE
NEIGHBORHOOD OF MARYHILL
(GLASGOW)

Along the north bank of the Kelvin River lies a working-class housing area known as "Kelvinside". The neighborhood lies largely between Kelvin Drive on the north bank of the Kelvin River over to the bridge on Great Western Road. On the north and east is Maryhill Road. Just to the south of the Kelvin River is the lovely Botanic Gardens, a gem of Glaswegian culture and charm.

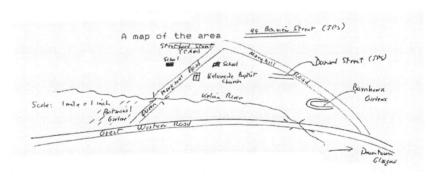

The names of the streets around my mother's home are: Shakespeare, Hotspur, Hathaway and Stratford, where she grew up at "92". My father's family live at 42 Dunard Street about eight blocks away. Both Clara Mill and John Sinclair grew up within a mile of each other and a short fifteen minute walk to the Kelvinside Baptist Church on Queen Margaret's Road.

Glasgow in the 1890's (1)

Between 1861 and World War I, the city of Glasgow and its satellite industrial towns grew apace, though more slowly than in the first half of the century. Glasgow's population tripled from 395,503 in 1861 to 1,034,174 in 1921. All the major industries grew. New iron and

15

steel works were built. The period was the heyday of the shipbuilding industry. The population attracted by the massive development of factories was housed in rapidly built tenements laid out in the grid form across the flat farmlands north and south of the Clyde River. During this period, the large, mainly industrial working-class communities of Clydebank, Partrick, Maryhill and others emerged around its industry. Kelvinidee and Cathcart meanwhile developed around squares of parklands and higher housing for Glasgow's managerial, professional and clerical workers.

Although the pace of growth quickened, so too popular interest in Christianity. Evangelical Non-conformity was at its height in England and Wales and its influence spread north of the border. There was vigorous mass evangelism by the Americans Moody and Sankey. Congregationalism grew and the related Evangelical Union built twelve churches between 1870 and 1914. Similarly a combination of a surge of population with a quickening of faith made this an era of Baptist advance.

Baptist growth in Glasgow

Twenty-five churches or missions were formed in this period and five were relocated. Baptist membership in Glasgow, estimated at around 1,000 in 1961, had risen to 6,241 in 1921, a rate of growth well beyond that of the population. The strength of the Baptist Church is its ability to develop gradually from an informal and independent association of believers living in a particular district. The new missions were not deliberate offshoots which grew out of inner dissent, but fed by members, at times leaving established churches, to help pioneer new work.

The Kelvinside Baptist Church did not enjoy the same kind of growth as nearby Hillhead Baptist, Adelaide Park Baptist and Cambridge Street Baptist. But by 1908, Kelvinside had 108 members, but declined in the mid-century and was closed in 1982. It had been organized in 1882. It was too close to the vigorous Hillhead Baptist which grew rapidly. The historical development of churches in inner city areas had left too many central churches and Kelvinside was only one of several churches closed between 1952 and 1982. The only records left in 1982 were two cash books and a list of members since 1926. So I had to turn to letters from my parents and Uncle Alex to recreate the life of this small mission congregation in a working-class section of Glasgow.

KELVINSIDE BAPTIST CHURCH SABBATH SCHOOL

On a mid-May Sunday afternoon in May, 1991 I went out walking to find this building which had been the spiritual home of my parents and Uncle Alex in their formative years. I had an address and the photo above with me. I had also been assured at the Hillhead Baptist Church earlier that day that the building was still standing, even though they told me it had been sold to a construction company. The pastor of the church also said, "You will not like what you see!"

I quickly found the church, next to the Shell Station on Queen Margaret's Road and Hotspur Street. The church hall was certainly a construction business but the church itself bore the name "Crosslands Bar and Lounge". I went in and sat down at a table near the bar. My gaze quickly fixed on the lovely arched windows and gabled ceiling; at the paneled walls and the rear balcony. I said to a man at the next table:

"Could this have been a church before the bar moved in?"

"Yeah, it could have been. But it's been a bar for over a year now."

I thanked him and walked out. Yes, this was the building where Mother, Dad and Uncle Alex spent so many hours of each week in their youth from 1897 to 1913. Here Alex and Clara were baptized in the same service in 1900 when Clara was 13 and Alex was 15.

Livingstone Sunday was annually observed in most of the churches of Scotland. This was the day designated in the church calendar on which the challenge was made to youth to dedicate themselves to foreign mission work. A decision card with the picture of David Livingstone was given out. The text read:

A WORTHY LIFE PURPOSE

David's Livingstone's: "I will place no value on anything I have or may possess, except in its relation to the Kingdom of Christ. If anything I have will advance that kingdom it shall be given up or kept, as by keeping or giving it I shall most promote the glory of Him to whom I owe all my hopes, both of time and eternity. May grace be given me to adhere to this.

And yours? (Write out a statement of your life purpose.)

On Livingstone Sunday, March 16, 1913, my father wrote his life purpose on the decision card which he kept on his desk for years. It read:

"Years ago through the reading of the life of David Livingstone as a boy, I resolved to devote my life to all that is highest and best. Once again when 'my hero' is being so specially referred to, I desire to record my still earnest desire to live to Christ. May this be in needy China! or in mystical India, or in materialistic Western Canada! My Master knows. John P. Sinclair. 16/3/13"

On the next day after visiting the former Kelvinside Baptist Chapel, I found myself perusing the BAPTIST RECORD at Baptist House, Glasgow to document my parents activities at Kelvinside. Here is what I found:

1908—"John P. Sinclair, 49 Benview Street, Firhill. President of the Senior Christian Endeavor Society. Five members of the society had joined the church during the last year."

1909—"Clara A. Mill, 92 Stratford Street, Secretary of the Senior C.E. Society. Thirty members were reported that year." (2)

Their names did not appear after 1910 since John had gone off to Canada to continue his theological studies and Clara was enrolled in the nearby Ladies' Missionary Training Home in Burbank Gardens. I did not go back to the records from 1900 on when Alec Mill was also active in the church. However Rev. Anderton wrote in his recommendation for Alex to the Baptist Missionary Society: "I have seen A.G. Mill engaged in Sunday School, Junior and Senior Christian Endeavor, open-air speaking, visitation and preaching. I can heartily recommend him as a good candidate for the Baptist Missionary Society." Alex wrote about his own "call" in his application papers:

"I formed my missionary call in my mind vaguely when a child of seven years of age through the influence of a missionary meeting and was expressed such as my desire at that time. When at the age of thirteen, my parents allowed me to take up architectural work as a possible experience for pioneer work as a missionary. When fourteen years of age, I formed my own definite resolve under strong inward convictions. The "purpose" was not arrived at by reasoning but by the combined feelings of anxiety for the fate of the Heathen and a desire to glorify Christ in their salvation." (3)

It was in this humble place of worship at the corner of Hotspur and Queen Margaret's Road that the Reverend A.W. Bean served as pastor to my parents and Uncle Alex from 1897 to 1902 and R.A. Edgar Anderton from 1902 to 1913. They were the Bible teachers and preachers who molded my parents' religious thought and set forth for them the standards for Christian discipleship. Mr. Bean and Mr. Anderton became household names for us as we grew up in California, New Mexico and Kansas.

Note

(1) Cf., BAPTISTS IN SCOTLAND, pp.169 ff.

(2) BAPTIST RECORD, Volumes for 1908 and 1909.

(3) Quoted from candidate application papers for Alexander George Mill, BMS Archives, Regent's Park College, Oxford.

David Livingstone: a model and inspiration for my parents

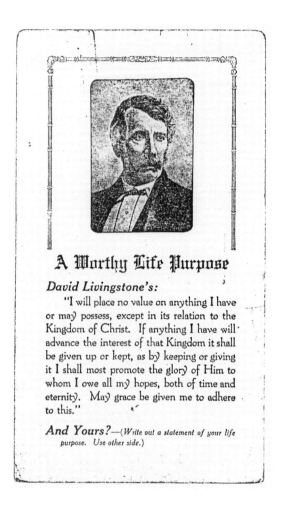

DAVID LIVINGSTONE was a model and inspiration for my parents, John Peat Sinclair and Clara Anna Mill Sinclair, and for Alexander G. Mill, her brother. My father kept this card he signed on "Livingstone Sunday" on March 16, 1913 before he left for Canada in May of that year. "Years ago thro' reading the life of David Livingstone as a boy, I resolved to devote my life to all that is highest and best. Once again when "my hero" is being so specially referred to, I desire to record my still earnest desire to live for Christ. May this be in needy China! Or in mystical India or in materialistic Western Canada! My Master knows. John P. Sinclair"

Uncle Alex, a close friend of my father, undoubtedly signed a similar card in which he also made the motto of Livingstone "A Worthy Life Purpose" his own.

PART TWO

UNCLE ALEC'S FORMATIVE YEARS (1885–1911)

C. UNCLE ALEC'S FORMATIVE YEARS (1885–1911)

1. The Kelvinside Baptist Sunday School and Church

The Mill family began to attend the Kelvinside Baptist Sunday School sometime in the late 1890's. When the children were smaller they went to a Gospel Mission, probably the St. George's Tabernacle in downtown Glasgow. They were definitely "non-conformist" church people, that is, they did not belong to the Church of Scotland. The parents of Catherine Mill (my grandmother), John and Margaret Goudie, were members of the United Secession Church (United Presbyterian ?). I know little of Grandfather Mill's religious background, but apparently he related to the United Presbyterian Church in which his wife had been reared. They were married by a minister of that small denomination in 1883.

"The little red hall" at the foot of Kelvinside Avenue at Queen Margaret's Road took on a semi-sacramental aura in the stories told to us by my parents. It was a neighbor Sunday School, established in 1882 as a mission outpost of a larger Baptist congregation nearby. Rev. R.A. Edgar Anderton was the pastor from 1902 to 1911 when he immigrated to Australia.

Alex spent long evenings and all day Sunday at the church. He led the Junior Christian Endeavor society, was secretary of the Senor Christian Endeavor, preached in their open air evangelistic meetings, taught Bible classes and carried out visitation of the sick.

2. His call to missionary service

He wrote in this application that the Congo was his objective and the work on the Upper Congo River at Yalemba was what he had in mind in particular. During the year before his appointment to the Congo (1910–11), the BMS considered sending him to India because they felt his health was not robust enough to stand the tropics. However he urged them to send him to the Congo after a minor health concern had been cleared up in mid-1911.

3. Alec, an architect's apprentice (1901–1908)

Alex had seven years as an apprentice in architecture. He took evening courses in Art, Building Construction, Engineering and Surveying. He obtained certificates in Building Construction, Engineering and General Drawing. The evidence of his mastery in these areas was seen in the buildings he designed and built during his years in the Congo. Free hand drawings embellished and illustrated his letters to his nephews and nieces across the years.

Mother, Dad and Alec: three close friends

Alec Mill, his younger sister Clara (my mother) and John Peat Sinclair (my father) were good friends from the year they met at the Kelvinside Baptist Church in 1899 when John's family moved from Wick to Glasgow. My mother would say that "John and I knew each other since we were thirteen" (1900). We have a brief note written to my father by Alex and Clara in April, 1903:

"Dear Peat; I got your letter o.k. . . We will have a Junior C.E. meeting tonight. . . I will not be able to meet you at the train (from Ratho) on Saturday. . . but I expect to see you on Sunday evening. . .C.A. Mill and A.G. Mill"

And on June 27, 1904, a somber letter was sent to John:

"Dear John; Mother is ill: apoplexy is the doctor's rather ominous diagnosis. . .and we are awaiting the return of consciousness to learn from him for which alternative we may hope. In life or death we have from our Saviour the full assurance for an anchor hope Hallelujah!. . .Mother died at 6:45 p.m. Yours, Alec." (Grandmother Catherine "Kate" Goudie Mill was 50 years of age when she died. Grandfather Frederick Mill was left a widower at age 41 with three children: Gladstone (21), Alex (19) and Clara (17).

On July 19, 1905, while the Mill family was on holiday another letter came to John from Alec:

"Dear John; I have had a letter from Clara but none from you as yet. But I suppose there is not much to say after her four pages of closely written information. . .Tell her she is a brick. (P.S. This is a compliment) . . .Yours ever, Alec."

It seems clear that by the time my mother and father were eighteen years of age they were "sweethearts". But John was to wait the more than seven years of Jacob's love to Rachael before Clara and John were married in 1913.

Alex's pastor, Mr. Anderton, wrote about him in a recommendation to the BMS:

"I should say that his mental power is above the average, education moderate and aptitude for learning good. . .He has a great command of his temper. . .I can heartily recommend him for missionary appointment."

4. Studies at Pastor's College ("Spurgeon College"), London (1907–1910)

Alec was accepted as a theological student at Pastor's College in the spring of 1907. He was then twenty-two years of age. He left by train in early August, 1907. He was traveling to London for the first time.

He sent his first letter to Clara on August 5, 1907:

"Dear Sister Clara: . . .I not only had a safe journey to London but a pleasant one. It commenced this way. Shortly after your faces, your handkerchiefs, the platform and the station of St. Enoch's had been left behind I was spoken to by a fellow traveler. . .I became aware that my companion was a brother. . .I was much strengthened by his company which came to an end at Dumfries. The country after this point developed into a most majestic cinematic through the carriage window. I caught the charm of the Yorkshire moors as we raced along. . .I have not been shocked with London yet, the people seem to be mild and industrious. . ."

He wrote vividly about his visit to Baptist House on Southampton Row which housed the Baptist Union, The Kingsgate Press and other Baptist organizations. "In the vestibule, somewhat dimly lighted stands the bronze station of C.H. Spurgeon with his finger raised in demonstration of some point of the doctrine of God I suppose. . .In the visitor's room are the beautiful leaded glass windows, the superb paintings of 'John the Baptist baptizing Jesus', 'St. Bartholomew's Massacre'. . .Above the large memorial fireplace there is a framed cast in terra-cotta of the scene in Pilgrim's Progress where Pilgrim becomes a Christian and receives the forgiveness of sins. . ." (AGM to CAM, September 12, 1907)

He visited Westminster Abbey for the first time and wrote about it in great detail:

". . .I have been twice inside this ancient and honorable heritage of our nation. . .I was never so honored in all my life to be within a step of the throne (this is all metaphor apart!). . .That old coronation chair, with its seat filled by the stone block. . . (Stone of Scone). The Abbey though often thronged with visitors and sightseers has always a larger congregation of the dead. . . While wandering among these dead stones one became alive to me as I read what it told of David Livingstone. I think you can sympathize with my feelings as I looked on it so I need not relate what they were. . ." (AGM to CAM, September 9, 1907)

About his studies, he wrote,

"I have now been to college two days but we have not really been in college since work is not commenced till next Tuesday. . . Here is a list of my textbooks:

INTRODUCTORY NEW TESTAMENT GREEK METHOD
SHORTER LATIN PRIMER
GREEK HISTORY
EUCLID
ELEMENTARY LOGIC. . . .

Outlines of Theology, Analogy and Sermons, Evidences of Christianity, On the Study of Words, English Grammar and English Lessons: How to write clearly: these are some of the classes I will take. . ."
He found lodgings with a Mrs. Saunders on 15 Warner Road, London, S.E. The next year (1907–08) he had a room at the college with two other students. He described the "collegiate" living and daily schedule in a letter to John.

John arrived in 1908 to begin his studies at Harley College in another section of London. Clara wrote to John faithfully as Alec said in a note to Clara: "John always writes. . .and he always keeps me posted on what happens back at the waxcloth covered table. . ." He was referring to the kitchen table at 92 Stratford Street, Glasgow, which was the center of daily conversation of the Mill household.

Alec usually did weekend preaching while at Spurgeon College. He was dead set against Sunday travel on public transportation, so he rode his bicycle. He writes in May, 1909:

"Dear Clara. . . .It was a very tiring weekend since my bicycle tires failed me as I was going to the church in the morning. I had to walk and wheel the machine for seven miles before taking the service. But all is well that ends well and I arrived home safe at 11 o'clock glad that I had been able to avoid train travel on: what has almost ceased to be in London: Sunday. . ."

"A Spy in the Promised Land": Alec makes
contacts for Dad on a visit to Harley House, London

My father had made his decision to study for the ministry in the winter of 1908. He was then twenty-one. Dad's initial inquiry was responded to quickly by Harley College sending him a schedule and arranging for him to conduct a service at Bell Street Church to get a report of his preaching ability. He asked Alex to visit Harley College and "spy out the land" for him. This was the report Alex sent to John on February 17, 1908:

"I arrived to find the whole college (consisting of about 50 men and 30 women students) gathered together in one of their halls, whose walls and balconies were decorated with crocodile hides and other emblems. I joined together with them in prayer for all the missionaries of the Regions Beyond Mission Union staff, led by that honored witness of Jesus,

Dr. Harry Guiness. . . .I talked to a student from Glasgow about the entrance examination. He said it was a very fair test for finding out if a man had had a good general education. From what I know of the examination and of you, I do not think you have anything to fear. . . .The chief factor in deciding your admission to the College would be the opinion formed by the Principal . . .

". . . Just at that point we had to stop our conversation, for up walked the Principal, Forbes Jackson himself. Kindly inquiring for my name and the purpose of my visit he reminded me that he had received your application, with the same 'Scotch sense' and 'modesty'. He expressed himself satisfactorily impressed. He then asked me to describe you and having received my account, he went on to speak of the interest he had in Mr. Anderton and the cause at Kelvinside. . ."

The reason is not clear why John chose to study at Harley College instead of Pastor's College where Alex was studying. It may be that John had made a decision to go out as a foreign missionary to China under the Regions Beyond Missionary Union and the approved place to study was Harley College. However Alex had also applied to the BMS for service in the Congo. It is also not clear why John left Harley College in the spring of 1910 and went out to Canada to continue his studies there. Was the Harley College course only for two years? Did he feel that he had made the wrong choice or that he did not stand a chance of an appointment with the RBMS? There is only one inkling in a comment that Alex makes in a letter to Clara on February 2, 1909:

"I know that this is a time of uncertainty in John's college career. . ."

Glimpses of London—1908

Alex visits Brockwell Park—"a park quite equal in cultivation to the Botanic Gardens of Glasgow. There is a great open space on the green hillside. There under the shade of the few spreading trees were little groups of men holding forth to little and big crowds of critical listeners on subjects of religion, socialism, landlordism and atheism. Each lecturer stood on a little platform with a small bookboard (lectern) in front. They all seemed intensely in earnest about their various subjects. . .The most badly attended crowd was a Gospel service being conducted by three old men. . .There was a great deal of shouting and stir which was unbecoming to God's Day. I am afraid there was very little listening for His Voice. . ." (March 8, 1908)

". . .the main cause of congestion in the London streets is the omnibus. The vehicle is almost as broad as it is long, as noisy as a coal bogie and as shaky as an earthquake. In all of which points it is a marked contrast to the fine electric trains with which it tries in vain to compete. . ."

"Besides the constantly grieving reminder of things Scotch which the 'whiskey advertisements' compel me to have, I often have vivid recollections of the old land of the sight of a kilted form in the street which makes me think of Gairbraid Street and the Barracks. . .but I am now on the street of a greater town. . ."

Alec and John: seminary pals in London from 1908 to 1910.

Alec wrote to John in September, 1908 that he would not be able to meet him at the Carron Wharf on the Thames River bank when John arrived to begin his studies at Harley College. Alex said he would be away preaching that day, so he gave him detailed instructions as to how to get to Harley Terrace, Bow, London East. John was bringing down Alex's bicycle with him on the boat, as well as his own trunk.

Alec and John seemed to see each nearly every weekend during the fall of 1908: Alex wrote to Clara: "I am afraid that I will have to come away before John gets back. I have not seen him this weekend on account of my being away preaching. . ." (December 14, 1908)

Alec told Clara about a pleasant day he and John spent at the British Museum looking at the manuscript collection. His finances were very limited: "Dear Clara: . . .The only respect in which I feel very bad is in respect of my pocket. My last penny goes to post this letter. If you could send me one shilling this week I may be able to get a preaching engagement next week which will provide enough to keep me going. . ." (AGM to CAM, March 8, 1909)

He sent his first letter Clara Mill's acceptance at the Ladies' Missionary Training Home in Burbank Gardens, Glasgow (February, 1910)

Alec responded to this welcome news with these lines on February 14, 1910:

"Dear Clara: . . .I have been rejoicing very much since I heard about your acceptance for I feel you are bound to me now in a closer union of service than you have ever been before. . .You will be under the strict rules of an institution and under the influence of company such as you have not had before. You will be under the authority and tutelage of superiors and teachers and you will feel quite young (even a child) again. . .And now I must go to work with added zeal for I have a sister, a coming student at Burnbank College!"

John left with Grandfather Sinclair and his younger brother, George, for Canada in May, 1910. His oldest brother, Henderson ("Harry"), had gone out the year before. John had been employed to serve a mission outpost of the Baptist Church in Lloydminster, Saskatchewan for the summer months before continuing his studies at Brandon College, Brandon, Manitoba.

Alec wrote to John on June 16, 1910:

"My dear John in the backwoods; I just received your informing letter and traveller's journal . . . It seems to me you would not live in a more primitive manner even in China if you have to partition your own room and to chop your own wood . . ."

Since Alec knew that John would be interested in the news of the World Missionary Conference in Edinburgh, held in June, 1910, Alec added a comment:

"The whole of London and the whole of the country generally seems to be interested in the World Missionary Conference just now. Our Dr. McCaig has gone there as one of the appointed delegates of the Baptist Missionary Society . . .".

Alex had a four weeks supply preaching assignment in the summer of 1910 in Dundee, but evidently was able also to attend the large Student Volunteer Movement conference in Barslow, England in late July. (This particular SVM conference had a great impact also on John Alexander Mackay, then a third year college student in Aberdeen. Several of the great world missionary leaders who had been at the Edinburgh Conference remained for this student gathering.)

Alec was graduated from Spurgeon College in late 1910 and moved on to Livingstone College at nearby Leyton, East London to begin six months of medical studies. Alex wrote John that he attained 91.6% on his Christmas exams and was among the first prizes. "I am afraid that the knowledge which I have gained will be retained with difficulty if it is retained at all since a good deal of it was cramming. I am often surprised at the small portion of our theoretical knowledge which we consciously put to use in our practical life. . ."

5. Livingstone College—basic medical training (January to June, 1911)

". . .I am just ploughing along in the elements of Medical Science and it looks as if I will not progress much beyond these elements. . .Half the students are returned missionaries . . .They come from China, India, Africa, Australia and the U.S.A. and their knowledge of the actual work of a missionary is a great help. . .The practical work which we got to do here is somewhat similar to Clara's work at Burnbank. We visit the wards of Poplar, Seamen's, Wathauisten hospitals. We help in bandaging up the wounds in the outpatients department. We accompany doctors to the medical mission in Bethual Green (sp?) and watch them deal with the cases. We also learn to extract teeth. My first dental operation was last Tuesday. I am thankful to say that (as far as I know) the patient is still alive. . ."

He writes about buying the basic equipment he will need as a pioneer missionary: camp bed, hurricane lamp, medicine chest, boots, canteen, mosquito nets, etc., "without having been into a camp, cooked with a canteen or even seen a mosquito, except in pictures!" (July 24, 1911) His outfit allowance from the BMS was forty pounds. He wrote that he spent 16 pounds on his "trousseau" (clothing and three trunks). He would be able to take two steamer trunks in the cabin and the "church presentation bag", Florrie Starte had given him five pounds to buy a camera. The Kelvinside Church in Glasgow gave him a parting gift of two pounds and three shilling "toward the cost of the medicine chest."

Alec thoroughly enjoyed his studies: ". . .The only fault about my studies at Livingstone is that it is far too interesting. I almost wish I had some years to give to the study of this wonderful, complex, harmonious temple in which the Spirit dwells."

Two letters of recommendation to the BMS from Professor Hackney and Principal McCaig of Spurgeon's College reflect Alex as seen by his teachers:

From Principal McCaig "He has considerable mental power, an independent way of looking at things. He had a fairly good education before coming to college and has done well in college. . .He has done well in Greek, Hebrew and Latin. He would hold his own opinion strongly and would not be easily led by another. He is amiable with all and gets on well with his fellow students. I really believe that Mr. Mill will make a good missionary. He is not an ordinary sort of man—his powers are somewhat special and of a high order. I believe he is fully consecrated to the Great Work. He will never be an echo of other voices, or a slavish imitator of other men, but in his own personality he will be absolutely devoted to the Great Master."

From Professor Hackney "He is a man of somewhat remarkable quality. A strong personality, talking (taking ?) his own way, resolute almost to a fault. When he is convinced, very thoughtful, a first class student and worker. Earnest and devoted in his own piety: a character with some Scotch drawbacks which will be rubbed off and leave a vigorous, dependable, brain and fruitful nature. His health is a care, as to whether it is firm enough for what he wants. If he can have a term at Livingstone it would be very good. Do you think that there is any rich man who would help him?"

(Note: "The rich man" did come forward and gave Alec most of the cost of his six months at Livingstone College—JHS)

He finished his studies in June, was interviewed and commissioned by the BMS in early July. He then spent most of July and August with his father and brother in Glasgow. Some college classmates and teachers came down to the train station to see him off for the ferry over to Antwerp. "They stood with bare heads and sang: 'All Hail the Power of Jesus Name' and 'The Cross it standeth fast'. I do not wish to describe a scene which so deeply stirred me. My medicine chest was brought down at the last minute and then we hurriedly shook hands." He sailed from Antwerp for Matadi, Belgian Congo on September 2, 1911. (AGM to CAM 9/1/1911)

PART THREE

AUNT ETHEL AND THE STARTE FAMILY OF CAMBRIDGE/SWAVESEY: ETHEL'S ENGLISH ROOTS

D. AUNT ETHEL AND THE STARTE FAMILY OF CAMBRIDGE

The Starte family

Ethel Clara Starte was born in 1880 in Cambridge, the second daughter and fourth child of Henry ("Harry") Starte and Mary Wilderspin Starte. There were six children in the family: Florence, Herbert, Harold, Ethel, Horace and Elsie. The family was related to the St. Andrew's Street Baptist Church, a historic congregation in the heart of Cambridge, dating from 1689. It appears that since the Starte family owned a small business in nearby Swavesey they were active also in a small Baptist mission there.

St. Andrew's Street Baptist Church had a tradition of sending young people into overseas missionary service. Two members and three children of the congregation were among the missionary martyrs during the Boxer Rebellion in China (1900) and another died of yellow fever in 1901 in Yakusu, Belgian Congo. They were:

Florence Emily I'Anson (nee Doggett), born 1867. Martyred with her husband and three children in the Boxer Rebellion, February 7, 1900. Aged 33.

Sydney W. Ennals, born 1872. Martyred in the Boxer Rebellion, Shensi. September 8, 1900. Aged 28.

Maud Frances Kenred Smith (nee Gregg), born 1869. Nurse and married to Kenred. Died of yellow fever in Yakusu, Belgian Congo, April 13, 1901. Aged 32.

No doubt the death of these young missionaries left a deep impression on Ethel Starte, then in her early twenties.

Grandfather William Starte was a "whitesmith", a worker in tin, galvanizer and polisher of iron. He was the son of James Start (without the "e"), born in 1831 who died in 1875. Henry, Ethel's father, had one brother William. William's grandson, Michael Nurse, born in 1927, is presently working on a Starte family genealogy. I have not been able to find out the profession of Henry "Harry" Starte, except that he owned a small business in Swavesey. They owned their own home in Cambridge. Ethel was working in a grocery store of her brother in Swavesey in July 1909. A postcard sent to Ethel, Florence and Elsie in Swavesey from Harold and Herbert who were vacationing in Rigi-Kulm, Lucerne, Switzerland confirms this date.

The Henry Starte home was devoutly Baptist. Alex Mill must have known the family through Florence "Florrie" Starte, an active supporter of Baptist missions. "Florrie" was a member of the governing board of the Ladies' Missionary Training Home in Glasgow which my mother attended from 1910–1912. It was probably through that connection that Alex got to know the Starte family when he came to London to study at Spurgeon College. Florrie later married Frank Dent and settled in Cambridge.

Herbert Starte went out as a missionary to the Belgian Congo in 1914 and served there until 1940. Horace and May "Maisie" Man Starte were active in the St. Andrew's Street Baptist Church, even though she had been reared in the Church of England. Maisie was a member of the Baptist Missionary Society Board when we met her in Cambridge in 1956. Ethel married Alexander G. Mill and served with him as a missionary nurse in the Belgian Congo, 1918–1946. Harold went out to India in 1909 (?) to serve in the Criminal Corrections of the British Colonial Service. Elsie married William Robinson and settled in England, Horace also went to India in 1911 and served in the Forestry Division of the Colonial Service.

Ethel Starte worked for several years in the family store in Swavesey. Father Starte wrote in 1909 that Ethel had attended "a dame's school" as a girl, but went to work shortly after her elementary schooling. Whether it was because of a lack of vocational desire or of opportunity, Ethel did not begin her professional training until 1913 at the age of thirty-three. She may have been "a late bloomer". She was not overly attractive and may have found it difficult to find her place in the family between a more vivacious older sister and a more attractive younger sister.

A romance not yet ready to blossom

It seems that Ethel Starte met Alex Mill through her sister Florrie's connection with Clara Mill at Burnbank Home in Glasgow. Since there were never more than fifteen or eighteen students at the Burnbank Home, it seems very probable that Florrie was Clara's "sponsor". Or it may have been through Alex's friendship with my father, John P. Sinclair, sometime between 1909 and 1910 when my father studied at Harley College, Bow, London and my Uncle Alex studied at Spurgeon College, London. The Baptist community in Great Britain was relatively small, so it is not surprising that students who were committed to serving in the foreign mission enterprise found their way to an important Baptist congregation like St. Andrew's Street Church in Cambridge. But by the end of Alex's third year at Spurgeon College, he had met Ethel Starte.

Alex wrote to Clara on May 6, 1910:

"I went to Cambridge. . ."; and to John on June 16: "The very personal affairs of your friend at Cambridge stand pretty much as they were and the hopes I have of its development are as pleasant as ever. . ."
And to Clara again on August 8: ". . .I have had a holiday at Cambridge which was not so much a season of retirement as of activity and pleasant excitement. I formed one of a party of 8. We made our headquarters at Ely and in two sailing boats we voyaged along the rivers and canals of the Fen country and enjoyed the novelty of a rough and ready camplife from morning till night. . ."
On October 5 to Clara: ". . .I still have a friendship at Cambridge, I have nothing dearer. . .". On November 10: "The friends in Cambridge are all well . . . .Horace, the son who was at Oxford, is now in Germany taking a course in Forestry. . ."
No further correspondence appeared among Alex's letters on how the romance fared during the first months of 1911, but we know that by July, 1911 Uncle Alex had written to John that Ethel Starte had turned down his marriage proposal before he left for the Congo in September, 1911. Uncle Alex wrote to John in July 9, 1913, after my mother and father were married in Canada, "I can well remember how you sympathized with me. . .in my love disappointment and now my happiness is to sympathize with you in your love triumph. . .".

Ethel spends two years in India

Ethel went to India with her bachelor brother, Harold, when he returned in November, 1911. They landed in Bombay and traveled some five hundred miles across India to Bijapour in East Central India. She had been living with her other unmarried brother, Horace, in Swavesey, and worked with him in the family store. Horace was considering going also to India to work in the Forestry Service and took a forestry course in Germany in 1910–1911.

Ethel was very active in the Baptist Sunday School in Swavesey since they collected a special fund in her honor on the eve of her departure to refurbish their meeting hall. Father and Mother Starte wrote to Harold and Ethel a very detailed report of the dedication of the new Sunday School room. Ethel, according to her father, was "quiet and unassuming. . . She would not accept any personal gift and expressed the wish for no formal farewell, saying she would call on each friend and say goodbye to each one." Father Starte to Ethel and Harold a twelve page narrative report about the dedication of the new room. It was dated November 24, 1911: ". . .Without doubt Ethel will be very much occupied at the first learning a new language, saddle riding and new modes of home life under canvas. This will take up much of her time. We hope she will improve her playing of the portable harmonium. We also hope she will be able to learn to use the camera, so as to let us have some of the many photos Harold has already taken. . .Now we commend you both to the Heavenly Father and to His safe keeping, both in body and spirit. You will find great help and comfort from daily reading of your Bible, and prayer and song will be a helpful closing to each day's work. . .".

Then Father Starte proceeded to describe Harold's work as an itinerating magistrate in the British Colonial Service: "His work was that of a magistrate committing evildoers to prison. But he, as a Christian man as well as a magistrate, felt sorry for the prisoners he had to pass sentence on. . . He had submitted different proposals to the government of India on how to deal with these people, of how to utilize the money spent upon their prosecution and imprisonment in the future for their uplift. The government had accepted one of these methods which has also received the sanction of the Home Government Office. Harold had received the appointment to carry it out. . ."

Father Starte then lays out the lay missionary task which Ethel planned to carry out while journeying with her brother: ". . . As a government official he was pledged to have nothing to do with the religion of those under his charge, but to be neutral to one and all. They could now see how the sister could come in for good and useful service. She had no government restrictions and was free with no opposition from any source to come in her way. But first she must learn a new language to be able to talk to the people. Harold had proposed that some hospital and nursing should be learned and then as a sort of traveling Florence Nightingale she would travel with her brother and try to help him and serve the Lord Jesus by doing what her hand could find to do. . ."

Ethel stayed for about two years with her brother Harold in India and returned sometime in late 1913. She then began her studies at Guy's Hospital in London. It seemed that during her stay in India she caught a vision of preparing as a nurse.

Guy's Hospital was named in honor of Thomas Guy, one of the pioneers of modern medicine. This institution was one of the early public funded teaching hospitals in Britain. Nurses were registered only in Great Britain beginning in 1888. Ethel was probably received in the category of "intelligent, working class students" which required a course in general subjects as well as practical nursing experience. This was a three-year course of study. We know that she also did some nursing in Holland between 1916–17.

Since this was during World War I, she probably was on assignment with a military hospital, but there are no details, simply a reference "to time spent in Holland". This may have been the equivalent of practical work required before graduation. She studied from early 1914 through the end of 1916. There was also another category of "probationary students" who came with better general education and were able to finish the course in two years, but Ethel took the three year course.

Alex did not forget Ethel . . .

Alex did not forget Ethel when he sailed to the Congo in September, 1911, nor did she when she sailed to India in November, 1911. Alex wrote my mother on June 5, 1913:

"Do not think, Clara, because you are not my only dear one now that you are not as dear as ever. You are and you would love the one I love too if you knew her. . ."

He also sent Clara some new words to the old tune, "Way down upon the Swanee River", as he pined for Ethel:

"One little sister in the Homeland;
One other girl
Those make my heart a world of fancy
Thronging my memory still!. . .". (AGM to CAM, March 8, 1913)

We do not have any evidence that they wrote to each other during the years 1911–13. We can assume that news from each filtered through the Starte family to both Ethel and Alex, but we have no letters to document this.

Alex seemed to get mildly interested in a single or widowed missionary colleague in the Congo, but he wrote Clara in December, 1913:

"Don't speak to me about Mrs. Wright. I have gone wrong so often in thinking myself to be Mr. Wright."

Alex's first furlough (December, 1913 to August, 1914)

First term missionaries of the BMS were given a two-year probationary period to prove their fitness for overseas service. Alex returned to Britain in late December, 1913 to do language study and be interviewed by the mission board for appointment as a career missionary.

He first spent a few weeks with Father Mill and his brother Gladstone's family in Glasgow. He was interviewed in Glasgow by Mr. Fullerton of the B.M.S. home staff regarding his language study plans. (Letter to CMS from AGM February 11, 1913). He then returned to England and left his baggage at Mrs. Saunder's in London. This was the family with whom he stayed when he studied at Spurgeon's College. He wrote Clara on April 4, 1913 from 5 Willow Walk, Cambridge, the family home of the Startes: ". . . Do write, Clara, to Florrie Starte for my sake if possible though I know you are very busy. . ." Alex was looking for "a friend in court!".

Evidently by this time he was more than an occasional visitor at the Starte's family home, even though Ethel was away studying at Guy's Hospital in London.

Alex went to Brussels in mid-April, lived at the YMCA and took an intensive French course. He wrote in detail about the gathering clouds of war. He returned to London in late June. He wrote to Clara and John in Canada that he had given up the possibility of visiting them in Winnipeg before he returned to the Congo. His words of "wisdom" to recently married sister, Clara, were:

"Whatever you do with that leopard's claw, first wash it before you scratch John for the poison of a leopard's claw is well known". (AGM to CMS May 23, 1914 from Brussels).

The family members get "romantically" involved. . .

The Starte family was evidently interested that Ethel and Alex get together. It seems that Ethel thought that Alex was still angry at her since she turned down his marriage proposal before she went to India in 1911.

But events moved quickly in the romance during July, 1914. He wrote to Clara on July 22, 1914 and gave her the good news: "Your prayers for me were answered. . .I am sure that you could not guess what I am going to buy with that money you gave me a birthday present. . .an engagement ring." (Alex celebrated his 29th birthday on July 20).

He tells Clara the story of the whirlwind three-day courtship in Cambridge on July 21, 22 and 23:

"I could not have told you myself last Saturday night as I said farewell to all the Startes and to Ethel who is now in training to become a nurse. But on Monday morning as I was packing up at Mrs. Saunder's to go off to Congo, Ethel's brother noticed after as I left the Starte home that Ethel seemed sad. He sent his sister to ask her the reason and I think she said something about me. At any rate, he gave me a hint in a little note that I ought to have spoken to Ethel."

"I left everything that morning (for my heart has been hungry for a long time) and I found more of love than ever I had hoped for at the begging in the bosom of Ethel—and all of it for me. She thought I had been angry after her refusal. Well, Clara, I have put off my return for Congo for three weeks just to get to know her better and then after two or two and a half years of nurse's training she hopes to come out and spend her service for Jesus with me at Yakusu. . .Clara, God will bring about things in His own way—for it is far better than if I had arranged it all myself. . .Tell John that I passed the place in London today, the spot near "Old Bailey" where I told him of my disappointment and he tried to justify God's ways to me, but my soul was deaf at that time. . ." (AGM to CMS, July 22, 1914)

Ethel's older sister, Florrie, wrote to my mother in early August her version of the rapid train of events (in which she may have been a participant!):

"Dear Clara: You will have received Alex's letter with the rejoicing with us that God has led them together and given Ethel love beyond doubt at last. I know she earnestly prayed for it before she went to India, rather than give Alex pain, but God's wisdom knew best how long to withhold and through what paths to lead them before they were ready for the joy. . . For Ethel had her time of darkness thinking Alex had probably begun to care for one of the young ladies on his station (in the Congo) which was our most earnest prayer for him in the earlier days. Her life in India was saddened because she began to realize that she had made a mistake. After taking the path she thought right at the time she realized she did need Alex sadly and Harold couldn't take his place. . .".

Alex wrote in jubilation to Father Mill in Glasgow on July 21, 1914:

"Now the Mill has got a Starte,
Cambridge air has helped his heart. . ."

"What I could not accomplish by entreaty or courting years ago has been accomplished in one day through God's providence and by the help and kindly hint of Herbert and Elsie. I am now engaged to. . . my early and true sweetheart Ethel Starte. . . I am going on a little holiday with Harold, Herbert, Elsie and Ethel to the seaside. . ."

Ethel wrote to Father Mill (no date on the letter, but that is understandable!)

"Dear Mr. Mill; Alex has written to you and asked me if I would like to enclose a note too. I know Alex now better than I did years ago and am looking forward to the holiday we are all spending together (except Father,

Mother and Auntie) somewhere on the East Coast. I hope I shall never hurt again as I did when first I knew Alex but I didn't know him as you know him. . .We went down the river today and had a paddling race taking the boat in pairs. Needless to say Elsie and Harold won by three minutes. . . Yours affectionately, Ethel."

Father Mill journeyed to Cambridge to meet the Starte family. Ethel wrote on his return to Glasgow:

"We were all glad to know that you arrived home safely and we hope you will have a lovely time for the rest of your holiday. It will be nice and quiet with no such disturbing elements that nearly drove you to distraction here!"

Alex wrote on August 23, "Ethel is busy writing at my side. . .Now the question is 'How can I get back to the Congo with the war beginning'?" On September 9 at the Central YMCA, London:

"I am waiting for the BMS to make a decision on going out in the light of war and transportation problems. . ."

And on September 17:

"I leave on September from Liverpool. Lights are flashing over London, searching for any approach of hostile aircraft. . ."

By September 26 Alex was on the train to Liverpool. On October 19, he wrote from the Cape Verde Island at Principe. He told Clara that he only had time to say goodbye to Ethel in London on a street corner outside Guy's Hospital since she had to slip out between classes to see him before he left for Liverpool.

We are sure that there were many letters flowing between them back and forth over the submarine infested Atlantic Ocean during the long winter, spring and summer of 1914–15. One precious letter survived. It was found among his personal effects at the nursing home where he died in 1969. Among his scant possessions was a worn leather folder which contained some precious papers. On the first page of the letter were two roses which Ethel had artfully drawn in pen, probably written in June, 1915:

"My dearest boy;

I went home with them after Chapel this morning and had supper. It was beautifully light and Father cut me two lovely half-open roses from his own rambler which he has been training along the wall. It is really a standard rose only Dad has let the suckers grow and he has never had so many roses before. . . .One rose I would like you to have so I call it yours; it's not quite so open as mine. I smell them both, but they are very like us. We shall be a sort of revelation to each other when we unfold.

Right inside yours there looks as if there will be a depth of beauty and so there is in mine. The scent is lovely just the sweet old fashioned smell. Goodnight.

"I wish I could come with this letter, but instead of looking after Africans I must stay and look after an Indian (one of her patients at the hospital). I like it when I am busiest then I don't have time to think about things but does it matter for I suppose this is all planned for us. . . .Ever yours, Ethel."

Ethel Clara Starte—a profile

There are no missionary candidate files on record for Ethel Starte in the BMS files at Angus Library, Regent's College, Oxford. Evidently the wives of approved missionaries did not have to go through the personnel selection process. It seemed to have sufficed that Alex Mill had chosen Ethel Starte to be his wife!

Missionary colleagues described her as "a plain person" and about five feet five inches tall. She stood nearly a foot shorter than Alex who was nearly six feet four. She was not given to fancy stuff and small talk. Alex was "the leader" in the couple; Ethel was "the follower". But as missionary colleagues commented to me "that Ethel usually got her way!" She did things in "her own way" and was not given to putting her attention on fashions and frills.

Ethel loved to cook. Her missionary colleagues said she could cook and served up a wonderful three course meal on the mission river boat "for a crowd of us".

Barbara Mary, their only daughter, was born in July, 1920 in Yakusu. Ethel was then forty years of age. They were concerned about Barbara's health since some missionary children had died in the Congo in recent years. So on April 27, 1921 Ethel and Barbara returned to England. Alex accompanied them on the 1200–mile river trip to Matadi, the port of embarkation. He would not see them again for two years when he went home on furlough. This separation wore heavily on both of them since they had just been married for three years when they had to be separated for over two years.

Ethel gave the impression of being stern and abrupt, yet from time to time her face would break out in a broad, warm smile. When a child would come into a room of adults, the little one would invariably go to Ethel. She was "a character". During mission meetings, she seldom spoke and kept herself busy sewing and remaking Alex's clothes. One missionary said that she remembers the noise of Ethel's ripping up some of Alex's old clothes during a committee meeting.

Early in her missionary days she was given a group of unruly school girls who were referred to as "Mrs. Mill's lambs". "We pressed Mrs. Mill into service. . .since they were too much for a native teacher. They were meek in school, but riotous out of it. Formerly they used to leap through the open windows to get to their classroom with a sheepish look to the accompaniment of un, deux; un, deux!" Ethel was such a stern disciplinarian that "at the sound of a large hand bell, the girls galloped off to the Yakusu school like a troop of young colts". (YN, July, 1921)

Ethel was known as "Mama Bandombele" to thousands of Africans in the Yakusu District. She and Alex were "in journeyings oft", on foot, on cycle, motorbike, by river steamer and later by motor boat, visiting the growing Christian community in the Esoo and Bambole forests, and in countless riverine villages from Yanjali on the Congo River to Opala on the Upper Lomami River. One colleague remembers seeing Alex on the motorbike and Ethel coming along behind on her bicycle!

She, with Alex, had the spirit of the early pioneer missionaries and the call of the "unreached" was ever with them. Unwearyingly they sowed, never once putting self first. Ethel, as a nurse, was always on call for the sick and suffering by day and night. Her medicine chest was the last load to be packed when breaking camp, and the first box to be unpacked upon arrival at the next village. Even though she would be dead tired from the day's journey and in need of her cup of afternoon tea, if a sick person needed care, she went right to work.

A colleague wrote about Ethel

"Whether examining a village school, or a candidate for baptism and church membership or in personal visits with church members or assisting in a teacher training course or tending the sick, Mama Bandombele was always ready to do "whatsoever my Lord and King shall appoint. . ." (Gladys C. Ennals)

Ethel was a poor linguist and did not pass her first Lokele language exam until ten years after arriving on the field. She mixed phrases of Lokele, French and English much to the quiet amusement of her more linguistically apt colleagues.

In the late 1940s, Ethel was informed that the Belgian Government had awarded her "The Medal of Gold of the Legion of the Lion" (translation of French words). She wrote to the mission headquarters to inquire what it was all about. She was told that the colonial government had asked for a list of missionaries who had served for many years in the Congo in humanitarian work and Ethel was chosen. But when she was told that she would have to buy the medal, she said she didn't want to spend the money!

Ethel was a puritan through and through. This made her relationships with her daughter, Barbara Mary, difficult. Ethel had been in Africa so long and was so far removed psychologically from life in England that when she tried to relate to Barbara as a young adult—and that by letter at a distance of six thousand miles—the results were sad, if not tragic. A missionary colleague confided in me that Ethel was so upset because Barbara (who was very gifted as a seamstress) was working as a designer of garments for dancers in the ballet. The missionary friend thought that the garments she had sewed were so lovely that Ethel should take delight in her daughter's achievements. But for Ethel this was "the devil's work" and sinful! The friend replied, "Why, Ethel, how can you say that designing such a lovely dress is sinful—how can such beauty be sinful!" This happened when Barbara was just in her early twenties and trying to find a meaningful vocation after the pressures of her war service in the Women's Auxiliary Air Force.

Ethel was a daughter of the Victorian Age. She reflected in her life the emerging independence of the English woman of the early part of this century. The nursing profession opened up to her a meaningful vocation through which she could express her Christian faith. Her Baptist piety and sense of call to world mission was only three generations removed from the missionary call of William Carey, the founder of the Baptist Missionary Society in 1792. The young missionary martyrs of St. Andrew's Street Baptist Church in Cambridge certainly cast a spell over her and dissuaded her of "cheap grace".

The two years in India with Harold and the continuing connection with India through both Harold and Horace made a lasting impression on her life. The service of Herbert in the Congo, beginning in 1914, gave her a deeper understanding of the kind of sacrifices she would have to make if she married Alex Mill. All these influences conspired to give her a world view of a kind, even though it was largely through the eyes of the British Colonial Service of her brothers. She was therefore a more cosmopolitan person than Alex. But she did not have the benefit of the rich classical education of Alex in the liberal arts and his theological training.

Alex and Ethel were "a pair of characters" in the best sense of that term. They were both non-conformists, not only church-wise, but in the society of their time. Ethel was at times stubborn, judgmental and withdrawn; but also a warm, loving and caring person. Both Ethel and Alex reflected the best (and perhaps the worst) of their English and Scottish cultural and temperamental heritage. Alex was a lyrical romantic—more like the High-landers than the more down-to-earth practical Lowlanders. Ethel had some of the abruptness and stern character of the English middle class. Her tenderness was down deep inside and only welled up occasionally; Alex wore his tenderness and warmth on his sleeve!

Ethel Starte and Alex Mill were well-matched as a couple. Their personalities complemented each and seemed to draw out the best from their inner selves.

PART FOUR

THE MISSIONARY SERVICE OF UNCLE ALEX AND AUNT ETHEL IN THE BELGIAN CONGO (1911–1946 AGM; 1919–1946 ECM)

E. THE MISSIONARY SERVICE OF UNCLE ALEX AND AUNT ETHEL IN THE BELGIAN CONGO (1911–1946 AGM; 1919–1946 ECM)

1. ALONE IN AFRICA (1911–1918)

A. Alex's first voyage to Africa (September–October, 1911)

From Queen's Hotel, Antwerp:

"My dear Clara: . . .I can never forget you, Clara, for I think that like as you have sewed on tabs to all my clothing, so you have a 'tab' on to me. Sewed it on with a little gold chain which like all the other tabs will speak to me, not of A.M. but of C.M. I have watched them securing the great ship to the stone quays with steel wire ropes and chains but no tie can ever be so strong as that little bond between you and me.

And now I must soon leave from Antwerp. Tomorrow morning, D.V. will see us free from Antwerp and sailing south to the sunny shore of Africa. 'As his is the part that goeth forth to the battle, so shall his part be that tarrieth with the stuff.'" (AGM to CAM 9/1/1911)

Their steamer was to call at the following places on the voyage out:

September   5 La Rochelle
               9 Tenerife
           12 Dakar
           14 Conarkry, Sierra Leone
           17 Grand Bassam
           21 Banana; Boma, Congo
           23 Matadi, Congo

Now on board, he wrote on September 4 on the "S.S. Leopoldville" in the Bay of Biscay:

". . .The last piece of land we saw distinctly was the 'Hook of Holland' with its church tower, its windmill and its beacon light. We have on board our own missionary party of eleven. . .There are also eleven Catholic missionaries from Belgium dressed like monks and three Sisters of Mercy. . . .

Yesterday was Sunday and we had a nice prayer meeting among the missionaries and we hope to have one daily now. Today we saw the coast of France and the fishing fleet and also a school of dolphins followed the ship for some time. . ." The Protestant missionaries traveled First Class. Alex reports that the ship has a "Marconigraph station fitted upon the top deck and the current newspaper news is published and printed daily on board in a 'Journal de l'Atlantique'. We all speak French here (or else try to!)"

September 7. From the "Mid-Atlantic":

"Now that I have been for about a week on the bosom of the voiceless deep my thoughts have settled themselves sufficiently to enable me to write a few of my experiences during the eventful days which preceded my departure. . . . (he recounts the farewell service at Kelvinside a few weeks before. Mr. Anderton, their beloved pastor, was going out alone to serve in Western Australia.). . . .

"The sunlight has hardly left the sea since we started and everything grows better as we approach the Land of Promise—except the heat. . . .It is even difficult to get cold water to drink. . .News from John will be even much older when I get it but I hope it will get better with the keeping and that soon he will be able to ask you to board a ship and become the first (and last) mate with him on his life's voyage. . .Here we are in the ocean—hundreds of people and thousands of tons of weight but the mighty ocean all around easily bears us up. How like the mighty love of God? We fear some time that we are going to sink but that is just the dipping down of the ship as we pass over the surface and soon shall be lifted high on the next wave and realize that underneath us are the Everlasting Arms. . ."

B. Alex begins his work in Africa
(October, 1911 to December, 1912)

Alex had arrived now at "The Land of Promise". The next lap of the journey was the 1200-mile riverboat ride on the "S.S. Endeavor" up the Congo River to Yakusu where he arrived in November, 1914. He wrote John in Brandon, Manitoba on October 20 from Bolenge where he stopped for a conference of the Protestant Missionary Societies working in the Congo:

"Dear John; I suppose this will reach you in the middle of your exams and in the depth of winter. . .I have been asked to take over the oversight of the supply of drinking water for the steamer. Well! Before we left Kinshasa (on Stanley Pool), we got about 8 large glass bottles and 3 large tin water butts and told the boys to fill them from a spring which was on shore some distance off. They filled them but when we came to pour them out after we had been some time on the journey; we found that only the glass bottles had the spring water in them but the tin butts (where you could not so easily inspect the contents) were filled with dirty river water. I suppose they did this because it saved them the work of carrying it from the spring and thought it would not be seen because it was not in the glass bottles. The next time I took in water, which was at Ikau, I went out with them to the spring and witnessed with my own eyes the contents which were in all the bottles. . ."

The Protestant work ethic is challenged!

"Another job I had taken part in has been the loading up of the vessel with firewood for engine fuel. We stop the vessel at a place where wood is stacked for sale and then a few of us go with the men to see that they do not lift too much or overhurry themselves!! It generally happens that we have to stop as short a time as possible at such places. But to see the men you would think that they had come to the end of the voyage and that the ship was laid up for repairs. They stroll up to the bundles of wood and wait for one another to start. To make it appear that they are carrying a lot they selected the thinnest faggots they can find and think that because they have a great number they have a great load. Once instead of carrying it in bundles they stood in a line and handed it along (5 of them) faggot by faggot to one another! Sometimes to hurry matters we lift the wood up to their shoulders for them but while you are turning around for another piece to complete their load they hurry off to avoid carrying as much as they should.

"One can only laugh at the barefaced shirking and laziness. But it is a vice which the Congolese must overcome if they are ever to rise to anything. I have heard from the missionaries that they have absolutely no idea of foresight or providence and will spend all their wages on Saturday night on fancy articles or dress and will be starving by the middle of the week. But still, John, I like them. I find them a simple, cheerful, contented folk and I believe God is going to make something of them. . ."

Alex witnesses his first baptisms in Africa

"At 8:30 o'clock the stillness of the air was broken by the bell ringing which summoned the candidates to the appointed place. It was the beach of the broad Congo River which stretched like a level lake to its green forest boundary beyond. This place was now to be the centre of interest to all within the hearing of the floating notes of that bell. And they all came too! The rising, terraced slope behind the beach was calculated to suit the convenient assemblage of a vast company as spectators being a rising, terraced slope.

"The candidates were arranged facing the water in 4 long ranks, one behind the other close to the edge. They formed a compact oblong containing 194 sun-stained children of Africa. They stood forward in a space from the native crowd which draped the overlooking slope with expectant and interested faces all directed toward the candidates. At a sign of the four missionaries who stood up to the armpits in the river, the front rank moved forward in silence. The sound of their feet striking the water seems ringing in my ears yet, for it seemed as if they were leaving the shore of their own land and their old life and washing their feet from their sinful habits. They came forward and were immersed one by one into the Triune Name. After all had been immersed to the accompaniment of the singing of choruses by the Christians on the bank, they turned toward the Chapel.

"It was a race who should get there first and they filled a building seating 1000 people. When the missionaries had changed their clothes they led the great company in worship. They began with a hymn and you can judge my surprise to hear them singing it to the tune of "Auld Lang Syne" which they sang as heartily as any kilted Clan. It was beautiful to hear them sing the Doxology to the tune of 'Old Hundredth'". . . .

"I may say that since everything is strange to me for the first day or two out here that I am now feeling as much at home here (in a way) as I did among the Scotch hills and fir forests. . . But I would like Africa much more indeed if it were not so hot and if I could learn the language. . . ."

Alex's first experiences in Yakusu

"Working for 'Bosongo' (the white man)":

Alex wrote to Clara on January 30, 1914 about his work with his workforce of "boys":

". . .My work has been mostly in the open air. I was getting my boys to clear out a part of the station which is infested with weeds. I was also directing others who were making a road. . .This afternoon I had all the boys gathered to receive their pay and after that there was some grumbling and discontent to settle. One boy had a grievance with another about a little white jacket which he had sold to him a few days before. The other boy had promised to give him one and one-half francs for it when payday came but when the time came to pay up he said it was only worth one franc.

"They wanted me to settle the dispute by passing my opinion on the value of the jacket, but I had no more idea than about the price of one of your hats. But when I found that there were witnesses that he had made the promise I told him that he could not go back on his word—or as they say, 'He could not change his heart' but must pay up. I often wonder if I do anything to lead them into the Kingdom because I am able to understand so little of the language that I cannot preach to them. But I try to deal justly with them and to encourage them when they do right and attend to their work. But when I catch them idling (which is much more often) and when they tell lies and quarrel among themselves I have to be strict with them. . .They call themselves my "children" as it is the custom of all the boys who serve the missionaries to use this phrase. . .But two of the 15 are in the enquirers class. . ."

And the next day (January 31), he added,

"I am getting a little more accustomed to the heat and since affairs on this beautiful station are going on pretty even and the staff is keeping in good health, I am almost renewing my youth. The feeling of apprenticeship however still hangs upon me and keeps me from striking out in any new direction for myself."

"A Scotsman with a great sense of humor. . ."

The senior missionaries at Yakusu, Rev William Millman, known as "Mokili", and his wife "Mama Mokili" returned in 1913 to reinforce a pitifully small staff. More and more Mokili was concerned with administration and teacher training, and left itineration to Mr. and Mrs. Wilford, Mr. and Mrs. Pugh, M. Lambotte and A.G. Mill. Mr. Millman wrote a few very descriptive lines about the most recently arrived missionary, A.G. Mill:

"THE LATTER HAD ARRIVED IN 1911 . . . A SCOTSMAN WITH A GREAT SENSE OF HUMOR, AN ALMOST FEMININE SENSITIVENESS IN PERSONAL RELATIONSHIPS AND AN UTTERLY INFLEXIBLE WILL WHICH DROVE HIM CONTINUALLY TO EXTEND FRONTIERS."

This insightful description of Uncle Alex is found in the memoirs of Mr. Millman compiled by his step-daughter, Jane Millman Butterworth, born in 1898 in Yakusu. (Alex visited her in England as a young girl when he was on his first furlough in 1914.) These words summarize well how many colleagues remembered "Uncle Alex".

"John, you ask what have I been doing? Well. .

"I was dancing in the moonlight with some of our workmen and boys! It is good exercise and I want to get as much in touch with them as possible and to know their ways and language. .

"I was also setting up type for our native monthly magazine. . .

"I was also in the village close by doctoring one poor man who I think has malaria. . ."

Alex laments those who "fall way"

"A lot of the Station hands have showed evidence of a changed life and made public profession of their faith by baptism. But one has just gone off to his distant village and we hear his friends have persuaded him to leave us. One prominent member of a few years back is now stirring up partisan war between his own village and another. Two promising clever young men who were printers at the Station . . .have given up their work for us and gone off with their wages to their villages. Yet another boy who had seemed very earnest and had written a "hymn" in his own language was convicted the next day of stealing from the house of the missionary who employed him. I feel I am in constant danger of distrusting everyone and yet there is another side which I dare not forget and perhaps it is harder for them to do right than we think. . .Yet I believe that the image of Christ will yet be reproduced in them. . ."

Will Clara and John go to China?

On July 10, 1912, Alex has heard from Clara that she will definitely be going to Canada to be married to John in July, 1913. He writes:

"Just a year from the time of my writing this and just about four months before I (D.V.) will be leaving here to go home for my first furlough. I do not know how you have been led about your further training after leaving Burnbank. But all the training you can get will be of use especially if you go to China as it seems possible you may do. . ."

Glimpses of life aboard the "S.S. Grenfell"

Alex wrote in the MISIONARY HERALD in April 1913, a brief article "The Congo: glimpses of the Great River"

". . .Its flow is strong and steady but there is no tide, for it is far from its journey's end at Yakusu, some twelve hundred miles of tree-land and human habitations have to be passed before it sinks into the Ocean's embrace. Its bank is an unbroken palisade of forest, which prevents all view of the country through which you are passing. The clay bank, however, when cleared, and washed by the torrential rains, makes a suitable and healthy site for a native village, and when high, can be seen far across the sunlit waters, shining like a golden shore. . ."

"Dear Clara; As I write this the black steamer workmen are singing hymns. . . 'All hail the power of Jesus' name'. I am sitting in the cabin of the "Grenfell" on my way up river to Yakusu. It is Sunday and the men have nothing to do. I am tired of reading and I cannot go out because it is wet.

"This little cabin serves for a dining room during the day and two sleep in it at night. It is also the place where we keep the ships crockery and the ship's library. On the back of the white painted door there hangs the portrait of "George Grenfell" in a little frame. The memory of him gives an influence to the place. There is a little cabin for the Captain which opens off one end and out of the other end you look into the Galley, Larder, Store, Cookhouse and Washing house of the steamer combined. Just behind this is the passage space by which you go up on deck where you see the engines. Everything is compact however and the good nature which all arrangements are carried out on the steamer makes it impossible that you should feel discomfort. . .

"The Steering wheel and Compass and chart house and Engine Telegraph are in a space chained off at the front. At the back the constant splashing of the two stern paddle wheels makes the spray rise almost to the deck. . .

"We had a terrific storm on Saturday. The midday sky became dark and the rolling clouds were driven darkly down upon us by a mighty wind, but our anchors held and the little steamer bore it all as steadily as a swan. . .

"Last night before going to bed I was enraptured with the view of the star spangled sky. The text came to mind: 'We are compassed about with a great cloud of witnesses'. I thought of George Grenfell . . .was he one of those stars?. . .Then I thought of someone else who might be thinking of me. I said to myself 'Those are all who may be watching my career'. But then I remembered that Jesus is "The Star" to which we must look. And I saw the evening star Venus glowing with a soft, clear glory which all the other stars seemed to worship and I knew that He was looking on me and you too. I amuse myself with these fancies sometimes for the steamer life becomes very vacant at times. . ."

The temptation "to play God"

Alex wrote to Clara on October 2:

"Dear Clara: . . . .You will be surprised I think when I tell you that I maintain my dignity with all the natives and from my workboys and the other workmen on the Station I will not take the slightest disrespect. I will not take a word from them. As for their opinions I have not the slightest respect for them and if they are not willing to be teachable I dismiss them. As for their desires and inclinations they are so fleshly and selfish and material that I always reckon it is best to refuse them what they would like themselves. To do thus, you see, is to sort of 'rule' them and sometimes I feel there is a danger of setting myself up as a 'little God' among the workmen of my departments.

"I suppose you will wonder how I can do this and yet follow in the lines laid down by Christ. But it is only as I am ruled firmly by He himself that I can hold with a helpful authority the rule of others. The Apostles spoke with true authority and used it. I hope I can get the same spiritual secret as they had because there is such a danger of authority that is fleshly.

"I am in danger of worrying too much over their unfitness to rise to the standard of Christian men or of thinking too much of myself by comparing myself with them. I have only the right to rule them if I do it in the name of Christ and most of them are content to submit while I do it as I think Christ would until they can be fit to rule themselves. I trust I do it goodnaturedly and of course I try to help them when they are ill and try to teach them a little. . .Of course they get their wages and houseroom but we do not want them to come or stay only for that. . . My native boy 'Lianyongo' is asking for you. He wrote you a little letter which I think I enclosed and sent to you. He was asking if you had got it. . ."

. . .and about the single ladies. . .

"You asked me about what sort the single ladies were and what were my relations with them. In answer to the second part of the question I may say 'none'. Their house is a little distance down the front Station road. I pass within sight of it when on my working rounds. We all meet together on Wednesday evenings and I hear them talk. Then on Sunday evenings we are all present at the little English service. . . They work hard on the language and have a set of 7 unruly native girls to manage in the house. One takes full control of the medical work of the dispensary and the other conducts the school for village girls. . .I am glad that you have come through your 'college course' (refers to the two-years at the Ladies' Missionary Training Home) without a swollen head. . ."

Alex's bachelor colleague—Henri Lambotte

Henri Lambotte served in the Congo from 1909 until his untimely death July 31, 1918. He was a Belgian citizen. He had heard the call to missionary service during the visit of the Camerons (BMS personnel) in Belgium in 1908. He was a native of Flemelle Grande, born October 23, 1884. Henri was less than a year younger than Alex.

While he worked days in a factory, Henri had attended university classes in Leige in the evenings until 10 p.m., getting up at 4 a.m. to study his lecture notes. (Cf. Jane Millman Butterworth's comments in MOKILI IN CONGO. Her mother was known as "Lutwasi" and was the granddaughter of William Millman. Lutwasi was born September 28, 1898). M. Lambotte had a diploma in mechanics and metallurgy and ten years of experience in a factory of John Cockwell Sercing. (?) He had been influenced by the YMCA as a youth and taught Sunday School. His decision to come to the Congo provided an interesting and helpful link between the Protestant Missionary Church of Belgium and Baptist missionary work in the Belgium's only colony.

Henri was not ordained, but Mokili insisted that he should have full status as a missionary and rejected the idea that a man with such eager initiative be called an "aide missionaire"! He was supported financially by the Robert Arthington Fund. Henri must have been a good linguist because he had passed both his first and second exams in the Lokele language by July, 1911. Lambotte went on furlough to England in 1916–17, was baptized by immersion there and received as a member of a Baptist congregation. He said to Alex that "I have certainly been able to help my colleagues more since I was baptized. I can now take my share in the baptisms." (MISSIONARY HERALD, 1918. A.G. Mill)

Henri Lambotte and Alexander Mill were both bachelors at Yakusu during the years 1911–1914 and shared quarters. Henri met Nurse E.N. Whitemore at Yakusu when she arrived in 1913. They were married in Yakusu in 1914. Alex preserved a lovely wedding picture of them. She had to return to England for medical treatment in 1915. In 1916–17 Henri went on furlough to England and they were reunited. Yvonne Lambotte, their only daughter, was born on June 5, 1917 in Yakusu. (Cf Jane Butterworth, page 283)

On the day that she was dedicated in the church at Yakusu, Henri left on an extended trip. He was retracing the exploration journey of three years before among the Foma people. The Foma River is a tributary of the Lomami. Mrs. Lambotte had taken Yvonne downriver to Upoto to stay with friends while Henri was away.

Henri took ill on this journey and died on July 31, 1918. "After his departure on June 5th, Lambotte was not heard from for three weeks. It became later known that it was a difficult journey. Two of his teachers became involved with women in villages where they stayed. Quarrels occurred between his porters and villagers. For two days they had drenching storms, the marshes filled up and the mosquitoes swarmed. At the end of the second week fever came on. He hurried forward and reached the Lomami on the 24th of July since Pugh was due to meet him there with the 'Grenfell' on the 28th. . .When Pugh met him and put him to bed on the steamer and made all possible speed, the "Greenfell" reached Yakusu at midnight. But now Lambotte obviously had blackwater fever. As they got him into his own bed he said: 'I don't know what this may mean for me, but I don't think we have done a good piece of work this time.'. . . Lambotte seemed to recover considerably and a radio telegram was sent to his wife at Upoto saying that he had haematuria, but was better. But his strength was exhausted and he died at 10:45 on the last night of July. At this same hour, Mrs. Lambotte says she was kneeling praying for the recovery of her husband. She felt that her husband himself came and knelt beside her and said: 'God has permitted me to come and say goodbye to you. Be brave for Yvonne's sake. It may not be long." Mrs. Lambotte says that she touched her husband."

Alex and Ethel received the news of his death in Oban, Scotland while on their honeymoon. (Cf. page 85). Alex penned these words of tribute to his dear friend Henri:

"My colleague has died and the world seems to me a little darker. His bright spirit and cheery word, and quick and lively step, made bearable many a dull hour of my early days in Yakusu. A worker, too, has died. He never thought twice what the difficulties of a new building, or a long journey, or a new responsibility might be. He never ceased labour till he had produced the thing the need of the time demanded. As at work, so in enterprise he showed a fearless genius . . . With the coming of the 'Grenfell' came the responsibilities of engineering oversight. With characteristic enthusiasm he took up her overhauling, even to the novel expedient of dry-docking her on an African beach. . . .

"He pioneered and struggled most of all for extension—the extension which has killed many a modern Henry Martyn. Well do I remember his first extended tour into the unreached regions of the great Foma forest. It was not considered expedient that I should have my wish fulfilled to go with him, I can see him in imagination crossing those flooded streams and pushing his way through these dense thickets. He came back with a report of all the land right through to the Lomami River, which is now one of the most promising fields of extension. . .,

"He procured and copied out a map of our yet unopened Mabondo station and district. Lambotte sent a pleading letter to Mr. Wilson to be allowed to go forward and open up the new field. Henri has now entrusted it to my care. . ." (MISSIONARY HERALD, 1918)

C. The year 1913 at Yakusu

There are eight letters in the correspondence archives from 1913. Alex celebrated his 28th birthday on July 22, 1913. This is the same year that John and Clara were married in Winnipeg, Manitoba on July 8. Grandfather Mill was very lonely after Clara's departure in June, 1913 so Alex planned his furlough so he would arrive in London in December, 1913. Grandfather Mill offered to journey to London to be with Alex from December 31–January 5. Then they would travel together to Glasgow to be with his brother Gladstone, sister-in-law Jean, niece Mari and nephew Freddie in Glasgow.

Alex made rapid progress in the language. He took his first language exam on Hogmanay Day and New Year's Day. "I wrote my three hours written Exam paper in a tent which was quiet though hot. I have not yet been told the details of the result but I have been told that I passed. This makes me free for more work and I will soon be asked to take my turn at the Sunday morning service for the whole station."

Letters from England took about six weeks and parcels from 4 to 6 months. His health seemed to be robust, after a fortnight of illness in August, 1912 after which he had a month of holiday on the "S.S. Grenfell" traveling down the Congo to the Bololo Station.

He wrote that he would like to leave in the beginning of November and have a change of climate in South Africa perhaps before coming home, if he can afford it, "though I may not be able to afford Canada". (He was thinking of visiting Clara and John in Canada in 1914.)

Alex lived with another bachelor, Monsieur Henri Lambotte, a Belgian lay missionary. "He is a very energetic and capable man, whose character I much admire. He has been very kind to me. I have given him charge of all my provisions and he looks after the cooking while I look after the garden."

Pining for his "lost love", Ethel

"As the time draws near for your wedding, I am sorry that I cannot be there. . .In a frivolous mood the other night I saw down and in the spirit of the "homesick darkie" wrote a new verse to "Way down upon the Swanee River", viz:

"One little sister in the Homeland; one other girl, (sic, Ethel Starte)
Those make my heart a world of fancy
Thronging my memory still . . ."

He added: "We do get up to jokes here but that is to prevent an almost too great depression which would come upon us if we took everything seriously."

January 2, 1913: A picnic in the forest

"Last Saturday Mr. Lambotte, Captain Hynes and myself invited all the other missionaries on the Station to a picnic in the forest close by. We three made cakes, shortbread, rock cakes, tarts and ordinary cake. Much to the astonishment of the guests they were not all spoiled and with good tea we made a nice picnic beside a forest stream. Afterwards we crept through the tangled bush to where a canoe was waiting for us downstream and embarking in this we followed the narrow stream down to the great Congo and paddled back to Yakusu. It did me good physically and mentally by lifting my mind off the troubles of the Station. . ."

March 8, 1913: "I trespassed upon the secret native ceremony"

One of the most difficult of African rites for the missionaries to understand was "the coming of age" custom for young men. It was generally referred to as the "libeli" and condemned by the missionaries.

"I trespassed upon the secret native ceremony which was being held in a village nearby by walking through a maze of circuitous paths in the forest and coming upon them by surprise. I did this, I feel sure, by God's Guidance; and because I knew that several of my young men were being initiated there and because an ex-church member was a leader in the superstition. Arriving in the sacred clearing I was threatened and opposed but I did not leave til I had spoken a warning to my two old school lads and had openly defied in the name of God the spirits which are supposed to inhabit the place.

"I am odious to some of my colleagues for doing this for they thought it was imprudent but had they felt as I did I feel sure they would have done the same. We were along one of the forest paths today for a picnic with Christie Davies of Yalemba and the new single lady Miss Whitmore (who later married Lambotte). I saw the tree stump again beside which I knelt to pray for the guidance through the forest which was so surely given. . ."

May 18, 1913: A brother thanks his sister

"When I think of how we have grown up together, played together, done wrong together, planned together, been baptized together, sorrowed together, sympathized, prayed, worked: I wonder what thanks I can render to God for guiding and guarding both our lives so that we are not yet parted. You have been a great help to me this year by your letters; and your solid missionary work and collecting makes me feel as if you were my banker at home. . ."

June 25, 1913: Journeying out in the bush

"I am writing you from Yalemba, having arrived here on June 21. I have been out just over four weeks. I visited 60 schools in all and held communion services on the Sundays. I then came down here to rest until the 'S.S. Endeavor' passes on her upward journey and lets me get back to our Station. . .

"This time was very full of interest and sometimes of anxiety. I am just now getting time to look over many things which I did hurriedly on the journey and which may have lessons for me. I met with all sorts and conditions of natives from the black boys and girls who held their finger-marked reading cards fondly and tightly; to the chiefs of villages who walked surrounded by their train and displayed their barbaric finery with flagrant pride. But one and all, high and low, vied in honoring me as their teacher and welcoming me as their guest.

"This does not mean that I always enjoyed the way they did it (i.e., the welcome) nor that I acknowledged the friendship as desirable for I am the servant of a Master and the representative of a community and a race. I will explain to you that even a bad white man would have been received as I was just because he is looked upon as the representative of wealth, knowledge and power and has proved himself a dangerous foe or a helpful friend.

"But after the initial delight on seeing all my bed-things unpacked and my tent put up and my tidily furnished table set and cleared, there still was an interest left in the minds of some, especially the teachers, in what books I had brought and what teaching or instruction I was bringing to them. . ."

July 9, 1913: To my brother-in-law

"Dear John; You are also my brother-in-law by this time (their wedding was July 8), but that is only another confirmation of our brotherly connection which has always existed between us. So you are now settled in an Institution and Church in the midst of a mixed and rather poor population, in a Colony which is facing a lot of new problems."

Is service in China still an option?

In this letter to John, there appears to be an inclination reflected that John and Clara are thinking now that their call to missionary service is in Canada, not in China. Alex comments on an article which Dad wrote:

"Your recent letters and your printed article showed that your heart was longing to apply the healing and power of the Gospel to the weak and disorganized society of the new Colony (Canada) which has become so much to you. I did not reply in open approbation because I was jealous for my missionary friends in China. But I felt strongly the force of your arguments in favor of a living interpretation of the Living Christ and a fearless but fair handling of all criticism of the Bible and our work . . . . The Chinese will not be altogether foreign to you though you are not in China for they are today in Canada and the United States. . ."

In commenting on John's work with the boys at MacDonald Memorial Institute in Winnipeg, Alex writes: ". . .Perhaps you may yet be able to send out your own substitute to China. . ."

"John, you sympathized with me. . ."

It was with some pain that Alex sees John and Clara happily married and he is still longing for a life partner. Ethel had turned down his first offer in 1911. He writes to John:

"I can well remember how you sympathized with me in my love disappointment. Now my happiness is to sympathize with you in your love triumph! I want to come to see you and Clara in Canada and where there's a will, there's a way. But I cannot say the date yet. If time and temperature permit it will be during this first furlough which falls due in December of this year."

Do I fit in here in Yakusu?

Alex was aware that he had to find a place for himself in relation to his older missionary colleagues. There had been some minor (?) differences over mission policy and his way of doing missionary work. . . He writes: "I am trying to find a sphere of my own in the many-sided work which our district presents. During a four-week itineration I went practically through the length and breadth of it and I have just to sample a few branches of station work and then will finish my period of probation. Whether I will think about marriage then in the same way as I do now I do not know. But the desire for it (marriage) is almost distracting now."

September 11, 1913: "I have just received your wedding cake by this mail and have given a taste of it to everyone on the Station. Mr. Lambotte and I ate our pieces of the cake after supper in the evening and we gave 3 united cheers for your blessing-in-the-work, health and happiness. We then explained to the "boys" who keep the house that marriage in our country and according to our custom is because of love. . .The boys were thinking of my sister's marriage in their terms and wondered if a part of the marriage price would be sent to me. But we told them that Love was king in those matters and that Love gives all and expects nothing."

September 27, 1913: What about your fiancée?

". . .In the marriage question, I have not much to say except concerning the customs of the natives. They come to me and enquire about my own fiancée and tell me about their own prospects and method of going about the business. They start with the mouth first, of course. If they see a young woman who can cook food well and is healthy and strong, they find out if she is eligible for marriage and offer her a present of food. If she accepts it, it is understood that she wishes her father to get her sold to the man who gave her the food. . ."

Arrival back in London, December, 1913

Alex had now completed his probationary period of 28 months in the Congo. His first impression of England are recorded in a letter written from the BMS offices, 19 Furnival St., London on December 23, 1913:

"I arrived in Liverpool St. Station at 7:30 a.m. on December 10th and was met by Mr. Saunders who took him on the tube railway out of London about six miles to a little villa in a row of semidetached houses on the top of a beautiful hill . . . You know that was 100 Pepys Road, New Cross, London, S.E." (The Saunders family who had Glasgow roots hosted Alex and John often during their student days in London).

"I feel the cold (not 40 degrees below as you have in Canada), but not too much. . .I have bought a large Ulster overcoat, flannel lined and a big pair of wool lined gloves like John's Father gave me before I went to College. By doing this and wearing two pairs of socks and soles in my boots, I both feel and look so comfortable and warm that nobody gives me any sympathy. . ."

"I always read two pages of the Lokele Scriptures each day to keep me in touch with the language. . .Father is coming down on December 31st and will stay until January 5th. (They attended an evening service at St. Paul's Cathedral in London "listening to the reading of Scripture—Revelation 22.) I thought it very strange when I came back to civilization to see so many women: for white women are the rarity in the Congo and I had forgotten that after all the proportion of women is three to one man in the British Isles." (Note: Where did Alex get this figure?)

He assumed that he would be formally appointed to the Congo at the close of his furlough in July. He wanted to get a good command of French "to enable me to be left alone if necessary on the Station and to speak with the officials of the Government". He planned to take two months of classes at the Berlitz School in Glasgow. Then he wanted to go to Brussels for three months' medical training "so I can be taught to diagnose cases of Sleeping Sickness and so prevent the spread of the disease which has brought so much suffering and sorrow in our Land. . .My deputation work takes me to Scotland in March. . .".

D. The Year 1914: deputation, language, medical training and his engagement to Ethel

After three weeks in England (no mention of visiting Cambridge or of being in touch with Ethel), he wrote on January 13, 1914 from the old family address "92 Stratford Street, Maryhill, Glasgow". How happy Grandfather Mill must be to have his son at home again! Alex wrote that he is busy studying French at the Berlitz School. He felt he had to practice French before entering the College of Tropical Medicine in Brussels on April 15th. He planned to go directly from Belgium back to the Congo in August. He indicated that upon arrival in the Congo that he would spend a month in Leopoldville taking a special course related to Sleeping Sickness, arriving at Yakusu by the end of October. He wrote to Clara and John that "this schedule crowds out Canada relentlessly, but you see I cannot consider my time my own and being busy keeps me from thinking. . . Whatever prospects there are for Father in Canada as a hen farmer will be most welcome to me. . .Today I have my Congo mail which makes me all the more convinced that I must soon be back. . .".

He writes on February 11 that he has met with the Secretary of the Baptist Missionary Society. He asked me if I was engaged and I said NO. I told him I wanted to get my sleeping sickness training in Brussels and get back to Yakusu as quickly as possible. He then asked me about my family so I told him (as Father had said) that Father was willing to let me go. . . Mr. Fullerton then said YES to my furlough plans, so my plans will be as I have outlined to you: study Berlitz until March 5th; deputation in south Scotland and the Midland Scotland (March 5–April 5 or 12); classes in Belgium from April 15–July 30; then go straight to the Congo; spend one month at the State School in Leopoldville and then go up river to Yakusu "Home" by the end of October. . ."

A vignette of deputation "ease"

Alex wrote from Galashiels on March 21: "I am staying at Galasheils with the wealthy widow of a doctor. I have been happy in the exceeding great kindness of the friends with whom I have stayed all of whom have petted and spoiled me. I have had a hot water bottle in bed and hot water to wash with in every home where I have been. . ."

A detour to Brussels via Cambridge

He had promised to visit "Litwasi", the orphaned daughter of Mrs. Millman of Yakusu in Rochdale, Lancashire, near Manchester. (Litwasi was the daughter of Mr. and Mrs. Stapleton. Her father died when she was small and her mother married Mr. Millman whose wife had also died.) Litwasi was about ten years of age. "She had forgotten seeing me at Yakusu but she took to me and before evening, when I again had to leave for another night journey, she had kissed me and played with me in a way which quite touched my heart. . .".

On April 10, 1914 he wrote from "5 Willow Walk, Cambridge", the home of the Henry Starte family. In some way he had gotten an invitation (probably through Florence Starte, Ethel's maiden sister) to visit the Starte family en route to Brussels. He had left his things at Mrs. Saunder's home in London so he needed to pick them up there. Alex does not mention seeing Ethel in Cambridge, but simply comments that "Thursday night I came down here. I just did as I liked and had such a comfortable time and such a helpful fellowship that I hope to be going on my way rejoicing (perhaps tonight). Do write to Florrie Starte for my sake if possible. . . Address your next letter to 11–13 Rue Ernest Allard, Bruxcelles, Belgium. . ." (This was the address of the Chez l'Union Chretienne de Jeunes Gens.)

Springtime in Brussels: April to July

Three letters came to Canada from Alex during his sojourn in Belgium. "If I can't come to Canada I can at least try to bring Bruxelles a little closer to you. You would be surprised to see how much the city resembles any well built British city. . .It is more like London in respect to having many open spaces. But London is nothing to Brussels in the way of monuments and squares! Every street corner almost has its statue, good, bad and indifferent. Fountains flow along the middle of some streets. . . The streets are washed daily and frequently by hose pipes in the dry weather."

He mentions little about his classes in French and at the Tropical Medicine Institute. "I hope, towards the end of the term, to understand the lectures and to acquire some facility in the use of the medical microscope". However Alex did get a diploma from the Institute which I have in my possession. He was shocked by the ritualism of the Roman Catholic Church and their outdoor processionals. He visited several congregations of the Belgium Protestant Church. Alex also refrains from any comments of the clouds of war which are looming treacherously over Western Europe. Alex sent to Canada that summer several of our family curios which have survived eight decades: two little carved canoes "which David Botela of Yalikina made for you. . .also the leopard's claw which the natives use as a charm, but can serve you for 'Good Luck'. . ."

An invitation to return to Cambridge and "a whirlwind courtship"

Alex tells John and Clara that the Starte family has invited him for a week of holiday. He commented that it was too expensive to go back to Scotland and he needed two weeks of rest and time to pack before returning to the Congo.

The stage was set for Ethel and Alex to finally get together. The Starte family was certainly cooperating in every way possible. He arrived in Cambridge on July 15 and wrote to Clara:

"I am too lazy to write much and I have some other business arrangements to make for my departure from Cambridge the day after tomorrow or next day so I will continue this letter from on board the boat when I am on my way back 'Home'." But he stayed July 17, 18, 19 and 21. The details of the events of July 18, 19 and 20 are graphically chronicled in his letters to Clara and Grandfather Mill dated July 21 and 22 and an undated letter from Ethel to Grandfather Mill after he had come down in early August to meet the Starte family. (See PART TWO D. pp. 38–39 on Ethel Clara Starte.) The essence of the letter was poetically expressed by Alex to his father in the words:

"NOW THE MILL HAS GOT A STARTE!!"

Alex said that he could now sing "with the repaired cords of my heart a song which throbbed there long ago" and "I am now engaged to as well as by my early and true sweetheart Ethel Starte". Ethel responded in writing with her typical reserve to Grandfather Mill,

"I hope that I shall never hurt him again as I did when first I knew him. But I didn't know him as you (Father Mill) know him. . .".

Three weeks of reprieve!

The mission board granted Alex an extra three weeks before he had to be ready to leave on September 1. It was one of the happiest times for both Alex, Ethel and their families. Grandfather Mill came down for a visit to Cambridge. I have a photo of him boating on the Cam River with the Starte brothers, Alex and Ethel. The Starte family took the newly engaged couple on a holiday to the beach near Harwich. Florrie Starte wrote to Clara a long letter about all the fun and frolic they had together.

But by late August 1914 World War I had broken out between Great Britain, Belgium and France and the Axis Powers. Alex wrote on August 23:

"Ethel is busy writing at my side. . . Now the question is 'How can I get back to the Congo with the war now beginning?'"

On September 17 he informed Clara and John: "I leave on September 26 from Liverpool . . .Lights are flashing over London, searching for any approach of hostile aircraft. . ."

Alex and Ethel had to say farewell under adverse circumstances. Alex wrote from aboard the "S.S. Loauda" between Cape Verde Islands and Principe on October 19:

"By the exigencies of the situation I was denied the opportunity for a private farewell. Hospital rules are very strict and as I was going to leave at a time on Saturday when Ethel was to be on duty she could not possibly get off for that. On the Friday night previous too it was the night of her examination on the subject of nursing. I was sorry for her just to have to run out between the close of the exam and closing time (and against the rules too) to say goodbye. The only place we had to go was the railway station and we had to say goodbye at the corner of a street just within view of the Hospital . . ."

Arriving in the Congo for his second term

Alex evidently arrived in early November and spent a month at the government Sleeping Sickness Department in Leopoldville. "The government Department treated me very handsomely and paid my expenses and more while there by giving me 441 francs or about 25 pounds sterling. I have also got on the steamer with me 9 cases from them including microscope, balances and medicines for my medical work in Yakusu." By December 7 he was aboard the "S.S. Sagetini" on the Congo River, arriving at Yakusu on December 24. He wrote to Clara en route about "Ethel's practical Christianity and kindness. . .I will try to be worthy of her in what I do." On December 31, in a long letter to Grandfather Mill he told him how the box of chemicals had been soaked in water on the voyage and many of the contents broken. However the things in the tin trunk had arrived well: the bootlaces, drill, saw, watch and little electric bell set . . .".

"Dear Father, you have made this 'homecoming' very nice for me both by the willingness with which to let me go and by your numerous letters and the gifts and requisites which you sent out packed in the box and the trunk. . ."

THE YEARS 1915 to 1919

The next five years of Alex's life in the Belgian Congo and Britain, 1915–1919, seem to form a distinct period in the formation of his style of missionary endeavor and his attitudes toward African people. During this period, important events were also transpiring in the life of Clara and John in Canada and in the life of Ethel Starte in England. 1919 marked the birth of my wife, Maxine Banta Sinclair near Topeka, Kansas.

1915

John and Clara in September began their third year at the MacDonald Memorial Baptist Mission, East Elmwood, Winnipeg. Catherine Grace celebrated her first birthday on August 31. The family of Uncle Gladstone in Glasgow had now grown to four: Fred, Mari, Gladdie and Archie.

1916

Mona Jamesina, Clara and John's second daughter, was born on July 12 in Winnipeg. Ethel completed her nursing training at Guy's Hospital, London and had hopes of going out to Africa to be married to Alex in 1917.

1917

The United States declared war on the Axis Powers. John graduated with the theological degree "Associate of Theology" from the Northern Baptist Seminary, Chicago on June 1. Henderson Peat Sinclair, ("Uncle Harry") was killed in action with the Canadian troops in France, August 29 at the age of 32. He left his widow, Margaret, and two children, aged four and seven.

1918

Martha Muriel Sinclair was born on March 14 in Winnipeg. Clara and John moved to Cranbrook, B.C. in the summer, just before the devastating flu epidemic in the fall of 1918. Alex and Ethel were married in Cambridge, England on August 1. Grandfather Mill immigrated to Canada on September 26. Robert Peat Sinclair ("wee Bobbie"), John's youngest brother left home in Winnipeg for the U.S.A.

1919

Alex and Ethel sailed to the Congo on March 28. Lillian Maxine Banta was born on September 19.

E. THE YEAR 1915: Alex settles in a four year term

Alex often shared with Clara and John vignettes of individual African friends. His sensitivity to the uniqueness of the natives is reflected as he writes:

"Dear Clara: . . .I wonder how I am succeeding. . .I asked our teacher about a man whom I examined how his life in the village compared with his profession. He told me that this man is wonderfully patient and even if struck by another he would refrain from retaliation. He would give to the church collection even if it meant that he had to give his loin cloth itself. This being all he had, we did not advise that!

"Our preaching still gets a respectful hearing and a goodly number of hearers receive the seed. The main problems are: growth as in the young convert who starts teaching his village before he realizes his own weakness and the nature of the conflict with evil and growth arrested as in the case of the successful evangelist who wearies in the work because of. . .the deadening influence of the environment. The Foma tribe has some 100 villages standing open to us. The Esoo tribe has 66 and we have only slightly touched them. . ." (7/26/15)

". . .Another woman whom I examined told me that she was much impressed with the story of Christ's treatment of the Canaanite woman whose daughter was cured by Christ after his insistent preaching. In relating the story to me the woman made the story wind up very curiously for she said that when the woman returned to the house she found even the dog 'dancing' for joy!!

"Clara. . .I unexpectedly boarded a river steamer to go up to Stanleyville and I found among the native passengers a member of our Church. He was going to give evidence on the death of a man who died of Sleeping Sickness. His face was most terribly scarred by smallpox and he had only one good eye. But when I asked him whether he was daily remembering to pray, he produced at once from the fold of his robe the copy of the Psalms which had been given to him at his baptism. He was reading it with his companions morning and night. . ." (10/21/15)

Correspondence with Ethel

Alex and Ethel had said goodbye in London in late September before he sailed for the Congo. "Ethel and I are getting to understand each other alright in correspondence now but I wish I had known her longer." (1/17/15)

"Ethel hopes to be ready to leave Guy's Hospital in December 1916 and then she will come out to me and spend her two years of probationer missionary as my wife. I often wonder if I will be able to make home life important enough among my other duties to give Ethel her due of attention and consideration. I am getting quite careless and hard and matter of fact and feelingless out here. But I am counting on her coming out to have the softening and refining influence. Her letters are all that makes for this and make me think more than anything else. I don't think it would be wise for you to say too much to Ethel about her maternal prospects. Even kindly said, remarks on this subject might hurt. . ." (Note: Was Alex thinking that Ethel at age 35 might not be able to have children?) (4/26/15)

There is a lovely letter from Ethel to Alex written over several days from the "Nursing Hostel" which began on June 16 (1915 ?). Alex kept this letter in a worn leather folder with a few other personal items which he took to the nursing home in 1967.

"My dearest boy. . .Fancy Matron asked me if I would like to go out in a punt with her and her friends so I did. We sat under a tree in the punt near St. John's College and then went and had tea near Clare College. I had a little methy spirit stove in the end of the punt. We had a really delicious time. . .

". . .had an operation this morning at 8 a.m., cancer of the breast. . . today two tonsils and adenoids removed: one boy and one girl. . .an Indian patient Mr. Ramanujan for gastric ulcers. . .

"You poor old thing what are you doing tonight—reading a nice book? Cuffing somebody's ears? Translating? Think how you would be hindered if I were there! Thank your lucky stars that you are left in peace for a little longer yet. . . .

"I am nursing Mr. Hillyer, a Fellow of Magdalene College. He is about 60 and his wife about 56. I think he is one of the nicest patients that I've ever nursed. A gentleman through and through. Not a bit of humour, word, joke or action out of taste. I shall be sorry when he goes on Friday. . .

"Mother dreamt that she saw you and boys at home all together, if only it were a reality! (Horace and Harold in India; Alex in the Congo and Herbert soon to leave for the Congo.) Shall I ever see you? They tell me the war is going to last five years and there'll hardly be anyone left. . .I go round and say goodnight to all my patients and you are the last but first. Goodnight, Sunny Jim. . . .

"Matron let me go home for tea Sunday and I was out till ten. Of course I found you there when I got home sitting on the edge of my chair. Do you remember the photo on the piano? . . .Dad is going to get the boat out and give it an oiling. Dad's a brick. Goodnight Alex. I wish you were coming. . .

"Elsie (younger sister) is home and we had a most glorious half day down the River yesterday. Aunt Rose came with us. She had the post of knocking the weeds off the end of the boat. We had just sat down to tea and then discovered that the milk was left behind. So Elsie and I jumped into the boat and went to the other side of the river to a dairy farm and got the coveted fluid. . ." (Note: The River Cam is quite shallow at Cambridge, filled with aquatic plants and meanders along through farmland.)

"Elsie went into Furnival Street (offices of the Baptist Missionary Society) and got the necessary money to pay for your things—14 pounds. Will you be ruined? The beauty of it was they mistook Elsie for me and told her how sorry they were to still see her in England instead of Africa. So she said she gasped and then enlightened them! Here's how I spent your money:

For my bracelet	3.10.0
Two white suits sent for you	2.10.0
1 pair Chrone Canvas Boots	16.6
2 pair white shorts	3.00.0
2 pair khaki shorts	2.17.0
	12.13.6

So you see I still have on hand 1.6.6. I am buying you a "fountain pen" for your birthday (July 22) which I am bringing out for fear it should get lost on the way. (Note: It is clear that Ethel was counting on sailing out to Africa sometime after December, 1916 when she would graduate from Guy's Hospital.)

". . .I wish I could come out with the mail which is out today. But instead of looking after Africans, I must stay and look after an Indian. Cheer up. The time will soon pass. I like it when I'm busiest then I don't have time to think about things but what does it matter for I suppose this is all planned for us. . . .Ever yours, Ethel."

Alex struggled with the issues which all the other missionaries faced in the Congo in the building of a Christian community among the thousands of newly baptized believers. One issue was the superstition of totemism.

On totemism

Totemism is the superstition that dead people are reincarnated into animals and inanimate objects. Alex wrote to his future brother-in-law Horace in India: "Totemism exists in a very crude and elementary form and has not been systematized into a cult. Many believe that dead men turn into leopards and lions. Today when examining medical cases I was told that a certain very efficacious remedy for "yaws" could be made from pounded bark mixed with a red stone which was supposed to be the coagulated blood of the dead ancestors petrified in the earth."

Comments on the course of the War

"Horace, how stubbornly Germany is maintaining her ill got territory in Belgium! The signs of disintegration in the Austrian Empire are very evident and alarming for them. The same thing among the Germany states would stop the war. . ." (1/31/15)

"Dear Father. . .I get the papers regularly and enjoy the History of the War very much. May our country at this time have God's Guidance and strength to sustain the strain of the conflict and the delirium of success (as I believe and hope for) . . . (2/25/15)

"Dear Clara and John. . .The Canadian Contingent has distinguished themselves very signally in the fighting at Neuve Chapelle. What a contrast with the United States? One wonders how the feeling runs between them and you Canadians. The sinking of the 'Lusitania' was a great sorrow to them it seems but not a great stimulus to action. . ." (July 26, 1915)

"Dear Clara and John. . .How war changes the conditions. This conflagration of Europe has I hope reached its boundary with the implication of Bulgaria and Romania. I feel apprehensive yet as to what Holland will do and successes for the Germans in the extreme East might carry the war to India. God forbid. In my heart of hearts I think the USA is being wisely guided to keep out of the struggle but I would not like to have the criticisms hurled at one that President Wilson is having. So you have lost your helper in the home now and her husband has gone to the war or to his grave. (This reference is to Margaret and Andrew Fyfe in Winnipeg). Which? No one but generals it seems to me will live through this war from the beginning to the end. . ." (12/2/15)

Herbert Starte (Ethel's brother) leaves for the Congo

The news from Cambridge is that Herbert Starte has been successful in his language examination and has been appointed by the Baptist Missionary Society to serve in the Congo. He will be going out in August or September. Alex wrote to Grandfather Starte: "I have just heard that Herbert has done me a great favor. . .He has promised, with Ethel's consent, to bring out the wedding ring when he comes. Perhaps you have seen it but it has no meaning yet. I am looking forward to the time when you shall see the ring carried by the hand which is carried by mine when I bring your daughter home to you as my wife. I promise you that God helping us we will fulfil your highest hopes. . ." (Letter is not dated but seems to be sent in June or July since Alex refers to a photograph of Herbert in the May issues of THE MISSIONARY HERALD.)

Alex "captains" the "S.S. Grenfell" for the first time

"We got our turn of use of the little steamer Grenfell. On the first run Mr. Lambotte captained her; on the second and fourth Mr. Pugh; on the third Mr. Millman and by watching him and risking a little I have now taken the direction most of the voyage. We have been out now 4 days from our station and have visited 16 towns about 70 miles down river from Yakusu." (1/31/15)

"We are able to preach from her deck; sleep and eat in her. We have communion services, marriage services and enquirers classes on her upper deck and so get quite close to the people in their village life. I am also able to give medicine to people with simple ailments. They are not slow to ask for it. Crowds come every day. . ." (2/25/15)

Work with Sleeping Sickness patients

"I have been hardly able to give time to the treatment of Sleeping Sickness cases because of the other demands of the school and church work. I have found however some 11 cases this last week without much searching and this looks ominous. An island has been deforested by the State and a segregation settlement formed there. We put grave cases there so as to keep them from infecting others. However few natives will trust the State enough to go and live there if they have the disease. I am trying to persuade them to go and trying to help the State treat them. . . The natives have a great dislike of being sent to the Island and try to hide when they have the disease. . ." (1/31/15) (2/25/15)

"To make sure that they have the disease I have to take the microscope round with me and examine a specimen of the gland juice of suspected persons. This takes some time but I have found up to the present some 25 positively deadly cases and am trying to persuade them to go to the Island. To help them to get confidence in the State native doctors, I try to go to the Island myself and superintend the giving of the injections and the treatment. The State is treating them well. They have cleared the forest from the Island so that the Tsetse fly may be exterminated. They have built good mud and grass houses and have given them free medical treatment—only they are prisoners while there!" (2/25/15)

"Father. . .There is enough to do and enough people to preach to and advise to occupy many lifetimes. Besides there is all the Sleeping Sickness work. I have already over 60 patients scattered over 80 miles of river in 30 different villages. This is only a part of the number who are tainted with this incurable disease. Incurable and unlikely to be cured too for no one man can do this work of a weekly injection to such a number under such conditions and especially when they have a superstitious fear of injection needle and generally run away. . .I am looking for a black assistant to train who might help me in my microscopic examinations for I find it a strain on my eyes. . ." (5/19/15)

"Clara. . .I have tried my best at the Sleeping Sickness prophylaxis but the natives fight against their best interests and fear my medicine. If they are known by their parents to have swollen glands they are hidden by their parents lest the family should get a bad reputation as being diseased. . .they are despised and sent to the forest to live. They prefer even this to coming to the segregation Island to live. . .They would prefer to die than to come and have their glands pierced by a needle to see whether they have the germ there or not.

"The chiefs have been told that it is a spreading disease and they ought to compel their people to have treatment but—they are not scientific— they are not reasonable and only when stirred up to act by the presence of a white man do they exert their authority. . ." (6/7/15)

"John. . .I still find time. . .for the work of medicine, especially that of administering treatment to Sleeping Sickness cases. I cannot yet speak of a single cure but I have several cases who are hopeful of it. That is to say that they are hopeful but am not. . .I continue to work in the Dispensary and treat about 50 patients daily. . .I may soon be able to take in patients from a distance for I am finishing the building for a place which will accommodate about 12. . .Now pray for a suitable native male nurse with inclination and capacity for such work. . ." (9/27/15)

How I use the "Glasgow Herald"

"Father, I never forget to take some of your 'Glasgow Heralds' with me on my journeys. I do not read them; that is not them all. There are other uses for newspapers. Here are some of them: floor mat when living in a 'jigger' infected hut. Wrappers for books. Parceling up medicines. Tablecloth, etc. etc. This morning I wakened to find that the rain was coming through the roof. So I groped for the matches and found a 'Glasgow Herald' and spread it on the top of my mosquito net to catch the drops. So there is some use for a Tory paper after all!

"However the copies of 'Punch' which you sent are not submitted to such ignominious treatment but I only get time to glance through them. I then give them to one or another State official who knows a little English and so make friends with them. . ." (4/1/15)

Descriptions of "his boys" and helpers

"One is a preacher heart and soul. One is a cook. One is a little 'jack of all trades'. Another is a boy who attends my table and follows we everywhere and whose marking or marring I have in my own hands. He is a sharp lad.

"I have recently taken on an elderly man to teach him how to dispense the medicines in my absence and to nurse serious cases with me when they come in. His name is Liaocho (pronouned Lee-ah-o-choo) . . .He knows how to bandage up pretty well but he forgets to clean out a wound thoroughly. He is a terror for giving 'Caster Oil'." (10/21/15)

Another is the clown of the company. He does not know it but he thinks he is the commander-in-chief, but serves best at woodcutting and the like. . ." (4/1/15)

Some glimpses of itineration journeys

"I have been doing some stiff marching during the last week 20 miles a day sometimes through the forest. . ." (4/1/15)

"I have just made a cursory tour of 77 villages in one section of my parish. 30 of them have schools and teachers. All of them are engulfed in the great green forest whose limits I have never reached. This meant that I travelled with a train of men carrying loads in front of me. I carry as little provisions and clothing as possible. I shave about once a week. Mr. Millman lent me a shotgun and my helper shot 4 monkeys and 35 bats, all of which the carriers greedily ate.

"The collections from the schools were queer. One was sugarcane, another little knives and native hairpins and finery. Here I am now at the headwaters of a forest stream awaiting a canoe to take me back to the river. As it is behind time, I am just going down in a small canoe with 3 or 4 boys to look for it. If I don't find it I shall just have to sleep out—or in a hut. If my food gets short I can buy native rice and cassava roots and bananas and sugarcane and monkey nuts and palm oil and so keep the machine working—granted good health. I hope however to be greeted by the 'S.S. Grenfell' on the Lomani River and to voyage on her back to Yakusu. . ." (1/20/16)

Concerns about Grandfather Mill

Since Clara has been away in Canada for nearly two years and Alex has been away over six months, he is concerned about how Father Mill is dealing with his loneliness. "Clara. . .I think Gladstone and Jeannie ought to think it a privilege to make their next home big enough to enable him to lodge there free of charge if he liked. Of course he would not do it unless he were compelled. But we do not know how soon he might be ill . . ." (4/25/15)

Alex, Gladstone and Clara continue their concern about Father. Perhaps he can marry again? "Dear Clara. . .Father writes that Miss Brown was giving up business. I thought that perhaps he thought she should marry him. But I think he is almost past the marrying age. . ." (Note: Grandfather Mill was 55 years old in 1915.)

Again Alex is hopeful that Miss Brown may be the solution for his Father.

"Clara, you seem to have had the same idea I had: Father's weekend visits to Miss Brown at Burnside meant the prelude to a proposal for marriage. I wonder if we both have been deluded for I have heard of no developments." (7/26/15)

"Clara. . .the hen farming and Miss Brown for Father seem to have gone where most dreams go. . ." (12/2/15)

"John. . .I have just heard of Father's venture to break with his old occupation which had grown irksome to him. I am sorry that he succeeded in the way he did before settling down elsewhere. I don't know what the provocation was. . ." (3/3/16) (Note: It seems that after about 30 years as a clerk in the ironmonger's business, either Father Mill quit in disgust over something or he was fired. I remember that Mother wrote that he was let out without any pension after serving the company faithfully for many years.)

By late 1916, Father Mill had gone to Wales to work in agriculture. Alex wrote that "I fear it is too rigorous for him although he pretends to like it. . ."

Brick making, dispensing and teaching

"Dear Clara. . . I am either brick-building, road-mending, school teaching or dispensing and so I get diverted from the main issue of working with people. Then besides I am still a long way off from the people even though I know their language. I do not feel quite as they feel and they feel that I do not feel quite as they feel. I do not understand all their customs. I must try to give myself more to this. . .Goodbye my dear little sister. You would be surprised to know that I can now say that because I have a beard! . . .I must close now. The mail boat comes down tomorrow morning. . ." (4/26/15)

Just call me "Solomon"!

"Dear Clara. . . My work is pretty much keeping the eager ones from going too fast and stirring up the indifferent ones to do their part and giving to all 'Wisdom'. . .Everything I do is taken to have a meaning. I am supposed to know all things, especially about disease and sickness and to be able to put all troublesome affairs straight by my advice—especially matrimonial affairs! I simply can't do it. I go about from village to village and preach and try to get the people to exercise their own common sense and to settle their own affairs. Often I feel that my example falls short of the Message I preach of love and perfect deliverance from sin by the power of Christ. . ." (6/7/15)

Mixed motives and desires

"Yesterday 25 men came from a village 2 days journey away willing to carry my bed, my food, my chair, my table, my lamp, my clothes, my salt (money), etc. if I would come with teachers to their villages and stay a day or two. I hope to go but what about the teachers?. . .I do not know if the desire of the people for learning is altogether purely from desire to know about God. But, pure desire! Why, it is a thing almost non-existent—we all have mixed desires and mixed motives. But I take it as an opportunity to give them a chance of knowing and wishing for higher things than they ever realized themselves. . ." (6/7/15)

Making bricks like the Children of Israel

"Clara, I have a little building scheme on hand. I am getting the natives of one village to make 10,000 sun-dried bricks (like the Children of Israel made in Egypt) to build a little brick schoolhouse. It will be the first of its kind. Only 5,000 bricks have been made in three months!" (6/7/15)

"I am building the new brick wing of the 'Ward' of the Dispensary and attending to the printing of the native monthly magazine. . ." (7/26/15)

You ask what I am reading

"John, I don't do much else beside reading in my spare time. I divide my reading time for the present between 'The Life of Judson' and 'Punch'. I think the one counterbalances the other!" (9/27/15)

I am still too "Scotch"

"Dear Clara. . .I am well, but hardly quite 'enjoying life' as you would say. Perhaps I am still too 'Scotch' to enjoy life but you seem certainly to have been quite assimilated to the Canadian climate and ideal. . . .I think that Father is losing a little of the joy of old age because of some of these things which he neglected, or thought it unnecessary to tell us about when children. At any rate, this is for your ear alone, I would like to have been told a little more. How grateful we would have been to him then when we had come up against the real experience." (10/21/15)

F. THE YEAR 1916

I am trying to imagine what. . .

". . .the wooden Mission home at the corner of Grey and Castle Avenues in Winnipeg is like inside. Perhaps it will only be when I have my own heart and home full that I will be able to conceive it. I imagine that there is not much grass or garden about there although there are plenty of grain elevators and shops for gardening and farmer tools. . ." (12/2/15)

You ask what my garden is like

"Dear Mother and Dad (Starte) . . .When I have some spare time I do a little gardening. When I think of your tiny patch behind Willow Walk and look at my own big garden back and front, I feel ashamed that I do not look after it better. I could get any amount of ground for gardening if I liked. The ground grows things almost so quickly that you can see them rise. But that just make us have all the more pruning to do for nothing that grows rank preserves the neatness of a garden.

"Today I have been cutting down my line hedges. I have also orange trees which are now beginning to bear. I have mango trees which give a lovely shade and bear fruit. Bushes like holly and other flowering bushes and palms are the other trees. Flowers are rare at present but I have marigolds, a pink creeper and a few roses. The best and most decorative bushes are called "crotons". The variegated leaves range from green to yellow, orange scarlet and brown and looks like a bush afire. All this green stuff growing close together makes the place very damp and keep the ground wet for a long time after our thunderstorms so I try to cut it down as much as possible. . .".

My daily schedule at Yakusu during
the Advanced Teacher Training School

"Dear John and Clara. . .We have between 30 and 40 of the advanced class in session at Yakusu just now. They have lessons from morning till night and many complain of writer's cramp!

6 a.m. Early morning prayers
6: 30   Recitation of a Psalm by heart (set the day before)
7:30   Break
8:30   Homiletics, Mr. Pugh
10:00 French, Mr. Millman
11:00 Exercise and Drill

11:30 Arithmetic
12:00 Break
3:00 Singing (solfa)
4:00 Elementary physiology, Mr. Mill

This is their daily program. After it is all over the teaching staff gathers to talk over about half the things we would like to talk of and then get off to preparation for the next day's classes. Three of the new teachers are from the new work on the Lomami 100 miles away. Two trusted teachers have disgraced themselves by doing what in the native eyes is looked upon as only adultery. . ." (4/14/16)

How I get along with my colleagues

"John, we are pretty congenial spirits but our unit is more complementary than identical, more potential than realized. I find much unity in spirit in association with Mr. Millman, but he towers above me in intellect, experience and office and we have little time to confer. . ." (3/3/16)

News from Ethel: "I may not be able to come out this year"

Alex writes Clara, "Ethel says that she may not be able to come out at the end of 1916 because she may have to give four extra months to get her C.M.B. certificate. I can only hope that the time will go swiftly. . ." (Certificate of Midwifery ?) (5/7/16)

The Monday morning blues

"Dear John. . .I am in a bad mood tonight partly because I let my mind dwell too much on my own interests during the day and partly because of the reaction after the recent ten days' busy journey through the Bamanga country. I can quite understand you feeling the same on a Monday morning after an exciting and busy Sunday. . ." (5/20/16)

An invitation to serve as army chaplain

"I received news that I am requested to go forward as a Chaplain to the troops which are fighting in East Africa. I accepted, though with a few thoughts of reluctance, for the work is so needy just now in our Yakusu district. . .I am waiting for orders from the Governor of Congo to know when I am to go and where I shall be placed. . . .As it is the only chance I shall likely have of taking any part in the War, I shall enjoy taking the risk. Of course I do not expect I shall be in any fighting. I pray that the strife may soon cease but the life will be rougher I expect than here at Yakusu. . ." (5/20/16)

SERVICE AS ARMY CHAPLAIN TO
CONGOLESE TROOPS

(June–December, 1916)

Since Alex had responded positively to the Governor-General in Boma on May 26, 1916 that he was willing to serve as chaplain and since there is no correspondence from Alex to my parents from May 20, 1916 to January 20, 1917, it can be presumed that he did go on that assignment. The secrecy required for troop movements in East Africa during World War I probably made it necessary for him not to write during that period.

However in later years, he never mentioned this period of service with the Congolese troops. Was it that his deep revulsion to war made it difficult for him to comment about that experience in his life?

Hochschild's book on King Leopold I has only the following reference to the use of Congolese troops during World War I in East Africa:

". . .Forced labor became particularly brutal during the first World War. In 1916, an expanded Force Publique invaded German West Africa, today's Tanzania. Enormous numbers of Congolese were conscripted as soldiers or porters. In 1916, by colonial official's count, one area in the eastern Congo, with a population of 83,518 adult men, supplied more than three million man days of porterage during that year. 1,359 of these porters were worked to death or died of disease. . ." (p. 278)

This experience was the only part of Alex's missionary career that he chose to try to forget.

4 FURNIVAL STREET, LONDON.

telegraphique:
ASIATIC MATADI.

MATADI,
CONGO BELGE,
WEST CENTRAL AFR

MAy 26th 1916.

To
His Excellency
The Governor General of Congo Belge
Boma.

Sir

In further reference to your Excellency's
letter No 4555 under date the Ist May, I have the
honour to state that we have received a telegram today
informing us that the Rev A G Mill has agreed to fill
the Chaplaincy post which your Excellency has done us
the honour to offer. The Rev A G Mill has signified
his desire to accept the "indemnité en lieu du ravitaille-
ment. He will await your instructions at the address
given in full below.

I have the honour to be,

Sir

Your Excellency's most obedient
servant

Rev A G Mill
B M S,
Yakusu

We have no correspondence written by Uncle Alex before, during or after his service as chaplain with the Congolese native troops on the Eastern frontier during World War I. It is presumed that these were African colonial troops which supported the European military. The secrecy of troop movements may well have been the reason for no correspondence.

Born at
Glasgow.
22nd July,
1885

MR. A. G. MILL.

Mr. Mill was brought to Christ at the age of seven, and the desire to be a Missionary was early awakened by a lime-light display dealing with Africa's sorrows. After he was baptised, at Kelvinside Baptist Church in 1898, the definite call came through one of his Pastor's Missionary addresses. Mr. Mill's parents gave him seven years' architectural apprenticeship with a view to a Missionary career, and during that time he had the opportunity of working for Christ in the Open-air, Christian Endeavour, and Sunday-school work. He has also had a four years' Theological course at the Pastors' College, and a six months' medical course at Livingstone College.

1911

NEWS has been received that Lieutenant Frank Longland has passed Stanley Falls, beyond Yakusu, on his way to the Eastern Congo frontier in his capacity of chaplain with the Belgian Congo army. The Rev. A. G. Mill of Yakusu is also serving as a chaplain. The Rev. David Jones, of Wathen, has reached England on furlough, the Rev. A. A. Lambourne is in Lisbon studying Portuguese, and the Rev. W. D. Reynolds, B.A., B.D., is taking up service in connection with the Y.M.C.A. abroad for six months before his return to Congo after furlough.

Appointed 1911
Yakusu, 1911 —
(On Belgian Colonial Chaplaincy Service
during the war)

(Note: I obtained from the BMS archives a copy of the letter which the BMS home office had been sent "To His Excellency the Governor General of the Congo Belge, Boma" in which Alex's affirmative answer by telegraph been received on May 26, 1916 in London. The letter concluded: "The Rev. A.G. Mill will await your instructions. . .". My opinion is that the Congolese troops were used as support personnel for the East Africa campaign around Lake Tanganyika, but I have not researched this matter further. I note that he was evidently away for most of the remaining months of 1916, since there is no correspondence from Yakusu to document his activities.)

G. THE YEAR 1917

January, 1917 finds Alex out in the forest again. He writes in pencil since "I only took one fountain pen full for the whole three weeks-odd journey." There are only five letters to document his 1917 activities: January 20, April 6 and 22, October 18 and November 3. The Henri Lambottes now have a baby girl "Yvonne", born in 1916. Alex enjoyed having the little one to hold. Plans for Ethel coming out were still uncertain since the BMS had cancelled all travel plans for single missionaries because of the submarine danger in the Atlantic Ocean. Alex wrote on April 4, 1917:

"What a disappointment it must have been for Ethel when she had already said goodbye practically to her friends and had received ever so many marriage presents! I can only faintly imagine and being so far away from her my letters of condolence can only arrive about 2 months after all the worst of the trial is over. It is good that we both have a mutual friend who can comfort us both. How terrible the war is getting! President Wilson cannot hope to get a hearing in arranging peace terms unless he has staked something precious on the great dispute of arms which locks us in its grip. . . .I don't think that the Allies can impose too rigorous a peace on the German people when she still holds intact all her native soil and has the prospect of ever friendly trade with the U.S.A. . ." (4/6/17). (Note: The United States had still not declared war.)

John and Clara had inquired about missionary service in South America (Regions Beyond Mission Union or the Canadian Baptist Mission Board), but decided that going out with two little girls would be too risky. The China missionary appointment possibility is mentioned only once by Alex. John was awarded the Associate of Theology degree from the Northern Baptist Theological Seminary in Chicago in June, 1917. Apparently that seminary took his credits from Harley College and Brandon College, examined him by correspondence and found him qualified for the Associate of Theology degree.

Uncle Harry killed in France

The great sadness in the Sinclair family household was the death of Henderson "Harry" Sinclair in France on August 29, 1917 at the age of 32. He was John's eldest brother. Harry left his widow, Margaret Lechars Sinclair and two children: Henderson, Jr. "Harry" of six years and Margaret "Greta" of four years. They were living in Vancouver, B.C. at the time of Harry's enlistment in the 231 Battalion on March 25, 1916. He went to Britain on April 10, 1917 and proceeded to France, May 22, 1917. He was killed in action in the battle of Vimy Ridge as a private in the 72nd Bn. of Canadian Infantry (British Columbia). I have seen his name inscribed in the Scottish War Memorial in Edinburgh Castle.

Uncle Harry was awarded the British Cross of Honor and the Victory Medal. He is buried in Plot 10, Row F, Grave 14 in the Villers Station Cemetery near Villers-au-Bois, France. Clayton Sinclair has visited his grave. Uncle Harry's war medals were in the possession of Christina Peat Walker in Edinburgh until the late 1970s when Clayton brought them back to North America and presented them to "Harry" Sinclair in Port Charlotte, Florida. I have in my possession several beautiful letters which Aunt Margaret Sinclair wrote to my parents after Uncle Harry's death. She remarried a few years later in Big Rapids, Michigan, USA to a Mr. Van Alstine. Clayton Sinclair has made contact with that branch of the family. The children of Margaret "Greta" Sinclair Sarracino have kept in contact with the Van Alstine relatives.

My "art gallery"

"Dear Jonathan. . .I have a book of Scotch views which forms my art gallery on the sideboard and day about I open it to different pages. Yesterday it showed Lybster Harbour and Dornoch Church (Northeastern Scotland) and I thought I could hear your voice saying these names. Still I cannot imagine the stern simplicity and practicality of such places. Perhaps a struggle for existence in such an inhospitable environment breeds a philosophical and meditative strain!. . .".

Life on the Yakusu station

"Dear Clara and John. . .I am giving my spare time just now to making a tea tray for Ethel. Besides I have some fowls and chicks of my own, 2 boys in my cabbage garden, 3 boys cooking and keeping house, 3 assistants to keep watch over in the Dispensary and Hospital and 12 boys keeping station fields and roads in order. I do revision of the Old

Testament stories in the afternoons. The evenings are taken up in carrying about Baby Yvonne Lambotte. Then I have a night school for the old blockheads among the workmen and so all the time is taken up. . .We have had no mail for six weeks and no prospect of any for a month yet. I am anxious to hear how your plans for South America are maturing and also to hear from Ethel as her last was dated June. . .I hope to get home in 1918. . ." (11/13/17)

H. THE YEAR 1918: Home again! Marriage and the close of World War I

"Dear Clara. . .Our work is now in 250 villages and we are trying to get a visit in to all of them before I go home. So I will be like a washed out rag when I get on board for 'Blighty'. . ." (1/5/18) However there was a further delay of five months in leaving the Congo for Britain. The wife of Mr. Cooke of Upoto fell ill and Alex was asked to stay to relieve him until Mr. Pugh got back from furlough. Finally by June, 1918 he was on his way to Britain.

"Aboard the 'S.S. Duc de Brabant'. . .Dear Clara and John. . .I'm afraid I'll be prevented from getting home to marry Ethel on her birthday. I had built myself up for it and her too. The reason for delay is imperious. Mrs. Cook of Upoto has been dangerously ill and Cook has to go home with her at once. So I am to wait in his place at Upoto till Mr. Pugh comes out to relieve me.

"I can't bring myself contentedly to resign to God's will until I have struggled to the best of my ability to get home and fulfill the claims of love to Ethel. In any case, if I don't get home for April 27th, it will not be much later than May. She has told me that she can wait but I think it is rather ignoble and spiritless for me to wait! You see while I am waiting there is not the keen full interest in my work. It is merely marking time. . .it is a fragmentary existence. I want my mate, too!. . .I hear you are considering moving to British Columbia—getting farther away still—or nearer China is it?"

On the way "home" at last!

"Aboard the 'S.S. Anversille', Bordeaux, 25 June, 1918. . .My dear and only Sister. . .I am sending this as my reply to your letter of January 1, 1918. . .Your letter was sent to London, then forwarded to me in the Congo. I put off answering it until I was actually nearly home. God has brought me safely through the dangers of my ocean voyage. The ship will be here for ten days unloading cargo. . .German prisoners are working at the discharge of the cargo for nearly all French men are at the Front.

"This is a big ship of 8,000 tons and has brought thousands of bags of palm kernels which are made into margarine for food and provide glycerine for explosives. She also carries India rubber for motor tyres and cotton and palm oil for soap and clothing. In addition she carries 200 passengers and 12 lifeboats at which we were drilled 4 times on the journey. She carries 4 guns which practiced shooting at a floating barrel in mid ocean at about 3 miles range. Among the passengers are 7 missionaries and some Christian friends who sat at one round table at meals and played games together . . .

"The ship. . .is not out of danger yet but we hope to make the run from here to Brest by night (moonlight after 2 a.m. unfortunately) and then to wait there one day and try to run the following night from Brest to Falmouth and safety and joy and unrationed love! . . .". (6/25/18)

And on the evening of June 30 he wrote from Falmouth Harbour, "As the lovely summer sun was setting we slid safely into the harbour. We shouted hurrah when the Pilot came on board for very relief because all the way from Bordeaux we had required and were granted the escort of a French torpedo boat and had been in danger of submarines and mines.

"After we had got rested and had supper we called those of the passengers together who were willing and sang the Doxology. . . We were searched and examined by the officials when our ship arrived at Falmouth. But we gladly put up with any inconvenience so long as we ultimately got loose to run wild over the streets and fields of our native land. . ." (6/30/18)

TOGETHER AGAIN AFTER 45 MONTHS!

"CAMBRIDGE. . .I met my true and loving Ethel on the station platform. She went with me to get measured for a new pair of trousers and to get a new hat. She herself is busy nursing her mother who has been ill for six weeks with neuritis which has brought on 'herpes facialis' along two of the facial nerves. . .We will be married on August 1 in the large St. Andrew Street Baptist Church in Cambridge by the Rev. Ussher of Swavesey, the former pastor of Ethel.

". . .Ethel's love for me is so discreet and so warm (yet she can't help showing it) that I feel that I have a girl with all the wisdom and candour of my only sister with the difference that she is my own. . .Will write you on our honeymoon . . ." (7/10/18)

Who will be at our wedding?

". . .George Sinclair who is just coming out of the hospital will come down for a day or two if he is allowed to come out of the Hospital . . . Father Mill, Gladstone and Jean will probably come . . .(Gladstone was the best man) . . .Mr. Wooding, the Congo missionary from Matadi . . .Mr. and

Mrs. Starte, Elsie and Herbert. . .Aunt Rose as well as a number of friends of the Starte family. They will be opening their homes for lodgings for the visitors and never could greater kindness be purposed than is being arranged for them. . .".

Ethel's remarks on the wedding preparations

"Alex is an awful man. He wants most of my time. I don't know what for, still I've handed the nursing of Mother over to Elsie now since she is home from the hospital for a month's holiday. If only the two boys were home from India (Harold and Horace), we should all be home together for the wedding."

"I am looking forward to Oban on our honeymoon. I have never been Scotland way. Alex is thinking of us spending a day in Edinburgh. He is so fond of looking in shops. Yes, it is exciting when they both arrived (her brother Herbert and Alex). We were in the seventh heaven. . .". (7/9/18)

Alex recounts the wedding details

"Dear Clara. . .One of the difficult tasks was to arrange the transport for the guests from the chapel to the wedding tea which was held at a married cousin's house. The government does not allow petrol to be used for marriage conveyances. Even if we had wanted horse carriages it would have been difficult for August 1 fell on "Newmarket" week and horses were at a premium. At last we got 3 taxi cabs and decked in white ribbon and flowers they called at the cousin's house. . .".

"The St. Andrew Street Chapel is beautiful in itself and the communion table which stands on a circular raised dias had a huge vase of margaritas and ferns on it. I met Ethel when she came just in front outside the rail. The minister stood just behind it. He told me what I had to do and I said 'I will' before the time. Then he gave us both such homely and practical advice. Then we went out into the vestry and signed the marriage register. I then carried off my bride down the aisle amid smiling and well-wishing friends and was met in the vestibule with showers of confetti. When we had escaped into the taxi cab we found the floor strewn with rose petals and a horseshoe mirror stuck up in front! . . . At the marriage tea there were speeches. Father's was the last—and almost the best. I never heard Father speak more fittingly or more elegantly in public than on that occasion. . . We will send a copy of the bridal group with Father when he goes out to British Colombia next month . . .

"We left the same evening and seeing Peterborough by twilight left for Edinburgh, passing York and Durham in the night. We crossed the Tweed at Berwick in the misty light of a wet Scotch morning. We saw the rock-bound shore and the sheep in the hills and the stone dykes as we held each other's hands unreservedly.

"We put up at Waverly Hotel and then I forget what happened until I paid the 4 guinea bill for lodging three days later. . .". (8/7/18)

Honeymoon echoes from Oban

"Dearest sister . . .c/o Mrs. McDonald, Victoria Place, Oban. . . .It doesn't seem possible that it is only a week since the wedding. Alex has taken me about so much that it seems impossible to have seen all that we have in a week. It has been simply lovely. I had no idea that Scotland was so beautiful and strong. I can quite understand why she would turn out fine rugged characters. . .

". . .At the present month Alex has dropped off to sleep on top of this Oban Hill. We are surrounded here by a very massive stone circular wall which has the appearance of a colosseum. There are three tiers of windows all around. We are in fact rather curious to know what the builders intended to build! From where we sit it is a lovely view over the 'Lock' or rather (I'm corrected by my superior husband) 'The Firth of Lorn'!"

I thought I would give Alec a surprise when he woke up so I just slipped outside the wall and sat down to write. But my pleasure was short lived. He was around in three minutes! . . .". (8/7/18)

"Dear John. . .Ethel and I can stand a lot of each other's company. We are on our honeymoon as you have guessed (as also has the landlady and the other boarders) but we have not yet seen the moon—so dreary and wet has been the weather. . .

"We cycled in lowering weather at the start to Melford Pass 12 miles from Oban. By the time we were half an hour on the road, it was raining and the further we went the wetter it got till when we were well up in the wooded pass we had to eat our lunch under my mackintosh; and then we cycled back like "drooned crabs". But we simply can't be gloomy. I suppose the text is true: 'Many waters cannot quench love.'"

News of the death of Henri Lambotte

The honeymoon joy was dampened by the news via wireless of the sudden death of Alex's dear colleague Henri Lambotte in Yakusu on July 31st. He writes, "I was struck dumb for some time. . .but after a few hours I made up my mind to continue enjoying my holiday with the thought that my grief stricken colleagues and the sorrowing wife and young mother would find their best solace where no human can come, in the communion of the eternal voice which is unheard. . .". (8/8/18) (See pages 54–56 for the details of the death of Henri Lambotte.)

I. SIX MONTHS DEPUTATION WORK IN ENGLAND
(September, 1918 to February, 1919)

These were very happy months for everyone in the Mill and Sinclair families. Father Mill finally set sail for British Columbia via New York on September 26. Alex and Gladstone put together 45 pounds to cover his passage, plus 10 pounds for his landing fees in New York. He went by rail across the U.S.A. to Winnipeg where he spent some days with Grandfather and Grandmother Sinclair whom he had not seen for over eight years. John and Clara agreed to pay back to Alex and Gladstone one-third of the expenses of Father's passage as they were able. It was understood that the three of them would share in his weekly room and board costs (the estimate was one-half pound a week (US$2.50) in Cranbrook, B.C. until he could become self-supporting.

Alex and Ethel enjoyed traveling together as they spoke in Baptist churches in England. Ethel writes: "I've seen much more of England than I ever expected to: Newcastle, Kent, Leeds, etc." (10/12/18). Alex took his interpretation work very seriously since he states "I am the only man in the British Isles, much less from the B.M.S., who really knows the great extent and deep needs of our work in Central Africa. . .". (9/26/18)

At times they shared the platform with Ethel's brother Herbert Starte. After a two-month stay at Goldsmith College near London taking special courses on "Tropical Diseases", and "How to Teach", Alex and Ethel were busy packing to leave on March 28, 1919 on the "S.S. Albertville" for Matadi. At last they were together and going to the Congo for what turned out to be 26 years of missionary service.

2. TOGETHER IN THE CONGO 1919–1946

A. The Upper Congo Field of the
Baptist Missionary Society

This field comprised some 17,000 square miles which is an area about two and a half times the size of Wales. The area is bisected by the mighty Congo River. The second main river is the Lomami and the third the Lindi. The seat of colonial administration (until independence in 1960) of the Haute Congo Beige was Stanleyville, located just above Stanley Falls. The first and largest station of the BMS was at Yakusu, just 12 miles by land or river from Stanleyville. It is located close to the point at which the Lindi River flows into the Congo.

The area served by the BMS included ten major tribes, as described in YAKUSU NOTES in April, 1941. Each one of these tribes had its own language. The Lokele were the virile riverine people, having villages on both banks of the Congo and Lomami Rivers. They were the tribes which were always more open to new ideas because of their constant contact with "the outsiders". The Torubu were a forest people occupying the North bank and hinterland. The Foma, originally a forest people, now were living on the main river and in the forest.

The Baena were a fishing tribe around the Stanley Falls and the Lualaba. The Bambole, a more primitive tribe, lived back from the river, inhabited the forest in the south of the BMS field between the Congo and Lomani Rivers and beyond. The Esoo formed a forest tribe living west of the Congo and Lomami Rivers; the Boyela, another forest tribe lived to the south of the Esoo; the Bakumu, a forest tribe with riverine villages opposite Yakusu; the Bamanga, a tribe to the north with villages on the banks of the Lindi, and in the forest; and finally, the Bangelema, a tribe to the north of the Bamangas.

The three mission station where the Mills served were:

Yakusu	(Alex 1911–1924)
	(Ethel 1919–1921)
Yalikina	(Alex and Ethel 1924–1940)
Irema	(Alex and Ethel 1940–1946)

i. The Yakusu Station

Yakusu was the first station to be founded in the Upper Congo by the BMS in 1895. The first missionary was Harry White who was there alone for seven months until C.J. Dodds arrived in May, 1896. Mrs. White joined her husband in October, 1896 and they both left to go back to England in April, 1897. Harry White died at sea on July 4, 1897 en route to England.

Alex arrived at Yakusu in late December, 1911. He was 26 years of age. Ethel arrived with Alex in April, 1919 at age 39. Alex and Ethel were to become the 28th and 30th missionaries to served at Yakusu since 1895. Six of these were buried in the little cemetery behind the chapel. A total of one hundred-four missionaries served in Yakusu for a total of 826 years from 1895 to 1954. (The years of service of Alex and Ethel comprised sixty-three years of that total.)

Ethel has left us a moving description of their arrival at Yakusu:

"As we neared Yakusu, it was not a secret that we were on board. In some mysterious way the natives knew for there were wavings from the bank.

Children were swimming toward the boat calling out our names. . .Several teachers came out in canoes with some of the church members to welcome us as we passed. . .The boys and girls were lined up on the steps of the cliff and the girls were arranged on either side of the road as we walked up to our house—my new home! All the girls were holding palms so that we walked along under an arch. Mr. Mill missed the familiar face of 'Kambale' (Mons. Lambotte) so we walked to the little cemetery to see his grave. . .". (Henri Lambotte had died on July 31, 1918 in Yakusu). (MH, ECM, 1919)

Alex describes Yakusu

"I may describe its physical features, its geographical situation and its arrangements, but at the same time fail to show its real beauty. . .It is shut in on all sides by forest, except on the river side, which is a bank fifty feet high with a grass-covered top. This height forms a sort of miniature 'Dover Cliff' from which you can view the opposite bank dotted with villages."

Sutton Smith quotes a phrase from an American settler of 150 years ago to describe the land claimed from the forest for the mission station: "From every direction the forest appeared to be rushing in upon the perilous little reef of a clearing. . . The all-conquering wilderness is all around us and will scarcely be repressed. Six months unattended would see grass higher than your knees on all the paths and round the buildings, and in a year it would be the wilderness again, the roofs of the buildings alone visible above the tall saplings." (p. 114) "The clearing is a large area of about 300,000 square meters. Our workmen live on it, and some are engaged in cultivating it. Others tend the sheep and goats which we have to keep in order to have fresh milk daily and fresh meat occasionally. It has all been cut out of the dense bush. . .". (MH, AGM, 1913)

Alex described the buildings as they stood in 1913, just eighteen years after the station was founded. "Immediately behind the cliff edge and parallel with the river runs the broad main path of the station. From this main path, the roads branch off to various parts of the station buildings and offices. On the front road stand the missionary houses, each in its own garden and each built up on piles or arches to be kept free from the destructive inroads of the white ants. One of the houses is of wood, built by our late honored leader, Rev. W.H. Stapleton, The other three are of brick. All have verandahs and corrugated iron roofs."

Alex wrote on September 14, 1921 about the house where he lived temporarily while Ethel and Barbara were in England:

"I am fortunately well housed. I have a cement floor under my feet, a high wooden ceiling over my head and two large rooms with verandahs to live on. An open air cook shed and servants' sleeping places complete the establishment. It was built for the State Doctor but seeing that post is vacant for the present and I am supposed (underlined) to be doing the Sleeping Sickness work of the district as I could. . . not knowing what arrangements the Yakusu Station Committee had made for me. It turns out that I will only be here one month out of six. Nevertheless I have brought down a writing desk, some books, provisions, a good lamp and have a few pictures and texts about the wall and feel a bit set up." (AGM to JPS 9/14/21)

"The gardens which surround them have flowers which grow with luxuriant beauty and remarkable rapidity. . .The white men have shown the natives, as they rolled up their sleeves and persisted in the work, the dignity of labour. They have shown them how to dig the clay and burn the bricks which now stand in those compact and healthy dwellings; they have sanctified them by the lives they have lived. . ."

He then imagines that Yakusu is like a British town with its own church, "university", bank, market and Exchange—"the Regent Street of this part of the country". "The most commodious structure is of brick and tiles, dignified in structure and stands as a tower of testimony. It is the School-Church for workmen's school, Sunday services and annual assemblies. The plainer building serves as bank-market-exchange. Here on paydays the workmen draw their wages and the more thrifty bank some. Here daily the natives exchange raw material, live stock and native vegetables for European goods. Here they can learn the purchasing power of money and the value of a regular currency. They are encouraged also by it to purchase the clothing of decency and the articles of thrift. . .".

"And not far away stands the most mundane of structures—the University! It is, at any rate, the seat of highest education . . . in this part of the country. It is the Yakusu Training Institute for Native Teachers. Its wall drapings of maps, charts, modulators, and natural history specimens testify to the wide range of the curriculum. . .There is no breach between theoretical and practical learning, for the back door of the Institute opens to the carpenter's square, where a well-equipped shop with benches and trestles provides the opportunity for profitable labour. . .

"Yet another path leads off from the front of the station. It leads past a quiet spot where we seldom go, but of which we often think. It is a little tree-shaded enclosure which we call the Churchyard." By the time Ethel Mill arrived in 1919, the following missionaries had been buried in this graveyard behind the Yakusu Church:

George Moore	1902	Henri Lambotte	1918
A.E. Wherrett	1896	Mrs. Kenred Smith	1901
S.O. Kempton	1908	Salumu (servant of Mrs. Millman)	(1903)
E.E. Wilford	1914		

The forest beyond

". . .You cannot go farther than our borders, however, at present. There are no roads. It is the domain of the leopard, the boar, the chimpanzee and the elephant. The little paths are only known well by the bush-dwelling natives. You must return to the river. Down river is the only way home. And the only steamer which leaves makes a call once in four months. . . Yet we do not feel marooned. We may be insulated but we are not isolated; we are a touch with home by thought and in touch with Heaven by faith. . .

". . .The bugle has just been blown by the soldier at the State police post close by as the sign for retiring, so good night. . .". (9/12/21)

Impression of Station Surroundings

Sutton Smith has left us lovely and moving impressions of his years at Yakusu from 1899–1910. (He left the field in 1912.)

River steamers and dugout canoes

"There are some things the resident never grows weary of. This place is redeemed from any possibility of monotony by the varying charm of the river. It is a poem of life; a moving picture of surpassing interest. The modern steamer passes frequently, the beat of the stern-wheels being heard often before it is in sight. . .A little island called 'Ile Bertha', nine miles long by one and a half wide, breaks the river immediately below the station. The course, being dangerous, is carefully charted and buoyed. The course is ever changing and the pilot has to spend much time with the lead, rebuoying and recharting it.

"The ancient dugout, the sole craft for centuries on its broad bosom, is seen meeting the mail steamer. The progress against a rapid current and over a difficult course is naturally slow for the steamer, but when the water is high and the vessel is coming down from the Falls, we frequently but barely catch it and safely dispatch our letters. . ." (Note: The steamer had only a short trip from Yakusu to Stanleyville where it started its return trip to the coast within a few hours of the time it passed Yakusu on its way up river to Stanleyville.) On one occasion, I had finished my letters, but none were stamped. As the steamer was rapidly approaching, aided by a swift current, I pushed another letter into my home-envelope and rushed to the beach. Millman ran across to his house to see if he could get me a couple of stamps. We had already pushed off when Millman reached the beach for the steamer had had to slow down and turn in to meet us. So he gave the stamps to a boy who swam out to us holding them above his head. . . .

"There is still to be heard the catching lilt of the river song from fifty dusky throats, the entrancing sight of nodding red plumes, glistening bodies and long graceful paddles, which swiftly plied, gleam as though glass in the sunlight. . .Poverty and wealth glide side by side. A woman sitting in the stern of a small canoe, the bow of which is out of the water, plies her paddle with perfect 'sang froid'. Leaks abound below the water line, but she knows her business and will reach her port by many a dexterous stroke. A native chief parades in a huge canoe, with a crowd of painted warriors. A decorous Arab in long white tunic reclines under his awning, as his neatly dressed domestic slaves propels him, to the accompaniment of harsh, discordant cries." (H. Sutton Smith, pages 104–105)

Oppressive heat. . .healing messengers

"The day has been unusually hot, the vertical rays of the sun almost insupportable. The oppressive heat is the most marked feature of our equatorial station. The natives speak of the two hours after noon as the time of 'the maddening heat which blisters the feet'.

"On this particular day, the afternoon witnessed a rapid change. Westward sweeps the wind and all the eastern horizon of river is dark with ominous portent of storm. It roars through the trees. It lashes the quiet water to fury of foam-flecked waves. Limbs of the forest giants crack and crash. Flying dust blinds the eyes. How glorious to face and drink in this rush of air from cooler places. After the heat, it comes as a healing messenger to the throbbing pain.

"The wind has gone, destroying and purifying with the same breath. There is a hush; all nature waits expectant. Behold an unbroken wall of hissing rain comes, smiting the water to stillness. Far up river the magical line can be seen approaching. It drops like a sheet and conquers each foot of its path. Once the storm was suddenly stayed when scarcely five hundred yards away. Athwart the dark wall of falling rain the glorious hues of a magnificent rainbow arch scintillated. . . .". (pages 105–106)

Moonlight nights

"When smiles the silent moon in full-orbed splendour, native dance songs and drums are heard as though on the path outside, so little do the sounds lose in their way over the quiet river. Who is sufficient to describe the moonlight nights of Africa? They are dim, cool days. The burden of the heat has lifted and the oppressiveness of the sun has passed. Why sleep when nature has conspired to make gaiety pleasant and every movement a delight? What hide and seek the children play in its deep shadows. The gently beating silver rays seem to cast a spell over all.

"The missionary with his reading lamp and evening work is in danger of neglecting the quiet enjoyment of those evening hours, through his stern devotion to thronging duties. Still, he will recall in after days with some renewal of the feeling of joyous satisfaction, how much he appreciated those strolls in the cool night air in earnest converse or lightly chatting, a world of beauty around him unblemished, for the soft rays hide the spots. The garden plot looks perfect, which in the hard unsparing rays of the sun is full of spots.

"Perhaps one's outlook upon life in Africa tends to become hard and critical and lacks the tempering shadows, the softer light of compassion and sympathy. We have all entered the same lofty temples whose dim, quiet aisles minister silent healing to the fretted spirit. So we give thanks for the light that hides, as well as the light that reveals, for the dim cool nights of tropical Africa." (pages 106–107)

What we do not see in the night

"Dark is the night when the stars are hid and the moon has ceased to rise. Man is asleep and the birds are at roost, save the watchful owl whose call vies with the many shrill-voiced insects in startling the night air. In his search for food he has no respect for the slumbers of the recumbent missionary. A sudden commotion above the ceiling-boards awakens him from a sound sleep. The squeaks of a rat in torment, growing fainter and fainter, with patter of scurrying feet, tell of eyes that can see far in the dark, as well as some long-tailing pests that have escaped.

"How much we miss by our keeness of daylight vision. . . .the lightning-like movements of the monster, hairy tarantula on the track of some small animal or bird. . .the gliding snake across the path; the prowling leopard and the quick, little steps of the bush-cat after some stray fowl. The advancing swarms of red (driver) ants. Long, brown cockroaches that are busily scratching away as they eat the leather off the bookbindings or nibble away at the gum labels of bottles. The spiders nimbly find a safe retreat and a quietly slumbering lizard will emerge from under a cushion to find a better hiding place. . .".

The hordes of driver ants

"But the countless hordes of driver ants come on relentlessly. Through a crack in the door they pour into the house, their serried ranks unbroken until the signal is given. The giant soldier drivers guard and control the rank and file. They are several times larger and more powerful than the working driver. No lust of conquest will induce them to loot and destroy; they command the actions of the destroying host. Nothing escapes them, every lurking cockroach is found out, stung to death and carried away. Silent signals are quickly obeyed and this perfectly organized host of scavengers splendidly accomplishes its task. Soon after dawn they may elect to leave. In unbroken array they file out of the house they have cleansed, and you may enter it again in peace. Sometimes by repeated visits they become a nuisance. Seek then their rendezvous which perhaps will be found at the root of some neighboring tree, and burn them out with shavings and oil . . .". (page 108)

Sounds of the birds by day and night

"The cooing of the 'ekuku' (wood-pigeon) from the topmost branches of a high tree in the garden or on the cliff front is often heard from the verandah. It is never very long before a boy comes running up with the information and a hungry look in his eyes. An alighting parrot, or hawk or flying-fox will evoke the same beseeching request. Flocks of grey parrots, with red tail feathers, fly overhead morning and evening at different times of the year. The white eagle soars past, with widely spread, lordly beat of his wings as he watches the shore and the shallow water.

"The clear note of the 'shokoke' (wagtail) is a welcome sound. At some seasons they sing as rapturously as a canary. They are as common as a sparrow at home. They will pick up crumbs from the verandah. Then there is the bright-plumed weaver bird, with its dash of brilliant yellow. They come in scores to spoil the trees. With their sharp beaks they tear the graceful palm fronds to ribbons and carry away the streamers to cleverly weave a nest. . .They are noisy workers, but a clamour arises when a hawk comes near. . .

"There is also the tiny sunbird (Nectariniidae) visiting the flowerets of the variegated shrub at the foot of the step. Timid at first, it gathers courage with each passing moment and calls cheerfully to its dun-colored mate. Once a year, at least, we have a snowstorm of white butterflies. For hours they flit across the landscape like wind-driven flakes of snow. . . ." (pages 113–114)

. . .and the people come and go. . .

"The people come and go. The front path is a highway for all. The lime hedges of our front gardens border it and our homes are set some thirty feet back. Strange figures are seen on the path at times. In full career a crowd of women and girls and little children rush by holding or dragging fish baskets of all sizes. No silent procession is this: the dust flies and the air is rent with very audible laughter and queer cries. An hour or so later they return from the brook in straggling groups, having caught nothing, but having enjoyed immensely the excitement of it all and the impromptu shower bath under the shady trees.

"In the confidence begotten of long acquaintance little kiddies play about on the grass under the trees or sit on the path at their games or roll about in the dust. In the season of 'wa', they are looking for caterpillars and grasshoppers. At times they catch the caterpillars and the long blades of grass and string them on a piece of banana cord. . .".

Dark stains mark the path

"Noisy enough by day, the path is very still at night, What is that trail we find one morning, from end to end, as of some heavy object dragged along unresisting? Dark stains mark the path; it looks like blood. Later in the dark the workmen bring us one of our large billy goats that has had its head torn off. It was found a little beyond the station in the tall grass, the poor victim of a leopard. . .Dragging the lifeless animal, the leopard makes its way from the town . . . as though mockingly, in front of our houses, from end to end of the station until it can rest and complete its meal under cover of the thick foliage." (page 110)

The goats and sheep we have ever with us

"A fine flock of a hundred and twenty African sheep wander the station paths, cropping the grass. With a handful of salt you can gather twenty or thirty round you at any moment near the store door. They will lick the salt from your hand. The goats are more fond of the village rubbish heap, where plantain skins and bread root parings are to be found in plenty. They nose everything, and a nice little bit of fish hanging over a fire is considered a dainty." (page 111)

Sutton Smith places the immortal poem of Robert Louis Stevenson at the beginning of his chapters on "Impressions of Yakusu". (Note: After having lived for four years in the tropics in Venezuela at 9 degrees above the Equator, some of these same impressions are very vivid in my memory. JHS.)

"Tropic Rain" by R. L. Stevenson

As the single pang of the blow when the metal is mingled well,
Lives and rings and resounds in all the bounds of the bell,
So the thunder above spoke with a single tongue,
So in the heart of the mountain the sound of it rumbled and clung.

Sudden the thunder was drowned—quenched was the levin light
And the angel spirit of rain laughed out in the night.
Loud as the maddened river raves in the cloven glen
Angel of rain! you laughed, and leaped on the roofs of men.

And the sleepers sprang from their beds, and joyed and feared as you
fell,
You struck, and my cabin quailed; the roof it roared like a bell.
You spoke, and at once the mountains shouted and shook with brooks;
You ceased, and the day returned, rosy, with virgin looks.

And methought that beauty and terror are only one, not two;
And the world has room for love, and death, and thunder and dew;
And all the sinews of hell slumber in summer air,
And the face of God is a rock, but the face of rock is fair.
Beneficent streams of tears flow at the finger of pain:
And out of the cloud that smites, beneficent rivers of rain."

ii. The Yalikina Sub-Station (founded 1916)

Isangi is a government post at the mouth of the Lomami River where that river flows into the mighty Congo. Near Isangi, the first Yalikina Sub-station buildings were erected by Alex Mill in the years 1920–23 on a concession granted to the BMS in 1916. Isangi, the government post, is located fifty miles downriver from Yakusu. Before Alex went on furlough in 1918, he was looking for a way "to be on his own" and to stake out a piece of the BMS Upper Congo field where he could do pioneering work. He did not want "to build on another's foundation". The location at Yalikina was also good because it was halfway between Yakusu and the older station, Yalemba, about fifty miles farther up the Congo from Yakusu. He had explored the Lomami River in 1915 with Mr. Millman and felt a call to expand the work into that vast region. He had eyed Yalikina as the place to build a sub-station and use it as a base to evangelize along the Lomami River.

The people in the Yalikina region were also responsive to the Gospel and by 1920 there were 846 baptized members in the church there. These members were scattered in several surrounding villages where there were schools and chapels. "The two villages of Yanjali and Yalosambo have each built a brick-school this year of which they are justly proud. 250 bush-schools are functioning which represents about 7,500 school children. . .Of them 750 are doing a little writing and arithmetic. This year 562 passed from the Primer to a reader." (YN, date ?)

Across the years several buildings were erected at Yalikina. The map below was drawn in 1957 and shows the chapel, school, boarding department, dispensary and gardens laid out.[1] The Roman Catholic missionaries obtained a concession adjacent to the BMS property, laying mainly to the west and south of the BMS property.[3] The river was on the east, so the only possibility for expansion was on the north. The local police station was being built behind the Yalikina village, with its "centre comercial". Therefore the BMS was seeking more land[2] in 1957. (Letter from Alice Wilkinson of the BMS office in Stanleyville to Mr. Taylor at the London office. May 25, 1957).

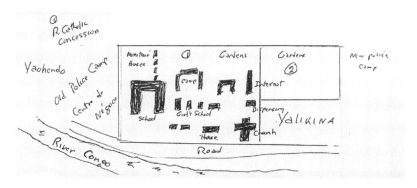

The correspondence of Alex tells the story of his tireless efforts to continue building in Yalikina, while he continued to carry heavy responsibilities while still living at the Yakusu station from 1919–1923.

"As it has been decided that we are to go ultimately to supervise the work at Yalikina at the mouth of the Lomami, I had been making a start in view of occupying the BMS site there although we have not the staff in sight yet for Yakusu to enable us to move there. I took down a Capita (foreman) 'Liaocho' by name who used to be my dispensary assistant. I left him with spades and axes to clear the site. He has also a case of medicines for sale and keeps me in touch with mission business down there. He does carpentry work at a small bench to augment his income. . .". (AGM to CMS 3/14/20)

"I am hanging in here as the work needs two men at least, but my arms are at Yalikina where the work needs more and more supervision. I have just had a note from the Administrator to say that the official formalities for the passing over of the piece of ground which was given to us are not in order and so we may have difficulty in installing ourselves. . . When Mr. Millman comes back in April the matter should be definitely settled. . .". (2/20/21)

 ". . .my colleagues are not quite as convinced as I am. . .".

It seems clear that the age-old struggle in mission strategy—expand or consolidate—was operative in Yakusu as Alex pressed forward to establish the Yalikina sub-station.

"I am feeling probable criticism from my colleagues for they are not all convinced as I am of the needs and prospects of Yalikina. In any case in 1923 I will pack up my troubles in my old kit bag: (my bag is getting a bit worn out) and smile, smile, smile. . .". (August 17, 1921)

But he kept traveling to Yakilina to supervise the brickmaking in between other tasks at Yakusu:

"I am going to continue brickmaking and gardening at the Yalikina site tomorrow morning in the interval between the spell of teaching and a river voyage up the Lomami River. . .". (September 14, 1921). And there were times when the brickmaking didn't go as well:

"I have got the building right up to the floor level now but I am leaving the work for a week to get round the district with Mr. Parris and then I will get on with it again. I had a great disappointment with the last kiln of bricks—15,000 breakages in the burning. That was about 50% of the whole. . .". (November 3, 1922)

Alex actually did much of the bricklaying himself. He writes:

"I have managed to get these last two months which allowed me for building the Yalikina house. I only do a little supervising and preaching at the same time but dirty myself with bricks and mud during the live-long day. The natives come and look on and sometimes help. But I am sometimes wild when they come and stare at me when I am perplexed about how to bond some bricks and trying to get them plumb. I think I can sympathize very much better with John's father now in his work. . ." (Note: Grandfather Sinclair was a stone mason in Scotland and Canada.) (AGM to JPS, July 10, 1922)

> ". . .an opportunity to use my seven years of
> architectural training. . ."

When Alex first felt called to become a missionary at the age of 15, he had in mind becoming an architect and a builder in missionary work. His parents encouraged him to begin an apprenticeship which lasted for seven years until 1907 when he went off to Pastor's College in London. He writes:

". . .It was my wish from early years to go to the wilds and build a home. I am getting some opportunity to apply my seven years of architectural training so I am happy. . .". (AGM to JPS, July 10, 1922)

According to Fred Drake, the early missionaries taught the Africans the art of brick-building. They also brought some bricklayers to the Congo from West Africa. Alex Mill loved to use "cloisters" in the buildings he designed to get away from the plain, traditional style. Alex would go off on a trip and leave instructions for the construction work to continue during his absence. At times he would return to find the work poorly done. He either had to tear it down or try to fix it. There was one wall which leaned, but Alex was able to plaster it so that it looked even! (Note: I am reminded of my first experience learning to lay cement blocks in the building of the church in Santa Barbara del Tuy, Venezuela in 1954. I got the four lower tiers of blocks out of plumb. But a local workman simply plastered it up to make it look even. To this day that section in the wall is called by the local people "Sinclair's barriga" or Sinclair's stomach!)

The Yalikina house was a beautiful structure as seen in the photograph. Aunt Ethel wrote to my sister Martha around 1925 (Martha was seven) her sentiments about the house that Alex had planned and built for her:

". . . Alex is so tired. I have just looked up and his eyes are shut and his head is nodding so we had better soon go to bed. He is making the house look so nice. I like it better than any I have been in on the Congo. The arches in the room are so pretty. . ." (ECM to Martha Muriel Sinclair, n.d.,1925–?)

iii. The Irema Substation (founded 1937)
(pronounced ee—ray—mah)

In an article by AGM published in 1939, "Still Pioneering: Forward on the Lomami", he describes the station location:
"This mission outpost is fourteen hundred miles up country from the Atlantic Ocean on the Lomami River. Just around the bend from the station (about a mile) is the village of Irema. In it stand two trees, gaunt and gigantic, under which the Arab slave-traders a generation before had sold their human merchandise. It was from this region that the little slave girl Salamu was captured and later saved by the missionaries from the slave traders on their way to the coast at Monsembe. Salamu was taken by Mr. Stapleton to Yakusu in 1895, was recognized as a native of those parts and became the first evangelist in the native language in Yakusu. However Salamu's home on the Lomami had long remained unevangelized. . .".

The work began in 1915 when I was privileged to take my first long itineration journey with Mr. Millman aboard the GRENFELL up the Lomami. We made friends with many chiefs for two hundred miles up the river to Irema. We sensed our responsibility for the Esoo and the Bambole tribes which live on the banks in the forest hinterland on the Lomami.

The founding of the work at Opala (The government
village, 20 miles from Irema)

From the sub-station in Yalikina, founded in 1916, my colleagues and I were constantly called on to supply the appeals for teachers. By 1928 two hundred and fifty Esoo villages had been occupied. This brought us to the Bambole tribe. Mr. Parris had been working on the east bank. In 1928 he crossed the Lomami River to Opala, the government administrative post of the Bambole tribe, on the west bank of the Lomami. He was told that there were probably eighty thousand of that tribe which were untouched by any Christian mission. The native Christians from the east bank and one devoted evangelist, Filipo Kewaita, died while endeavoring to push forward the boundaries of the Kingdom.

Alex pled for the extension of the BMS work into the upper Lomami in an article in the MH in 1929, "Diamonds or Dying Men". He pointed out that the Bambole people are exceptionally easy to reach since the steamer GRENFELL can run up the Lomami River for 250 miles to Bena Kamba. "Diamonds have been found at Litoko last year and already a Belgian company has surmounted all the obstacles of money, travel and men and are now exploiting them. . .We were on the verge of evangelizing them

when our staff has been reduced by illness and our funds by the Deficit. . .
Which are more precious? Diamonds or dying men?" (MH, AGM, 1929)

Roman Catholic missionaries enter

"The work had to wait for funds and the financial crisis of 1931 made it
impossible to start an outpost in Opala to coordinate the work. The Roman
Catholics started work in 1933, first in Yalikina and later at Opala, to make
Protestant Christians into superstitious Roman Catholics. We are now outnumbered by them by three to one. . .".

The palm oil industry

"Within ten miles of Irema three thousand are employed in the exploiting
of palm oil, coffee and rice at the mills at Yalulwe. There one hears the
constant sound of the whirr and clank of industrial machinery—all among
primitive people, unclothed to an almost shocking extent. . .".

The first mission building at Irema

"In 1937 the missionaries were welcomed, even though a native teacher
had been there since 1920. A mud-house with a corrugated iron roof was
erected. Was not 1938 the Diamond Jubilee year of Congo Missions? The
loving gifts of supporters have made possible the building of the house. . .".
(MH, AGM, 1939)

Fred and Marjorie Drake recall the physical setting of the Irema station
as they first saw it in 1945 in an interview in May, 1991:

"It was 'paradise'. No Belgian administrator. No roads. No lights. The
buildings were set on the bank of the river: an old wooden house, a new
brick house, church building, dispensary and a school room. Perhaps there
were 200–300 people in Irema. The Church had 40–50 members. Some of
the nucleus of the congregation had moved with the Mills to Irema from
Yalikina. We remember Pastor Bufalulu, dressed in a pair of old riding
'jodhpurs'—too small for his big behind! These had evidently been sent
in a 'missionary barrel' by Horace or Harold Starte (Ethel's brothers) who
were working in India.

"There was a road for about ten miles south of Opala where the ferry
crossed the Lomami. From there the road went on to Kinsangani (formerly
Stanleyville). The village of Irema had a private trading post to buy palm
nuts and rice. The Lomami Company had leased about thirty kilometers
on either side of the river south of Opala. Alex always stopped to greet the
traders. He set a good example for us."

Alex and Ethel describe their first months at Irema in residence in 1940:

"...We are now comfortably installed in our own house around which flowers brought from Yakusu bloom. The sick were brought to us on the morning of our arrival and since then medicines have been distributed to large numbers of people. Every morning the Gospel has been preached to those who come. We have now nearly completed the dispensary building.

We have had gatherings for worship and prayer in the mud hall which the native pastor built before we arrived. This a simple building with an earth floor and fitted with rude benches. It has served for two conferences—refresher courses for study, fellowship and training for one hundred and forty teacher-evangelists in the Irema area. For a month at a time, living together and on the simplest fare, they have had classes from 5 a.m. to 5 p.m. They have also worked on the plantation and attended a practice school.

The first of the courses was for seventy Bambole teachers in the Lingala language. The second was for a similar number of men speaking the Lokele language...We have not gathered many in by baptism, but had ten baptized during the first conference and forty-six during a month's journey in the Esoo forest area. There are about five hundred inquirers in the district...". (MH, AGM, 1940)

Ethel adds other insights into their first days in Irema in YN:

"We started to fix up a two-room house, smoothing the inside walls with mud and then whitewash. The dispensary is still to be built. For the present, we decided to put all our things in the bedroom and have our meals there while the other room was being done. We were surrounded by our paraffin, flour, sugar, lamps, onions. Our nearest shop is 50 miles away so we are obliged to bring these things with us. There seems hardly a place to put the sole of one's foot. However, we do not mind since we are not on the spot.

"...At quarter of six the morning after our arrival I heard voices outside. I looked out and saw a crowd of sick folk had arrived. Oh! I said, 'Woe betide my wishes to get things done in the house!' We just had to lift the medicine boxes straight out on the earth of the verandah and commence. And so it has continued every day since. Two hundred fifty cases have been attended. A good many have gotten better, others are on their way and fresh cases keep coming. There were also 47 others who have injections every week for five weeks. Mr. Mill has hurried up with the Dispensary and it will be finished next month...". (ECM, YN, 1940)

Frederick Drake wrote in 1947 that the boys school in Irema has been enlarged and 68 boys, of whom 55 are boarders, are taking a four year course. Native crafts were encouraged. The schoolboys have built new sleeping quarters, classrooms and dispensary houses. During the year they made more than 30,000 pieces of roofing thatch. Mr. Drake commented to me in our interview in May, 1991 that "ndele" roofing mats were made by the boys by braiding palm leaves and then sewing them together.

Alex told about the trading companies to which the population is drifting:

"The Trading Companies' labour camps are still causing us grave concerns. In the Irema and Yalikina areas there are 11 of these camps and in only one have we any really effective Christian work. . .". (YN, 1947)

In an interview with the Drakes in 1991, I gleaned further information about Irema:

"The time for travel of the 150 miles to Irema from Yalikina was about two days by steamer launch. . . The Bambole people were much more primitive and less responsive to the Gospel than other tribes. They had bushy hairdos and painted their bodies. . .

"When we traveled with the Mills, we remember we stopped at each village, covering two, three or four villages during a day's journey. We had already done nine months of language study at Yakusu so were able to use some of the Lokele language on this trip. The purpose was to visit and inspect the schools, examine enquirers and give catechism classes. A crowd of people were always waiting for Ethel Mill and her medicines. We called it 'the medicine parade'. . .

"We ate very well, even though it took three to six hours to prepare the evening meal. That is why we had to stop by mid-afternoon. In the morning before leaving a village, they scooped out a place, filled it with wood, raked out the coals, put in the bread and covered the opening with a tin from a large lard can. . .

"We walked on the paths because there were no roads. We took along camp beds and mosquito netting, but relied on the local villages to provide food (vegetables, meat, often chicken). We stayed in 'a rest house' in each village which the local chief was obligated to keep in repair for 'the white visitors', government or others. We still used native carriers in those days. Alex had to negotiate (often daily) with the chiefs to get carriers. Later on the government outlawed the use of carriers. One day Alex was irate because a chief would not provide him with the carriers he needed."

"We played the gramophone with secular music to attract the people and at night showed Bible pictures with the magic lantern, powered by a pressured kerosene lamp."

B. Vignettes of the Mills' medical service

i. Uncle Alex's medical work

Alex had six months of practical medical training at Livingstone College before leaving for the field in 1911. Later he took a month course on Sleeping Sickness in Leopoldsville in November, 1914. He also had some studies in tropical medicine in Brussels from April to June, 1914. (In the book FOR THE HEALING OF THE NATIONS (1792–1951) which is the story of British medical missions, the author stated that Mr. Mill obtained the Belgian Diploma of Tropical Medicines.)

When he arrived in Yakusu in December, 1911, he was the only person with some specialized training and worked as a lay medical practitioner. A small hospital had just been erected in memory of Rev. Wm. H. Stapleton who died in 1906. A few months later the first missionary nurse arrived, Miss Rose E. Gee. She wrote in the MH in 1912:

"The medical work in Yakusu has been unavoidably neglected for a long time, owing to the station being undermanned. The missionary in charge of medical work, Mr. Mill, has had to leave his workmen to go to the dispensary, so very little time could be given to it.

"I now go to the Hospital every morning at 8 a.m. with Mr. Mill. As soon as I have mastered sufficient language I shall take it over altogether. There is much work to be done and no doctor. . .".

I have a photograph of Alex standing proudly in the dispensary, replete with two shelves of bottles and a set of scales in a glass case. However he did not just wait there for the sick to come to the dispensary. He writes in the MH in 1916 in an article about "Home Nursing in Congo":

". . .I do find it trouble to give medicine in a native house. You who know me will understand that my head often collides with the roof. (Note: Alex was 6 feet, 4 inches.) This brings down a shower of dust into the medicine spoon and on the dressings, and generally pollutes all the surroundings, Keeping in mind that the average native house of mud is six feet wide by nine feet deep, you will understand that there is very little standing room, especially when two people are lying down. And native pots and dishes usually cover half the floor.

"Two natives caught pneumonia in one such house. On visiting them I found that they had economised space by lying in the same rush bed; with their heels in each other's necks. One of them had an ulcer. In the dark it was difficult to sort out the one from the other.

"There was plenty of smoke in the house, but very little light. In the gloom of the evening, I read the thermometer, smoke permitting, by the aid of a humble match. The floor of the hut was unmentionable for they could not prevent damp, for the rain reached it. They care not to prevent dirt for they were used to it. It was useless to expect these people to keep clean. . .Do you wonder that I write in grateful appreciation of the Cottage Hospital which has recently been added to the Stapleton Memorial Dispensary. If I can get my patients there, I can go in now and relieve myself of my heavy sun helmet and breathe pure, fresh air. Clean water and clean beds give me a fair start in fighting a disease. . .I have the luxury of a table, a bench and sundry other hospital commonplaces. IT IS LOVELY. I only wish I had enough medicines to keep this healthful retreat in operation and to complete the work so well done. . .

"That is to put the case from the standpoint of my own comfort, but there are the patients to consider. . .I cannot record what they felt, but I can guess what a difference it was when they were removed from the discomforts of their 'home sweet home' to the only mission hospital within five hundred miles. How shall I justify myself when I say that the wing which has been built is only for MEN? Only by pleading that you will give us soon the funds to build the other wing and thus complete the little group of buildings. . .". (MH, AGM, 1916) (Note: According to researcher Nancy Hunt, the women's ward did not come until years later.)

Alex's "medical mistake" turns out well

Ethel wrote about this experience: "Alex had a case of a man who had ascites. Also a hernia in which his intestine had gone into his scrotum. But it was hard and big and Alex thought it was an abscess. So he waited for it to get ripe then later it became an awful sore as big as the palm of my hand. So one day Alex gave it a small cut to let the pus out as he thought. When to his horror he found faeces began to pour out. He had cut the intestine! Next day he tried to stitch it up but that didn't seem very successful. We had to be away for a time, but left instructions for the wound to be dressed daily. When we returned he looked ever so much better. The wound had healed and joined together . . .Do you know that Alex's mistake seemed to take care of his other ills. . .It seems as if God just took our mistake in His hands and turned it to good account!" (ECM to CMS, July 13, 1925)

B. Aunt Ethel's medical work

Ethel Clara Mill was a graduate of Guy's Hospital in London in 1917. It seems that nurses had been trained in the United Kingdom since 1848 but were not registered by the government until the latter part of the century. Midwifes had been trained since the early 1700s. Guy's Hospital, "a teaching hospital" was a publically funded hospital. Therefore it was obligated to receive as students:

a. Probationary students who paid their own way. This was a two-year program for those who came with better educational preparation;

b. "Intelligent working class" students who pursued a four-year course. They worked part-time and studied general educational courses as well as nursing. Ethel was a student in this category. She entered in the fall, 1913 and was graduated at the end of 1917.

(Note: This information was provided by John L. Greenwood, Burser of Regent's Park College, Oxford. He had served as an administrator of a nurse's training school of 480 students (plus 3,000 in continuing education courses) before he came to Regent's Park College in 1985.)

After Barbara's birth in July, 1920, Ethel seems not to have carried any formal medical assignment until they returned from furlough in 1924 and settled in Yalikina. She accompanied Alex on most of his missionary journeys. It was in the bush that Ethel exercised an important medical ministry. Frederick and Marjorie Drake accompanied Alex and Ethel on a three-week itineration in 1945. The Drakes were new missionaries in their late twenties; the Mills were in their early to mid sixties. In an interview with the Drakes in May 1991 in their retirement home near London they shared this vignette:

"Upon arrival at a village about 3 p.m., the first box to be unloaded was the medicine chest. At times, Ethel had to delay her cup of tea because the medical needs were so pressing. The medicine chest was the last box to be packed when the party moved on the next day. . .".

Times of disappointment

Alex writes on January 25, 1920: "Ethel too has some disappointments in her medical work. She has worked night and day over a little girl of the Baila tribe who had a wounded knee. When she found that it was impossible to keep the infection from getting into the knee joint she told them she could do no more but she would arrange for them to go to Stanleyville for the opening of the knee joint. Then they took fright. We tried to reassure them and reasoned with them that it was the child's only hope. But today, without a word of thanks or explanation, they left the hospital unobserved and by this time probably undoing all the work done by native methods in their own heathen village."

An epidemic of infantile paralysis

On March 14, 1920, Alex writes: "An epidemic of infantile paralysis or something of the sort has been sweeping the district. About 29 have died in our village. The other day a mother brought a baby in her arms which had been ill for a week as as she was too late coming for help, the child died in her lap on our veranda. The other child who was with her was also ill so we had to set to caring for it. It is infectious and so we do not feel justified in nursing the child in our station in the midst of our work people. So we feel our hands tied a bit. Under the circumstances I feel that I do well if I simply keep alive. . .".

A doctor at last!

In October 1920, Dr. and Mrs. Chesterman arrived. "They are now doing medical work and making great strides with the language. He has won his way to all our hearts by his graciousness and kindness. He is a M.D., London and has also Tropical Diseases. . . Doctor has patients from great distances—one has just come from the Lomami 100 miles at least by canoe. He is not undertaking any big operations as yet because he has not a nurse. Ethel would have helped him but we find it would demand too much of her time from her other missionary duties. . .". (AGM to CMS, November 27, 1920 and February 20, 1921).

Good news—sleeping sickness census down

Alex writes that he has been taking a sleeping sickness census of the people in Yalikina district for the government to see if sleeping sickness is on the increase. "I am glad to say it is NOT." (AGM to CMS, March 3, 1921)

"I act as physician and surgeon. . ."

"In between and at meal times at Yalikina, I have lanced boils and 'bubos' just to keep up my reputation and keep the goodwill of the people. I act as physician and surgeon. . .". (AGM to CBS, July 10, 1925)
In November 1922, Alex was asked by the government to take official charge of the medical work in the Yalikina district along with his missionary tasks. They promised to pay his expenses and give him about 4,000 francs (90 pounds) per annum. He responded to this request in a letter to Clara:
"I am going to do all I can as I have been doing for the last two years. When Ethel comes back I hope to be able to do even more. . ." (AGM to CMS, November 3, 1922)

C. Ministries related to the developing of congregations in the villages on the Lomami River; preaching, church discipline, examining members, training of pastors and catechists; theological issues; witchcraft, superstitions, etc.

By 1900 there were 230 Protestant and 150 Roman Catholic missionaries in the Congo Free State. Alex and Ethel came to the Congo a few years later, but the following description of the English-speaking missionaries was still quite accurate: (Cf. COLONIALISM IN CHRISTIAN MISSION by Stephen Neill, McGraw-Hill, 1966. pages 359–385)

"Even though the English-speaking missionaries carried with them into their stations their English mode of life, traditions and atmosphere, they had no intention of anglicizing their converts. As late as 1907 an American observer wrote about these missionaries: 'Although the currency is reckoned in francs and centimes, they talk about business and quote all prices in shilling and pence. . .They like their afternoon tea; they look with mild but some superiority upon all differing methods around them; few of them really talk French, the official language of the country; still fewer write it with any ease or corrections. . .'.Yet it must be said of the English-speaking missionaries that their intercourse with the Africans was carried on in the local dialect. They had given themselves to the task of learning the language. They had started with the translation of the Bible into many of the native languages. By 1958 over 50 Congolese languages were recorded as having the complete New Testament in their own language. . .".

As the years moved on from 1919 through 1946, Alex and Ethel blended more and more with the African forest and lost some of their British customs as they lived closer to the African. Yet when I came to know Uncle Alex in 1956, he was still a Britisher and a Scot in bold outline. It is this Britisher/Scot whom we now follow into the forest, together with Ethel who was a faithful copy of middle-class, early 20th century England.

The "educational" method of evangelism

It is difficult to separate the tasks of evangelism from educational tasks since these two aspects of missionary work were so intimately related in the work of the Baptist missionaries in the Congo. They were involved with an illiterate constituency and the total absence of public education. Many tribes had no written language or body of literature. The natives were eager to know "the white man's secrets" which they presumed were to be found in the books he read and the letters he wrote. The missionaries were convinced that the people could only become responsible citizens and true Christians if they could attain a degree of education and, above all, if they could learn to read well enough to read the Bible with understanding.

Not all the natives were enthusiastic about education. Alex writes: "Village headmen said we need not come to start work in their villages unless we offered some money gift first. The people as a whole seemed to think school learning was another burden beside tax collecting which was going to be put on them by the white men. . .". (March 14, 1920)

The "school/chapel" building in each village came to symbolize the merging of the two aspects of mission: education and evangelism. However many who learned to read and write in the village schools did not accept the Christian faith and become baptized. Yet the missionaries believed that even though every scholar did not become a Christian, they had an obligation before God to offer to everyone the opportunity for a better life which would come through education. The missionaries did not hide their evangelistic goal as they organized and administered village schools. But they felt called also to the broader task of "civilizing" and of offering a primitive people the chance to acquire some of the tools of the white man. It is not clear how much the missionaries understood that the education which they offered would undermine later the economic security and political power of the colonial overlords.

How did the Mills see their task of evangelizing and developing communities of Christians in the villages of the forests along the Lomami River? A glimpse into the psyche of Uncle Alex as an evangelist is found in his article "Southward Ho" in THE MISSIONARY HERALD in 1936 when they returned to the land of the Bamboles after an absence of a year:

"Armed with books and Scriptures, pictures and medicines, we went village to village, up and down the Lomami River, across the Equator, a hundred miles, a hundred and fifty miles, to the borders of the ramparts of pride and ignorance surrounding the Bambole people. Then we disembarked. . .and immediately found that Satan hindered us. We had to fight not only personal feelings in the villages, but the blatant godlessness which had said in its heart: 'Because the missionary only comes here for one visit a year, there is no God'! But our presence once more made them remember God and they were troubled. . .".

Another vignette showing the relation between education and evangelism: ". . .Again we plunged into the forest and reached a group of villages which we had visited for two years or more. . .From there the road diverges in three directions, all of which led to unevangelized territory. But we were only able to follow one, and it led to where last year a white missionary's face had been seen for the first time. . .There we found the chief and made a gift to him—not cloth, nor a mirror nor beads—but a fountain pen, and thanks to our teacher, he can now use. . .".

Itineration in primitive areas

The Mills had no alternative in their work but to travel extensively in these primitive areas. Their trips would often be six and eight weeks in duration. There were no roads so they journeyed on foot along paths through the forest. Each trip required careful preparation, a tremendous expenditure of emotional and physical energy and being absent from their home base in Yalikina and Irema. While they were away, unattended duties piled up which had to be faced upon their return.

While itinerating, they often visited two or three villages in a day and up to one hundred villages in six weeks. At times they would have the "Grenfell" take them to a certain point along the Lomami River. They would then strike off into the forest for several weeks and the "Grenfell" would meet them later at another point on the river on a fixed day.

They had to put together a great deal of equipment, provisions, books and medicines for each journey:

"The packing of literature for sale on the trip, of provisions of clothing, of wearable books, of medicines, etc. makes quite a week's work. And in the hurry one is apt to forget the preparation of the Spirit which is necessary. It may be that some will hear the Gospel from our lips for the first time and we are sure to be appealed to for guidance and decision on hundred and one points by young native Christians and teachers. I hope the weather keeps good. It is pouring rain tonight and our thatch roof here is none too good. I am looking for the iron sheets to come on every steamer. . .". (April 8, 1926)

"I will only be able to spend one month out here. In that month I am supposed to train 100 elementary teachers, visit local schools, treat Sleeping Sickness cases and proceed with materials for a building. Of course it is clear that work here at Yakusu will go back while I am away. By carefully planning my day I can supervise building work on my way from the Teacher Training classes. I can do dispensary and Sunday School work after breakfast and write up church books and correspondence after dark. But this is the utmost. I don't think it is a good programme either for it leaves me no time for play. Now that Ethel and baby have gone (back to England in June, 1921) I have no one to play with. . .". (September 14, 1921)

"We have 40 carriers with us. . ."

This is an example of the number of native carriers which they often needed to move their gear and provisions from one village to the next. At times the carriers were negotiated with a local chief to serve only for a particular stretch of the journey. Alex would then have to talk another chief or headman into providing him with another group of carriers. Native carriers were used by the missionaries for many years until around 19—when the use of hired human carriers was forbidden by law.

Ethel writes: "We have been out for three weeks and it will be close to four when we arrive back at Yalikina. Alex has gone to another village to exam a school and will come back here for dinner. Then we go on a fair distance and arrive there in time to sleep. . .One of them went out with Alec's gun and shot two large monkeys today so the men were pleased. There is plenty of monkey stew tonight. Alec says he has about 30 to baptize and we have already baptized 40 so far on this trip. . .". (ECM, January 29, 1927)

"We reached some hills in the distant forest. . ."

Most of the forest area was flat so they could not get a panoramic view of the hinterland. However on one trip they got to some hills from which the forest was viewed "as if looking from a cliff over the sea. . ."

". . .There we registered thousands of children in the schools and out of hundreds who applied for baptism we picked out 49 who had, we believe, been faithfully trying to serve God. . .and who had some intelligence in our examination of Scripture doctrines and were baptized. . . The teachers had taught 223 children to read. We sold 4000 francs worth of literature for Reading and Scriptures. . .

"Ethel had the daily burden of the sick and suffering who crowded to us everywhere we stopped and sometimes even stopped us on the road. She sold, with her native helper Kamanga, 5000 francs of medicines. . ."

"Books were soaked. . ."

"Well we had one mishap. On the last night of our journey when descending the Lomami River by canoe the rain descended and the floods came and the winds blew and all the boxes of books which we had left in the canoe got soaked. We have had such a job salvaging what we could . . ." (AGM, August 11, 1930)

"Another misfortune . . . just as we began our journey. . ."

As they began a trip in August, 1934, they experienced a serious storm: "We had packed up all our boxes and sent them on ahead of us about twenty miles by river in canoes. The two canoes were paddled by 5 and 6 boys respectively and the journey was made at night for the sake of coolness. About 2 o'clock in the morning a terrific tropical tornado came on. The boys with difficulty managed to beach the canoes near a village but the rains half filled the canoes. As a result the bottoms of all our boxes got filled with water.

"Our first job when we met our boxes after a bicycle ride the next day was to dry clothes and books as well as we could. But two bags of salt had been in the canoes and had melted all away so that the goods had been practically soaked in salt water and drew damp and rust galore. My gramophone was water-logged and the trumpet and the sound box was half filled with salt water. I have had to take it all apart two or three times to fix it up to run at all. When I went to use the Magic Lantern, the wicks would not light because the oil underneath was half full of water."

"Nevertheless that was the worst storm we had on our trip of three weeks. The second worst found us asleep in our camp beds under a native thatch roof. It began to leak so we got our macks and spread them over the top of the mosquito nets to catch the drips. It wound up with me sleeping with an enamel basin in bed with me and Ethel lying diagonally across her bed to get a dry place. Of course this is picnic fun even though it is a bit inconvenient!" (AGM, September 28, 1934).

A more typical travel "pen portrait"

Even though Alex and Ethel had some exciting adventures traveling by canoe, the following vignette is more typical of hundreds of days spent being paddled down the Lomami:

"We are now drifting down the Lomami River for 100 miles and have been two days on the journey. The Pastor steers in the stern and the house boys paddle back and front while we sit inside under a shade and write letters and do business. We then hope to go inland for a month visiting our native village schools. . .". (AGM, August 29, 1939)

Itinerating on "the house boat"

The regular use of the "Grenfell" became problematic as the number of missionaries and districts increased in the 1930s. Alex was pressing to go farther and farther into the Upper Lomami River. His idea of getting "a house boat" turned out to be both logical and practical.

A grateful patient at the Yakusu Hospital had given an iron "whaleboat" to the Mission. It was not being used on the Congo, since it lacked both motor and cabin. Alex offered to have it towed over to the Lomami River at Yalikina. He planned to build a cabin on the deck as living quarters for their riverine journeys. The "Grenfell" or a steamer of the Lomami Company would tow it upriver from Yalikina to the Upper Lomami region. The Mills would then float down river to the point at which they wished to embark, tie it on the bank for a day or a month and return at their pleasure to begin another leg on their homeward trip. (Note: The Lomami River follows a serpentine course.) Alex writes: "Today we have drifted down a long reach of the river and after 3 1/2 hours we are still only 1/2 hour walk from where we started because the river makes a big bend and circles back to form a "U"." (June 5, 1935)

Ethel writes about the convenience of the house boat for their itineration: "The Grenfell went back to Yakusu and we left our house boat moored and locked up on the riverside with a certain amount of stores. We then struck off inland for three weeks. . .There is a little place made of poles and a palm leaved roof in which the boys cook on the bank . . ." (ECM, June 5, 1936)

"The motor boat 'Lilemo'"

By late 1941, Alex had acquired an outboard motor boat which could pull one or two canoes. He called it "Lilemo" which was the African name of Mr. Pugh, once a Yakusu missionary and now Congo Mission Secretary. The first trip on which he used the "Lilemo" was a ten-hour run from Irema to the point on the Lomami where he left the boat to walk inland. Alex describes his new mode of transportation: "It is a 35 h.p. petrol-oil engine and starts by pulling at a cord—or doesn't start as the case may be. It then roars like a dozen lions till the journey ends or at last the petrol runs out. I had two big canoes with my luggage in them to tow with the motor boat.

"Before I was halfway there I had to beg 5 gallons of petrol from the Lomami Company factory. Even this did not get us to our journey's end and so, with a dry tank, we hailed one of our riverine school teachers in his village. They gave us 6 paddlers who, with our four paddlers, got us the length of the journey. It was my first long journey on it so I was not able to calculate our needs in advance. . .". (December 5, 1941)

"My motor bike ran into a palm tree. . ."

"Not a day passed without rain, although we were fortunate not to be often caught out in it, we could never get away from the effects of it. Most of the land is clay and the road crossed many deep ravines into which and out of which we had to struggle with the bicycle or in my case with the motorette. When it is slippery, it can be very dangerous."

"Struggling to get up one slippery slope, I spent 1/2 hour doing 10 yards and then had to wait to rest and hold the machine. Here Ethel and some native helpers whom I had left to follow caught up with me and even with their help it was with difficulty that I got to the top. These forest roads are very twisting and suddenly coming round a bend at a good speed one sees the dip of a steep hill in front and wants to stop.

"In my case it was not so easy. My back brake does not work and my front hub brake generally got oily and does not grip well. As in a case like that I generally stop by running into the forest at the side of the road or a soft earthbank if there is one. Well in doing so I ran into a palm tree which thrust my front wheel (which is well sprung) so far back that it banged on the cylinder of the engine and broke the spark plug, snapping the porcelain bobbin in two. I had no spare parts but joined the two pieces together and found the contact could be still made. . .

"Later I was going around a corner and lost control of the steering so I pitched off and got my leg caught under the engine of the bike. The leg was slightly burned before I dragged it out. This did not trouble me then and I rode on. But it festered the next day and it has kept a troublesome wound for three weeks now. In fact if it were not for it I would not be writing a few letters now. I would instead be mending a brick machine, whitewashing the houses or visiting a few of the outschools. But to get it better, I have to sit and put the leg up. . .". (AGM, December 5, 1941)

The "talking drums" locate Alex after a storm

"One day when at Irema Alex went to visit our natives who worked at a Lomami Company post on Sunday. He got held up by the storm. When he didn't turn up and it got to be 8 pm., on Pastor Bufululu's suggestion, I asked the cook's helper to drum up to villages asking if they knew of Alex's whereabouts. I listened to the distant drumming going on and in about ten minutes they came to me and said that the drums had replied that Alex was sleeping at Yalimi because of the storm. So I went to bed with an easy mind. How wonderful it was to be able to get the news about him. . .". (ECM, n.d. 1939)

Baptism and the Lord's Supper; worship; hymn tunes and
wedding rings; burial customs

Alex has few comments on the Lord's Supper, except that it was considered by the native Christians as a very sacred moment. Unless they felt that they were "in the Lord" and "in the proper spiritual condition", they would absent themselves from the Lord's Table. Alex comments on celebrating the sacrament in one village in which there were a hundred or more baptized members, but only ten came to the Lord's Supper. (December 29, 1920)

They carried with them a silver teapot which they used as the pitcher for the juice. It had been given to them by one of the relatives as a wedding present. Ethel occasionally makes reference to the silver teapot. For communion glasses they used fifty egg cups. The native "mata" was used for the communion bread.

A baptism "in the forest"

It was not difficult to find places to immerse the candidates for baptism. However the importance of the sacrament of baptism was given its proper place in church life. Every candidate for baptism had undergone extended instruction by Alex, Abraham or the local teacher. Each was to have bought a New Testament by the eve of his baptism.

"It was 11 o'clock when we reached the pool in the forest where water lilies crowded the edge. In view of 100 people, Pastor Abraham baptized twelve people and added a scripture name to their own native name. We then marched straight back to the worship service which was not over until 1 p.m. when we had dinner. We then had fourteen marriages (one was excluded when found he had been unfaithful to his wife) and dedicated eight children. Finally Abraham took the Communion service and now we are getting off to rest. . .". (February 6, 1932)

Alex provides another vignette of some baptisms: "A leper was one of those baptized today. He had a happy face. And a cripple boy who literally crawled on his hands and knees and could not keep his back stiff when he was being baptized. But he enjoys reading his New Testament and had a new light in his face." (February 20, 1936)

Some "logistics" of baptisms

"Within the last fortnight I baptized 30 in the forest villages behind Isangi. Such a solemn service as baptism would not, one would imagine, ever provoke humour especially as the natives take it so seriously and would count themselves mortally aggrieved if they left one hair of their heads which had not been under the water.

"Well the humorous side of it came to me because of the nature of the forest. I had to baptize in a forest stream. And as the 20 candidates varied from 4'0" to 6'0" in height I had to choose a depth fit for the smallest. Add to this the fact that some of the tall ones would not yield readily to lying back in my hands. So I had to put them down with force. Everyone of the onlookers thought it quite right and admirable but I who stood in the water knew that there was a sunken branch in the bed of the stream and that every candidate that was thus strongly plunged into the water felt the soreness of it on his back. . . ." (AGM, n.d.)

Alex literally baptized hundreds of candidates each year. He wrote on one occasion that he had baptized over 200 in the past three months.

"We provided the wedding rings. . ."

". . .Two couples were married this afternoon after the 4 o'clock Communion Service and four children were dedicated. We provide the wedding rings because we are introducing the custom. We want to give the woman the idea of being bound for life to the man she has married. . .". (ECM June 1, 1930)

Women and their efforts for recognition in the village churches

"Malia, a leading woman in the church said that the women church members were like a sore finger with pus. And so I put in the probe and asked the women what they thought they should do. They responded by saying that there should be a woman preacher in each village and six women should be chosen in each district who are capable of helping the weaker women. It would be nice if we could have an annual meeting of women to hear of their experiences and difficulties. Here are some of the suggestions which the women made: if a woman quarrels with her husband or leaves him, she should be read a portion of Scripture bearing on the problem and try to persuade her to make up, forgive and go back; we should try to find seats for women in the chapel; if we see girls running wild, give them counsel; not to go to markets on Sunday and to try to persuade other women to attend the services; try and stop witchcraft accusations; persuade the older church members who cannot read to go to the early morning service at 6 a.m. so that they can hear the Scripture read, hide these truths in their hearts and have food for their souls. . .".

Hymn tunes and other songs!

Alex always said that he didn't have a good voice for leading singing. "My own voice perhaps you remember. It is flat. When I reach for the high notes the scene (not to mention the sound) is serio-comic." (AGM, September 14, 1921) However he complained frequently when the natives invented their own variations of an old standard hymn tune. He would then proceed to line it out for them and make them sing it over and over again to preserve a vestige of the original tune. But Alex wrote words for several hymns and translated others which are still identifiable in the Lokele hymnbook with the initials "A.G.M.".

He also put his own words to old tunes. "Today I composed a little hymn about the Creation to the catchy tune of "It's a Long Way to Tipperary". They sang it seriously and cheerfully. "We also taught them the tune 'For All the Saints who from Their Labors Rest', besides their old favorites, 'Sweet Bye and Bye', 'There's No Friend Like the Lowly Jesus', and 'Stand Up for Jesus'. . .". (June 7, 1940)

"Did I tell you that I had set words to Harry Lauder's song 'She's the Lass for Me' for the school closing? . .The little tots did an action song to the tune of 'Here We Go Round the Mulberry Bush' showing how to wash and comb their hair and help their mothers. It was very pretty. . .". January 16, 1931). "I've been planning a musical drill to fit the tune of 'There's a Long, Long Trail Awinding' . . ."(AGM, 11/9/21)

When the young missionary, Douglas R. Chesterman was working with Alex and Ethel, the music life of the congregations blossomed. He was a gifted musician and organized an orchestra of 15 dulcimers. "He hopes to raise the standard of hymn tunes in the District Schools where the hymn tunes get murdered. . .". (August 30, 1935) Alex tells of the singing of a translation of "From Greenland's Icy Mountains . . ." with sweat running profusely down his face!

"A protest against a Sunday market. . ."

As I begin to write on the subject of Sabbath observance, I immediately go back in my memory to the stories that Mother told about Sabbath observance in their home in Glasgow in the 1890s. No work was done in the home on Sunday. They walked to church services and would not ride the tram on Sunday. In fact I do not believe that I made a purchase on Sunday in my life until I was sixteen years or age—and then with some sense of guilt. Alex was very committed to "keeping the Sabbath Day holy".

This he tried to do, along with the other Baptist missionaries. He writes in 1922: "We are trying to live Christ in the social organization for the sake of winning the next generation. We (the local church) won the other week on a protest against a Sunday market in Yalikina. . ." (November 3, 1922) Ethel wrote about censuring two women for selling puddings on Sunday behind their house so she would not see them. (January 29, 1927) However the odds were against Sabbath observance since the Belgiums adopted in the Congo "the Continental Sabbath". He writes in 1936: "4 or 5 miles down river is a Sunday forenoon market at Yaututu which is very large and has 4 white traders in attendance. 6 to 8 miles up river on the Lomami the large market at which all the Lomami Company workers buy their food is also held on Sunday morning. Also 8 to 10 miles away another company has its market. These latter markets oblige a certain amount of food to be brought for their employees and give them no other opportunity for buying. . .

"Our Yalikina people, especially the women, are a trading people and so although a few of the very devoted abstain from going at our request, yet the general audience is absent from the village till late on Sunday. I have seriously thought of changing our service to the later afternoon and having Sunday School in the morning instead. These people have very little to say in the arranging of their own life. . .". (September 9, 1936)

Use of fermented beverages

"The evils which we have to combat now are more the adoption of the white man's vices by the black. Shall I say smoking—we'll let that be for the present: but let's say vaunted immorality and drinking. A Sunday or two ago back Ethel and I visited a sick baby in the compound of the native chief after the morning service. Ethel pushed her way into the back verandah and found an impoverished native 'still' in full blast! Native beer is brewed, not distilled but the chief's wife seems to have learned from some Coast man how the stronger stuff could be made. I called the younger and acting chief and threatened him with government proceedings (It is forbidden by the government) unless he went to the Administrator and confessed to it. I lectured the children on the horrors which its abuse entailed. The chief reluctantly agreed to go next morning to the government post. . .

"Unfortunately when the native chief called the next morning to confess his sins he was unable to see the Administrator! And everybody guessed at the reason and with creditable restraint they told me without laughter. I felt pretty helpless . . .". (January 2, 1926)

By 1935 the BMS had enough influence in the region to prevent the sale of palm wine at the markets. But the Roman Catholics would not cooperate. Alex writes: "The R.C.s felt no compunction about breaking the rule and I found a woman selling a big pail of it at the market. I brought it away and poured it out. The woman complained to the Belgian Administrator. He said that I was against the law though morally correct. I had to pay 5 frs for the stuff because the R.C. priest claimed it for his employee's wife. . . (August 30, 1935) (Note: In an interview with Mrs. Nora Carrington in June, 1991, she told of her embarrassment when Alex kicked over in disgust a jug of palm wine in a public market.)

Hemp smoking

I am not sure what kind of drug this referred to, but it was probably a marihuana type plant. In YN in 1918 an article appeared on the subject.

"In May the out-post teachers sent a petition to the Vice Governor General of the province, called his attention to the increase in hemp smoking. They said that hemp is planted in almost all native gardens and sold in most markets and that it had injurious effects upon the minds of the scholars. The suppression of "bhang" smoking in the Stanleyville and Yanouge districts was immediate. However the prohibition seems not to have been effected in the Isangi and Lomami districts." (YAKUSU NOTES, Fall, 1918)

Indecent dancing

This is the term that Alex and Ethel use for a kind of primitive native dance with highly sexual overtones. The missionaries tried to stamp out the practices like this dancing which they considered an "unprogressive and superstitious" (AGM) part of the culture. The government administrator often supported them. However the populace sometimes rose up to re-institute their old customs. A particular dance was known as "Kewaya". Alex did not get too much support at the first since some of the local traders did not seem to be concerned about what kind of dances the natives danced. But Alex was adamant: "We have been encouraged by a message from the headquarters of the Lomami Company, advising its agents to do what they can to stop the 'Kewaya' dance. . . It is shortsighted policy to neglect these things, even on the part of a commercial company. For whatever lowers the morality of a people, lowers the vitality of a people and ultimately their ability." (October 9, 1927)

On one occasion the issue came to a showdown: "I had 100 of the teachers from the surrounding forest in for classes last fortnight. Last Sunday when 10 of them went to preach in a village, unexpectedly they found the indecent dance in full swing. They ordered them to stop but were only cheeked. Then they tried to appeal to the chief but he prevaricated. Then they took the 'law' into their own hands and rushed to seize the two drums by which the music for the dances kept up. They succeeded in getting away with them and brought them here. This resulted in a court case the next day. Five men were put to hard labour for a week for stirring up the dance. I have tried to show the teachers how the spirit of the people must be changed from believing in Darkness and Falsehood by the Spirit of God if the custom is really to be stamped out. I pray God it will be by the combination of Law and Grace." (AGM, July 30, 1926)

The struggle against witchcraft: a case study

This is a recurrent theme in the Mill correspondence. The following dramatizes the nature and seriousness of this problem. "The fight against witchcraft has still to go on within and without the church. Recently a native teacher died a strangely sudden death. His fellow teachers who went to the funeral were asked by the relatives to cut a piece of the flesh of the dead man to be used as a charm to discover the witch who had caused his death. The teachers refused but later on they compromised by suspecting a certain man on the evidence that he had been seen to go and extinguish a burning stick in the stream: this being a sign that he was conspiring the death of a man. The demons do all the rest even if the murdered man and the murderer do not even see each other face to face.

"Hours and hours were spent disputing these useless palavers by the natives themselves and by ourselves too. But reason proves nothing where prejudice reigns. . .". (AGM, January 20, 1926).

"No graven images, but. . ."

The natives in this part of the Congo do not make images. However they did have the practice of painting their bodies by smearing camwood (red) on their bodies. But Alex reports in 1921 that "the practice is being given up and the wooden troughs used for the preparation of this powder are being turned over in large quantities to Mr. Millman who is having them burnt. It is the nearest approach to 'idol burning'. . ." (AGM, November 9, 1921)

Violence erupts in a village

"Native passion and revenge showed itself the other day when a man was speared in mid-stream in his canoe by a rival section of his village. Subsequently they had a pitched battle before the State could interfere and two were killed. You will be surprised when I say that our church members were doubtless in the fight, but they act as a community and passion carries them away. . .". (AGM, November 9, 1921)

The rescue of a kidnapped young woman

"We found out on the first night of our journey into the forest that an injustice had been committed. One of the young women church members had been kidnapped while on a journey and taken to a family in a village who wished to have her in marriage to one of their sons whom the girl did not wish. At once I sent a native messenger to have the girl released and promised a legal hearing of the case the next day before an important native chief. The messenger returned to say that they refused to give the girl up and would pay damages if necessary. We journeyed on all the next day but could not get as far as the village where she was captive till nightfall.

We got our goods housed for the night and Mr. Chesterton and I got on our bicycles and made a night ride through a difficult path using our electric torches to guide us.

"Suddenly we came into the village to release her. We found the people very excited and rather unwilling to give her up. But by impressing the chief with our rights and of his duty to respect the new laws we were soon wheeling our bicycles back with the girl and a friend with her before us. She was soon met by her own relatives whom we had brought as near as they dared to the hostile village. We left her in their charge and rode back to our sleeping place. That same night a man was brought to us almost dead. . . It was a night!. . .". (AGM, February 20, 1936)

"Their lives are so different from ours. . .A woman who eats a fowl is supposed to be cursed with ankylostomiasis (worms ?) . . .A fisherman who opens his lips to talk when the nets are being loaded into the canoe is believed to cause bad luck to the expedition. How difficult it is to break from all of that. . .". (AGM to Grace Sinclair, 21/7/31)

A conversation with a young witch doctor

"The other morning a young native witch doctor came to buy a writing book. I gave him a lecture instead. He thought no doubt that our writing on paper was just another sort of charm which he could add to his repertoire. He said that there was a Roman Catholic teacher in his village but he did not seem to know much about Christ. I challenged him to take off his trappings, grease and chalk paint but he said that he dare not do that unless his fellow witch doctors assisted him or else he would be smitten with illness. He wore feathers in his hair, bands of forest creepers around his neck. He had a wooden bell suspended from his shoulder and a cane rattle in his hand. A hank of net was hung from his loins. His body was smeared with black oil and parts were lined with chalk. He seemed to listen intently to the rebuke I gave him and also the invitation to follow Jesus the great Physician. . .". (AGM, June 7, 1939)

Protecting a woman accused of witchcraft

"We are presently protecting a woman at Yalikina who was tied up by three church members and put on an island for a year. Six weeks ago she escaped to us for protection by making herself a funny little canoe to escape in it. A man fishing on an island nearby called to the Yalikina and Yaohendu folk to prevent her landing. They kept pushing her back but she eventually got ashore. With something under one arm and a paddle in the other, panting to get to us as I ran out to meet her. I sent her into the house and taking her paddle chased the Yalikina folk off and two workmen chased off the Yaohendu folk. The case was sent to the State. . .". (ECM, October 27, 1930)

The secret cult "Litecha"

"We came to Bondi section of the forest where the children had not been attending school and many church members had lapsed. . .Later we found out that the chiefs and chief women of the tribe had been running a secret cult called 'Litecha' which was cram full of superstition and lies. These were propagated by ceremonies, charms, potions and injunctions which promised to give courage, luck and safety. We asserted our influence as white people and told them the Government would be angry if they knew of it. So they agreed to give up their charms which we burnt. . . But oh, when will the idols be burnt in their hearts?" (AGM, October 23, 1930)

The "Libeli" cult reappears

"During this trip up the Lomami we have found that the superstitious secret cult of Libeli is being practiced with great effrontery. An important chief who professed to be a friend of our work has openly encouraged it. When our boys went to buy food in the village, the rowdies of the sect threatened to attack them. The school there is deserted since the young boys are sent off by their parents to live in booths in the forest and be initiated to the spirit mysteries. . .". (AGM, September 3, 1931)

Alex's views on witchcraft after 35 years

I had written to Uncle Alex from Princeton Theological Seminary in 1945 about specific aspects of his missionary work. Maxine and I were in the process of applying for missionary service in the French Cameroon. His reply on my question about witchcraft is as follows:

"To do any fundamental Christian work in Africa you will have to tackle the belief in witchcraft. . .After every effort to disprove to the natives the existence of witches and the occult power to bewitch, I and many other missionaries think that the native is still unconvinced. As a Christian he may rise by faith to a condition where he dares it or neglects it but I have never heard a native Christian preach to disprove it. . .". (AGM to JHS, August 9, 1945)

Two African pastors: colleagues of Alex

In the correspondence between 1919 and 1946 two names of African colleagues continue to appear from time to time: Pastor Abraham Akilabana

(1920s and 1930s) and Pastor Daniel Bufululu (late 1930s and 1940s). The fact that only two African associates are referred to seems to indicate that little attention was given to the training of pastors. Most of the attention was focused on training teachers/catechists for the village schools.

Pastor Abraham Akilabana

Alex writes in 1925: "My native helper, Abraham Akilabana has been consecrated by the Staff for the giving of the Lord's Supper and Baptism. So I hope he will help me with the visiting of the district. He is a worthy fellow but needs power from God if any real change is to come to the natives he preaches to." (AGM, July 14, 1925)

As the years went by, Abraham was given more authority. "I went to Yakusu and arranged for a new development in our area where Abraham, the native pastor, will be given more authority in a defined area to see if he will rise to the opportunity and get the people to be more self-supporting and devoted. . .". (February 2, 1936)

Abraham seemed to have periods in his ministry: for ten years (1925–35) he served as an itinerating pastor, sometimes traveling with Alex and Ethel; then for ten years (1936–46) he was placed in charge of an area ("the most difficult part of the forest work") to the west of Yalikina. He then went to live in Yabahondo, twenty miles inland from Yalikina. Malia, his wife, was a strong helpmate. His eldest son was trained in the Yakusu Central School and was able to be with his parents as a school teacher. He evidently died during the later years of the Mills' stay in Irema since Alex indicates in his tribute to Abraham that "I was on my way back to Yakusu when I heard of his death".

An article by Alex in the MISSIONARY HERALD in 1929 tells the story of Abraham's earlier life and ministry. It is entitled "The Bard". Alex asked him to write his story in his native language. However Alex was sure that Abraham would rather have sung and danced the important parts of his life than to sit down and write as he did. The people passed on their "history" every day in canoe songs and dance songs.

Listen to Abraham: "Here is the story of the beginning of the work of God in Yalikina. It was long ago, when I was about fifteen. (1890s ?) that I saw the white men, Grenfell and Stapleton, and the black woman Salamo, the mother of Neli, come in on the 'Goodwill' to the beach of Yalikina. But that time they did not tell us about their work. Later before we knew that the Good News was coming to us, they came again on the 'Peace' and looked at the land where the BMS now stands. Once they came and the black engineer, Baluti Dawidi, called us children, taught us a hymn, showed us a picture and preached to us about God. They taught us to read the signs "i.u." and "s.m.". Then he went back to Yakusu.

"We then had a visit for a few days from Botwafini and Waisangi, native teachers from the villages of Yangambi and Yaekela who taught us hymns and letters. Then they left before we knew enough. After some months we said the black engineer and Kilongosi, the black teacher, arrived. They gathered us together and preached from a picture. Then the white men of Yakusu asked our Chief Bonjuma a few months later if we wanted to have a teacher. All the village and the chief especially agreed. Then the BMS teacher Bosa Moses was sent to us. We liked him very much, and so did the chief. I don't remember the date when he started because at that time we were still blind. (illiterate ?)

"Those who went to school were our elders, our uncles, our big brothers and our little brothers. We built the house of God immediately and we had a big school of young men and young women who believe in it. We sang hymns, read the laws about the things which God had forbidden His people to do. We obeyed them carefully. After Bosa Moses had been with us for a long time and his preaching had entered our hearts, an elder called Lingomu and Mr. Millman came and approved of our work. Soon after the elder and two others were baptized. Since then many have passed through the school and been baptized.

"Even before they were baptized some started to open a road into the forest tribe of the Esoos, to teach them and in 1909, 1914, 1915 and 1916 we sent teachers to them. These teachers have done a great work in teaching people about the deeds of Jesus. They taught reading, writing and arithmetic; they prayed and preached and many of the Kombe (nearer) district were baptized. They in their turn went to the Bondi and Wilo districts beyond. Thus because of Yalikina the word of God spread in the Esoo tribe like the seed of Abraham. Those of Yalikina begat Kombe, Kombe began Bondi and Wilo and Bondo and Wilo begat Yaoleo (the farthest district) and Yaoleo has begotten even others.

"I, Abraham, am one of those who were taught by Bosa Moses and was baptized December 15, 1907. Then on June 15, 1915, I went to work in the garden of God in a very thick place of the Esoo forest. . ." (MH, "The Bard" by AGM, 1929)

"Black Shepherd" 'a memorial tribute

Alex wrote a moving tribute to his dear African friend, Abraham, in these words:

"He was tall, I can see his stance now, six feet of him, solid and smiling, with his kind thick lips and earnest white-rimmed negro eyes. . .What were his origins? Though he himself was not a cannibal, the chief of Yalikina, Bonjoma, gloried in the number of his Esoo enemies whom he had eaten.

"Akilabana chased hippos with his father in his youth (that was his name before he was given the name "Abraham" at his baptism). In his boyhood the first young Yakusu teacher came into his village. The youths were drawn together by the new message of the Young Man of Galilee and by the grace through faith the young man Akilabana. . .dared to be baptized. . .In a prayer meeting in a little mud chapel lit with palm oil flares, he responded to the call and went out to live in a village of the Esoo forest.

"He had not thought of marriage as yet, but with prudent African foresight his parents had. God provided in the Christian girl Bolaya a fine wife of whom he might have said with Robert L. Stevenson:

" 'Trusty, dusty, vivid, true
With eyes of gold and bramble dew
Steel ture, and blade straight,
The great Artificer made my mate'

"This young Christian pair did not fit into native life but were drawn into service with the white missionary who was beginning to build the Yalikina substation beside his village. Abraham built in brick and he built in men. His straight-forward manliness commanded obedience. But he did not dominate and could forgive personal injury with Christian self-control.

"The area of our district covered a hundred square miles of forest. He began to be a Pilgrim with me in staking out a claim for Christ in hundreds of villages. . .Many a man in the Esoo church looks him as their spiritual father. He gave of himself up to become an efficient teacher and in the training conferences at Yakusu where he taught periodically. . .

"In his own home which was first graced by twins and later by three other children, Abraham showed an example of Christian love and care. He kept the altar of family worship burning. God blessed his work but claimed his wholehearted faithfulness. Once when he had promised to follow me on a fixed date into the district, his children fell ill. Although the child was not yet better when the day arrived, he left the child with prayer and instruction in the arms of the mother. He told me that he was assured that he could not expect God to hear his prayer if he failed in faithfulness to His work. . ."

"Abraham fell ill. The shadow of the cloud of death began to come over him and the brightness of his faced was dulled. His solid frame wasted away with painful muscle swellings. He was unable to rise and get about in March. By the beginning of April he was unable to move his legs and arms. The missionaries then sent him to the Yakusu hospital for expert care, but he was too weak to recover. His last message to the teachers under his care was 'Do God's work courageously. I am going ahead to be with the Father in heaven and we shall meet again as Jesus said'. He passed away unconscious on April 26."

"Abraham has left us a rich heritage. These words express my personal feelings about him:

"I will not call him black; black is for death,
This man is living, and God's vital breath
Moves in the fleeting changes of his face.
A ready wit moves him to facile speech,
Keen sympathy commands a kind outreach.
Beneath the black skin, blood cells red like mine,
Impart a vivid glow to features fine
In which love, loyalty and laughter blend,
I will not call him black—he was my friend."

(Note: Certainly these words were not meant for black Africans to read. The relationship between the color black and death and evil is certainly a sad commentary on the cultural heritage of many of Alex's generation—and even of my own. However they do reflect an appreciation for the strength and beauty of Abraham as his friend. JHS)

Pastor Daniel Bufululu

We have little to describe this pastor who worked in the Upper Lomami field with Alex. There are only occasional references to his travels with the Mills. Ethel makes mention of him as the recipient of a pair of riding trousers which her brother had sent her from India among some used garments. Evidently Pastor Bufululu's body was of a different shape from Brother Harold's so the trousers did not fit very well!

A pathetic vignette of African grief at the loss of a child is recorded by Alex in 1943 when Bufululu and his wife, Sala, lost their five year old son, Ishamel. He was their youngest son. "He caught the measles and was complicated by his being unwisely exposed and catching a kind of pneumonia. This condition was accompanied by a painful septic throat and 104 degree temperature. For two weeks we wrestled for his life, but the heart was weak. The parents hardly slept and the old grandmother who wears hardly any clothes slept like a watchdog beside him all the time. Well the end came quickly at dusk by heart failure. I ran over with a needle of caffeine to reanimate the heart, but there was no result.

"You cannot believe the madness of African grief. The death of the little boy came as such a blow to Bufululu that he seemed to lose his reason. He had to be held by 3 or 4 men to calm him while other members of the family were rolling on the earth and the children were howling. I think the calmest was Sala the mother who seemed stupefied with grief while she held the little corpse in her arms. With great difficulty I gathered them together for a few seconds of prayer—everything was abnormal. I could not say much for I was sick at heart myself. The next day all the school scholars and about 50 native teachers and other friends gathered for the service at the grave. I could only liken it to the Good Shepherd having taken our lamb in His arms to carry him home first so that we might be constrained to follow to the heavenly land. . .". (AGM, October 13, 1943)

Some theological musings
on racial differences

Alex evidently had no training in modern anthropology or he chose to try to see cultural differences only through his own theological prism. Here are some of his thoughts on "the antipathy to coloured people":

"The antipathy toward coloured folk seems to be worldwide and although as a missionary and a Christian I don't share it I think it would be wrong to believe that in savage bosoms there are not lies, hates, yearnings and evils which we do not comprehend. And it is this, this lack of comprehension which dictates a prudent aloofness which easily gets exaggerated into vicious prejudice. I am still trying to understand the good and the bad of these people. And I am still a long way off for they are a surprise to me often. So much of their real self is under a different semblance. . .". (AGM, July 20, 1931)

On "liberté, egalité, fraternité"

"The Government seems to be feeling that they don't want many of the natives educated to read and write and to know our theories of 'liberté, egalité, fraternité' because so many natives use that knowledge to dress showily and forge signatures and shirk manual labour. The school of Christ is what they need to go through—but as attendance is voluntary not a sufficient number enter and the Government will force them by some other master. I can see trouble ahead. . .". (AGM, January 16, 1931)

On education vs. evangelism

Some of the missionaries may have seen Alex as a possible successor of Mr. Millman, the senior missionary, who was to retire in 1936. At least the

BMS Committee wanted him to take over Mr. Millman's administrative work in Yakusu in 1931 when the Millmans went on the furlough in 1931. Alex writes:

"I have recently been asked by the government to conduct a school for them on our lines in Isangi (the government post near Yalikina). This is the acknowledgement, after 30 years, of the value of our educational work and also the admission of the Belgian responsibility as colonizers to educate the people. The large commercial company which has the concession of the Lomami have also asked me to start a school at their post nearby.

"For this and other reasons I have asked the BMS Committee to relieve me of the post of successor to Mr. Millman at Yakusu during his absence on furlough and allow me to stay on here. They may think that I am shirking the office work which Yakusu affairs will involve but I want to be free for evangelistic work and the district here needs me."

In a letter in the same year, Alex comments on an article by Julian Huxley on the Sects War in Africa. "It is well aimed criticism and contains much truth. However when he says that what Africans need is education and not evangelization, he has not lived long enough in Africa to know the native. Evangelization is Education in its essence. For until a man knows himself—what is the use of his knowing geology or evolution. Until a man is saturated with the idea of a "living God", evolution, as one of His methods, is apt to be exalted into an idol of intellect in place of Him. . .". (AGM, March 7, 1931)

— — — — — — — — — —

WHAT WERE THE RESULTS OF 35 YEARS' WORK?

As I read hundreds of his letters written under the pressures of work and amidst the strain of the physical and intellectual isolation of Yakusu, Yalikina, Irema and dozens of villages in between, I asked myself many of the same questions my readers ask: Was it worth it all? What tangible results were left for succeeding generations in the Esoo Forest and beyond?

Certainly the life of the Mills as they served the physical, mental and spiritual needs of thousands of African villagers left behind memorable deeds which can never be erased from the oral history of these villages. "Bosongo Bandombele" walked among us and the stories we tell our children and grandchildren around the cooking fires and as we walk in the forest confirm the lasting impact of their life and ministry. "Bandombele" means "tall man walking in the forest". Aunt Ethel was

"Mama Bandombele", once described as a "a sitting mama", who sat with us in our huts in our darkness and suffering and brought us light and healing.

The ministry of the Mills reflected much of what we denote today as "missionary paternalism". Perhaps their anthropological assessment of African problems was often in error; their ethical standards seemed at times to be rigid and "Victorian"; yet the sum and total of their ministry across three and a half decades left an aroma of sweetness and rays of light in many lives, homes and villages. As I have tried to piece together a mosaic of their ministry of healing, teaching and preaching, the garment which was woven by their lives is whole. I now see their lives set in the context of a very primitive African society controlled by a self-seeking colonial administration. Even though the present chaos in Zaire is a serious step back into the modern "Dark Ages", the fundamental work of human transformation, educational advance, social and political evolution and development of Christian community will never be erased from the history of Zaire and her people. Recently I met a handsome young Zairian graduate student at a Presbyterian Church near the University of Minnesota campus from the Yalemba area—a Baptist! His poise, culture and education reflected several generations of Christian community of his native land. He was evidently drawn to the Presbyterian church because he could sing in their choir. Their little daughter had her feet washed at the Maundy Thursday service, so the father was still faithful to his Baptist upbringing!

One tangible evidence of the work of the Baptist missionaries in the first half of the 20th Century is the numerical growth of the Christian community. In Appendix A I have laid out an overview of the total Christianity community and its growth from 1900 to 1982. Here I have inserted some statistics to show the growth only over a twenty year period (1928–1947) in the Yakusu field. This field was only one of several mission fields in the Congo of the BMS and other Baptist missionary societies. The reader will note how the Baptist community doubled in size over this twenty year period.

– – – – – – – – – –

The growth of the Baptist community in the Yakusu field; 1928 and 1947 (comparison)

(From YAKUSU NOTES, October, 1928; May, 1947)

	1928	1947
Teachers and evangelists	400	740
Church members	3,300	6,000
Christian community	n.d.	14,000
Enquirers/catechumens	n.d.	2,000
Baptism during previous year	492	300
Church offerings	£ 120	£ 690
Attendance at hospital	30,000	58,000
Hospital assistants	20	50
Rural dispensaries	n.d.	18
Medical consultations (whole area)	n.d.	201,006
Scholars	n.d.	22,000
Girls in boarding school	30	40
Teachers in training	20	n.d.
Villages served	n.d.	540

To get some idea of the number of church members in the Yalikina sub-station area in 1928, Alex reports that there were 2,972 members. This is significant because the total membership for the entire Yakusu area in 1927 was only 3,300. The difference may be related to the fact that Alex reported in April, 1923 that 856 (about 30%) of the church members were presently under discipline. Did the figures in YAKUSU NOTES report only the number of church members in good standing?

D. Teacher Training, School Supervision and Sunday School Literature

There are educational aspects of the work of the Mills which are intimately intertwined with their evangelistic ministry. However I try in this section to lift up the uniquely educational aspects of his work and some of the problems they had to face in their role as teacher trainers and supervisors of schools.

School/Chapel Construction

Since the villages did not have any "public buildings", the building of school facilities was an indispensable part of developing an educational program. Of course many of the schools began to function under a palm tree with the scholars sitting on the ground, but that level of primitive education could not last for long.

Many of the first schools were hastily constructed of mud and wattle like the typical African hut. But these had to be replaced often and were unsuitable for education. Alex developed brick construction for village schools. This entailed hauling to the villages a simple brick-making machine which pressed the clay into bricks which were then sun-dried and fire-baked in a kiln. Parts of this simple machine would often break and Alex would have to stop operations until a local blacksmith could fashion a new iron rod or gear.

School books, paper and pencils

On every journey through the forest, the Mills had in their boxes large quantities of basic educational tools. When one thinks that there were literally thousands of scholars in the Yalikina substation area, you can imagine the quantity of material that had to be transported. These materials were not given out free; each scholar was responsible to come up with the cost of the notebook or primer. Some paid "in kind" and Alex had to dispose of the eggs, chickens, palm nuts, etc., which he received in payment.

Teacher training events

Teachers had to be brought together at Yalikina and Irema for what we would call today "intensive courses". Most of the teachers were just a few steps ahead of their pupils, so there was a lot to be taught. (See page 78 for a typical schedule of a teacher training institute in Yakusu in 1916.)

One of the most colorful vignettes of a two-week institute held at Yakusu is the following:

"They sleep on the ground in crowded huts (one begged some boards). They have to pay 1 franc per day for the plainest fare and we can only afford to give them one franc a week for food and a spoonful of salt. What do they get here? Bible instruction and memorization, reading, writing and arithmetic classes and a little French. We are starting a teacher training course at Yakusu for a three year period. We hope we can train the sharper intellects more fully. . .". (July 30, 1926)

"Lisongomi"—a kind of continuing education

"I had a 'Lisongomi' this month. That means I called all the teachers in for a month's training in Bible and general subjects such as reading, writing and arithmetic. During the time 120 of them lived in shacks beside me and got rations of food and classes from 6 a.m. to 5 p.m. with a two hour break in the heat of the day. To keep them from getting too stiff, I had outdoor drill from time to time. I have burst two pairs of trousers at the knees by bending in the exercise. We had a terrific rush about exam time with all the papers to correct and apportion the marks. I then took the occasion to pay them off their arrears in salary. Some were given 2 pence a month by the Church and others go as high as 4 pence and 6 pence. . .". (September 23, 1927)

Preparation for teacher training classes

"I was trying to cut back on my activities but soon I was involved in preparation for a gathering of teachers. I thought I had some notes of previous gatherings at Yakusu to fall back on. But when I looked for the notebooks I could not find them. So I have been working against time to get up 10 addresses on the books of Judges and Kings. Ethel has been a great help in keeping me free from callers and attending to minor pala-vers. . .". (March 31, 1925)

"I am using 'Stories of the Prophets' as my textbook for new addresses to the teachers. I shall soon be short of the O.T. stories which we printed in 1920. I wonder whether to apply for another edition or to enlarge or revise the present edition. Money is scarce so we only want the most essential books. The natives do not get much meaning out of any books they read so the result is that most missionaries confine themselves almost exclusively to N.T. stories. . .All the same I like the O.T. applications of the moral law to communal life and the unsophisticated religious motives which moved the primitive peoples of ancient times." (July 30, 1926)

Alex ends this comment on his attraction to simple primitive ways with the verse from Wordsworth:

"Great God! I'd rather be a pagan suckled in a creed outworn.

So might I, standing on this pleasant lea have glimpsed that would make me less forlorn;

Might see old Proteus rising from the sea and hear old Triton blow his wreathed horn."

"Mr. Parris and I try to keep a counterbalance on the O.T. by giving addresses, he on Paul's life and I on First and Second Timothy. This is like my teacher, Dr. McCaig used to do at Pastor's College, London. . .". (AGM, 22/9/31)

How a schoolhouse is constructed

"Yesterday was my birthday and I had six little black boys to make me happy. I went after breakfast to a village which I had not visited before although they had had a school for five years. Last year the schoolhouse fell down in disrepair and the people told our native superintendent that they would not have a school again unless the white man visited the village! I had intended to go there anyway. The first thing I told them on my arrival was that I wanted them to build the school right away. The men folk of the village went off at once for tree trunks and poles from the forest.

"I stepped off the house 3 yards wide by 7 yards long. The site was covered with sweet potatoes and grass but the boys and girls cleared that away. Then the holes for planting the tree trunks and poles had to be dug. (Note: I used the same kind of construction in Venezuela in the early 1950s to build a school/chapel using exactly the same method.) Six little boys who had dug them were quite an inspiration to me by their industry and goodwill. By midday the big half of the frame was built. In the afternoon I went on to a further village where I had not been before. When I called the roll I found a little boy had been named after me, 'Bandombele'. He was quite a stupid boy so I was not unduly flattered.

"The little boys had fun running after me on my bicycle. After I had nearly winded them, I dismounted and shook hands. They wished me the usual 'good journey' but one little lad added 'May God help you on your way' so with these black boys blessing I finished my birthday. . .". (July 18, 1937)

School under a palm leaf shelter

Sometimes Alex did not have the luxury of a schoolhouse, but gathered the scholars under a temporary shelter. He writes: "Today we had school at midday under a palm leaf shelter. And as the sun was getting through a lot, we just hung up our umbrellas to the roof by a vine and sat under them while we examined the school. We were out for a month trip this time. . .". (March 31, 1925)

The dedication of a brick schoolhouse

"The dedication of a brick schoolhouse in the Esoo Forest is just about to come off after 3 years labour at making, burning bricks, building and thatching. We want to make an event of it. We are getting a table made here for its platform and have arranged to have a reception there on Saturday and receive gifts to the collection. Then we are to have special singing and the gramophone. The scholars are some to have their photographs taken and we are to hand over the new bell. Then on Sunday we are to have a Communion Service. I do hope the weather will keep fine and that they will worthily celebrate the occasion.

"This village is Yalosambo which is the center of a group of villages and ought to be a rallying point for its best life. But unfortunately through backsliding it had become rather a disgrace to us. At another two centers we have brick schools in process of building and it means a lot of work. At one place a church member told that in a dream his father had come and told him to help the white man in this work. . .". (AGM, September 22, 1931)

A village school examination

"I am writing this while Abraham is at my right hand examining a native school and I am writing this letter at my traveling chair by his side. It is 9 o'clock and the sun is already hot and inside the walls of the mud walled school is still wet (having been brushed up for our visit). The air is damp and moist. There are about 80 in the building. They sit on wood bars for seats and they are not all quiet. What noise they make is the school boy (or girl) murmur which is unlocatable.

"As Abraham calls each name from the exercise book of the native teachers which serves as Register, each child comes forward with his or her book in hand, sometime biting the edge of it. The native teacher who stands at the side tells the examiner if the child is a good attender or not. The record book shows what progress has been made since last year's visit. Most of the little imps have been playing truant most of the year and when they come up they are put to shame and confusion and get the stick to their palms. Others who say they can read are tested by native helpers who sit at the sides of the sort of platform and have to read the words through a hole in the paper because they may know the whole primer book by heart (12 pages) and yet not be able to pick out letters and syllables by their names.

"Older lads and older men come up with the Book of the Stories of Jesus. Some read but don't grasp the meaning. Others have to be sent for. Abrahams says: 'Bolefo (his name 7 years old), where were you?' He answers, 'In the house'. 'Did you not hear the school drum?' 'Yes'. 'Were you hiding in the house?' 'No.' 'What?' 'No, just sitting down.' All this is said in an unsteady voice and the onlookers are all sniggering since they know that it is all lies. So the bad child is put in the corner for further consideration. . . .". (February 6, 1932)

Rounding up the kids for school

"I have so many children in the schools in this district that I don't know what to do to get them all taught. I have been assured that the Government would like them all taught. I am acting on that and collaring all the loose children I see in the villages till the schoolhouses will hardly hold them and my stock of books will not hold out to supply them."

"I have to keep them in hand or they would make light of the whole affair. But when I act like a Government official and appeal to the native authorities in the villages I get order enough to get the schools started. But how the native teachers will keep it up is another thing. Such is my work—recalling them all to their duty, inciting them to improve themselves and trying to let them see that the only adequate power for this is in Jesus Christ."

"I don't know whether I am losing my faith in human nature or not but I do not seem to expect anything but good natured deceit from any of them and no motive deeper than self-love in the crudest form in performing their duties to Christ and the Church. I have been feeling since our tours around the 150 villages in the Yalikina area, that the work of reproving, rebuking and exhorting is more of a burden than an inspiration. It has taken it out of my nerves more than I thought. . .". (AGM, en route, March 31, 1925)

Teacher training: ups and downs

"Last month we had a three week journey in the 'Grenfell' up the Lomami River where in 1916 I supervised the planting of seven teachers at points 150 miles up its course. This time I found only one of the original seven teachers at his post. Village headmen said that we need not come to start work in their villages unless we offered some money gift. People feel that school learning is another burden beside tax collecting which is put on them by the white men. . .But on the trip I found one man who has enthused his village to start learning to read although he himself has only just learnt and is considering putting away one of his two wives so he can be baptized. A young lad too who was one of our first school scholars in a new village was baptized on this visit along with one other man." (March 14, 1920)

"I recently had in a group of teachers for a fortnight of the 3 Rs and singing. They were a wonderfully contented lot though always begging for little favours in the way of medicine and books. . .They live on a little dried fish and cassava puddings which they market for themselves while not at classes. Boys who have followed them from their inland villages cook their food. They sleep ten in a little room and as accommodation was scarce some of them slept in the village jail which happened to be empty! There is the picture. You can fill in the palm trees and crocodiles as your aesthetic instincts dictate. . .". (September 14, 1921)

"The quality of our teacher's work is far from satisfactory. Laziness, unspirituality and tyranny over the Lord's heritage are common faults. We find it hard to get them to do the Lord's work along the Lord's lines only and bend their backs to His cross and humble their spirits. . .".

"There are some young teachers who have had an education superior to the others who are their elders. We hope that they will not get swelled heads but will grow up to establish the work. Two of them came to us last night with an exercise book filled with a criticism of heathen superstitious beliefs which showed that their minds were becoming emancipated from unthinking fears. But they need to have their hearts assured in things divine to keep the old ideas from reconquering them in times of calamity. I am afraid I am sceptical of a quick emancipation of negros from superstition. I remember a minister among negroes in Alabama (visited there in 1923) who told me that even negroes when civilized are very prone to charms. All the same it is encouraging to us to know some are facing the problem. . .". (October 23, 1930)

Government concern about influence of Marcos Garvey

"The Government looks on our work with satisfaction if it can scare the native chiefs into giving a portion of the male population for plantation labour and if it has sufficient clerks to keep an administrative check on the people. The officials have learned of late that educated natives from the Coast under the influence of Marcos Garvey have been stirring up discontent. A rumour was current all through the Belgian Congo that Americans are coming to occupy the colony and that the present whites are going to evacuate it to avoid trouble. But why, said the natives of Yalikina village, does Mr. Mill keep on building the new part of his house if he is going away! So the rumour was discounted here."

Writing textbooks for the teachers and other projects

Since Alex had medical training and drawing skills, he prepared a school text on Physiology and Hygiene. It was sent to Mr. Millman on furlough in England to be printed. (March 14, 1920)

"We have made an exhibition or 'exposition' as the French say to encourage the school children and folks in general to use their hands and keep up their ancient handicrafts instead of buying all machine-made European goods. Many fancy articles are being included. One is a river steamer model 4 feet in length with every detail shown down to the steam whistle and with a moveable paddle wheel. An aeroplane with 3 foot wing spread and body with dining room accommodations and pilot's cockpit with moveable rudders and helices is another marvellous bit of observation as well as handicraft.

"Some have made beds and tables and cupboards. Another has made vegetable ink. We hope the Administrator will come and preside and judge as he is keen on teaching the natives to work with their hands rather than to become clerks."

Ethel insisted that they clean up!

When Alex would bring in 100 teachers at a time for training, it often fell to Ethel the hassle of the physical arrangements for their housing. She writes: "I don't think they like me much for if they don't sweep out their places, I take hold of some goods or chattel and hold them till they report the place is cleaned up. . .". (July 30, 1926)

A son inherits a chiefdom. . .and four wives!

"I have just had news tonight that a lad who had grown to be a teacher and done great things for Christ has now inherited the chieftainship of his deceased father. In consequence he has also inherited his four wives. There are many called but few chosen in this sense. Although the idea of the Kingdom spread and the way of light and life is declared yet the road being narrow and the gate straight, few there be who find it. . .". (June 7, 1925)

A teacher's wife leaves her village

"One of our village girls has married a man who has gone to be a teacher to the Bambole folk. It is a long way from home for her—200 miles. Both she and her husband are church members. She cried at first but I told her to try to see what she could do amongst the women. We shall see her there in two months time. The chief in the new village welcomed her and gave them a house to live in and some plantain growing in the back of it. . .". (ECM, 24/9/31)

A very special educational opportunity

"Today we have been remembering the Death of Jesus and had a Good Friday service. By a coincidence there was a complete eclipse of the moon last night. Because of the blood-red appearance of the obscured moon, many thought it a portent and were recalled to think of the things of God."

"In fact the drums were heard beating on the other side of the river, calling the people of one village to come out of their houses and gather at the schoolhouse to pray as there was a serious portent in the heavens. Many came up to our house to ask us what it meant. We explained a little about the shadow of the earth being cast by the sun over the moon. But it did not get far in their brains since they said afterwards that the moon is a thing like a tin plate.

"However it gave us a crowded service and the chance to place in their minds that salutary ballast of the weight of guilt and sin which keeps us level in voyaging from time into eternity. On Easter Sunday we hope to rejoice in the fruit of the pain and vindication of that wrong by the Triumph of Jesus over sin and death."

A typical journey up the Lomami: headaches with schools

"I was timed to reach a certain limit on the Lomami and get the steamer back to Yakusu by ten days. So we made brief calls and only dealt with the most urgent matters. I put out a teacher who had been too long complaining about his people's laziness which I suspected was a cloak for his own. In another village, I chastised nearly the whole school with the stick because they had danced an indecent dance. We got into the next sleeping place after dark and were in danger of banging the steamer on some of the rocks which were there but we did not.

"The next day I put down a little teacher called 'Elephant' in a village where they had never had a faithful teacher yet. Another village was one which had split in two factions: R.C. and Protestant because one half wanted to learn to read and we have them a teacher to help them.

"Thereafter we did not stop at the villages longer than to pick up the boys who said they had completed their primer.

"These we told to be in their canoe alongside and went sailing on. On deck we examined them and then told them their fate. They then got into their canoe and we cast them off to drift back down the Lomami to their villages. Most of those who finished the primer bought the Stories of the Life of Jesus and so the story spreads. . .

"We stayed the Sunday at Yaisule, 150 miles up the Lomami, and as the Commissaire de District (sort of Governor) was there we told him our difficulties and aims. He was sympathetic and gave us some slates, books and pencils. Unhappily the small church of 2 which was here and the teacher have been ensnared by Satan and had to be put out of the church for fornication and polygamy. Such work as was going on in the school could not be as good as it would have been on that account. . .". (July 8, 1926).

Villages teachers and the head tax

"In a few days I will have to arrange for the teachers to go before the government collector of the tax and pay their tax for the current year. This involves urging them and their friends to their most heroic efforts to collect

48 francs/5 cms which is a lot of money in this year of acute depression. I contribute through the Native Church funds a small portion (about 16 frs.) which is due them as wages. Then if they cannot reach the total figure they risk being put in prison and given hard labour and rough usage until their relatives take pity on them and buy them out. It is not very easy being friendly with the local government official when one knows he is directing this tax affair. He himself says he hates the job but he does it all the same and his salary indirectly depends on it. . .We can never be content with it or cease seeking to replace it by fair encouragement to work and education for its necessity and dignity. . .

"We are trying to do this through education but we are disliked for it. Often a white man openly scoffs at the little village school and the honouring teacher and wishes he were out of the way. An educated native is not so easy to bully as an ignorant one. . .". (AGM, August 4, 1934)

Government harassment of scholars

"The officials are enraged at times with the 'aire' which the educated natives put on so that two of our Yakusu scholars were put in the block (prison) because when they were on holiday near the Government Post of Isangi they did not carry on their person the papers showing evidence: 1st that they were exempt from government head tax and 2nd that they had been examined by a doctor.

"Both of these papers could have been produced if they had give them time. But although I vouched for their word on these points the official was inexorable. They got out after two days and are now back at Yakusu. Well, I found out afterwards that the government touring doctor was offended at me for not inviting him to come with the Commissaire and perhaps he vented his dislike on the boys . . .". (AGM, January 16, 1931)

E. MISSION COLLEAGUES AND STATION BUSINESS: Policy Differences, Etc.

Their missionary colleagues (1911–1946)

From 1897 to 1954 there were 107 missionaries who served in the Yakusu field for a total of 826 years. Alex and Ethel Mill served there for a total of 63 years; he for 35 and Ethel for 28. This represents 7.5% of the total years served by BMS personnel in this 57 year period. However by the time that Alex Mill arrived in Yakusu in 1911, twenty-five missionaries had preceded him there. Upon his arrival only Mr. and Mrs. Millman,

Mr. C. E. Pugh, Mr. and Mrs. E. E. Wilford and Mr. Henri Lambotte were on the field. Four missionaries lay at rest in the small cemetery plot behind the Yakusu Church: Allbert E. Wherrett (1896); Mrs. Kenred Smith (1901); George Moore (1902); and S.D. Kempton (1908). Beside the remains of the white missionaries lay the body of Salumu, the servant of Mrs. Millman who was one of the first believers in the Yakusu area. In 1914, Mr. E.E. Wilford died and was also buried at Yakusu.

"The Old Guard"

"Mokili" (Mr. Wm. Millman) was the undisputed senior missionary. "Mama Mokili" was the first wife of the pioneer W.H. Stapleton (1897–1905). Stapleton died in 1905 and his widow married Millman in 1908. Mr. E.E. Wilford arrived in 1907 and his wife in 1906. C.E. Pugh had come in 1909 together with Henri Lambotte. Sutton Smith, another of the pioneers at Yakusu, had come in 1899 and his wife in 1909. The Sutton Smiths returned in late 1911 just as Alex Mill and Nurse Rose Gee and Miss James arrived.

The "younger" missionaries

Very few new personnel arrived from 1914–1919 because of World War I. Many new missionaries arrived in the 1920s and 1930s. Those whom Alex and Ethel mentioned most frequently were: Dr. and Mrs. C.C. Chesterton (1920–1936); Mr. and Mrs. Ennals (1921–1951; 1925–1951); Mr. and Mrs. Parris (1922–1950; 1923–1950); Mr. and Mrs. W.H. Ford (1922–1955; 1926–1927); Dr. F.G. Spear (1922–1923); Dr. and Mrs. K.W. Todd (1926–1929); Mr. and Mrs. Wilkerson (1928–1940); Mr. and Mrs. D.R. Chesterton (1935–1952; 1938–1952); Dr. and Mrs. S.G. Browne (1936–?; 1940–?)

New recruits who arrived as the Mills leave

I wish to mention two couples who arrived in the late 1930s and mid 1940s with whom I was privileged to be in touch in recent years: Dr. and Mrs. John F. Carrington (1938–1950; 1940–1950); and Mr. and Mrs. H.F. Drake (1945–1954). (Both couples returned to serve the BMS in the 1960s, but I need to ascertain these later dates.)

In 1975 when Maxine and I were traveling to the World Council of Churches Assembly in Nairobi we tried to arrange a meeting with the Carringtons in London. Even though the meeting did not work out, it gave me the opportunity to exchange several letters with the Carringtons about the Mills. Dr. Carrington died in the early 1980s, but I was able to interview

Mrs. Nora Carrington in Salisbury in 1991. Rev. and Mrs. Fred Drake also kindly received me in their home near London in 1991 and shared with them their brief acquaintance with the Mills in the Congo and in England. I am continuing my efforts to contact other aged BMS personnel who served in Yakusu from the 1930s through the mid 1940s who knew the Mills. I also hope to contact more people who knew them during their retirement years in Cambridge (1946–1969).

SOME VIGNETTES OF COLLEAGUES OF THE MILLS
(as described by them)

"Mokili"—William Millman

There was no doubt that Mr. Millman was "in charge" in the Yakusu field. An excellent pen portrait of him and of his work is "Mokili of the Congo" written by his granddaughter Jane Butterworth, daughter of "Lutwasi" Stapleton Butterworth. This is to be found in the Angus Library at Regent Park College, Oxford.

Alex writes about Mr. Millman: "He is clearly senior to us all—and I have drawn out from the Central Station affairs to superintend the Yali-kina area. It is likely that great changes will take place in our work when Mr. Millman retires. The missionaries who will be left when he retires are all about one stage and will form a Committee of quite a different type. . .". (AGM, 20/2/36). There was a time in the early 1920s when Alex was asked to be temporary head of Yakusu when Mr. Millman was on furlough. Alex was very reluctant even to consider the offer which finally did not happen. (AGM, 14/7/25) When "Mokili" retired in 1937, it was Mr. Ennals who became the senior missionary. Alex wrote that he preferred to be free to work the Upper Lomami field. (AGM, 15/10/37)

One of Mr. Millman's goals before retiring in 1937 was to complete the new church at Yakusu. Alex calls it "Mr. Millman's supreme activity and application". As a gift from the station, Alex made a model of the Yakusu Church as a farewell gift to "Mokili".

H. B. Parris

H. B. Parris came in 1922 as a single missionary. He stayed with Alex at Yakusu for a short time. Ethel and Barbara had gone to England the year before. Mr. Parris married Miss G.C. Owen on the field in 1923. Mr. and Mrs. Parris took over the Yalikina field when the Mills were on furlough in 1933–34. Ethel said "that they had to leave their own region of 100 villages to come to take over our field." (ECM, 28//33)

Alex describes the new probationary missionary:

"Mr. Parris, the new man who is staying with me, comes from Buckinghamshire and has very strong convictions. He came through some trying experiences during the war as a conscientious objector. He was put on to public utility works at last under a committee of the Society of Friends and did construction and relief work in France and Austria. He is a vegetarian so I have to learn quite a new department in cookery to be able to produce from nuts and roots things which are of the value of meat and fish which we receive regularly as they are naturally provided by God in living organisms. However he is pleasant about it. He does not object to taking a hand in the cooking so I hope we will have some more fun in that department soon. . .". (AGM, 12/9/22)

Mr. W.H. Ennals

He arrived in 1921. Alex comments: "Mr. Ennals, the other new man, is a Bristol College Baptist Theological student and has been set on missionary work with an earnest devotion which is evident in his conversation and prayers. He was also up and out first thing in the morning in order to commence taking his part in looking after the brick making boys. Both Mr. Ennals and Mr. Parris came out with me the first Sunday they were here to an open air service at a neighboring village. They were able to give out the hymns and read the Scriptures in the Lokele language. So that shows they have been working at it on the voyage out. I however will only be here with them for a few weeks now before I return to Yalikina. If, after a few months Mr. Millman agrees one may come with me to Yalikina and learn the work of that district . . .". (AGM, 12/9/22)

Alex does not hide his longing for a Scottish colleague when he writes in the same letter after describing Mr. Parris, Mr. Ennals and Dr. Spear: "They are all Englishmen but are such good and devoted fellows one forgets about that defect (being English!) and is sorry they were not born in Scotland. . .".

Dr. K.W. Todd (1926–1929)

"Dr. Todd is a Surrey man, has a very breezy disposition and a very open mind. Without deprecating his devotion to Christ, I may say that he is very advanced in religious thought and even the Virgin Birth needs more proof to him than the Bible gives. We have discussed Hosea too and he considers that God's love was revealed to him through his own love for an erring and unfaithful wife. I suppose he may be right but there is much more than that in the Book of Hosea. . .But in any case if perplexed in faith, he is pure in deed. He has taken on an orphan baby of two weeks old and is rearing it on the bottle himself just to show the natives that we are willing to take as much care of a black child as we would a white one. He is very interested in his boys and spends some evenings in explaining pictures to them. He also has classes to make medical students or nurses of them." (AGM, 7/11/27)

Douglas R. Chesterman (1935–1952)

Alex had been pressing the BMS to appoint a new missionary to work with him on the Lomami River. Finally in 1935, D.R. Chesterman was appointed. Alex writes:
"Our new colleague Mr. D.R. Chesterman, son of a minister in Worthing, is just getting to know the district. He saw about a fifth of it on a journey in January and February. In April he came up the Lomami with me as far as here but had some breakings out on his legs and returned to Yakusu to see the doctor. So he has no idea of the inland work in the area. He is a brilliant young man and has been purposely impressed with the importance of intensive educational work and sides with the Yakusu staff. He is naturally very keen on the Boarding School at Yakusu and the village school there. Whether the claim of the Forest and River Village work will come upon him I do not know. . .". (AGM, 20/2/36)

Clara and John: "The mental strain I have been having I cannot explain to anyone. . .As you know I have been given a colleague here but apparently I was not treating him properly. I did my best but he felt he was being repressed and in uncongenial company. He complained privately to Yakusu and the Doctor there agreed it was detrimental to his health and a medical report was sent home to the Mission. When the station heard however that the Mission proposed removing him from Yalikina to Yakusu, they thought the Mission had gone too far. In fact before the reply from the Mission had been received, I suggested a conference with him, the doctor, Mr. Millman and myself. After that, Mr. Chesterman and I agreed to pull along together and adjust things for the best interests of the work. That was three weeks ago and although I have kept up, my mind and feelings have been indescribable.

"He really wants to live alone and manage what part of the work is given to him on his own lines. He is capable and has fine qualities of character but I believe my friends (?) at Yakusu have made him feel that he must not ally himself with me. But as Ethel warned me, I must not let Satan make use of my feelings to upset me and the work. . .We went out to a sandbank in the middle of the river last Saturday and rigged up a shelter and bathed. Ethel enjoyed it. . .". (AGM, 24/7/36)

Alex and Ethel realized that in the long run they would have difficulty sharing leadership in the Yalikina substation with Mr. Chesterton:

"My colleague Mr. Chesterton is much easier to work with now but his complaints have led to the postponement of building his house even though we have some money towards it. In view of the shortness of staff he is not likely to be free for work in Yalikina with me after this term. This checks the work on the Upper Lomami unless I just go off and do it myself . . .". (AGM, 24/7/36). Ethel (usually much more blunt than Alex in her comments) writes about some specific complaints by Mr. Chesterton:

"Alex has written to the Home Committee because they want our new man (Chesterton) to live at Yakusu although the Yakusu Committee thought he should try and be master of himself. One of his complaints was that I was not punctual with meals on journeys. How could one be when often the boat stopped at a village just near chop time and perhaps Alex would say 'I'm going ashore' just to tell the people to get on with building the schoolhouse. He would say 'I shan't be more than ten minutes', but while he is gone up flocks any number of sick folk. Naturally I get on with the job and try and help the poor things. Alex then gets back before I've finished. Sometimes Alec would help me now and again and Mr. Chesterton would do the same. He has had exactly the same medical training as Alec.

"When we finished we would push away and start for the next village, eating our meal en route. We didn't know it at the time but Mr. Chesterton was annoyed. He reported this and other similar things to Yakusu and the Doctor sent a report home that unless the environment were altered Mr. Chesterton would have a breakdown. We were then told later of what had been done. We were annoyed to think he didn't mention things to us. . .". (ECM, 16/20/36)

By early 1937 it seems that Mr. Chesterman was reluctantly willing to stay on at Yalkina since the Mills would be going on furlough soon. Ethel writes: "Mr. Chesterton has now written home saying that he wishes to stay at Yalikina. He showed Alex his letter and wrote the same to Mr. Millman. I think he is sorry things went so far. He can hardly undo it but he is certainly much nicer. Moral is to pack up your troubles in your OWN kit bag when they are fiddling ones such as he complained about. . .". (ECM, 26/2/37)

Mr. Chesterman went home in the summer of 1938 and was married in Lowes, Surrey in September. The Mills were present at his wedding. But the Mills had decided before going on furlough in 1937 that they would return to settle in Irema and build an adobe style house there. "I can build a good mud house at Irema for about 70 pounds while a second brick house at Yalikina would cost about 600 pounds." The Chestermans would then occupy the mission house in Yalikina and the field would be divided. Alex would take the Upper Lomami region. It was clear that a second mission-ary residence was not needed now. Alex went ahead and burned the bricks he had prepared and built a storage unit instead of a second residence.

The BMS missionaries as linguists

Before I write about Dr. J.F. Carrington, who became one of the fore-most African linguists during his missionary career, (1938 through the early 1980s), we need to recognize the contributions of W.H. Stapleton, E. Sutton-Smith, W. Millman and W.H. Ford in the literature which they provided on the Kele (Lokele) language before the arrival of Dr. Car-rington in 1938. (Stapleton, W.H., COMPARATIVE HANDBOOK OF CONGO LANGUAGES, Yakusu 1903; Sutton-Smith, E, YAKUSU, THE VERY HEART OF AFRICA, London, 1910; Millman, W., AN OUT-LINE OF LOKELE GRAMMAR, Yakusu, 1926; ENGLISH-LOKELE VOCABULARY, Yakusu, 1926; Ford, W.H. A LOKELE GRAMMAR, Yakusu, 1936.)

The Kele (Lokele) language became the "market language" for a dis-trict far greater than that occupied by the Kele tribe alone which numbered (in 1940) about 26,000. The BMS in 1895 chose a site among the Kele people at the extreme corner of the Kele territory near the village of Ya-koso (Yakusu). Small groups of the tribe broke away from time to time and took up permanent residence as traders or fishers in points as far away as Kongolo (up-river) and Leopoldville (Kinshasa) (downriver). The early missionaries reduced the Kele language to writing and began to use this tongue as a medium for evangelistic and educational work.

Alex Mill learned the Lokele language at Yakusu and used it in his work, but since Lingala was the major language of the Lomami River ba-sin, he developed a high degree of fluency in Lingala.

Dr. and Mrs. John F. Carrington

The Carrington Papers have been cataloged carefully at the Angus Library and are available for scholarly research. I understand that one or more researchers have began work on these papers. Here are just a few of the catalogue headings in order to appreciate the extent of Dr. Carrington's research and writings. I am fortunate to have in my possession the entire listing of this valuable collection.

"Yakusu Papers. Outlines by W.H. Ford, of succession of Yakusu chiefs and 'Bekumi'. . . . .Plan of Yakusu Station. . .Letters from K.C. Parkinsoon to David Parkinson (1938–35) . . .Typed extracts from Mboli Ya Tengai 1928–29. . .etc."

"Unsorted Papers. Press cuttings on the Zaire River Expedition. . . 'Tone and Melody in a Congolese Popular Song' from AFRICAN MUSIC SOCIETY JOURNAL. . . 'Charcoal Burning near Kinshasa by JFC from AFRICAN STUDIES 27.1, 1968. .' etc. 'From mud school to university in seventy years by JFC. . . 'Gong languages' by JFC, SCIENTIFIC AMERICAN, Dec, 1971. . . 'Speech Surrogates: Drum and Whistle Systems' by Donna Jean Umiker. . .etc."

Alex Mill and John Carrington

I am fortunate to have had several exchanges of letters with Dr. Carrington in 1970 and 1975. He wrote about "Bandombele" in May, 1970 after I had come across two letters he had written to Uncle Alex before his death in 1969.

"Bandombele was indeed a great friend to us and a much admired one. He and 'Mama' were at Irema when we first joined the Yakusu staff (I in 1938 and Nora in 1940). We had the privilege of itinerating with them as well as meeting them at our annual station conference. From order of priority, 'Bandombele' should have been senior missionary when we got there—but he was always a pioneer missionary and could not abide the administrative duties which were necessary in the Station Senior Missionary's job. That work would have kept him away from journeys and personal contact with the Congolese people. . .

". . .The reference in your letter to his favorite hymn in Lokele, 'Swaka to ndako yae la bekeeli ya olau', is the one he composed in Lokele. It was one of the few that were probably original compositions and not mere translations from English. He had set it to the tune of 'See amid the Winter Snow. . .' It told verse by verse how a Christian builds the 'house' of his Faith and Witness. The hymn became a favourite among our Upper River brethren. . . We sang 'your' hymn in Lokele this morning by the way. . .". (John Carrington mentioned in a letter to Alex) (JFC to AGM, 16/5/66, Stanleyville, CDR)

I had sent Dr. Carrington an old photograph from Uncle Alex's collection. He replied:

". . .Thank you for the photo. We shall appreciate this all the more because many of our photos of Congo colleagues were destroyed when the 'Simba' rebels destroyed our Yalemba station in 1964. . .My wife and I were able to visit with him only a fortnight before he passed away in November, 1969 in Cambridge. I was able to put into his hands the first-page proofs, already corrected of the Lingala Bible in which he was so interested. . .". (JFC to JHS, 8/5/70)

John Carrington kept Alex up on the most recent news from the Yakusu field: "May 15, 1966. . .Pastor Bufululu is safe and well. He has been able to get to Yalikina from Irema area where he was hiding when the Basimba moved in. We hear that Basai came out at the same time, too. . .We were afraid for him because he is quite fearless when it comes to Christian witness and we feared that he might get shot telling the Basimba where they were disobeying God's law (or the ANC) . . .At the secondary school and university classes I meet with some of your old scholars. . .".

A February 28, 1968 letter brings good news: ". . .Work is being begun again at Irema. . .Evangelist Lifenya has recently gone back to the area together with Alafu. I understand also that Acholo is busy there. . .I have had a reply from Pasto Lititiyo who was glad to hear from you. He hopes to get Mokili, his son, to translate the English for him. Mokili Abalayama is a member of my English class at the University Extension classes and translating this will be an excellent exercise for him!" And in the last letter to Alex from JFC dated February 16, 1969 he reported: "We visited the Education office last week in Kinsangani (Stanleyville) and found Samuel Longo busy sweeping up around the building. He called us over to show us a letter he had recently received from you in which you had asked him to give us your best wishes. Thank you very much-the message got through. . .".

Station Business

Alex never looked forward to the meetings of the Yakusu Committees. Since he pressed so hard to open the Yalikina Substation, he felt that he was suspect of caring less for the Yakusu work. He writes:

"The last Yakusu Committees were not pleasant for me. Difficulties were made more difficult by the feeling that I was suspect of despising Yakusu work and favouring Yalikina work." (AGM, 8/11/26) (Note: Since my wife and I worked in a similar situation in Venezuela in 1949–56 when the first "substation" was opened, we know what Uncle Alex was talking about!)

His comments in a letter the following year reflect more of the problem: "We are now on our way up to Yakusu on the 'Grenfell' as Mr. Parris who was up the Lomami had just come down on Monday night. We are going up to meet Mr. Millman and plead for a larger portion of help from Yalikina in anticipation of the development of the district by the trade of the Lomami Company and in view of our furlough in 1928."

> Away at Yalemba for a while: a fresh breath or air, but the
> same administrative headaches!

"I was in Yalembe to relieve Mr. Palmer whose wife is dangerously ill. I had to go with just my camp kit from Isangi since I had already been out for three weeks. Yalemba is a beautiful station for flowers. I have brought away a lovely bunch of roses which are on the steamer table beside me as I write. . .".
"I went to Yalemba to take over the Station books and cash while Mr. Jackson the young missionary managed the workmen. I also took services in Lingala. I found mission business much more perplexing than other work. I only managed to take over from the retiring man and hand the work back again to Mr. Marker of Upoto who has come to fill his place. I lost some sleep over it. . .In any case in 1923, I'll pack up my troubles in my old kit bag—my kit is getting a bit worn out—and smile, smile, smile. . .". (17/8/21)

> "I've anchored my ship at the mouth of the Lomami . . ."

While on furlough in 1923–24 there was considerable talk in London and on the field about opening up new territory to the east of Yakusu. The strategy was to join up with the Church Missionary Society in Uganda. "I don't suppose I will have any part in it. I have as you know espoused the cause of the Yalikina area of the Yakusu district. I have anchored my ship at the mouth of the Lomami River where I have built the house. I should like before I do any other new work to build in a few lives. But that takes a long time settled in one place. . .". (AGM, 3/3/24)

It seems that Alex also enjoyed being "in charge" as he was on his own work in Yalikina. He even went so far as to confess this feeling to Clara and John: "You have no idea how pleased I am to be here and able to direct things in my own district . . .". (AGM, 4/20/24)

> "Another storm to be weathered. . ."

Alex's efforts to control his own section of the Yakusu field continued to cause tensions in the Mission. He writes about a particularly stormy mission meeting after a terrible, black stormy night when they thought that a native child had been drowned (later found sheltered in a house).

"Well we got over that night but the Station Committee meeting to which we went in August was almost more stormy. I stuck out for control in my own section of Yalikina District. Mr. Millman refused to admit that I had the right to pay a certain teacher whom he wants to pay from Yakusu. We parted good friends but we have not settled the matter yet. . .". (AGM, 22/9/31)

"My colleagues think I have pressed too far. . ."

Alex was always pushing out into the forest from the Lomami River and farther into the Upper Lomami region. This seemed to irk some of his colleagues at Yakusu. He and Mr. Parish had just returned from visiting some large villages and gotten permission from the Director of the Concession Company and from the local administrator to work in the area. In fact, they had received the best reception at the most distant village. From that village a road ran inland to link up with Mr. Parris's work. "Our station colleagues at Yakusu think that we have pushed too far afield and that we have not the resources to meet the present duties in our district if we add on this new center. I am ready to be blamed for pushing on too fast than for delaying. Our effort has already created fresh interest among our native helpers—especially as one of the oldest and most faithful of the native superintendents in the Upper Lomami region died while we were there. . .". (AGM, 22/9/31)

Alex pleads for decentralization

While on furlough in 1933, Alex told the BMS that he felt that every move he had made "for better development in the Yalikina area was shelved or blocked during the last eight years. . . The staff and direction at Yakusu . . . see in my desire for more autonomy as an attempt at schism in the work or opposition to central control and that opinion is only too easily reflected back to the home office. . .A reasonable amount of decentralization is helpful, I believe, for the work. I voluntarily gave up my place as successor to Mr. Millman at Yakusu so that I could secure the development of Yalikina. . .My spirit chafes under the apathy of Furnival Street (BMS office) . . .". (AGM, 23/8/33)

Decentralization finally took place just before Mr. Millman retired in 1937. By that time, Alex and Ethel had made the decision that they were the missionaries to occupy the Upper Lomami post at Irema. Yalikina as a duly recognized substation was then left to younger colleagues to manage.

Too much money put into large institutions

One of Alex's complaints to the BMS was that too much money and personnel was poured into large institutions. He writes: "I consider it treason to the tradition of William Carey who was so scholarly to depreciate higher training in our BMS. But as money is so scarce it takes a lot of faith to believe that we are doing the best with it to keep up colleges like Serampore (India) and leave whole areas of Africa unopened. . .". (AGM, 29/1/27)

MAJOR MISSION POLICY CONCERNS

It appears that at least two major issues faced the missionaries in the Congo in the 1920s: the Libeli practices and the Kimbangista movement.

Libeli practices

The early missionaries had repudiated these practices as early as 1903. The cult was binding the tribal life together in a solidarity hitherto unknown. There was nothing demonstrably immoral in the practice which, every few years, gathered the youth in every village and initiated them into full tribal membership. However there were some in the Christian churches who saw in the Libeli the counterfeit of the truth. The priests of the ceremonies were like the magicians of Pharaoh who deluded the unsophisticated. Fear was imposed by silence.

For some years there was a split in the young church over the condemnation of the Libeli. Alex had penetrated a Libeli meeting during his first year in Yakusu for which he was sharply criticized by the older missionaries (Cf. page 58).

Sutton-Smith describes in detail the ceremony: "Men hidden in the tree tops pulled cords to make branches move and packages of sticks and stones fell. Snakes, their fangs broken by teasing with rubber-tipped sticks, were used to cause fear; a trap door contraption in the ground ensured the disappearance of votive offerings, smoking fires to cause tears were built round the hut at the entrance of the sacred group where the initiates slept. The 'ancestor spirits' which were supposed to receive the novices into full tribal membership, were ordinary townsmen distinguished with feathers and animal tails and chalk-marks on their bodies. . .". (pages x)

Dr. C.C. Chesterton writes in "The Swan Song of the Libeli" (YAKUSU NOTES, January, 1926) about the agony of decision for the Christians to give up these cultic practices which held them in bondage to fear.

The Kimbangista movement

Cecilia Irvine has written the story of its beginnings in THE BIRTH OF THE KIMBANGISTA MOVEMENT IN THE BAS-ZAIRE, 1921. Simon Kimbangu had been instructed and baptized by a Protestant pastor. He was a member of the Baptist Church of Ngombe Lutete, near the Wathen Station of the BMS.

It is not surprising that the concern about the movement as it emerged came both from the Belgian administrators' fear of African unrest and a possible revolt in the Colony AND the conviction of the Roman Catholics that the Protestants were to blame for these socio-religious disturbances.

In fact, the Protestants were caught in the crossfire between the Administrators, the Roman Catholics and many African Protestant Christians who felt that the missionaries had abandoned first Simon Kimbangu and then hundreds of church members.

Simon Kimbangu seemed to become the scapegoat for the Africans who faithfully followed his teaching, as well as countless others who were confused by lesser prophets who claimed to follow Kimbangu but misconstrued his message by introducing their own political anti-white or non-Christian variations and interpretation.

The life of Simon Kimbangu was saved from death by hanging through the initiatives of the Protestant missionaries. The sentence of death was passed on him October 3, 1921 and was later commuted to life imprisonment by King Albert. On that same day, the BMS field secretary wrote the Governor General at Boma to consider a less severe penalty. Simon Kimbangu was inescapably the victim of the religious and political intolerance of the times.

The evidence for the above analysis is based on the following documentation:

(1) Three letters sent from the BMS in London to King Albert and the Belgian Colonial Minister which give evidence that the missionaries had expressed themselves strongly on behalf of reconsideration of their treatment of Simon Kimbangu.

(2) A letter from Rev. W.B. Frame which gives an eyewitness account of his encounter with some of the lesser prophets of Simon Kimbangu who distorted his teaching.

(3) A letter written in prison by three followers of Simon Kimbangu who had been deacons of the Baptist Church in Ngombe Lutete. This letter speaks for itself with almost Pauline strength and simplicity. It was sent to Rev. George R.R. Cameron (1884–1914) who translated it and sent it to the BMS in London. He had known the authors of the letter for over thirty years and vouched for their character.

It should be noted that much of the related correspondence of the BMS related to the Kimgangista movement was destroyed in the 1940 blitz bombing of London. Therefore few Protestant documents related to the movement have survived.

It seems that Alex knew little of the details of what was happening several hundred miles downstream on the Congo, when he wrote to Clara and John:

"In the lower Congo the revival headed by the Fetich-Prophet has been mistaken by the government for a political movement in connection with the Pan African propaganda. The 'Prophet' has been caught and sentenced to death. The missions have put in a plea for leniency. . .". (AGM, 9/11/21)

It appears that the Yakusu field did not feel the impact of the Kimbangista movement for many years.

Pressing for help on the Upper Lomami

Alex continued to press his case for "a new white man" for the Upper Lomami: "We had to come up to Yakusu about a fortnight after our return and have Committee meetings. We found that our colleagues had mistaken our zeal for extension as a kind of competition with the Yakusu importance. We had to 'apologize' in the classical sense for our work and to say we would still hold on to it even if we killed ourselves—but no good purpose would be served by that they feel and so they want us to curtail our work. I, on the other hand, want them to press for a new white man for the Upper Lomami. We are still pressing the home office for that. We all wound up with family worship in the right spirit however . . .". (AGM, 9/10/29)

F. DESIGNING AND BUILDING TWO MISSIONARY RESIDENCES AND MANY SCHOOL/CHAPELS: *Gardening, Maintenance Duties at the Station, Etc.*

Building the Yalikina house

Without doubt, this was the building project which meant the most to Alex. It was the African house to which he brought Ethel when she returned with him in 1924 after her absence from the field of over thirty months. He was rightly proud of the architecture with lovely arches around the verandah and throughout the interior of the house.

Ethel described her activities as they began to settle in at their new Yalikina home: "We are at last in the house that Alec built. It is very nice though unfinished as yet. Still we are here and something more gets done to the premises each day. We've got a watertank fixed up and that is one of the greatest boons. He is getting the garden in shape. Various friends have given us plants and seeds. We have bananas coming along and 20 palm trees. So we call our home 'Palm Beach House'. (ECM 30/9/24)

Alex writes on the same day that he is getting behind with a great many things which need to be done in the house. He has not got the window panes properly installed yet. "But Ethel is very good and does not mind waiting. She has made the house look very nice with curtains, etc. . . .". (AGM, 30/9/24)

"I've got a bedstead given from Yakusu and have made a mattress stuffed with box shavings. I also have a nice rose bedspread and some white curtains I am going to dye to match. I think the room will look very nice. Alex will soon plaster the walls and the wainscoting is on. . ." (ECM)

A year later there are still things to be finished. "At odd moments Alex has been trying to do various things which are necessary for the house. He has made a 'meat safe' and put mosquito gauze on the windows of the middle room. . .All this is worked in with the dispensary, school work, palavers and station management. . .". (ECM 25/9/25)

But Alex keeps at his home improvement tasks. "I have wanted to get the finishings of the house done. I have now embellished the back arch in the middle room by a plaster moulding round the edge of the woodwork. It is the first time I have done plastering myself. I now have a great deal of sympathy with plasterers. It took me the best part of a fortnight since I had to make the moulds, prepare the surface of the wall, mix putty lime and then clean up the whole mess. But it was worth it. It looks nice. And it only costs a little, The lime we have for pointing the bricks was what I used. The Plaster of Paris was a present from a man in East Orange, New Jersey!" (AGM, 20/10/25)

Adding on a Guest Room

Most missionaries in isolated areas are often called upon to furnish accommodations for travelers. The room could also be used for an additional missionary who could come and help "when we are pressed". The guest room project was urgent but it took over six years to complete. . . By October, 1929 he could proudly write: "We have about 30,000 bricks waiting to be burnt for an addition to our house. . .". (3/10/29) By March, 1931 the walls of the addition were up and the finishing was underway. "The room at the end of our present house is nearly fitted with doors and could accommodate an assistant missionary or a visitor. . .". (AGM, 26/3/31) The "annex" was completed by August 25, 1931 "and very convenient for a visitor. But I hope they all won't have boys like Mr. Parris' one!", (ECM, 25/8/31)

The adobe house at Irema

When the Mills decided that they were the ones to go "forward" and locate permanently at Irema in the Upper Lomami field, there was a severe BMS budget shortage. A brick house would cost 500 to 600 pounds. Alex said he could put up an adobe house with a corrugated iron roof for 70 pounds. (Alex finally got 50 pounds for the construction.) They had to move out of the Yalikina missionary residence in the summer of 1938, so that the D.R. Chestermans could move in when they arrived in October, 1938.

The Irema building project was underway before they went on furlough in 1938, but they did not settle in at Irema until their return from furlough in June, 1939. Ethel relates that "we have three flying trips to make to Irema to get the mud house built and to get our furniture in there before we go to England. . .". (ECM, 8/26/37). They also planted some fruit trees at Irema before they left "to get the trees started so we can save funds. . .". Off Alex and Ethel went to England to prepare for what would be their final term of missionary service, (which turned out to be over six years) before their retirement in 1946.

Alex wrote on arrival at Irema: "We had to struggle with a great conglomeration of baggage, dust and disorder when we opened up the room where our stuff had been stored for a year. The place had also to be plastered and whitewashed and planks put on to form a ceiling. All this added to the muddle. We have now got the front room smoothed and whitewashed but things are still in need of repair in many places. . .". (AGM, 7/6/39)

But by August, he wrote: "We are beginning to like our new mud house very well. It is now whitewashed with a mixture or lime and palm oil which resists the rain and it is very useful for our work. . .". (AGM, 29/8/39) They named the house "Breezy Bay" since the Lomami River takes a bend in front of the house and usually there is a good breeze blowing off the river.

"The house is built on trunks of trees put in the ground. They can go under the house by stooping to see if ants or insects have eaten into the wooden posts. We have windowlite in the windows instead of glass which was cheaper. I didn't like it at first but now I am getting used to it. Alex has placed the house in the best position for the sun so that the house is always cool. It faces the river and we really have a beautiful view. When the verandah is finished I expect we shall have nearly all our meals out there."

On milk goats, ducks, flowers and vegetables

From the early years at Yalikina, the Mills had success with milk goats. "We get milk daily from the three of them who are with kids. However they have to be brought in in the evenings and need a little medical attention. . .". They brought back from England in 1924 a pen of a special breed of ducks (which cost them one pound each!). They did quite well until they got in the habit of going to the big river. "One evening the night came on quickly while the ducks were about one mile out stream. Two lads went after them in a canoe but before they reached them, their canoe filled and sank. That seemed to frighten the ducks still further away and we never saw them again after that night. . .but we have had success with our goats." (AGM, 20/11/25)

The flowers and vegetable gardens seemed to flourish at both Yalikina and Irema. The only exception were the seeds which they brought back from the United States and England which were not resistant to the tropical insects. Here is a lovely description of the Irema gardens:

"On the side of the house is a red bougainvillea in full bloom and a mauve colored one at one end of the sit. I hope to plant another at the other end so that it looks well from the passing boats. We have some rose and mulberry bushes. The orange, rose apple and coconut trees are beginning to grow. We succeeded in bringing out with us a root of cultivated blackberry and we are wondering if it will take root. I am getting some vegetables seeds planted behind our house. A geranium we brought has died and we are doubtful about a hydrangea we got in a pot from the chief steward on the ship on which we came out. . .". (ECM, 12/6/39 and AGM, 6/6/39). Here is the floor plan of the house: (ECM, 12/6/39)

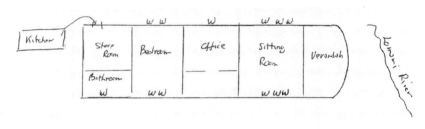

The driver ants invade

Once the driver ants invaded: "They got in the house last week in the cupboard, up the walls, over Alex's bookcase and they swept the floor. We had to sit on seats with our feet up. They were in for three hours: bedroom and sitting room from 7:30 to 10:30 p.m. They were in the bathroom all night! But they have driven out every cockroach. The spiders ran but they caught one big one. And there is not a sign of a rat. So they do some good though it is very inconvenient while they stay. I think their home is about 20 yards off. . .". (ECM, 20/11/39)

(See page 100 for a more detailed description of the Irema House.)

G. PERSONAL LIFE: good and bad feelings; disappointments and frustrations; health; intellectual and theological concerns

Alex was very revealing of his personal feelings as he corresponded with my parents. However there are very few expressions of Ethel's inner feelings in her letters. Therefore much of this section reflects Alex's personal ideas and feelings.

One lone Scot among a host of English colleagues

Alex had a strong cultural identification with Scotland. Perhaps this increased across the years by living with an English wife and English colleagues! This feeling came out clearly in his comments on the arrival of three new missionaries:

Alex recognized the trait of "dourness" in his personality.

"I believe we are having things ordered for us in our shift to Irema. If I can keep my Scotch dourness from being too apparent, people might support me better. . .". (AGM, 18/7/37)

When he was traveling in Northern England on furlough, he visited Newcastle-upon-Tyne. In his letter to niece Mona he commented: "I am writing in this city where the castle is located in which Baliol the Scotch King did homage to Edward I of England. It makes my blood boil!" (AGM, 28/9/33)

Upon reading THE JOURNAL OF A TOUR THROUGH THE HEBRIDES WITH DR. SAMUEL JOHNSON by James Boswell which reflects on Scottish idiosyncrasies, Alex writes:

"The criticism by this robust English mind of our race is a wholesome corrective for the vanity of any Scotsman even though he may say that Johnson is prejudiced against Presbyterianism and extravagant in dispraise. . .". (5/12/41)

Intellectual and theological concerns

Since I spent nearly four years at a semi-isolated rural mission station in tropical Venezuela, I have some empathy for the intellectual isolation which Alex experienced in the Congo. He tried to keep up his reading of British theological journals which his father (Grandfather Mill) sent him from 1911 to 1918 and many periodicals which my father sent out nearly every month.

Alex also tried to develop a library of French books. He was proud to write in 1929 that he had added twenty French books to his library acquired during his stay that year in Grenoble, France. I still have a few of Alex's books in English, his Lokele Bible and hymnal and his Lingala Bible. Several of these books have the marks of Congo insects within their covers. (I also have marks of some Venezuela insects "inscribed" in a few of my books.)

He was concerned, as were most missionaries in 1932, when the LAYMEN'S REPORT ON FOREIGN MISSIONS came out in the United States. It was highly critical of traditional missionary efforts.

The BMS was an active participant in the International Missionary Council which organized the World Missionary Conferences in Jerusalem (1928) and Madras (1938). The BMS requested missionaries to have input on the doctrinal basis for mission in the light of modern world problems. Alex writes:

"I have been so busy that I have written nothing down. . .Emphasis must be more on God's immense nature to comfort them with man's extended knowledge of many realms of creation. A more restrained admiration for the person of Christ as our brother in spirit is needed to purge our concept of everything but the essentials of His Message. A much grander expectation of the moral glory of His coming back in power must uplift and awe us while living a triumphant life before the world which has such tawdry morals. . .". (AGM, 11/11/36)

In my opinion, Alex did not really speak to the concerns of the International Missionary Council as they posed this question to missionary personnel. It seems to me that Alex was not able to think theologically beyond the narrow limits of a personal understanding of Christian faith and practice. I recognize that I may be wrong in this opinion. However what Alex lacked in theological insights, he proved in effective Christian witness by word and deed.

Alex's physical and mental health

Alex had a magnificent endowment of physical strength and stamina. He stood well over six feet and had an impressive physique. As I read his correspondence over the years and realize the exposure he had to disease and danger on his travels, I am constantly amazed at his resistance to disease and chronic ailments in the rigorous tropical climate. He also knew well practical medications and "doctored" himself carefully. I am sure that the hundreds of miles he tramped each month along the forest trails gave him good exercise! As a nurse, Ethel cared for his health also with an eagle's eye.

Ethel seemed to enjoy consistently good health. She did have a bout with Blackwater Fever, but had only one serious medical problem in the Congo. In 1931 Ethel got a carbuncle of a very virulent kind on the lower phalange of the middle finger of her left hand. It was operated on three times. They feared for blood poisoning. Finally after two years of continued pain, she had the finger removed in England when they were on furlough in 1933. (AGM, 16/1/31)

In regard to mental health, Alex certainly had his moments of depression. However he seemed to be able to write and talk about these feelings which probably saved him from a nervous breakdown. Here are some glimpses of moments of stress:

"I have been feeling since our tours round the 150 villages in the Yalikina area, that the work of reproving, rebuking and exhorting is more of a burden than an inspiration. It has taken it out on my nerves more than thought. . .". (AGM, 31/3/25)

". . .I am steadily losing confidence in myself. It is perhaps not to be wondered at for some days bring work more than I can tackle. One day when I came back from a week at Yakusu, I found that my dispenser was ill so I had to run the dispensary with the two boys. We had a large and varied attendance: a mad woman was raving with sleeping sickness, then there was a screaming baby with burns. In the midst of all this there was a man carried in unconscious and apparently obsessed by evil spirit ideas. I tried to keep in touch with these three bad cases while at the same time examining specimens of dysentery stools under the microscope and giving intravenous and intramuscular injections and advice. . . The fact that Jesus was in the Dispensary came home to me forcibly. . .". (AGM, 14/7/25)

"Ethel has kept wonderfully well but the climate tries our nerves. I have not had a breakdown but I have been walking very gingerly and have side stepped (a good U.S. word!) many hard things to just get through. This is not good for the work but till we get more help, I still believe that 'a living dog is better than a dead lion'. . .". (AGM, 23/1/30)

"I had bad headaches of late and asked Dr. Chesterman to take my blood pressure. He said it was just about normal! I suppose I have just about the same amount of aches and pains as the majority of mankind— but I don't agree that I ought to have them. I have such a small store of energy left that I don't get over them quickly. Besides I have no philosophy now which takes them all in and can give them all a meaning and a purpose. The world is too big and old and complex for me. . .".(AGM, 4/6/31) Five months earlier he had written: "I nearly had a nervous breakdown at Yalikina because of the worries of the friction with Government, the backsliding of the church and misunderstandings with my colleagues. You see I have not yet learned quite how to roll all my burdens on to the Lord. . .". (AGM, 16/1/31)

One of the greatest strains on both Alex and Ethel was in 1935–37 when they were trying to work with the new missionary, Douglas R. Chesterson.

They were an unfortunate match of personalities, but Alex seemed to feel some guilt that he was not able to work comfortably with his younger colleague. There are several letters during these years which reflect Alex's condition of depression, probably related to personnel.

Toward the end of his final term of service (1939–1946, with a brief six months visit to South Africa), it is clear that the Mills were struggling to make it through to retirement. He said that they even forgot each other's birthdays. Evidently several letters between Alex and Ethel and my parents and letters from relatives in Britain were lost at sea in 1943 and 1944, since Alex writes: "I might as well not have a brother for all I hear from him (Gladstone), but who knows how many of his letters to me are in Davy Jones' locker and mine to him? . . .". (AGM, 11/1/45)

Yet there were moments of encouragement such as the three-day retreat with native pastors. On the long motor boat ride up the Congo and Lomami Rivers to Irema, he wrote of one of these experiences. He noted that the vibrations of the motor boat made his hand tremble as he wrote. "At the Yakusu retreat we studied the First Letter of John. I had never met with our church leaders in a discussion like this. You have no idea what a pleasure it was to me to find that their souls were thirsty for exposition and discussion. They also helped me by their evident knowledge of what the vital issues are in our work. I was amazed at the rich scriptural repertoire of some of them. So I left Yakusu less tired than when I went since I was well fed by my colleagues. . .".

"A Litany of Disappointments"

The year before the Mills returned to England to begin their retirement, Alex shares some deep feelings with Clara and John:

"I suppose I should let you know how we are getting on here—but it seems to me that we are not getting on: disappointments with native helpers since several teachers have of late backslidden into polygamy; disappointments in the level of intelligence of native Christians. They often drop Bible study after baptism and when they come to school it is nonreligious subjects to which they give most attention. Disappointment in the reception given by the Government to the Gospel by the outsiders who seem too tired out with Government work and their own money grubbing to consider their spiritual state and their peace with God.

Disappointment in our daughter who seems to have drawn further away from us than every so far as correspondence is concerned. Disappointments in our Missionary Society which has no more tolerance to the work we have done at Irema and have not yet appointed our successors. I may be wearing dark spectacles owing to poor health. Perhaps in your church work you have the same disappointments. I can hear Clara quoting the hymn to me which begins with the words: 'He is not a disappointment; Jesus is much more to me than in all any golden fancy I imagined Him to be.' Well, He had His disappointments. Ah, but what He made of them!. . .". (AGM, 20/8/45)

Sailing home to retirement in England: February, 1946

When Alex and Ethel returned to England in early 1946, they were evidently exhausted physically and mentally and ready for the peace and quiet in Cambridge. They were still concerned about their relationships with Barbara who had taken a job with a traveling acting company as "scene designer" and would not be living near them.

He confessed in a letter to his niece Clara (then aged 26 and a mother for the first time):

"Auntie Ethel and I have reached the retirement age and will not see the Congo again. In fact I broke down before we left Irema and can see no way to regain content and interest in life. It is stupid and futile I know but you must excuse me. We do hope you are well and baby and your father and mother-in-law and that you can say with Whittier:

'In the maddening maze of things and spite of storm and flood; To one fixed trust my spirit clings, I know that God is good.'" (AGM to Clara Mill Sinclair Hurn, 12/1/63).

"We brought with us 26 cases of goods. . ."

". . . The less I think about that the better. We left Yakusu on January 4th and got to Kinshasa on the 12th. . .The time in Leopoldville (Kinshasa) was spent in getting all our formalities with Consul, Government officials, transport people and customs officials properly put in order. . . The day before we left the Governor General of Congo, M. Rykmans did our Society the honor of asking Ethel and myself to go to see him at his office. He thanked us personally for the work we had done for the Colony and wished us well on our retirement. I admire him as a man and as a Governor. He has been very fair and carried the Belgian Congo through the very difficult period of the War. I told him that I believed that not only missionaries worked for God on the Congo but that he did too. We had went last run down the picturesque Lower Congo Railway and went through Customs and aboard in the same evening. . .". (AGM, 15/2/46 "Off Dakar, aboard the 'M.V. Copacabana', a ship used during the War on the South American—Antwerp route".)

Alex had served in the Congo for 35 years and Ethel for 27 years. She was 65 years of age; Alex was 60.

PART FIVE

RETIREMENT YEARS
IN CAMBRIDGE

F. THE RETIREMENT YEARS IN CAMBRIDGE

(Ethel Clara Mill; 1946–1956; Alexander George Mill; 1946–1969)

This chapter is a reconstruction of their retirement years, based on correspondence, interviews, cash books, pocket diaries for 1956, 1966, 1967, 1968 and 1969, and several miscellaneous pocket "reminder" books.

If I could imagine two places which offered more contrast in terms of culture, language, customs, fauna and flora, it would be Irema, Belgian Congo and Cambridge, England. Alex and Ethel moved eight thousand miles from Irema to Cambridge within the period of less than two months! Perhaps the only common aspect of these two habitats of human abode were flowers and gardens. The rest was stark contrast: mud huts with grass roofs and ancient stone edifices with ivy creeping up the walls; dusty, forest trails and concrete streets with traffic signals.

But they were coming "home"—back to England, back to Britain, returning to the Baptist congregations which had so loyally supported them over nearly four decades. Alex would now be able to attend lectures, visit great libraries, frequent art galleries and museums and do mission interpretation in the churches. Ethel would enjoy keeping house with some of the "modern" comforts of England. She writes: "I am in the middle of changing the eider down into a new cover. . . I dyed some fine calico I had with an 'old rose' color and it doesn't look too bad. Now I must tackle making covers for the cushions in the sitting room before winter. . .". (ECM to CMS, 22/9/48).

But they returned to find England still reeling from the dislocation and destruction of World War II, with shortages of nearly everything which British people consider necessary for comfortable living. But the Mills had been used to deprivations in the Congo, even in times of prosperity and peace in England. Perhaps the impact was much less severe on them than on their neighbors. The Mill and Starte relatives in England and Scotland were not wealthy, but they were comfortable middle-class urban families. Several nephews and daughter, Barbara, had been in military service and were now back in civilian life trying to find their place in business and industry. Barbara was traveling as a scene designer with a theater company and was "distant" from her parents in more ways than one.

The Starte brothers, Herbert, Harold and Horace had also returned from overseas service and were preparing to retire. Elsie (Mrs. William Robinson lived and Florrie (Mrs. Frank Dent) in Cambridge. Brother Gladstone Mill in Glasgow was 63 years of age and planned to take retirement at age 70 in 1953. Clara and John were both 59 years of age and situated in a pastorate in Kansas. John could retire at age 65, but his health was not the best and might choose to retire early.

Some of the younger relatives visited with the Mills across their retirement years: Edith's sister-in-law, Liz Downing (1947) on her return from the World Youth Conference in Oslo; Paula Hurn on her way to Vienna for a semester abroad program; William C. Knapp returning from military service in Europe: Donna Knapp and her husband (1968 ?) en route to medical service in Tanzania.

1. The relatives in Cambridge, Glasgow and the United States; the death of Ethel (1956) and of Barbara (1966)

It was to Sister Florrie's home in Cambridge that they went upon their arrival in February, 1946. They evidently lived with her in a rented home until June 1, 1948 when they moved into the old Starte family home at 5 Willow Walk. Later they acquired a small bungalow at 40 Blinco Grove sometime around 1955. Uncle Alex lived there until his health required him to move to a nursing home in 1967. Ethel died at the Blinco Grove home in June, 1956.

Reunited with Clara and John after 25 years

Clara and John fulfilled a dream of many years to visit Great Britain again. Neither had been back to "the old country" since 1910 (Dad) and 1913 (Mother). Dad was 23 when he left and they was returning for the first time, now at age 61. Mother was 26 when she sailed to Canada to be married; she was returning to Britain also at age 61. They had not seen Alex and Ethel since they visited the Sinclair family in Belen, New Mexico in 1923.

Since my father had maintained a keen interest in the world missionary movement and the emerging ecumenical movement, he wanted to attend the First Assembly of the World Council of Churches in Amsterdam in August, 1948.

His file of materials from that event indicates how much he relished this "magna" event in Christian history. Alex had been in touch with the Dutch Baptists for years and they were planning to send personnel to the Upper Lomami field in the Congo. So he was interested in renewing these contacts. The Mills and the Sinclairs visited Holland together. Alex wrote about the World Council Assembly's impact in Britain:

". . .The BBC talks on the Assembly admit that it was disappointing in certain ways but it tried to do what was needed. It is a beginning . . . of a very good thing. God knows the Churches need to repent as Pastor Niemoller said in Amsterdam. . .". (AGM to CMS, 22/9/48)

My mother and father visited the relatives in Glasgow, Edinburgh and Wick, as well as a distant cousin, Audrey Turner in Gloucester. One of Dad's favorite cousins, Margaret Mattison lived in Wick but did not have room to accommodate them. So two maiden ladies (the Malcolm sisters), primary school classmates in Wick, received them royally in their home. Cousin Nelly Walker Macfarlane (Dad's niece) in Edinburgh got to know her Uncle John and Aunt Clara for the first time. Since that visit of Clara and John in 1948 to the home of Nelly and David Macfarlane in Edinburgh, many of us have enjoyed the warmth and love of their genuine Scottish hospitality on more than one occasion across the past four decades.

Alex accompanied them to Southampton when they sailed back to the United States on September 14, 1948. Alex wrote us on that day: "It will take me some time to adjust my mind to normal life again after the wonderful time we have had together. My mind seems all of a whirl. And yet our visit seemed all too short. . .". (AGM to CMS, 14/9/48)

Ethel's stroke in April, 1949

"Aunt Ethel had a near fatal cerebral hemorrhage when she seemed to be in abounding health and it has plunged us into acute anxiety, confusion of faith and many nursing problems. The credit side of the account is the way in which the goodness, thoughtfulness and sympathy of our relatives and friends was shown . . .The way one looks on the homecall of a life partner after passing through the Valley of the Shadow is solemn but glad for the one who goes. It was touch and go for 2 days. Now in extreme weakness she is battling to regain health. The doctor has suspended judgement so far. . .", (AGM to JHS, 22/9/49). However Ethel was able to recover enough to carry on most of her household duties. But her health steadily declined over the next six years and she died in Alex's arms on June 15, 1956.

Alex meets John, Maxine and David: June, 1956

We planned our first visit to Britain during our second term of service in Venezuela. It seems incredible now that we were able to save up about $1,500 for our air tickets from New York to London. We sold the tiny cabin near Stroudsburg, Pennsylvania where Mother and Dad had retired in 1953. After paying off a $2,000 loan used to purchase it in 1953, we had $1,000 left which proved enough for our expenses for travel in Britain. David was nine years of age and ready for the adventure, as were we. Paul was about three years old and stayed with Eleanor (Maxine's younger sister) and her family in Sedalia, Missouri with his little cousin, Jim, who was eighteen months old.

I had been able to get a study grant of $500 to make a field visit to Greece, Turkey, Syria and Lebanon. I had written my Master of Theology thesis on three Pauline Churches (Philippi, Ephesus and Colossae) in 1952–53, I wanted to visit those archeological sites and develop materials and filmstrips for my teaching in the mission field on the Acts of the Apostles and the Pauline Letters. The plan was for the three of us to spend a month in Britain. Maxine and David flew home on July 31st and I boarded a train from London to Salonika, Greece to begin my pilgrimage "in the steps of St. Paul". I traveled eastbound on the famous "Simplon-Orient Express" from Victoria Station on July 31 (Third Class coach) and arrived in Salonika at midnight on August 4. Quite an adventure!

Diaries and photo albums tell the story of our stay with Uncle Alex, boating on the Cam River, visiting the historic churches and colleges and the days we spent with him in Old London. We could not have had a more knowledgeable and willing guide. Since Ethel had died only two weeks before we arrived, Alex was worn out and sad, but he pulled himself together and received us "with all his wits about him", as Mother often said. Perhaps our visit helped him in part take his mind off his own sorrow. "John, Maxine and David will be off to Scotland today and I will go to Worthing for five days. Even with the excitement and changes of their cheering visit, the deeps of my heart still remain the same and it will take a long time to get an occasional light heart again. Barbara was out with us for a picnic lunch and tea and was as good as I have known her to be. . .". (AGM to CMS, 12/7/56)

Death of Brother Gladstone in November, 1957

Just sixteen months after Ethel's death, his brother Gladstone died in Glasgow at the age of 74. His wife, Jean, had preceded him by death in early 1956 (?). She was a very happy person, with an outgoing personality.

Jean was a good correspondent with my parents, while Gladstone wrote only occasionally.

Alex was present at Gladstone's funeral, but it was apparent that there was deep tensions between his niece, Mari, and her brothers, Gladdie and Fred. Our family was mildly aware of these tensions, and it was not until two letters surfaced among Uncle Alex's papers that we understood some of the reasons behind these unhappy feelings. (Mari Beveridge to AGM 25/11/57) (Fred Mill to AGM 11/57).

Certainly the fact that Mari and Willie made their home with Gladstone and Jean for some twenty years did not help the situation. He and Uncle Gladstone never hit it off and perhaps he was always jealous that Willie had "stolen" the affection of his only daughter. Fred, the older brother, never seemed close to his sister, while Gladdie, the more easygoing brother, appeared to be able to relate to Mari.

When we visited the Mills in Glasgow in 1956, we sensed certain tensions between the siblings. Again in 1969 we found that some of the same feelings lingered, but a family dinner was arranged for us. Mari died in 1976 (?), Gladdie in 1989 and Fred in 1990.

Needless to say, the family relationships seemed to fall completely apart after Aunt Jean died. She was a reconciler and either ignored or overlooked the problems which Uncle Gladstone seemed to have with Willie and Mari. However in any human relationships there are two sides to most problems. It is enough to say that Alex, sensitive to every human hurt, was affected deeply by the fallings out among his Glasgow relatives. I choose to reveal the general contents of these letters after the passing of both Mari and Fred so that the family will know their respective positions. There were certainly two sides to tensions in the inner circle of the Mill family in Glasgow. Two of the three spouses, Dorie Mill and Willie Beveridge, are still living in Glasgow and are in their early eighties. Dorie continues to be very cordial toward her husband's American cousins; Willie, temperamental and a loner, relates to us as he chooses. But when niece Andrea Downing and her friend were in Glasgow in July, 1991, Willie was their willing host and entertained them with his beloved fiddle.

Billy Beveridge the son of Mari and Willie never regained his mental health and died in his upper thirties in the mid-1970s. We have no connections with the descendents of our Grandfather Mill's three brothers (Lorimer, Gladstone and Alex) and sister Colina. Lorimer was the only one to survive to full maturity. The others died of tuberculosis in early maturity. The descendents of Lorimer are probably scattered around Glasgow and other Scottish cities. But as far as the Sinclairs know, upon the death of Alexander George Mill in 1969, the branch of the Mill family to which we are related ended.

Barbara Mary Mill; her final years

It seems that by May, 1946 that Barbara was under psychiatric care and Alex shared with Clara and John that "Barbara has stated that the cause of her problems is being left by us at home!" (AGM to CMS, 27/5/46). Mona's husband, Robert C. Knapp, then a chaplain with the U.S. Air Force in England visited with Barbara on some occasion in 1944 or 45. He spoke with the German psychiatrist who was treating Barbara. He was told that Barbara's problem seemed to stem from the fact that she had no one to confide in and no one who really cared for her welfare. (Mona J. Sinclair Knapp letter to JHS 10/92)

It seemed that her mental breakdown came sometime during 1945. Alex wrote in October, 1945 that "Barbara is living in lodgings under the Mental Health Department of the government." (AGM to CMS, 17/10/45) She was eventually admitted to the Fulbourn Hospital, Cambridge sometime in 1946 or 47. She was then 27 years of age.

When we visited Alex in July, 1956, Barbara was able to get permission to leave the hospital with her father for short visits. Barbara liked to attend Evening Prayers at the Church of England parish on Sunday evening. The church was a short distance from Alex's home on Blinco Grove. After Ethel's death, some degree of bonding between Barbara and Alex took place despite her mental illness and her feelings towards her parents. Alex's need for human companionship and Barbara's need for attention certainly provided opportunity for a relationship, tenuous as it may have been. For some years she spent several weekends each month with him at 40 Blinco Grove. Maxine, David and I had a picnic with Uncle Alex and Barbara near Cambridge on a July afternoon, 1956. Yet Alex wrote us in 1958 that "Barbara is still a bit confused but much better than she was. We keep praying for her full stability, although full intellectual ability is not to be expected since she has lost about fourteen years of thought life. . .". (AGM to JHS, 17/11/58) I have not been able to find record of her psychiatric diagnosis. Barbara did obtain a British "visitor's passport" in July, 1965 to be able to travel with Alex to Holland.

She was evidently released to live with Alex for a period of time around 1965 since I found a certificate from the Fulbourn Hospital for a 13 week extension dated March 3, 1965. Barbara died on March 15, 1966. (AGM to CMS, 11/5/66)

The relatives of the Starte family

In the summer of 1991 with the help of Robin Henry Starte (b. 20/1/32), son of Horace Starte and May "Maisie" Man Starte, and Michael J.D. Nurse (b. 23/4/27), son of Doris Starte Nurse and Leslie Frank Nurse of Cambridge I was able to gather some data about the Starte family relatives. Michael Nurse is presently working on a family genealogy. Robin is an active layman in the local Baptist Church in Great Shelford, near Cambridge and employed in the University of Cambridge library system. They have two children. Michael is a lay leader in the Church of England parish in nearby Stapleford. He is a retired employee of the Philips Corporation and active in the district Boy Scouts Council. Michael and Heather Mary have two married children.

Florence ("Florrie") Starte and Frank Dent had no children. Herbert and Harriet Starte had one son, Harvey, a lawyer, and served as the executor of Alex's will. Harold and Mary Starte had four children: Ruth Quadling, Roger Starte, Mary and Gordon Starte, M.D. Horace and Maisie had three children: Joan, Robin and Margaret. Elsie and William Robinson had two children: Frank and Giles.

Since Alex and Ethel lived for several years in retirement in Cambridge, there were, without doubt, some occasions for family gatherings. However I do not have any record of these, nor do I know if there was much "togetherness" in the Starte family. I visited with Robin and Muriel Starte and their daughter in June, 1991. They told me that they would pick Alex up regularly and take him to church in the 1960s. Michael Nurse remembers going with his mother in 1968 to clean out the Blinco Grove house when Alex had to move to the nursing home. "We had a bonfire in the yard to clean out a bunch of papers", he said. Perhaps much of the correspondence of Alex's later years disappeared in that blaze! Michael does not remember much about these details, but he is very committed to recording the family history as well as their genealogical chart.

John spends a memorable day with Uncle Alex in 1961

In April, 1961, I had the unexpected pleasure to be with Uncle Alex for twenty-four hours in London where I made air connections to the U.S.A. on my return from a conference in Asmara, Ethiopia, a week in the Holy Land and three days in Rome. I arranged to meet Uncle Alex at the Heathrow Airport on Saturday afternoon, April 4. He had arranged for us to stay at a mission guesthouse in London. We had a leisurely dinner and chat in the evening. On Sunday we shared an informal service in the guest home, walked around Trafalgar Square and worshipped together at St. Martins-in-the-fields.

It was the year the new nation of Zaire was in tragic post-independence turmoil. Uncle Alex seemed confident that the new nation would be able to work its way through the chaos. He said that he had word from Kinsangani (Stanleyville) that one of his former school boys was now a provincial supervisor of schools. Since the village teachers had not been paid for several months, he was entrusted by the central government with a large sum of money to travel through his district and personally pay the teachers. I was impressed by his confidence in Zairian leadership. I wonder what he would think today after three decades of national turmoil in Zaire.

I think back on that short, but memorable visit as one of the best visits I ever had with my uncle. I was able to share with him some of my own missionary experience and also the initial experiences of seven months in a mission administrative post. I was beginning to see the issues of modern missions "from both ends": the field and the home office!

2. Travel experiences during retirement years

The grand tour of the United States: Summer, 1967

At the age of 82, Uncle Alex traveled to the United States for six weeks to visit Clara and all his nieces and nephews and their families. He had to travel from New Jersey, to Pennsylvania, to Ohio, to Chicago, to Kansas City and out to Phoenix, Arizona. Since the World Baptist Alliance was to meet in Miami in 1967 and he wanted to see the meeting site there we routed him to Florida and back to New Jersey for his final days with us. A missionary friend, Dr. Gaspar Langella, kindly hosted him in Miami. Gaspar said that he was fascinated with Mr. Mill since he was the first missionary "of the old school" he had ever met!

Uncle Alex recorded in his 1967 pocket memo book some interesting impressions of his U.S. tour. Each one of the families which hosted him also has its own photos, stories and memories of his sojourn in their homes. I only record here a few lines from his travel diary:

June 23 Arrived on B.O.A.C. at Kennedy Airport, 3 p.m.

June 24 John drove me to Newton, NJ to be reunited with my sister Clara. There I met Rev. Wylie, the superintendent of the retirement home, who had been a missionary in the French Cameroon.

June 25 Communion at the Presbyterian Church. All were invited to partake.

June 26 Clara took me to buy a light Palm Beach suit—trousers wanted more space!

July 1 Great evening seeing Mr. Wylie's collection of Cameroon curios, death masks and signal drums.

July 5 Visited Westminster College (Presbyterian) with the Knapps

July 10 Taken by Grace and Lowell to a stylish "Scotch" restaurant;

July 11 Ate "chop suey" in Valparaiso. Saw their ultra modern chapel with the motto "In Thy light we shall see Light".

July 12 Got a haircut with most modern style and a "Hoover" cleaning of neck.

July 13 Saw Katherine House and its ministry to underprivileged children.

July 14 Now at the Downings in Circleville. Took a picnic with the boys, Kay and Andrea to "Old Man's Cave".

July 16 Met "Goldie", Martha's colored maid and went with her to a Coloured Southern Baptist Church—10 a.m. to 1:30 p.m. Such singing and pleading for "decisions". Evening went to "Chop Sticks" Restaurant; ice cream parlor by moonlight.

July 18 Spent forenoon in Judge's Court with Hon. Judge Koenigsdorf and heard a trial for receiving stolen property. Took three hours. Finally the judge sentenced the man to 15 years of imprisonment. In the afternoon Martha dropped me off to visit Rev. Allan of the Presbyterian Congo Mission.

July 19 Visited Jewel Baptist College founded in 1852. The library has the complete collection of books by C.H. Spurgeon. Clara's plane had a dangerous accident en route from Earlham College to Kansas City—it caught on fire and she didn't arrive until midnight.

July 20 With Clara we visited the Kansas City Art Gallery.

July 21 Flew with Clara to Phoenix. Were delayed by a dust storm.

July 22 Marilyn showed me the high school with cement mushrooms instead of trees! Showed me their meeting house near Camelback Mountain. Saw Cactus Garden.

July 23 Worshipped with family at the Friends Meeting House. Five people spoke, some about the cessation of the war in Vietnam. In the afternoon visited Indian Art Gallery. I had a wakeful, wonderful night.

July 24 Flew to Miami via Dallas and was met at the barrier by smiling face of an Italian, Dr. Gaspar Langella. He took me to the Dixie Land Motel and the next day showed me Miami Beach. Also an evening car ride around the Everglades Swamp.

July 26 Flew to New York. John took me to the United Nations for a guided tour. Then we visited Riverside Church and climbed the bell tower. While at the top, we heard and saw the giant bells ring at 3 p.m. The view of this great city from that tower was very striking. At home in Glen Rock that evening we sang hymns around the piano and had evening worship together. Great nieces Kay and Andrea Downing were visiting the Sinclairs that day.

July 30 Worshipped with John and family in Glen Rock Community Church.

July 31 through August 11 stayed with Clara in Newton. Found the camera I thought I had lost. . .played Scrabble and Chinese checkers. . . watched television. . .

August 12 Left Kennedy Airport and arrived London at 7:10 a.m. My great nephew, David, drove me to the airport. I had a hard time getting to Cambridge from the airport but finally made it home in time for a late lunch.

3. Alex Mill; pacifist and peace activist

I have not been able to ascertain at what point in his life he arrived at his pacifist convictions. These seemed to arise from both humanitarian and Christian motives. As I moved into my late teens, I was aware that he had deep concerns about World War II and struggled in his letters to express his feelings to us as young people. However I do not seem to find pacifist convictions articulated in that period of his life. However in his retirement years after the explosion of the first atomic bomb in 1945 and after the development of the hydrogen bomb, he definitely embraced a pacifist position.

"This year of the Sputniks and 'Zeta' high temperatures demonstrates how wonderful are the secrets of God's creation and how wonderful is the science which has penetrated them. Man seems to have mastered the HOW of many material phenomena but the WHY of how to use them seems limited to crude display and destruction. Hydrogen bombs now can be transformed into electrical power but will they all be so transformed?" (AGM to JHS, 28/1/58)

Alex was active in the Fellowship of Reconciliation: and attended a two day Council meeting in London as the delegate of the Cambridge branch. "It was well worthwhile to meet such a lot of high-minded friendly people working for Peace. And how it needs to be worked for! . . .". (AGM to JHS, 12/5/58)

Comments on space exploration and atomic energy

"The international situation does not conduce to gaiety and yet the simple man everywhere wants Peace but he does not want the sacrifices of economic luxury or the restraints to national sovereignty which it demands.

'The fruit of righteousness is sown in peace of them that make peace.' Now after 13 years dabbling in destructive atomics we are ill fitted to do anything but to fear and suspect each other. I don't wonder that some wish to shoot off to the moon, forgetting that they take their sinful hearts with them. However these efforts are thrilling but horribly expensive. Besides, to what purpose would we put our acquired knowledge if God permitted us to make contact with other bodies in space?. . .". (AGM to JHS, 17/11/58)

Participation in a peace protest at age 74

"I went down to the East Anglican country where bases for the launching of American nuclear weapons are spread out in barbed wire acres of land. I went because I supported in spirit the 40 brave protesters who had entered the Pickenham Base in course of construction and trust to get the workers to stop and to blockade vehicles bringing supplies. They suffered blows and were arrested by the police but the matter was thus lighted up by the press and wireless all over the country. The Rev. Michael Scott went to prison among them. It cannot be said that I or you or anyone, if he felt strongly enough about it, could have done as they did—but apparently martyrdom is not a popular line today. . .". (AGM to JHS 20/1/59)

Two years later he wrote "I would have been in a "sit down" prison by this time perhaps if I had not the responsibility for Barbara and could not stick the cold! Well it has all got to be judged one day by that Child who came to bring in God's kingdom. Let us see it advanced. . .". (AGM to JHS 28/12/61).

"I hope as a pacifist I do not refuse. . ."

As the confrontation between the super powers became more intense in late 1961 related to the Berlin crisis, Alex wrote to Clara:

"Unfortunately the military rivalry between East and West Berlin has been kept up and foreign arms and forces from Russian and NATO nations have made it an armed frontier. I hope that as a pacifist I do not refuse to share the common burdens of people in distress but I refuse to use the carnal weapons but try first to find spiritual ones. . .". (AGM to CMS, 8/10/61)

On the obsession with nuclear power

"The political concerns of the Western world seem to be still obsessed with the possession of nuclear power. Diffenbaker (Canadian prime minister) seems alone in declining it. If Britain drops her own manufacture, only to secure weapons from NATO, it is still the same policy which provokes the Russian counter moves. Can we hope anything from international conferences when fear and suspicion rule the negotiations? I have read of some of the courageous protests in the United States and I saw a film of the San Francisco march to Moscow which had parts like the 'Pilgrim's Progress'!" (AGM to JHS, 24/2/63)

On Vietnam

"The world situation calls for a firm stand by the People of God to try to bring about peace in Vietnam. . .which seems so evil. I still hold to my conviction that it is better to be killed oneself than to kill others in trials of war. . .". (AGM to JHS, 11/6/66) Again he writes: "The Vietnam War is much written up and the dangers of escalation into a nuclear war seems possible. The United Nations can only make recommendations because Formosa only figures on her roll of members! The intelligent feeling in your country seems to back a "peace party" and influential persons such as Senator Robert Kennedy, even to the possibility he will run for president. However this does not help outspoken pacifists being fined and imprisoned for their conscientious objections. It is very courageous how some of the field ambulance doctors and nurses continue to operate and tend both friend and foe on the field. . .". (AGM to JHS, 8/3/68)

4. Activities around Cambridge: Christian Aid Committee; evangelism; international friends; etc.

The Christian Aid Committee of Cambridge

"Christian Aid" in Britain can be compared to Church World Service in the United States. It is a cooperative effort of all the major denominations to collect and distribute world relief. Alex was secretary of this ecumenical committee, beginning in 1965, according to a small notebook he left behind in his personal effects. His notes from the monthly meetings were abundant with notes on particular situations in Rhodesia, Ghana and Zaire.

A Baptist layman remembers Uncle Alex

In June, 1991 I was warmly received at the St. Andrew's Street Baptist Church by Mr. Geoffrey Smart who had known Alex well in his retirement years and had helped him prepare his will. Mr. Smart recalls: "Mr. Mill was well known around Cambridge because he rode a bicycle with a small trailer with a flag on it. A Bible text was emblazoned on his bicycle trailer. You can be sure that the traffic separated when he came along!"

Miss Dorothy Hurst (in her 80s) remembered Mr. Mill because her mother was active in the Fellowship of Reconciliation with him. Mr. Smart told me how Uncle Alex was very zealous in inviting people to come to the evening preaching service at St. Andrew's Street. One of his "strategies" was not too popular with some of the more staid leadership of the congregation. There was a graveyard on one side of the church which was separated by a wall from the cinema next door. Alex (who was 6 feet and 4 inches) would stand on the highest tombstone from which he could see over the wall and "preach to" the people in the queue waiting to enter the cinema. He urged them to spend the hour hearing the Gospel in his church rather than attending the cinema! Robin Starte commented on the story to say that his mother, Maisie, a former Anglican, was not too pleased with Uncle Alex's evangelizing techniques! But Mr. Smart added that "everyone respected Mr. Mill and accepted him for who he was."

He kept informed on the Baptist efforts to evangelize England by means of the campaign "Alive unto God" which sought first spiritual renewal among ministers, deacons and church members. "It is deeply true that 'judgement must begin with the house of God'. There is a branch of the St. Andrew's Street Church at Barnevall in a new housing estate which is led by a young pastor. Twelve of his earnest members are going and visiting in pairs every second Wednesday to invite people to come and hear the Gospel. Records are kept on all the 1000 houses in the Estate. I have the job of keeping these records which enables me to have a share in this ministry. The work of the Sunday School and among young people is already bearing fruit. Last Sunday three young ladies and a married couple were baptized by immersion and at the close five others came forward to confess their faith in Christ in His appointed way. . .". (AGM to JHS, 17/11/58)

I had an interesting experience in 1991 when I visited a small suburban Baptist congregation in Cambridge on a Sunday evening to hear a Baptist pastor from Nicaragua speak. Visitors were asked to identify themselves. I said that I was the nephew of A.G. Mill, a retired Baptist missionary who spent his last years in Cambridge. Afterwards a woman in her late forties came up and showed me a New Testament which had been given her by Uncle Alex. He had inscribed it with a Bible verse and his name. She had been considering missionary service as a young woman in the 1960s and Alex took a particular interest in her.

Alex was concerned about evangelism among the Cambridge students and faculty. "The Cambridge Intercollegiate Christian Union (C.I.C.U. pronounced 'kick you') is sponsoring this week a Dr. Vidler who is conducting a mission on Christian faith and practice. The largest church in

Cambridge is filled nightly and we feel it is sincere interest in the subject which brings them. . .". (29/1/47)
Alex soon became aware of the complexity of Cambridge student life. "There are all kinds of queer societies, 126 different student societies, competing for their spare time interests! . . .The students have their religious societies among these groups which pray and study the Bible. It is good to look in on them as they do it. The 'conservative' C.I.C.U. is commencing an evangelistic mission for students tonight. . .". (AGM to JHS, 11/11/61)
He also enjoyed his contacts with African students who studied in Cambridge. He reached out to other international students. "I had a seat mate on the coach returning from London who remarked that he did not like London but did like the English countryside. I noticed that he had a foreign accent and he turned out to be a Swedish engineering student on a four months holiday and was winding up with Cambridge, Today he came over to 5 Willow Walk for tea. . .". (AGM to CMS 14/9/48)

Some special moments in his retirement years
Contacts with Congolese "national missionaries"

An early missionary effort was made by the BMS in São Salvador on the Atlantic Coast which subsequently became a part of a Portuguese colony, later Angola. The work in 1953 was focused on Santo Antonio de Zaire, on the southern bank of the Congo estuary. The four tribes which were related to this work were all Kikingo speaking. The work continued to be related to the BMS and Alex corresponded with a group of African leaders there, with names like Castelo, Garcia and Castro! They answered his letters in English.

Alex baptizes a Zairian student from Stanleyville

Guestan John Bells Philippe was his name. He was studying Pharmacology in Leige, Belgium in 1961 on scholarship. "His father was one of our own converts in 1921. I was asked to meet him in the London Terminus and baptize him here by immersion on Sunday, December 17. . .". (AGM to JHS, 28/12/61)

He mourns the death of Tetya, an African colleague

"Tetya was a boy whom Ethel and I cared for as a boy about 40 years ago. He was a faithful Christian layman and a deacon in the congregation in Stanleyville. His son, Filemon Henry, was able to study in English at the

University of Addis Ababa. Tetya had sacrificed all his life for his son's education. Teyta was not ill but a diabetic and renal crisis took him suddenly. . .". (AGM to CMS, 22/7/64)

The Brussels Exhibition

Alex spent ten days there in 1958. He had had word from Guestan Etienne Nyama, who had worked for them as a little boy and now was high up in the government medical service that he would be at the Exhibition. He wanted to see us and some of the other older missionaries if he could get a visa to England. "I may be able to bring him over to spend a fortnight in England visiting friends and churches. . .". (AGM to JHS, 12/5/58)

Son of an ex-German prisoner of war

I would like to know more of this event in the life of Alex and Ethel which evidently took place after the end of World War I in Cambridge before they returned to the Congo in early 1919. "A young man who appears in this photo is the son of an ex-German prisoner of war whom Ethel and I befriended in Cambridge after the Armistice. He is now a deacon at a Baptist Church near here. He has a car and came to take us over for the day last Sunday week. . .". (AGM to CMS, 22/7/64) Whatever the story might have been of their meeting in 1918, this sequel is certainly an evidence of some contact made with the family over 40 or more years.

5. Uncle Alex's last two years

Our last visit with Uncle Alex was a two-day stop in Cambridge in July, 1969 with John Mark and Paul. We were celebrating our twenty-fifth wedding anniversary with a trip to England, Scotland, Holland, Belgium, France, Spain, Switzerland and Austria. David came over to Europe for a youth study experience in Czechoslovakia in late June and met us in Spain in mid-July for the final stage of the vacation trip. John had a three-day meeting in Geneva with representatives from the Reformed Presbyterian Church of Cuba. They were only able to travel to Switzerland to meet with a representative of the Presbyterian Church, U.S.A. due to the travel embargo imposed on Cuba by the United States.

My "old Ford" constitution not "a Cadillac"

Such as he expressed himself about his declining health in April, 1968. Soon after that he had an accident on his bicycle and was badly shaken up. He was only 83 when he was forced to exchange his cycle for "a walking frame"! But he seems to have gotten well enough to get out for the May Day convention of the Baptist Union and the Baptist Missionary Society.

Uncle Alex moved out of the Blinco Grove home, first to a home for elderly folk at 39 Hartington Grove (1967–68), and then to "Edwinstowe", a nursing home operated by the Red Cross at 9 Chaucer Road when he needed more care after his accident. (1968–69). His roommate there, the Reverend Stevens, a Baptist minister, died shortly after our visit in July, 1969. We visited Uncle Alex there for the last time. We had tea on the patio and our sons (ages 16 and 12) played a memorable game of lawn croquet with their octogenarian great uncle. They were very impressed by his ability to put the balls through the wickets with force and precision! One of the attendants told me that he would sometimes walk through the gardens of the home with his African finger piano humming hymn tunes.

Clara had sent him with us in 1969 a lounging robe and pajamas for his 84th birthday. He wrote and thanked her with these words: "I feel like a Roman emperor with my new lounging robe. . .". (AGM to CMS)

On July 16 he suffered a fall which bruised his left hand. But he continued to write Clara up to August 8: "My own condition is only mediocre but people are very good. Yes, dear, we have been able to be something to each other all through our lives. . .Your loving brother, Alex". (AGM to CMS, 6/8/69). Ethel's cousin, Doris Nurse, continued to be very attentive to Alex in his last days: "I found Alex resting in bed. He talked to me quite happily but the sister told me that he was often in bed during the day but not because he was ill. . .". (Doris Nurse to CMS, 5/10/69). A final entry in his pocket memo book was for October 25 "United Nations Day".

His last visitor with Congo connections was Dr. John Carrington who had just returned from Zaire and brought him fresh news of his beloved Zairian colleagues. He visited him on the last Sunday of his earthly life which was November 23, 1969. Alex died the following Saturday, November 29 on the eve of "St. Andrew's Day". That was a remarkable coincidence since Andrew, the Apostle, has been a symbol of the missionary outreach of the Christian Church since earliest times. Andrew was the disciple who went out and brought his brother to meet Jesus.

We received the cable informing us of his death on Sunday evening, November 30 in Glen Rock, New Jersey. We were sitting at the dinner table with three of David's college friends: Sunny from Afghanistan; Denize from Tanzania and Sunny from Kenya; Muslim, Hindu and Christian. At that moment, symbolically, I felt the peoples of the world gathered around a New Jersey suburban dinner table.

Alex's final will and testament made on September 27, 1966 reflected his priorities and commitments: "To Clara Anna Sinclair, my sister the sum of 200 pounds; and the remainder of my estate to be divided in six parts: three for the Baptist Missionary Society; and one part each to the Fellowship of Reconciliation, Inter-Church Aid Service and Spurgeon College." Among his personal effects were three photo albums, a complete set of Shakespeare's Works, a few pieces of ivory (a clinical thermometer holder, an umbrella handle and two napkin rings), an African "finger piano", a worn leather folder with a few "precious papers" from Ethel, two worn Lokele New Testaments, a Lingala New Testament, a very worn Lokele hymnal and an English Bible. He died as he lived—simply and free of material encumbrance. Uncle Alex traveled lightly across eighty-four exciting and productive years.

I was privileged to preach at his funeral service at the St. Andrew's Street Baptist Church, Cambridge on December 7, 1969. (The text of the message is found in the Appendices.) I then accompanied a few members of the family and friends to the City Crematorium. The mortal remains of Uncle Alex disappeared into the crematorium furnace to emerge as a small box of ashes. These ashes were comingled on the lawn of the Memorial Park adjacent to the Crematorium with the ashes of his beloved wife and daughter.

PART SIX

THE LIFE STORY OF COUSIN BARBARA MILL

G. THE LIFE STORY OF COUSIN BARBARA

1. An overview of her life—46 short years

This chapter is perhaps the most painful to write. In our family circle as I was growing up, a reference to "Cousin Barbara" was usually responded to with the comment: "poor Barbara". Only my older sisters met her once on the visit of the Mill family to Belen, New Mexico in the summer of 1923 when Barbara was three. Mother and Dad saw her in 1948 when they visited the Mills in Cambridge. Maxine, David and I spent a few hours with her on a picnic near Cambridge in 1956. Barbara was largely unknown to us. She was one of five Mill cousins; the other four were Frederick, Gladstone, Archibald and Mari Mill of Glasgow. "Archie" died as a child on February 24, 1920. He was the twin brother of "Gladdie". None of us ever knew Archie but we got to know the other Glasgow cousins rather well. Mari Mill Beveridge and William Beveridge had a son Billy, whose entire life was marred by mental illness. Billy died in his late-thirties in the early 1970s in an institution in Scotland. Frederick and Dorie Mill and Gladstone and Mae Mill had no children.

The story of Barbara Mill is particularly poignant since there were at least four factors in her life story which seemed to form a tapestry of unhappiness. Perhaps there were years of joy and mirth in her life which we will never know. Robin Starte shared with me a dozen letters written by Barbara when she was in "Sevenoaks" boarding school when she was eight and nine years of age. But as a family we were made aware by our parents of problems which Barbara had to face in life.

Barbara was born with a rather large "port wine" birthmark on her lower check and upper neck. It is difficult to judge the extent which this physical blemish had on her personal development. Other than the birthmark, Barbara was an attractive person of moderate stature (5 feet, 4 inches), grey eyes and comely features. The second factor was related to her upbringing from age four by her mother's relatives in England and being placed at the age of six years in a boarding school for missionary children. It is hard to judge the intellectual capacity of an eight-year-old girl by her letters, but it appeared early on that her talents were more in art and imagination, than in reading, writing and numbers.

The third factor which seems to have left an impact on her life was the four years (1940–44) in the Woman's Auxiliary Army Force (The "WAAFs"), largely spent at a lonely aircraft watch site in England and at post in the Orkney Islands in early 1943. While in the Orkney she suffered a nervous breakdown and was sent to Inverness to convalesce. In recent correspondence with the Ministry of Defence, I was able to ascertain that once the family has established a "Certificate of Kinship" that Barbara's official personnel records can be released. One neatly typed letter from Barbara to my mother, dated June 18, 1942 written at an "RAF station. . . near Devon, England" has survived. The letter, however, is one that reveals her feelings and outlook as a young woman of twenty-two. During this period in her life she had a love affair with an RAF pilot who subsequently jilted her. It is not clear how deeply she became involved with "Toby", but the betrayal of his love for her appears to have been a crushing blow. The only record of his full name is a personal card with the printed name: "J. Christopher Carter, Corpus Christi College, Cambridge" and the penned words "With all my love, Toby". There is also an address written on the card: "P.S. Haron's (sp ?) address: Mrs. H.R. Atchison, Drummore, York Road, Weteridge, Surrey". This card was found in Uncle Alex's personal effects among his "precious papers".

In March, 1992 I wrote the Ministry of Defence to see if they could identify J. Christopher Carter as a former crew member of the Royal Air Force during World War II. A reply came several months ago that J.C. Carter, "Ex-aircraftman 2nd Class J.C. Carter, 3023022, is apparently still living. He was discharged from service in October, 1947. They offered to redirect a prepaid letter to him at his last known addressed recorded on discharge. We had understood that "Toby" was a pilot, but it seems that he was probably a member of a bomber crew. My interest is not to seek out any details of his life, but simply to ascertain that such an RAF airman does or did live.

Barbara was a gifted seamstress and worked at this for a short time when she was demobilized after World War II. She worked for a theater or ballet company for a time in 1946–47.

The fourth factor is harder to define. It seems to have been a conflict of a religious and personal nature with her mother (and perhaps also with her father). Barbara was "a freer spirit" than her parents. She was not a conformist in terms of orthodox religious beliefs. Her mother, Ethel Starte Mill, was very conservative and "Victorian" in her attitudes. She felt that Barbara was wrong in some of her choices as a young woman. I have gleaned in at least one interview with a woman missionary something about this. This younger colleague of the Mills in the Congo told me that Ethel was very upset with Barbara since she was working on ballet and dance outfits, saying "that's the work of the devil". The friend was shocked with Ethel's narrow attitude toward the arts and said, "But, Ethel, the dance is one of the fine arts that we should encourage as a cultural expression. It is not the work of the devil!"

The fact that Barbara was institutionalized in the late 1940s around the age of 28 or 29 may have been the result of a variety of pressures in her life. When we met her in 1956 she was a patient at Fulbourn Hospital, Cambridge. She was able to live with her father during the last years that he was in his own home in Cambridge from about 1964 to 1965. However this was possible because of the advanced medication which she was given at the hospital, not because there was a significant improvement in her condition. Barbara went with her father on a vacation trip to Holland in August, 1964 according to the British Visitor's passport in my possession. She died in the Fulbourn Hospital in 1966 at the age of 46. Her remains were cremated and her ashes are scattered, together with the ashes of her mother and father, on the turf of the Memorial Garden in Cambridge.

2. The birth of Barbara Mary Mill—July 31, 1920

She was born in Stanleyville, Congo. Her mother was 40 years of age and her father 35. I have the elaborate, worn "Acte de Naissance" signed by the Belgian civil officer in Stanleyville on August 2, 1920. Alex writes that "Ethel came to the Stanleyville Hospital (12 miles from Yakusu by river launch) to have her baby. As there are not enough nurses I had to come in too!"

There are two letters, dated August 4 (Alex) and August 8 (Ethel) just after Barbara's birth.

"Dear Clara and John. . .The news of your having your 4th baby on May 2nd just came to us while we were a two-days old Father and Mother! You need not be so long in doubt over our daughter's name. It is Barbara (after our Aunt Barbara) and Mary (after Ethel's mother) and Mill after us. We call her the B.M.M. (Baptist Missionary Movement).

". . .Barbara was 2 kilos 450 grammes or about 5 pounds 6 ounces but it was quite enough for Ethel for the travail lasted sixteen hours from 2 o'clock in the morning until 5:50 p.m. It was just the day before the second anniversary of our marriage. The doctor's fee was 10 pounds and our food and lodging here costs 70 pence per day. This will bring down our credit or bring up our deficit at the end of the year alarmingly. I wonder if during the coming year we will be able to recover ourselves to be able to bear the expenses, if it is considered possible with the baby, to visit Canada. . . .I am sure that if it can be done by means of economy that Ethel will do it.

"Why, you may ask, did we not get the doctor to come to Yakusu? 1st because it requires six hours to call him; 2nd because if he has other urgent cases he cannot come and 3rd because no one else on our station knows anything about nursing. Most of the natives have not heard about the birth of our child as the Hospital forms part of our Roman Catholic convent and is rather secluded. But the few who have heard have expressed hearty pleasure. . . One who is a mother of one of our black boys slapped her sides and executed a sort of dance and then suddenly stopped and blew out a spray of spittle in the direction of the Hospital and said a blessing to the child of Mama Bandombele. . .".

Ethel writes on August 8: "Dear Clara. . .So you have a little black haired girl. Our little baby girl is fair haired and blue eyed. They say half of her features are like Alex (mouth and chin) and forehead and nose like mine. Perhaps her eyes will change to a blue grey afterwards like Alex's. She is only a little thing at 5 1/2 pounds but wiry and soon lets you know when meal time comes round. I'm sorry I can't feed her. I can only get a teaspoonful from my breast in a day and that won't keep her going so we had two goats brought up from Yakusu to the hospital . . . .

"You would like to see Alex at this present moment walking up and down the verandah with the baby in his arms getting her off to sleep! The doctor here is an Italian named Grossule (employed by the State) who speaks French and the nursing is done by Roman Catholic sisters. The property is owned by the Great Lakes Railway Company. There is a little crucifix hung up in the room in which both our beds are. I have not thought it necessary to ask for its removal but we have hung up our BMS prayer calender on the wall opposite to it. . . The Roman Catholic sister apparently thought the birth was going to be hard with Ethel. When I was out of the room she seemed to have offered a prayer for I just found her rising from it. Her prayers were answered as well as mine. . . .

"It is so strange somethings they don't do. For instance when baby was born they departed and Alec had to help. Many other times I've needed attention and the doctor has had to do what I consider a nurse's job or else I've had to do it myself . . . .

"The S.S. Grenfell is coming up on Tuesday and then we three go back to Yakusu. It has been so nice having Alex with me all the time. . .the last few days seemed like a holiday and very likely it is all we'll get this year. We came five days too soon to the hospital, but Alex did a little work in the schools in the district round. One day we went out in a canoe to the rocks by the river to eat our lunch. We listened to the roar of the water as it rushed along. These are the Stanley Falls. . . We've already spent a fortnight here and Alex was previously ill a fortnight, so that's our vacation finished for this year. If Barbara had arrived two months later, Dr. Chesterman would have been out and settled at Yakusu station and attended me as one of the B.M.S. staff.

"We are sitting out on the verandah today and Alex brought the baby out in the cot. She likes it and has been as good as gold and will soon turn brown. When we get to Yakusu we've plenty of verandah so she can nearly live out of doors. . . Mrs. Grosulle, the doctor's wife is coming back to Yakusu with me for two days. She is Italian from Milan and is going to show me how to make macaroni since she says she makes her own. She is about 22 and the doctor is about 56. They are exceedingly fond of each other but he looks more like her father. . .".

"Dear Clara and John. . .How pretty the baby ways are. Barbara is a little darling, fair with blue-grey eyes. I am going to weigh her tomorrow (October 7) and I expect her to be 9 pounds. . .Alex rubs his hairy head on her face. . .she enjoys it and gives such coy smiles. . .It will be Alex that will spoil her. She looked so pretty this evening. Alex was carrying her with her head over his shoulders, sucking away at her fists. I've short frocked her hair so that she can kick about to her heart's content. I put her on the table near me while I was machining today and she was kicking away, enjoyed herself. . .It is a developing experience to be a mother and brings one in touch with parents. Already I have felt a connecting link with one mother whose baby died. She comes periodically to see Barbara and nurse her. She brings with her 3 or 4 other women too. . . . Alex has made me a foot stool to make it easier for me to feed the baby. He just makes life full of joy. Baby wants her bottle now so must close. . . . Ethel". (October 6, 1920)

". . .Baby Barbara is asleep now. She is a good wee girl except when she is hungry or ill. I recall with amusement what Father once repeated to Clara as a little girl: "When they're nice, they're very nice; and when they're not, they're horrid". Ethel says that Barbara is just like the weather in smiles and sunshine and rain and storm. I say that she is like an airplane for she likes me to hold her up in my hands face down and her legs kicking out behind. . .The heat during the middle of the day makes her often feel exhausted and fretful. . .She is now 9 pounds, 7 ounces at the end of 12 weeks. She has just commenced to make sounds of her own and "ga" and "ge" seems to be the first of them. What is Clara Mill junior saying now?. . .".(Letter from Alex, October 19, 1920)

". . .I have made a little carriage for baby but its rather ramshackle. (Ethel adds: 'No it isn't!')

"I am likely to have to go and live at Yalikina during the early months of 1921 so as to get our temporary sun dried house materials prepared. (They were scheduled to move to the sub-station at Yalikina, about fifty miles from Yakusu at the mouth of the Lomami River and the Congo.) It will be very hard to move because you have no idea how nice a home we have gathered here. But that will depend upon how much Dr. and Mrs. Chesterton (whom we expect any day) will be able to do to carry on station work here . . .". (October 19, 1920)

"We are now in the midst of sweltering rains and hot blazing suns and the sugar cane is growing 10 feet high in the garden around us. . . Our best little flower of course is Barbara. . .". (November 27, 1920) ". . .Ethel has to mind the baby pretty much. . . even though we have black boy for we don't want her looked after as a black boy would. Nyama is the name of the black boy and this means "animal". We can literally say that our child was brought up by an animal! Romulus and Remus aren't in on it. . .". (4/10/1920)

Regarding health conditions in the area in 1920

"Dear Clara and John. . .An epidemic of Infantile Paralysis or something of the sort has been sweeping the district. About 29 have died in our village. The other day a mother brought a baby in her arms which had been ill for a week—and as she was late coming for help, the baby died in her lap on our verandah. Her other child who was with her was also ill so we had to set to caring for it. It is infectious and so we do not feel justified in nursing the child on our station in the midst of our work people and so I feel our hands tied a bit. Under the circumstances I feel that I do well if I simply keep alive though that does not get much done. I read somewhere the other day. . . 'that the action of presence has its own power'. . .". (March 13, 1920) ". . .We are terribly understaffed. 3 men have died and their wives have gone home to England, making six workers less in our Congo Mission. . .". (3/28/20)

3. The childhood of Barbara in England (ages 1–4)

On April 27, 1921 when Barbara was less than nine months old, Ethel and Barbara returned to England. Alex accompanied them to Matadi, the port of embarkation which is 1200 miles down river from Yakusu. Alex would not see Ethel and Barbara again until May, 1923 when he returned to England on furlough. There is a gap in the correspondence between early February and early June, 1923. It was in this period that something came up which caused Ethel to take Barbara back to England. It is not clear whether it was the health of Ethel's parents, her own health, Barbara's health or some other reason. Alex seems resigned to this fact as he wrote on June 5, 1921: "When I get home again Barbara will be 2 and 1/2 years old, but we hope to get my term shortened to October, 1922."

"Dear Clara and John. . .Ethel's letters tell me of the wonderful progress in health, intelligence and contentment which Barbara has made since reaching home. She now sits up and eats biscuits and drinks from a cup. 'Pat a Cake' biscuits being hers by special request!" (9/14/21) ". . .I have good news of Barbara and am prompted to fuller gratitude when I think that so far she has been spared serious illness. . .". (1/30/22)

By July 10, 1922, Barbara seems to be "feeling her oats". Alex comments on a letter from Ethel: "Baby Barbara is now the terror of the household and takes up all her mother's time. She has been to one missionary meeting and faced the audience but that may be more to her mother's credit than hers. At any rate God has blessed her with red cheeks and a clear brain so we have the basis of much in that."

Alex did not get home as he had hoped in October, 1922, but arrived in May, 1923. He traveled home to England with two couples of the Swedish Baptist Mission and an American Baptist (Northern Convention) single woman missionary. The four Swedes didn't speak much English, but there were three other English-speaking passengers. "We stopped at Tenerife where the Spaniards were having a 'May fete' of 11 days and the streets were festooned with flowers. . .".

Alex received the word of Father Mill's death in Creston, B.C. on February 23, 1923 a short time before he left the Congo for England. His dreams of visiting Canada, the Canadian Rockies and seeing his beloved father after nearly five years were now only dreams. No letters survive to record his response to Father Mill's sudden passing at age sixty.

In June, 1923, Alex, Ethel and Barbara (now nearly three years of age) were reunited and traveled to Belen, New Mexico to visit John, Clara and their five daughters (ages 9, 7, 5, 3 and 1). John had not seen Alex for thirteen years and Clara for twelve. The cost of the trip was really beyond their means, but Alex wrote to Clara before he left the Congo (3/18/23):

"It appears it will cost 200 pounds in fares alone to come to Belen, go to Creston and then take 'a colonist ticket' back to Montreal and 2nd class home. However I am prepared to sink all my savings in it. Ethel, too, is willing except not to use what we have for Barbara's education. I hope to get home May 8th and by June 8th to be leaving for New York. . .". (This was written before he received word of Father Mill's death which eliminated the trip to Western Canada.)

(Note: My sister, Mona J. Sinclair Knapp, said that our mother and father wanted to keep Barbara as a part of our family but the parents felt that it would be too far for them to visit when they came on furlough.)

Alex visited the Negro Training Institute at Tuskegee, Alabama while in the United States. He was very interested in the initiation of industrial education at Yakusu. It seems that their contact in New York City was the A.B.F.M.U. (American Baptist Foreign Mission Union) at 276 Fifth Avenue where they picked up their mail. They visited Mrs. McKellar (a Glasgow church friend now living in New Jersey) before sailing on the T.S.S. "Cameronia" of the Anchor Line on August 8, 1923. A reporter from the NEW YORK HERALD TRIBUNE was waiting at the dock with three photographers to prepare a story about the Mill family as they sailed back to England and then to Africa. (I have a copy of the photo and brief comment under the picture.) Ethel records this vignette of their brief encounter with the press:

"We got away just by the skin of our teeth. Alex left me in the waiting room at the New York Anchor Line wharf while he went into the City to finish up a little business. He came up just as the bridge was about to be drawn up. We were surrounded by officials also photographers immediately as we arrived on the deck. They had us out in the sunlight and 3 photographers took two photographs each. Then they bolted off the steamer saying they were going to write up an article. Goodness knows what they will put into it. . .". (8/19/23)

4. The hardest decision of their married life: leaving Barbara with relatives in England

This was the decision they reached in early April, 1924. The idea was beginning to form in their minds in the fall of 1923 since Alex wrote:

". . .Elsie (Ethel's younger sister) has written to say that she will be home from India in June. This is much later than we had expected so the arrangements for Barbara settling may be delayed a little. We would like to make some housing arrangements for Elsie before she comes home but some things might have to await her personal return. . .Horace expects to be home for Christmas. Herbert and his wife (BMS missionaries in the Congo) are now in Brussels studying Tropical Medicine at the government school. Their little baby Harvey is with them and is getting big and fat. . .". (9/28/23)

". . .Ethel is almost altogether responsible for the bringing up of Barbara. It is a great thing that she is content and able to do it. I cannot dare to think what it will be to Ethel to leave her. . .". (11/3/23)

". . .Tell Clara that Barbara can now put on her shoes and socks and can lace up her shoes but not tie the bows yet. Can Martha accomplish this feat yet?. . ."

". . .We are going to see Miss Shadwell for a couple of days on March 27. This will be Barbara's future home. Horace will be back on Saturday from sightseeing in Milan, etc. . . .". (3/6/24)

Alex and Ethel were scheduled to leave Cambridge on June 7 and sail from Antwerp on June 10. There are three letters, two from Ethel and one from Alex written on April 4, April 7 and May 5 which give the details of the plans to leave Barbara with relatives for the next two years, until she could be received at the age of six in the school for missionary children.

"Dear Clara and John. . .We propose taking Barbara to Ashwell on June 5th and leave on the Saturday morning for Cambridge. . .Changes in plan as regards Barbara have taken place as you will see. We were visiting Herbert's wife's mother one weekend and just as we were about to come away she offered to take Barbara . . . Herbert's mother-in-law is taking their baby 12 months old, too, so it is nice for Barbara to be with another child and that her own cousin. She will be there for two years. After that she goes to Sevenoaks, a school for missionaries' children. We are going to see it on Thursday so that when she goes she will have some dim recollection of having seen the place before. . .".

(Letters written 4/6 and 5/5/24)

Alex wrote about his feelings: ". . .Ethel has written you to tell you of our final arrangements for Barbara. I am sure that in writing the letter she thought a great deal more than she has put down on paper for it must have brought the parting much nearer. She did not say so to me but she took a long time to write it. I am afraid I cannot quite enter into the feeling of it as baby likes her so much more than she likes me. However I feel she will be happy at Ashwell when she has forgotten about us."

He continued writing about the numerous details of purchasing supplies for the coming four-year term in Africa: "I have been busy getting our orders out for provisions and crockery. . .I am taking out a maize grinder and a palm kernel grinder to make maize flour and kernel butter. I had hoped to have enough subscriptions (sic, offerings) to get a sugar cane crusher, but I decided that with the money I received that I will purchase drawing paper and materials so that I can teach the natives drawing. They will thus acquire a new language as it were: the language of sizes and shapes and be able to interpret pictures and especially drawings and mechanical plans. . .". (4/7/24)

Ethel and Alex sailed back to the Congo from Antwerp on June 7. They got passage up the Congo River on the Lever Company steamer "Duc de Brabant", arriving in Yakusu on August 10, 1924. Ethel had been away from Africa for over three years; Alex for only fifteen months. Barbara, aged four, was left in Ashwell playing with her year old cousin, Harvey, in the care of Ethel's brother's mother-in-law.

Ethel reminisced to "Clara, John and the bairns" about Barbara in letters written aboard the S.S. "Anversville" on the first day on the high seas (June 8, 1924) and again "Duc de Brabant" on the Congo River (August 5, 1924):

"It all seems a sort of dream and I hardly seem to realize that we have left England and yet I know we have. . . .Barbara is very happy at Ashwell. Several times I saw her holding Harvey's hand and walking him around. (Harvey is her little cousin of fourteen months whom she looks after like an older sister.) He can now walk and is very proud of himself. Alex asked Uncle Bryant to let her have a piece of garden. So before we came away, Alex dug up a piece of ground and she sowed some gaillardia and some cabbages. She was delighted to have the job of watering them with a little watering can about five inches high. We also bought her a little push car with a hood. Her auntie sent her a doll that cries "Mumma" which I handed her just as we drove away at the last. I don't think she realized we were going for a long time. And, too, I think she has an idea that Africa isn't very far off. It is as well it should be so.

". . .There is a big garden at the back of the house where the children can play when not walking. Mrs. Bryant has set a room apart to be used as a nursery where the two children have their meals with Connie. I watched them through the window and they seemed as happy as can be. . . .

"Alex has been thinking every night of some saying or doing of Barbara's and reminding me of them. I am very glad we are traveling together. I think if I had had to come alone, I should not have been able to keep from fretting. . .I'm indeed glad that we have been guided to such a home. He just led us a step at a time until He had brought us to the right place He had chosen. We can see that it is the best of all for all concerned. . .".

Shortly after their arrival back at Yakusu, the wife of the overseer named their new baby girl "Barbara". Alex commented that "we'll have to look after this little girl well". (29/9/24)

When Barbara was six, she was placed as a boarder in "Sevenoaks" School for missionary children. Holidays were spent with her grandparents in Cambridge and other relatives.

Reunited again after four years

Barbara was nearly nine years of age when they saw her again on May 14, 1928 when they went to "Sevenoaks" to bring her to a little home at 5 Grafton Street in Cambridge where they were to live during their furlough.

Alex wrote: "As far as Barbara's welcome to us is concerned, there was nothing wanting. She took us as her property as soon as she saw us. After a little quiet shyness she burst out into an afternoon of horseplay which only stopped for sleep and was renewed early next morning. We were allowed to take her with us right away to Cambridge for a holiday. . .Her little errors were quickly corrected but she likes to get her own way if she can. . . She is an independent little spirit. . .she really loves dogs and cats most of all. . .and a pigeon of her own would be heaven to her. But at the school the authorities cannot allow it. . .".

"She loves helping her mother in the housework even if she cannot spell words of two syllables correctly. She enjoys being dressed and will be delighted with the one you have sent her when she gets back next time from school. She gets holidays from July 26th to September 9th. . ." (Alex informs Clara and John that Ethel's brother Horace will be married to Maisie Mann, daughter of a retired naval captain at Grimsby on September 5th.) (AGM to CMS, July 4, 1928)

The house on Grafton Street was close to Ethel's mother. Mother Starte died after a long illness on June 9, a few weeks after their arrival. Father Starte had passed away five months before on January 28. Three precious letters written in February, March and April, 1927 by Father Starte to Ethel and Alex provide deep insight into his abiding Christian faith, his loving care for his wife and his continuing support for his daughter's calling as a missionary.

5. The Mills in Grenoble, France (March–June, 1929)

"Alex got 55% on his exams; I have only a nodding acquaintance with the French language. . .". (ECM)

The BMS permitted the Mills to do four months of French language study in Grenoble, France from March to June, 1929. Barbara attended a school where all the instruction was in French. "At first she hated it and cried every morning and wanted to get out of going. But now she goes off smiling. They say her accent is good. She understands quite a bit and can talk a little. One day was looking out the window and saw two dogs get hold of a fowl and run off with it. Barbara ran round to the people and told them in French what had happened. And then she stayed and saw the dogs whacked. . .". (ECM to CMS/JPS, May 19, 1929)

Vignettes of life in Grenoble, 1929

"Barbara is sick of nothing in France except 'school'. She is not putting her heart into her work there for she talks nothing but English the moment she gets home. The country all around here is teeming with flowers. You know what a little 'Florentine' Barbara is. So she simply goes into raptures over fields full of primroses and cowslips and climbs like a little chamois on the mountains for crocus, hyacinth and daffodils which grow quite wild. . .We live on the outskirts of a university town. We are under the shadow of two great mountains. From our windows at both sides of our house we see the Alps clad with eternal snow. We have only one room in the hostel with three beds, but with food and extras it is costing us about four pounds a week. . .". (AGM to CMS/JPS, April 3, 1929)

A family visit to Brussels

After the four months in Grenoble, the Mills spent a fortnight in Brussels. "We stayed with M. Marecaux, a French Wesleyan, where several missionaries of other societies are staying. We went to the Waterloo Battlefield and in the great Diorama which is housed in a domed building beside the great Lion Monument. Barbara saw how terrible a battle was and is now strongly in favor of peace. . .We were able also to see the Congo Museum which is Belgium's glory. But Barbara was more interested in a baby frog which she caught in a pond on (the grounds) and kept it in her hand till it nearly died . . . .

"We saw the great Palais de Justice (the largest in Europe) where 2000 German soldiers were billeted during the occupation. They took away all the bronze they could for shells. . . We spent some of our money in Brussels too on foodstuffs in tins. . .and palm oil lamps which we will use for evening meetings or a boys club which we hope to start to enable them to profitably employ their evenings. . .". (July 11, 1929)

The Mills sailed back to the Congo in mid-July, 1929. Barbara remained at "Sevenoaks" School.

6. Barbara's schooling in England (ages 9 through 20): furloughs with her parents in England (1933–34) and 1938–39

She wrote to me in 1929 when I was on vacation with my mother and sisters at Ruidoso, New Mexico. I was five and she was nine.

"Dear John. We got a letter from Congo telling us Lunia is well. Love from Uncle Alex and Love from Barbara (her signature)."

The years of her schooling between 1929 and 1939 have only passing references in Uncle Alex and Aunt Ethel's letters. I am sure that there are memories of visits with Cousins Robin, Harvey, Margaret and other cousins who knew her during those years which could be shared with the family. Perhaps there are records at "Sevenoaks" school which could be reviewed. Barbara definitely struggled academically to get through school. She was interested in flowers, animals, drawing and sewing more than the basic academic fare. Ethel wrote in 1936: "Barbara is no good at studies, but good in art. . .she shows no reasoning powers." Barbara saw her parents quite often during their two furloughs in 1933–34 (at age 14) and in 1938–39 (at age 19).

When Barbara was seventeen she enrolled in the Barret's Trade School in London. (January 1, 1938). She visited Grenoble, France in August, 1939 and got back just before the war broke out. By November, 1939 she was in an Aeroplane Drawing Office working as a "plotter". In March, 1940 she was already in the W.A.A.F. and had just been moved from Suffolk to Sussex.

7. Her service in the W.A.A.F. (1940–44)

Ethel wrote to Clara, John and everybody on December 30, 1941 en route to Stanleyville from Irema (a 200 mile river trip) to buy provisions for six months. She writes about news from Barbara:

"Barbara had her 21st birthday and all the family, aunts and uncles combined together to buy her a gold watch for the event. We sent her cash but we have not heard yet whether she got it. She got her commission (WAAF) and the last we heard she and some other girl officers were billeted with a Major and his wife. She is not a very good correspondent."

"The affair with Toby in whom she was interested (and is still) is off we think definitely. He was called off to go abroad the night that they had a little difference of opinion and she has not heard from him since, three letters having been returned. We are sorry for her for I believe she sincerely loved him and she is very loyal in her affections. Of course it may be he is a prisoner or has been killed. For six months she couldn't write to us because. . .she felt she must tell us but couldn't bear to put it down on paper. So pray for her that she may find solace at the only sure place where it is to be found. Yours, Ethel."

Alex made an interesting comment on Toby in a letter dated March 15, 1943: "Barbara is now in the Orkneys. Toby gave Barbara as a last gift "A Modern Reader's Bible".

The only letter from Barbara which reveals her feelings about the war and her feelings about "Toby" is dated June 16, 1942 "R.A.F. Station, West Prawle, Near Kingsbridge, Devon, England":

"My dear Aunt Clara:

Yes I am well, always am, one of the most fortunate people in that respect. It is good to hear from a person who has so many varied activities and of such an open mind. Yes, I knew of a friend who is like John. (Note: I had expressed to my parents in 1942 my position as a conscientious objector to war as I faced the possibility of being drafted into the army.) He too will never kill. He has given up his job in the Stock Exchange. He did at once, just as soon as the war broke out. He has been a pacifist all his life—sometimes having caused a little sorrow to his little mother's heart. His faith comes as high in his esteem. But even she could understand in the end. She would always rather see him give up everything even her own Lady-self rather than give up his faith. Needless to say I love her for that. She is a dear old lady. I call her my little mother. She has helped me all the time I have been alone.

"As I say, he gave up his job and joined the Friends ambulance—went to China—was along the Burma Road, helping, helping all the time. Wonderful stories of how they had to almost tie the engine of their ambulance up with string! and bring it over miles of that road—which is evidently terrible on its surface and finally managed to bring to a safe destination 120,000 pounds of drugs they had rescued. He is now in Canada after having been in America and is soon to make his way home to render his report. Perhaps you've heard of him—Christopher Sharman. He has many friends all over the world—perhaps you have read his name in the newspaper at some time or other. As I say—good old John—if he has a faith he holds as dear as that he will do well—

"I am sure you are longing to see your grandson (refers to either Lowell Sinclair Robertson or Robert Sinclair Knapp) . . .I was a little taken back when I read the next part of your letter! But then I do not know you Americans very well, but I think I know you well enough to know that you are wise and wouldn't tell me so much about your near surroundings. On the other hand, I am young and use rather the 'say naught at all method' rather than judge for myself what I may and what I may not say for England's sake during the war—

"You've been told over the wireless, by books, and by people, but I will tell you again for myself—thank God for America and your President. We couldn't have gone on without you to win.

"Toby was reported missing from Singapore, but he is safe and as John his brother-in-law says, 'he has been serving in France, Norway, the London blitz and now Singapore. I think that Toby cannot have completed the purpose for which he was sent into the world just yet, that he should have come through all that'. . . .what every purpose that may be. Toby does not deserve a death like that—it is only a heroic death because it is so freely accepted by those who meet it as a cause worth fighting for—nobody who fights that way deserves a death like that—to be killed by fellow creatures with minds who love beauty. That is why war is so terrible and that is why I must fight it. To help those to fight who have the courage to fight for us even against their own hearts—and each does it in their own way—pacifist, soldier, sailor, airman and so many other minds with methods all their own. We have just moved into our new rooms—

"We are terribly busy and I love it. My rank is equivalent to lieutenant in the army and sub-lieutenant in the navy (and flying officer in the air force). I like it, but I can only hope that other people like the work I'm doing in the same way. All one can do is try—it is all everyone is doing. I have some beautiful pinks in my bedroom with a lovely scent. With my love to all of you. Barbara."

The sequel to the story of Barbara and Toby is that he did survive the war. He never contacted Barbara again. According to one family story, one day she read in the newspaper the account of his marriage. Uncle Alex felt that this blow was responsible for the beginning of Barbara's mental breakdown.

Aunt Ethel sent word to Clara (August 21, 1944): "Toby wrote that he was married and to forget about him." In 1991 when I visited an old friend of the Uncle Alex who knew the story of Barbara and Toby, he confirmed the detail of Barbara's having learned of Toby's marriage through the society notes in a newspaper.

(Note: I researched the Friends Ambulance Unit in which Christopher J. Sharman served. This was the son of the friend of Barbara when she was stationed in Devon. The information about the Friends Ambulance Unit is found, "A. Tegla Davies, FRIENDS AMBULANCE UNIT: The story of the F.A.U. in the Second

World War, 1939–1946 published by George Allen and Unwin Limited, 1947. I also located a Quaker who lives in Minnesota, Mr. Robert S. Arthur who served with Sharman in the Friends Ambulance Unit on the Burma Road in 1941–42.)

8. Work as a seamstress after the war; mental illness; institutionalization and her later years (1945–1966)

Barbara was evidently mustered out of the W.A.A.F. in late 1944 or early 1945. Her official records should reveal if she received a medical discharge. Alex wrote in October, 1945 that she was living in lodgings under the government's Mental Health Department and will go into "stage designing". He added: "We are anything but pleased!"

As Alex and Ethel sailed back to England to begin their retirement in February, 1945, Ethel wrote to Clara:

"We have not heard from Barbara recently and probably she is on a 'scene designer's' job with a traveling company and will not be living near us. . .".

She continued to have serious mental illness and was institutionalized in the Fulbourn Hospital, Cambridge, sometime in late 1946 or early 1947. She died there in 1966.

A C T E   D E   N A I S S A N C E .

L'an Mil neuf cent vingt le deuxième jour du mois
d'Août devant nous BUTTICAZ LOUIS officier de l'Etat-Civil
à STANLEYVILLE a comparu le nommé MILL ALEXANDER GEORGE
âgé de trente-cinq ans, missionaire lequel nous a déclaré
en présence de D'HONDT VICTOR âgé de trente-cinq ans, agent
territorial et de DELVIGNE ADRIEN EDOUARD âgé de trente-trois
ans, agent territorial que le trente unième jour du mois de
juillet mil neuf cent vingt, est né à STANLEYVILLE de lui
déclarant âgé de trente-cinq ans, missionaire domicilié à
LONDRES et de STARTE ETHEL CLARA âgé de quarante ans, infirmière
domiciliée à CAMBRIDGE conjoints un enfant du sexe féminin auquel
il a été donné les prénoms de BARBARA MARY le déclarant nous a
présenté son livret de mariage.

En foi de quoi nous avons dressé le présent acte et, après
que connaissance en a été donnée aux comparants, nous l'avons
signé avec eux

SIGNATURE DU DECLARANT ET DES TEMOINS,   L'OFFICIER DE L'ETAT-CIVIL,

(s) A.G. MILL   (s) L. BUTTICAZ.

(s) A DELVIGNE

D'HONDT

Pour Copie Certifiée Conforme:

Stanleyville, le 2 Août 1920.

L'Officier de l'Etat-Civil

(s) BUTTICAZ.

I certify that this is a correct copy of the Birth Certificate
of BARBARA MARY MILL.

Mabellu Deed.

CONGO BELGE
—
ETAT-CIVIL
N° *55*
—
VOLUME : *VIII.*
—

ACTE DE NAISSANCE

L'an mil neuf cent *Vingt* — le *deuxième* — jour
du mois d' *Aout* — devant nous *Butticaz Louis*

officier de l'Etat-Civil à *Stanleyville* — a comparu
le nommé *Mill Alexander George*
âgé de *trente-cinq* ans, *Missionnaire*

lequel nous a déclaré en présence de *D'Hondt Victor*
— âgé de *trente-cinq* ans, *agent*
territorial — et de *Delvigne Odile*
Edouard — âgé de *trente-trois* ans, *agent*
territorial — que le *trente unième* jour du mois de *juillet*
— mil neuf cent *Vingt* — est né à *Stanleyville*
de *lui déclarant* —
âgé de *trente-cinq* ans, *Missionnaire*

domicilié à Londres

et de Starte Ethel Clara

âgée de Quarante *ans,* infirmière

domiciliée à Cambridge

Conjoints — *un enfant du sexe* féminin *auquel, il a été donné*

les prénoms de Barbara Jary

Le déclarant nous a présenté son livret de

mariage

En foi de quoi nous avons dressé le présent acte et, après que connaissance en a été donnée aux

comparants, nous l'avons signé avec eux

Signature du déclarant et des témoins,   L'Officier de l'Etat-Civil,

(s.) E. F. Mili   (s.) L. Butteux

(s.) A. Delvigne

Dr. Houd   POUR COPIE CERTIFIÉE CONFORME :

                                 Léopoldville, le 2 Aout 1920.

                                 L'Officier de l'Etat-Civil,

noas and too ghots come in and wun of them was corld the ghot of kodliveroull. and he had a big spoon like this and a botol and hera it is, here she is in bed, the ghoto sed to her you, will, have your punishmen now for not, beleving, in ghots.

Altem and cuming even to see us, if Harve was thee I wad be abel to see him.

It is a lovely day to day, but it is windy and cold, but the sun is shining.

With love
from

Barbara

XXXOOOXXXOOO
Mammy
XXX OOO XXXOOO
Daddy

RAF Station
West Prawle
Near Kingsbridge
Devon, England
6/16/42

My Dear Aunt Clara::

..... Yes I am well, always am--are of the very fortunate people in that respect.
it is good to hear of a person who has so many varied activites and of such an open
mind. Yes, I know of a friend who is like John. He too will never kill. He has given
up his job in the Stock Exchange. He did at once, just as soon as war broke out. He
has been a pacifist all his life---sometimes having caused a little sorrow in his little
mother's heart. His faith comes so high in his esteem. But even she could understand
in the end. She would always rather see him give up everything even her own Lady-self
rather than give up his faith. Needless to say I love her for that. She is a dear
old lady. I call her my little mother. She has helped me all the time I have been alone.
As I say, he gave up his job and joined the Friends ambulance--went to China--was along
the Burma road, helping, helping all the time. Wonderful stories of how they had to
almost tie the engine of their ambulance up with string! and bring it over miles of that
road--which is evidently terrible on its surface and finally managed to bring to a safe destination £120,000 worth of drugs they had rescued. He is now in Canada after having been
in America and is soon to make his way home to render his report. Perhaps you've heard
of him--Christopher Tharman. He has many friends all over the world--perhps you may
have read his name in the newspaper at some time or other.   As I say--good old John--
if he has a faith he holds as dear as that he will do well--

      I am sure you are longing to see your grandson......I was a little taken back
when I read the next part of your letter! But then I do not know you Americans very well,
but I think I know you well enough to know that you are wise, and wouldn't tell me so much
about your near surroundings. On the other hand I am young and use rather the "say naught
at all method" rather than judge for myself what I may and what I may not say for England's
sake during the war--

     You've been told over the wireless, by books, and by people, but I will tell you,
again for myself--thank God for America and your President. We couldn't have gone on without you to win.

     Toby was reported missing from Singapore, but he is safe and as John his brother
in-law says, "he has been serving in France, Norway, the London blitz, and now Singapore.
I think that Toby cannot have completed the purpose for which he was sent into this world
"just yet, that he should have come through all that". .... what ever purpose that may be.
Toby does not deserve a death like that--it is only a heroic death because it is so freely accepted by those who meet it as a cause worth fighting for--nobody who fights the
way deserves a death like that--to be killed by fellow creatures with minds who love beauty.
That is why war is so terrible and that is why I must fith it. To help those to fight who
have the courage to fight for us even against their own hearts--and each one does it in
their own way--Pacifist, soldier, sailor, airman and so many other minds with methods
of their own. We have just moved into our new rooms--

      We are terribly busy and I love it. My rank is equivalent to lieutenant in the
army and sub-lt. in the navy (and flying officer in the air force). I like it, but I
can only hope that other people like the work I'm doing in the same way. All one can
can do is try--its is all everyone is doing..

    I have some beautiful pinks in my bedroom with such a lovely scent---

                              With my love to all of you--
                              BARBARA

APPENDIX A

The Baptist Missionary Society in the Congo: notes on the early explorations and missionary endeavors; King Leopold and his exploitations of the native people, the first BMS stations in the Lower and Upper Congo; the story of Salamu and the atrocities of the Congo Free State.

APPENDIX A

THE BAPTIST MISSIONARY SOCIETY IN THE BELGIAN CONGO, 1878–1909: early explorations and missionary endeavors; the Congo River; Leopold I and exploitation; first B.M.S. stations in Lower and Upper Congo; the story of Salamu; and the alleged atrocities in the Congo Free State.

1. Early explorations and missionary endeavors

Portuguese Roman Catholic missions were established in the Congo soon after 1482 when Diago Cao, an explorer, set up stone pillars (padraos) to claim this strange new land for the Portuguese crown. The early missionaries arrived with Rui de Sousa at the end of March, 1491. The Congo king, Nsaku, was baptized and took the name "Joao da Silva". This took place over three centuries before the first offering was received in a snuff box by William Carey on October 2, 1792 to begin the Baptist Missionary Society.

When the first Baptist missionaries entered the Lower Congo in 1879, they found little evidence of the missionary activity which had been carried on four hundred years before. (Cf. Duffy, James, PORTUGUESE AFRICA, Cambridge/Harvard University Press, 1959. Also Forbath, Peter, THE RIVER CONGO: The discovery, exploration and exploitation of the World's most dramatic river, Houghton Mifflin, Boston, 1977.)

Livingstone, Stanley and Central Africa

Interest in the Congo was certainly triggered in Britain by the journeys of David Livingstone. The great explorer of Central Africa first saw the Lualaba (Congo) at Nyangwe, an Arab trading town on its banks, on March 1, 1871. He believed that the Lualaba (the Congo) was a major river and that it flowed a northward direction. He wrote:

"I went down to take a good look at the Lualaba here. It is. . .a mighty river, at least 3000 yards wide and always deep; it can never be waded at any point, or at any time of the year; the people unhesitatingly declare that if any one tried to ford it, he would assuredly be lost".

Livingstone concluded that it could be the river he had been searching for. He stayed there until July 30, 1871. He believed it to be the Nile River for which he had long sought. Livingstone died in Chitamba Village on May 1, 1873, not knowing that the river he thought to be the Nile was actually the Congo which emptied into the Atlantic Ocean some 2500 miles to the northwest of Nyangwe.

2. A description of the Congo River (now known as the Zaire River)

"The Zaire River cuts an enormous arc through the heart of the African continent—'an immense snake uncoiled', Joseph Conrad wrote, with its head in the sea. . .and its tail lost in the depth of the land. Lying almost entirely within the country of Zaire, the river flows 2,700 miles from the headwaters of the Lualaba, crossing the Equator twice, draining the vast rain forest nestled in the Congo Basin. Some would add two hundred miles to the Zaire's length, by considering the Chambeshi River as its source.

"Countless tributaries lace the forest, feeding the waters that make the Zaire, at ten million gallons a second, the most powerful river, after the Amazon, in the world. This river system offers more than 8,500 miles of navigable waterways, an unparalleled network of virtually maintenance-free highways reaching into every corner of the country and beyond.

"The river is divided into three parts. For the first 1,300 miles from the source it is called the Lualaba. It flows due north, draining the upland savannas of mineral-rich Shaba Province. Navigable reaches are interrupted by thunderous rapids and gorges with names like Fortes d'Enfer (Gates of Hell). In one immense valley the Lualaba spreads out in a sheet of lakes and swamps choked with papyrus and reeds, seasonal home to hundreds of thousands of people attracted by abundant fish.

"At Kinsangani the river, now called the Zaire, begins its long, easy curl through the central forest. As it bends around to the southwest, the river widens to nine miles, its glassy waters dotted with myriad islands. Kinshasa lies at the head of Livingstone Falls, actually 220 miles of cataracts and rapids, where the river crashes through the Crystal Mountains, the western rim of the Congo Basin. The ocean port, Matadi, lies at the foot of the Falls."

"Now called the *bas flueve* (lower river), it once again spreads out, wide and deep enough for oceangoing snips to sail down the final one hundred miles to the Atlantic. The current is so strong that its brown waters are hurled nearly one hundred miles into the sea and have gouged a 4,000 foot canyon in the ocean floor.

"The river appears today just as it had to Conrad a hundred years ago: 'Going up that river was like traveling back to the earliest beginnings of the world. . .when vegetation rioted on the earth and the big tress were kings. An empty stream, a great silence, an impenetrable forest.'" (Quotations from NATIONAL GEOGRAPHICAL MAGAZINE, November, 1991, pp. 10–29.)

Henry Morton Stanley wrote: "The Indus, the Ganges, the Irawaddy, the Euphrates and the Nile. . .the Amazon—I think of them all and I see no beauty on their shores that is not excelled many fold by the natural beauty of this scenery."

It was Henry M. Stanley, the American explorer, who found Livingstone at Ujiji in 1873. Livingstone was to be found "dead or alive" said the NEW YORK TIMES. Livingstone told Stanley that the great river he had seen was called by the Africans "Lualaba". Stanley returned to Africa the next year to continue his explorations of the great river, 1874–1877. Stanley began his final journey across Africa from Zanzibar in 1874 and on the 999th day arrived on August 9, 1877 in Boma on the Atlantic coast at the mouth of the Congo. He had come 7000 miles through "the dark continent"!

On September 17, 1877 THE DAILY TELEGRAPH reported in giant headlines that Stanley had arrived at the mouth of the Congo. This news swept across the world, but was caught in particular by the Baptist missionary community in Great Britain.

3. The initial steps to establish the Congo Mission

It was a single-minded, stubborn, visionary from Leeds, Robert Arthington, who provided the initial funds for the venture. The Yorkshire millionaire poured over his maps of the world while living in penury so that he could devout his riches to the spread of Christ's Kingdom. He was described as "a very wealthy man . . .a very spirited man, too, but with his peculiarities. . ." by Ludwig Kraft the who had a dream of establishing a chain of missions across Africa. Arthington suggested in a letter to the Church Missionary Society that they might expect a contribution from him if they would begin a mission in Uganda. He offered the London Missionary Society 5,000 pounds if they would establish work on Lake Tanganyika since he believed that Central Africa should be evangelized from the East by the London Missionary Society and the Baptist Missionary Society working then in the Cameroons would move forward from the West. The missionaries of both societies would meet in the region of the Central Lakes.

When the news came of the success of Stanley's expedition, Arthington approached the BMS with an offer of 1,000 pounds for an exploratory expedition to the Congo in 1878. Mr. Arthington had been greatly moved by the report of Lieutenant Grandy who visited San Salvador on his way to the interior of Africa in his search for Livingstone. A Mr. Wathen of Bristol gave another 500 pounds toward the same expedition. (Arthington continued to push the BMS across the years to enter new fields. In 1910 he offered the society a considerable sum to begin work in South America.)

The first Baptist missionaries were warmly received by the old king, Pedro V and his people. The BMS had chosen George Grenfell, who had been working in the Cameroon since 1875, and Thomas J. Comber to carry out the expedition. They were joined later by Bentley, Crudgington and Harland in 1879. In that year they founded the San Salvador mission station.

Portugal was then responsible for the coast south of the mouth of the Congo. By 1878 Portugal had abolished the slave trade. The mission site chosen was on a plateau 1,800 feet above the sea, about 90 miles southeast of the river ports of Matadi and Noqui. In 1874 a terrible outbreak of smallpox swept away eight persons out of ten. When the mission was established there were fewer than 1,200 people in the village.

"They found old Roman Catholic images used as fetishes and the cross as a hunting charm. The missionaries began schools, preached and gave medical and surgical aid, not asking whether they were Catholic, Protestant or Heathen. They stood firmly for the rights and liberties of their native parishioners against tyranny and oppression in every form, and especially against slavery." Two years after the arrival of the Baptist missionaries, the Portuguese priests returned. But in spite of persecution and abuse, the Baptist Mission in San Salvador put down roots. By 1901 the mission reported 1,167 church members.

4. The Congo becomes the property of Leopold I of Belgium

In 1885 in the Anglo-Portuguese Conference of Berlin, called by Bismarck, Portuguese sovereignty over the coastal territory was limited to that lying between 5 and 8 degrees south of the Equator. The treaty gave Belgium the right to organize "The Congo Free State" which became in effect the personal estate of King Leopold I. He divided it into districts which he leased to trading companies for exploitation. Here begins a chapter in the sad story of the Congo and its people. The details of these events are presented in graphic detail in THE SCRAMBLE FOR AFRICA by Thomas Pakenham in the chapter "Resistance and Reform".

5. The establishment of new stations: Tumba (1884); Kibokolo (Zomba) (1898); Wathen (1898); Matadi (1899) in the Lower River area

Robert Arthington gave another 1,000 pounds to purchase a twin-screw steel river steamer, 71 feet long and of very shallow draft. It was named "The Peace". Grenfell actually assembled its 800 sections himself on a beach since the three engineers from England died on their way to the Congo. This river steamer become the vital link for supplies between England and the BMS stations along the Congo River.

In the Upper River area six stations were built from 1882 to 1896: Arthington (1882); Bolobo (1884); Bopoto (1888); Lukolela (1891); Monsembe (1891) and Yakusu (1896).

The story of Salamu

One of the first converts in the Upper Congo field was Salamu, a nine year old girl who was captured by Arab slave-traders about the time that Stanley was passing through the Yakusu district. Her story and that of her descendents is summarized in THE MISSIONARY HERALD in 1928: "Four Generations: Salamu, Neli, Damaris and Basuli".

"About the year 1876 when Stanley descended the Congo for the first time, a little chocolate-coloured girl was born in a village some forty miles from Yakusu. Her parents called her Lifoka, 'wealth'; but she was known by the name Salamu, 'greeting'. Before any white man had so much as seen her village, and some twenty years before the B.M.S. had thought of establishing a mission station at Yakusu, God chose Salamu to be the first native messenger of the Gospel to her tribe.

"Salamu was taken from her village by Arab slave raiders. Some of the inhabitants managed to flee for safety to the nearby forest; others were killed in the fight which took place, and many were captured. Salamu was separated from her parents when she was captured. The long procession of chained prisoners started the weary journey to the slave markets on the far east coast to be sold. But God willed otherwise concerning Salamu. When many weary miles had been traversed she was miraculously liberated by pioneering Europeans. They decided to take the child with them on their journey through the Congo forest and down the great river until they could find a mission station where she could be placed.

"Through the dense forest and down the mighty waterway for many hundreds of miles Salamu was taken by her liberators to the B.M.S. station at Bolobo. There in the mission school she learned to know of the love of God in Christ and later became a member of the church at Monsembe. She was sad that no one could tell her to which tribe she belonged or where in the vast Congo country her people might be found. Daily she prayed that God would guide her to them. When she had grown to young womanhood and married, the missionaries were asked to undertake work at the newly-established station of Yakusu. Salamu and her husband went with them some seven hundred fifty miles from the mission station where she had first begun to ask God for guidance to find her tribe again. At Yakusu her prayer was answered.

"She found the tribe in the Yakusu district from which she had been separated and discovered the village where she was born. To her joy she was reunited with one surviving parent, her father. Hers were the first native lips to tell the Gospel story in that region. Grenfell wrote of her:

'Here at Yakusu station, Salamu takes part as interpreter in all the services. But what is better still, she interprets Christianity by her daily life among the people in a manner that is more eloquent than words.'

"Salamu died in August, 1903, a victim of sleeping sickness. One of her last conscious acts was to confide to her missionary friends her three year old daughter, Neli, with the request that she be trained for the service of the Saviour. Neli was brought up in the home of Mrs. Millman, who had cared for and trained her mother, Salamu. . .The span of Neli's life was only a little longer than that of her mother: she died at the age of thirty-two. She also confided to the care of her mother's missionary friends, her own daughter, Damaris, then thirteen years old.

"At the age of seventeen she married Tetiya, a fine Christian youth and valued helper at the Yakusu sub-station of Yalikina. . .She went to Leopold-ville with her husband who was training to be a telegraph operator. While there Damaris attended the Diamond Jubilee of Protestant Missions in the Congo. Damaris and Tetiya have just had a son named Basuli, Salamu's great-grandson. . .!'"

The Yakusu station

Yakusu was built on a high bank, some 30 to 40 feet above the highwater mark. It had a spring of fresh water at the back of the property and was surrounded on three sides by forest. The mission station was comprised of about 300,00 square meters of land. Pages and pages of fascinating descriptions of the Yakusu station and surrounding area can be found in YAKUSU: THE VERY HEART OF AFRICA (1912) by H. Sutton Smith.

6. The alleged atrocities (1885–1909) (The word "alleged" is really redundant!)

Arab slave traders had roamed without control over this region for long years before the arrival of Livingstone and Stanley. In 1967 Dr. Arden Almquist of the Evangelical Covenant Mission Board reflected on the tremendous suffering caused by the slave trade:

"It is estimated that 13,000,000 people were sent out of the Congo alone in chains. It is a memory etched in blood with whips and chains, of long marches as beasts of burden, a memory of broken homes, of sorrow, of suffering, torture and death." In 1957, a victim of the Arab slavery, a Lokele woman, Sulila, was still living in Yakusu to greet Millman's daughter who was returning to her birthplace at Yakusu. The first convert in Yakusu, Salamu, had been a slave girl who knew the native Lokele tongue.

Today there are lineal descendents of those who suffered the atrocities a hundred or more years ago and who have shared through oral history their experiences to their children, grandchildren and great grandchildren.

The urgency to deal with the atrocities in the Congo was pressed hard by the British Consul in the Congo Free State, Sir Roger Casement. He had a connection with the BMS, having served as a lay worker for a period with the mission. Sir Roger came upriver to interview Mr. Millman to get evidence of cruelty by soldiers and forced payment of taxes. The report to London was a major factor in causing Leopold I to set up a special Investigating Commission made up of three Roman Catholic priests and three Baptist missionaries (two British and one American). The BMS tried to play a reconciling role and, at the same time, to keep the missionaries out of politics. But it was a very delicate situation in which the privileged status of the BMS with the government could have been lost.

Grenfell was bitterly attacked for having covered up by his eulogies to the State the true state of affairs. Also the Home Committee of the BMS was accused of failure even to acknowledge his letter to them on the subject. The press took up the cause of the atrocities in the Congo. A story "Are All Men Liars?", prepared by Dr. Gratton Guiness of the Congo Bololo Mission was answered by Grenfell: "There is an incontrovertible case for reform and I believe it will come; the good sense of the Belgian people will demand it when they know the truth. The Commission which has just returned will greatly enlighten them. I am hoping for great things as the outcome." (George Grenfell to Gratton Guiness, written in Bolobo, Upper Congo, March 20, 1905) Several letters between Gratton Guiness and George Grenfell can be found in the B.M.S. archives in the Angus Library, Oxford about the atrocities and the report of the Royal Commission.

Another article "Baskets of Hands" was published in the English press about the same time. It was based on the stories of cutting off hands of living natives because they refused to bring in the allocated amount of rubber. A photo of a boy thus maimed can be seen in the Millman papers at Regent's Park College. Millman also related how six people were forced to eat raw rubber.

Unfortunately some of the field reports of the BMS seem to have been destroyed when the BMS archives at Furnival Street, London, were fire bombed in 1940. We do know that George Grenfell returned the decoration he had received from the King when Grenfell failed to effect a change in the colonial authorities through his personal influence.

According to the Millman biography, in 1907 the Belgian government took over the territory from Leopold I and began to "lift the administration beyond reproach". At last in 1909, Prince Albert went to the Congo on a tour of inspection and recommended that the Congo become a responsibly governed colony of Belgium and cease to be a royal estate.

APPENDIX B
"The Scramble for Africa"

Thomas Pakenham in his comprehensive survey of the white man's conquest of the Dark Continent from 1876 to 1911 provides a monumental record of THE SCRAMBLE FOR AFRICA of the major European powers. (Pakenham, T. THE SCRAMBLE FOR AFRICA, Random House, New YOrk, 1991) The book describes in detail the story of British, French, German, Belgian, Spanish and Italian colonial intrigues, failures and successes.

Livingstone's last words inlaid in brass on his tomb in Westminster Abbey express the idealistic motivation of exploration and colonial development:

"All I can add in my solitude is, may heaven's rich blessing come down on every one, American, English or Turk, who will help to heal this open sore of the world."

However the "blessing to heal" seemed to exacerbate that "open sore of the world" as colonial powers imposed their imperial wills on the peoples of Africa. Europe imposed its will on Africa at the point of a gun during the 1876–1912 period. Livingstone had pressed for the three C's: Christianity, civilization and commerce. But Pakenham writes that "the Maxim gun, not trade or the cross, became the symbol of that age in Africa." The fourth "C" was added which was conquest and that gradually predominated. So it was not strange that the epilogue of Pakenham's volume is entitled "Scrambling Out"! What is ahead for the continent after 85 years of colonial exploitation and paternalism followed by three decades and more of independence for most of the African nations? What is the meaning of this double legacy of self-serving colonialism and strife-ridden independence for the continent as it moves toward the next millennium? I can only say that Africa deserves a better future.

CONTENTS

Part One The Open Path

Part Two The Race Begins

Part Three The Rights of Conquest

Part Four Resistance and Reform

Epilogue Scrambling Out

Zimbabwe, Africa and Europe; 18 April 1980, before and after

— — — — — — — — — —

Summary of contents: "The Scramble for Africa" is one of the most extraordinary phenomena in history. In 1880 most of the continent was barely explored. Yet by 1902, five European powers—Britain, France, Germany, Belgium and Italy—had grabbed almost all of its ten million square miles, awarding themselves thirty new colonies and protectorates and 110 million bewildered subjects.

"The sudden race for African territory swept the political masters of Europe off of their feet. The British colonial secretary protested this 'absurd scamble'. The German chancellor, Prince Bismarck, complained that he was being led into a 'colonial whirl'. The French prime minister called it a 'steeple chase into the unknown'."

"Ironically, the provocation for this massive display of greed on the part of the European powers came from the heroic death in 1873 of the missionary-explorer David Livingstone, who had exposed the horrors of the African slave trade then in progress. His call for Africa to be redeemed by the three C's—Commerce, Christianity and Civilization—was aimed at the conscience of the civilized world. However, the initial response came from rival colonial enthusiasts like Henry Stanley, mariners like Pierre de Brazza, soldiers like Edward Lugard, pedagogues like Karl Peters, and gold-and-diamond tycoons like Cecil Rhoades. . . ."

**An early document which moved Alex to apply for
missionary service**

(c 1906)

*"May Heaven's rich blessing come down upon every one who will help to
heal this OPEN SORE OF THE WORLD."* Livingstone's Prayer for the friends
of Africa.
"In as much as ye have done it unto one of the least of these." Matt. 25:40.

Conditions in the Congo State
Testimony from Many Witnesses

The Promise

"Our only program, I am anxious to repeat, is the work of moral and
material regeneration." *Leopold II, 1885.*

The Fulfillment

"The inhabitants have fled. They have burned their huts, and great heaps of
cinders mark the sites. The terror caused by the memory of inhuman floggings, of massacres and abductions, haunts their poor brains and they go as
fugitives to seek shelter in the recesses of the hospitable bush or across the
frontiers to find it in French or Portuguese Congo." *M. Edouard Pickard,
Member of Belgian Senate, 1896.*

"Everywhere I hear the same news—rubber and murder—slavery in
its worst form." *E. J. Glave, companion of H. M. Stanley, in "Century
Magazine," 1899.*

"Upon the least resistance the men were shot down, and the women
were captured as slaves and made to work. It was a sad sight to behold
these poor creatures driven like dogs here and there, and kept hard at their
toil from morning to night." *Semliki region. Mr. Lloyd, 1899.*

"Imprisoning 60 women and putting them in the chain, where all but
five died of starvation." *One of the counts in the indictment drawn up
against the agents of the Anversoise in the Mongala massacres in 1900.*

"Men are first applied for, and if they do not present themselves, soldiers are sent, who tie up the women or the chiefs until the workmen are
forthcoming." *Rev. A. Billington, Bwemba, 1903.*

"M——, went to the factory and released 106 prisoners. We saw them
pass our stations—living skeletons—among them grey-headed old men
and women. Many children were born in prison. One poor woman was
working in the sun three days after the child was born." *Mr. Ruskin, 1903.*

"This man himself, when I visited him in Boma, in March, 1901, said that more than 100 women and children had died of starvation at his hands, but that the responsibility was due to his superiors' orders and neglect." *Cyrus Smith to Consul Casement.*

"At the different Congo Government stations, women are kept for the following purposes. In the daytime they do all the station work—at night they are obliged to be at the disposal of the soldiers.—The women are slaves captured by the Government soldiers when raiding the country." *Katanga region. Affidavit. March, 1903.*

"In an open shed I found two sentries of the La Lulanga Company guarding fifteen women, five of whom had infants at the breast, and three of whom were about to become mothers.—They said they were detaining them as prisoners to compel their husbands to bring in the right amount of india rubber. 'Why do you catch the women and not the men?' I asked. 'Don't you see,' was the answer, 'if I caught and kept the men, who would work the rubber? But if I catch their wives, the husbands are anxious to have them home again, and so the rubber is brought in quickly.'—At nightfall the fifteen women in the shed were tied together, either neck to neck, or ankle to ankle, for the night. *Lulonga district. Consul Casement, 1903.*

APPENDIX C
A Statistical overview of the Christian Community in Zaire (1982)

(Data based on David R. Barrett, STATISTICAL SURVEY OF WORLD CHRISTIAN POPULATIONS (name ?), 1982)

A. Basic statistics

Total inhabitants	49,500,000	(1982)
	12,500,000	(1900)
Per capita income	US$126	
Doctors	818	
Hospital beds	67,624	
Hospitals	1,380	
Adult literacy	31%	
Universities	3	
University students	5,324	

B. The Roman Catholic Church

Founded in 1482. Today there are 1,682 congregations with 5,765,700 baptized adults and an estimated constituency of 9,940,873.(?) The Roman Catholics received an annual government subsidy in 1930 of 26 million francs.

C. Comparative statistics on total Christian Community

	1900	1982	2000 (est.)
Total Christians	124,650	26,414,000	47,957,000
Total Roman Catholics	74,600	13,322,000	24,551,000
Total Protestants	50,000	8,166,000	14,538,000
Total African Independent	000	4,777,000	8,848,000

By percentages

Christians	1.4	94.5	97.0
Roman Catholics	0.8	47.6	48.4
Protestants	0.6	29.0	29.4
African Independent	0.0	16.2	17.9

D. Baptist Constituency in Eglise du Christ au Zaire

(Note: Eglise de Christ au Zaire includes 19,540 congregations composed of 1,519,499 adults and an affiliated community of 4,728,280)

Year	Congtns.	Adults	Community
Com. Baptiste au Flueve Kivu (1928)	592	32,753	60,000
Com. Baptiste de Flueve Zaire (1878)	600	60,000	450,000
Com. Baptiste de Zaire (Ouest) (1878)	700	100,000	450,000
Com. Bap. Automome entre Wambi-Bakili (1949)	15	1,940	7,500
Com. "du Bas-Uélé (1918)	219	16,000	35,000
Com. "du Sud-Swango (1961)	15	833	12,000
Com. "de Bandundu (1892)	192	18,812	50,000
Com. "Independente Ev. (1932)	226	10,592	25,000
Totals	2,550	240,930	1,089,500

E. Missions working with Baptist groups

Com. Baptiste au Kivu Flueve	Conservative Baptists (USA)
Com. Baptiste du Flueve Zaire	Baptist Missionary Soc. (UK)
Com. Baptiste du Zaire (Ouest)	American Baptists (USA)
Com. Baptiste Automome W.B.	Swedish Baptists
Com. Baptiste du Bas-Uélé	Norwegian Baptists
Com. Baptiste du Sud-Kwango	Independent Baptists (USA)
Com. Baptiste du Bandundu	Swedish Baptist
Com. Baptiste Independente	Independent Baptists (USA)

The Dutch Baptist missionaries began to work in the Upper Congo in the 1940's

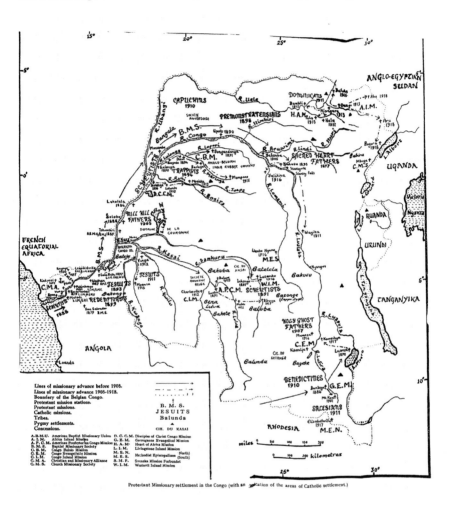

Protestant Missionary settlement in the Congo (with an indication of the areas of Catholic settlement.)

APPENDIX D

THE STARTE FAMILY OF CAMBRIDGE

1. WILLIAM START "a whitesmith"—without the "e"
2. JAMES STARTE, his son and WILLIAM STARTE, a second son
3. HENRY "Harry" STARTE, Ethel Mill's father. b. 1850; m. 1871
A storekeeper in Swavesey, near Cambridge

4. THE SIX STARTE SIBLINGS

Florrie (married Fred Dent) b. 1872
Oliver Harold B. ("O.H.B.") b. 1874 (married Muriel Harriet Dywer, 1920)
Horace b. 1876 (married Maisie Man)
James Herbert b. 1878
Ethel Clara b. 1880 (married Alexander George Mill, 1918)
Elsie b. 1882 (?) (married William Robinson)

5. ETHEL'S NIECES, NEPHEWS and COUSIN

Children of Maisie and Horace: Jean; Margaret Ann (Hampton-Chubb); Robin (married Muriel) _____.
Daughter of her GREAT UNCLE WILLIAM START - Mrs. Nurse, whose grandson Michael Nurse (b. 1927) was reported to be working on a Starte family history.

6. OTHER FAMILY INFORMATION

1. Henry Starte was a leader in the St. Andrew's Street Baptist Church, Cambridge.
2. Horacio Starte served with the Forestry Service of the Colonial Civil Service in India. Ethel spent two years traveling with him in India as his "housekeeper", 1911–13.

3. James Herbert Starte and his wife, Ruth Quadley Starte, were commissioned as Baptist missionaries to the Congo, 1915–1940. He died in 1963.
4. Maisie Starte, reared an Anglican, became active in the Baptist missionary movement and served on the board of the Baptist Missionary Society.
5. Robin and Muriel Starte live in suburban Cambridge and are active in the St. Andrew's Street Baptist Church. Muriel had been an office secretary to Rev. Robert Thompson, the Ass't General Secretary of the Baptist Union of Great Britain and Ireland before her marriage. Robin and Muriel took Uncle Alex to church and to their home for dinner every Sunday after Aunt Ethel died.
6. Mrs. Nurse, Ethel's cousin, was very attentive to Aunt Ethel and Uncle Alex during their retirement years in Cambridge.
7. The sons of James Herbert and Ruth Quadley Herbert were Gordon (a medical doctor) and Harvey (a lawyer).

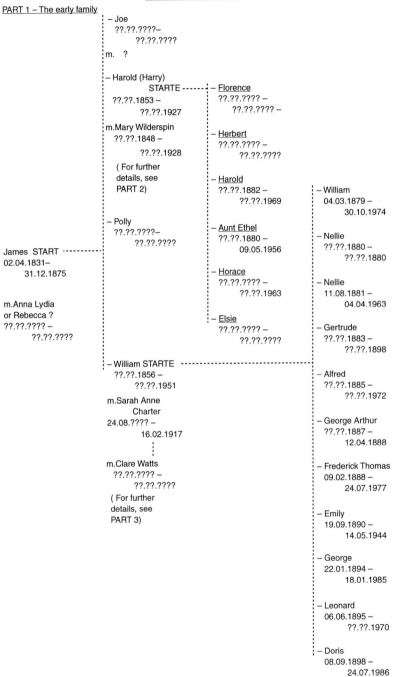

FAMILY TREE – STARTE

PART 1 – The early family

- Joe
  ??.??.????–
  ??.??.????
m. ?

- Harold (Harry)
  STARTE
  ??.??.1853 –
  ??.??.1927

m.Mary Wilderspin
  ??.??.1848 –
  ??.??.1928
(For further
details, see
PART 2)

- Polly
  ??.??.????–
  ??.??.????

- Florence
  ??.??.???? –
  ??.??.???? –

- Herbert
  ??.??.???? –
  ??.??.????

- Harold
  ??.??.1882 –
  ??.??.1969

- Aunt Ethel
  ??.??.1880 –
  09.05.1956

- Horace
  ??.??.???? –
  ??.??.1963

- Elsie
  ??.??.???? –
  ??.??.????

James START
02.04.1831–
31.12.1875

m.Anna Lydia
or Rebecca ?
??.??.???? –
??.??.????

- William STARTE
  ??.??.1856 –
  ??.??.1951

m.Sarah Anne
  Charter
24.08.???? –
  16.02.1917

m.Clare Watts
  ??.??.???? –
  ??.??.????
(For further
details, see
PART 3)

- William
  04.03.1879 –
  30.10.1974

- Nellie
  ??.??.1880 –
  ??.??.1880

- Nellie
  11.08.1881 –
  04.04.1963

- Gertrude
  ??.??.1883 –
  ??.??.1898

- Alfred
  ??.??.1885 –
  ??.??.1972

- George Arthur
  ??.??.1887 –
  12.04.1888

- Frederick Thomas
  09.02.1888 –
  24.07.1977

- Emily
  19.09.1890 –
  14.05.1944

- George
  22.01.1894 –
  18.01.1985

- Leonard
  06.06.1895 –
  ??.??.1970

- Doris
  08.09.1898 –
  24.07.1986

PART 2 – The 'HAROLD' family in detail
Florence
??.??.??–??.??.??
m.at (town) ?
 (date) to
Frank DENT
??.??.??–??.??.??

Herbert ----------+–Harvey ----------+–Harvey
??.??.??–??.??.??   ??.??.??–   ??.??.??–
m.at (town) ?   m.at (town) ?
 (date) to   (date) to
Harriet ?   Olive ?
??.??.??–??.??.??   ??.??.??–

Harold -----------+–Ruth
??.??.82–??.??.69 | ??.??.21–
m.at (town) ? | m.at (town) ?
 (date) to | (date) to
Mary Bushel | Douglas ?
??.??.??–??.??.?? | ??.??.??–
                   |
                   | – Roger
                   | ??.??.23 –
                   | m.at (town) ?
                   | (date) to
                   | ? ?
                   | ??.??.??–
                   |
                   | – Gordon----------+–David
                   | ??.??.26 –   ??.??.?? –
                   | m.at (town) ?
                   | (date) to
                   | Mary ?
                   | ??.??.??–
                   (Emigrated to Melbourne, Australia (date)?)

Ethel – – – – – – – – – + – Barbara Mary
??.??. 80–09.05.56   ?? . ?? . 20 –?? . ?? . 66
m. at Cambridge
 07.18 to
Alexander George MILL
22.07.85 – 29.11.69

Horace -----------+ – Joan Rodney -----+ – Virginia May
??.??.??–20.07.63 | 14.01.30 – | 06.12.60 –
m.at (town) ? | m.at (town) ? |
 (date) to | (date) to | – Richard Thomas
May Rodney Man | Thomas CLARKE | 29.05.62 –
01.11.96–19.07.81 | ??. ??. ??– |
                   | | – Emma
                   | | 26.05.70 –
                   |

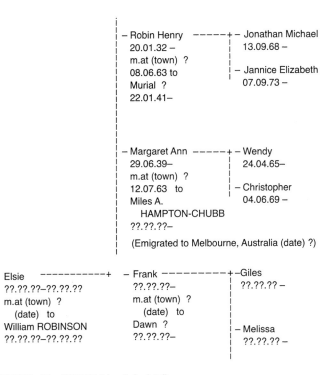

– Robin Henry ─────+ – Jonathan Michael
20.01.32 – | 13.09.68 –
m.at (town) ? |
08.06.63 to | – Jannice Elizabeth
Murial ? | 07.09.73 –
22.01.41–

– Margaret Ann ─────+ – Wendy
29.06.39– | 24.04.65–
m.at (town) ? |
12.07.63 to | – Christopher
Miles A. | 04.06.69 –
HAMPTON-CHUBB
??.??.??–

(Emigrated to Melbourne, Australia (date) ?)

Elsie ──────────+ – Frank ─────────+–Giles
??.??.??–??.??.?? | ??.??.??– | ??.??.?? –
m.at (town) ? | m.at (town) ? |
(date) to | (date) to |
William ROBINSON | Dawn ? | – Melissa
??.??.??–??.??.?? | ??.??.??– | ??.??.?? –

PART 3 – The 'WILLIAM' family in detail

William ─────────+–Alexander ─────────+– Anthony ────────+–Anthony
04.03.79 – 30.10.74 | William | 04.09.34 – | 22.11.61–
m.at (town) ? | 04.10.04–06.10.35 | m.at Oporto |
(date) to | m.at Carcavelos | (Portugal) | –Michele
Sarah Anne (Ciss) | (Portugal) | (date) to | 24.03.63 –
Christmas | 1930 to | Sally Kendal | m. at (town) ?
30.04.78 – 11.01.58 | Dorothy Bull | 13.03.35 | (date) to
| 01.12.04 – | | Boudouin
| | | DEFFENCE
| – Gladys Anne | | ??.??.?? –
| 06.10.08 – |
| m.at (town)? | –Marina
| 24.08.33 to | 18.01.65 –
| Geoffrey MILLER |
| 24.12.04 –15.07.85 | –Christina
| 08.01.70 –

Nellie ─────────+–Joycylin Mary ─────+–Timothy Griffith ───+– David
11.08.81– 04.04.63 | 18.12.07– 09.12.65 | 27.07.41 – 29.10.89 | Griffith
m.at (town) ? | m.at (town) ? | m.at (town) ? | 12.03.73 –
(date) to | David Howard | (date) to |
Archibald Shedd | DAVIES | Joseene Fletcher | – Robin Edward
RAYNER | 26.11.10 – 07.04.69 | 07.08.42 – | 04.07.75 –
??.??.82 –10.11.55 |

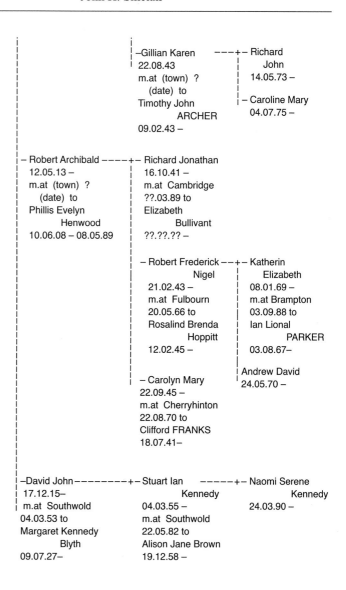

–Gillian Karen   ———+— Richard
22.08.43 | John
m.at (town) ? | 14.05.73 –
(date) to |
Timothy John |— Caroline Mary
      ARCHER | 04.07.75 –
09.02.43 –

– Robert Archibald ————+— Richard Jonathan
12.05.13 – | 16.10.41 –
m.at (town) ? | m.at Cambridge
(date) to | ??.03.89 to
Phillis Evelyn | Elizabeth
     Henwood | Bullivant
10.06.08 – 08.05.89 | ??.??.?? –

                          |— Robert Frederick ——+— Katherin
                          | Nigel | Elizabeth
                          | 21.02.43 – | 08.01.69 –
                          | m.at Fulbourn | m.at Brampton
                          | 20.05.66 to | 03.09.88 to
                          | Rosalind Brenda| Ian Lional
                          | Hoppitt | PARKER
                          | 12.02.45 – | 03.08.67–
                          | |
                          |— Carolyn Mary | Andrew David
                          | 22.09.45 – | 24.05.70 –
                          | m.at Cherryhinton
                          | 22.08.70 to
                          | Clifford FRANKS
                          | 18.07.41–

–David John ————————+— Stuart Ian   ————+— Naomi Serene
17.12.15– | Kennedy | Kennedy
m.at Southwold | 04.03.55 – | 24.03.90 –
04.03.53 to | m.at Southwold
Margaret Kennedy | 22.05.82 to
     Blyth | Alison Jane Brown
09.07.27– | 19.12.58 –

Alfred
??.??.85 –??.??.72

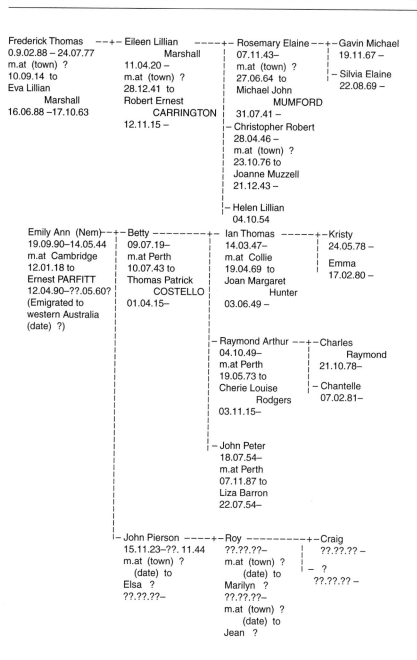

Frederick Thomas
0.9.02.88 – 24.07.77
m.at (town) ?
10.09.14 to
Eva Lillian
Marshall
16.06.88 –17.10.63

Eileen Lillian
Marshall
11.04.20 –
m.at (town) ?
28.12.41 to
Robert Ernest
CARRINGTON
12.11.15 –

Rosemary Elaine
07.11.43–
m.at (town) ?
27.06.64 to
Michael John
MUMFORD
31.07.41 –

Gavin Michael
19.11.67 –

Silvia Elaine
22.08.69 –

– Christopher Robert
28.04.46 –
m.at (town) ?
23.10.76 to
Joanne Muzzell
21.12.43 –

– Helen Lillian
04.10.54

Emily Ann (Nem)
19.09.90–14.05.44
m.at Cambridge
12.01.18 to
Ernest PARFITT
12.04.90–??.05.60?
(Emigrated to
western Australia
(date) ?)

Betty
09.07.19–
m.at Perth
10.07.43 to
Thomas Patrick
COSTELLO
01.04.15–

Ian Thomas
14.03.47–
m.at Collie
19.04.69 to
Joan Margaret
Hunter
03.06.49 –

Kristy
24.05.78 –

Emma
17.02.80 –

– Raymond Arthur
04.10.49–
m.at Perth
19.05.73 to
Cherie Louise
Rodgers
03.11.15–

Charles
Raymond
21.10.78–

– Chantelle
07.02.81–

– John Peter
18.07.54–
m.at Perth
07.11.87 to
Liza Barron
22.07.54–

– John Pierson
15.11.23–??. 11.44
m.at (town) ?
(date) to
Elsa ?
??.??.??–

Roy
??.??.??–
m.at (town) ?
(date) to
Marilyn ?
??.??.??–
m.at (town) ?
(date) to
Jean ?

Craig
??.??.?? –

– ?
??.??.?? –

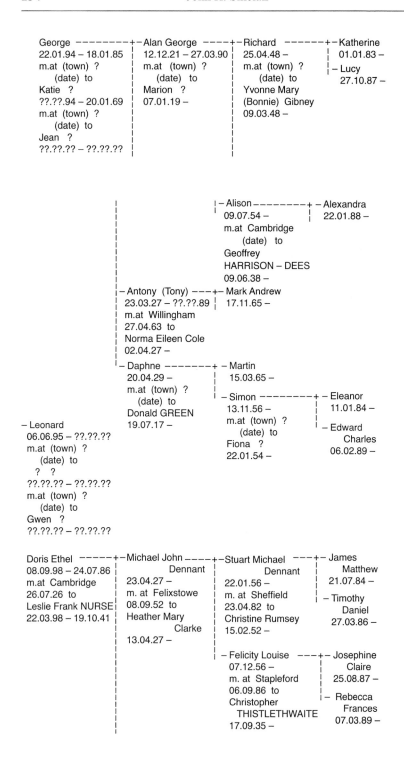

George ————————+—Alan George ————+—Richard ———————+—Katherine
22.01.94 – 18.01.85 | 12.12.21 – 27.03.90 | 25.04.48 – | 01.01.83 –
m.at (town) ? | m.at (town) ? | m.at (town) ? | | – Lucy
   (date) to | (date) to | (date) to | 27.10.87 –
Katie ? | Marion ? | Yvonne Mary |
??.??.94 – 20.01.69 | 07.01.19 – | (Bonnie) Gibney |
m.at (town) ? | | 09.03.48 – |
   (date) to | | |
Jean ? | | |
??.??.?? – ??.??.?? | | |

| – Alison ————————+ – Alexandra
| 09.07.54 – | 22.01.88 –
| m.at Cambridge |
| (date) to
| Geoffrey
| HARRISON – DEES
| 09.06.38 –

– Antony (Tony) ———+– Mark Andrew
23.03.27 – ??.??.89 | 17.11.65 –
m.at Willingham
27.04.63 to
Norma Eileen Cole
02.04.27 –

'– Daphne ————————+ – Martin
20.04.29 – | 15.03.65 –
m.at (town) ? |
   (date) to | – Simon ————————+ – Eleanor
Donald GREEN | 13.11.56 – | 11.01.84 –
19.07.17 – | m.at (town) ? |
| (date) to | – Edward
– Leonard | Fiona ? | Charles
06.06.95 – ??.??.?? | 22.01.54 – | 06.02.89 –
m.at (town) ?
   (date) to
? ?
??.??.?? – ??.??.??
m.at (town) ?
   (date) to
Gwen ?
??.??.?? – ??.??.??

Doris Ethel ———————+—Michael John ————+—Stuart Michael ————+— James
08.09.98 – 24.07.86 | Dennant | Dennant | Matthew
m.at Cambridge | 23.04.27 – | 22.01.56 – | 21.07.84 –
26.07.26 to | m. at Felixstowe | m. at Sheffield | | – Timothy
Leslie Frank NURSE | 08.09.52 to | 23.04.82 to | Daniel
22.03.98 – 19.10.41 | Heather Mary | Christine Rumsey | 27.03.86 –
| Clarke | 15.02.52 –
| 13.04.27 –
| | – Felicity Louise ————+— Josephine
| | 07.12.56 – | Claire
| | m. at Stapleford | 25.08.87 –
| | 06.09.86 to
| | Christopher | – Rebecca
| | THISTLETHWAITE | Frances
| | 17.09.35 – | 07.03.89 –

```
¦ — Lynette Mary ————+— Susan ———————+— Andrew
¦   29.05.30–           ¦  03.04.54 –      ¦  28.10.78 –
¦   m. at Cambridge     ¦  m. at Edinburgh ¦
    ??.??.53 to         ¦  ??.??.76 to     ¦ — Neil
    Clifford John       ¦  Iain MORRISON      03.04.82 –
       DODSON           ¦  ??.??.49 –
    28.10.30–19.08.81   ¦ — David
                        ¦   04.11.58 –
                            m. at Belfast
                            ??.08.86 to
                            Julie Crowe
                            ??.??.?? –
```

Doris Ethel Starte who we met in Cambridge in 1956

APPENDIX E

"Picture Letters" written by Uncle Alex to his nieces and nephews
1927–1940

B. M. S.
Yalikina
12/10/27

LOVE TO JOHN's LITTLE SON.

Here is what grows in my garden.
What grows in yours!

RICE

peanuts (monkey nuts)

FROM UNCLE ALEX

B. M. S
Yalikina
November 7th
1929.

My dear Johnnie/

I have not got a Christmas card to send you and I can't buy one for none of the shops here sell them. So I am just sending you a Christmas Tree and I hope you will get all the things which are on it.

You will enjoy climbing the tree to get the presents and if you try hard to be good you wont miss any of them.

Your loxing Uncle
ALEX.

12/2/29.

My big John/ What do you think of trousers? I once had a pair cut off at the knees like Scouts' and I liked them best of all.

I had to swing a hatchet as hard as I could on the ice on top of the water butt this morning to break it. It was great fun. I am glad you can sit still in Church now and Daddy and Mother will be proud when you can go to School. Love from Uncle Alex.

B. M. S.
YALIKINA.
11/4/30

My dear John./ I had to go to School in a canoe like this because the floods were up. Wasn't it fun!

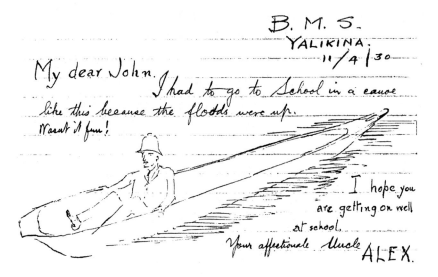

I hope you are getting on well at school. Your affectionate Uncle ALEX.

B. M. S.
YALIKIIYA.
2 : 6 : 1930

Dear Johnny.
We are on a journey
among a people who wear their hair
done up like this
and all covered with
red powder.
They are called Bamboles.
I had a nice Xmas and I liked
your letter. Love from
Uncle Alex + Auntie·Ethel.

B.M.S.
YALIKINA.

13 November 1930

DEAR JOHNNIE/

We saw a crocodile in the Congo River today and we wished we had had a gun to shoot it with

It was swimming along with its head above the water like this but as soon as it heard us it went below the water like a Submarine.

Auntie Ethel & I were in the little steamer Grenfell with a lot of black men and boys and so we were quite safe.

We hope you will have a very Happy Christmas and that you will pray for the black boys & girls out here.

Your loving Uncle Alec

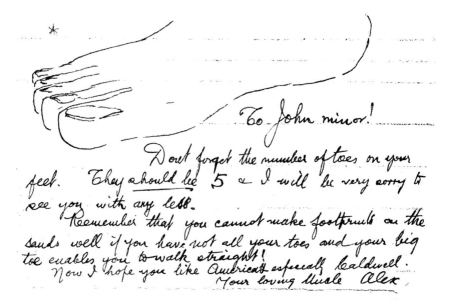

To John minor!

Don't forget the number of toes on your feet. They should be 5 & I will be very sorry to see you with any less.

Remember that you cannot make footprints on the sands well if you have not all your toes and your big toe enables you to walk straight!

Now I hope you like America especially Caldwell.

Your loving Uncle Alex

Note: I had nearly severed a toe when I was cutting flowers for my mother. JHS

Uncle & Auntie say. "What a shame Johnnie should be in bed on Christmas day!"

B.M.'s
Yalikina
21/7/31.

My Dear Johnnie/

I hope you like your teacher at School and are able to do all that she tells you. Do you know how I knew that I had a Birthday yesterday? It was because of which measures all my days & a which measures all my years.

I am now 46 years old. How many are you? Be sure you don't lose a birthday by neglecting the time. Your loving Uncle Alec

Bill's
Valikuia
11/4/30

My dear Niece Edith — Thanks for your letter wishing Aunt Ethel & I a Merry Christmas & a Happy New Year. We are still having it. I am glad you liked the letter from Barbara. I liked the photograph of you & Clara very much. I hope Mother is well & I know you will help her in the work in the house. I had some nice flowers in the garden & the sheep came & trod on them all. Wern't they silly sheep.
Your loving Uncle
Alex.

12/2/29

My dear Edith /
I was glad to hear that you gave Daddy a Blotter for Christmas. I got one too from Barbara and a Calendar like this (It was nicer) with blue sky & green hill & 3 bunnies with cotton wool stuck on for tails.

I am glad you liked being a Chinese girl in the play and are trying to help them.
Your loving Uncle Alex.

My dear EDITH

Do you remember
your Uncle Alex and
Auntie Clara who
came from AFRICA
to see you? When
are you coming to
see us?

You must grow up to be
a good big girl first.
We have no Peaches IN
Congo except what come in.
cans. But we have
pawpaws.
Your loving Uncle ALEX X C

72. M.S.
Yalikuna

My dear Clara / You did draw a very nice
picture on your letter to me and I hope
you like writing & reading & drawing and
all the other things you are taught at school.
Barbara writes her own letters to me at school
now and says she likes her lessons.
She had to have her tonsils taken out this
year but she is better now.
Your loving Uncle
Alex X X

This is a big
red flower which grows
in our garden.

I salute these
ensigns which
have such a
deservedly high

EXCELSIOR.

Grace's Family Crest.

reputation throughout
the World!
Glad to hear you are a
trusted leader in this
International army of
Good.
Your loving Uncle Alex

B.M.S
Yalikina
2/6/30.

My Dear Clara

That was a nice letter which you wrote me. Barbara had measles because a girl went back to school with Measles infection & gave it to all the other girls. We got another curio ~~who belonds to~~ in this journey. It was a Tortoise.
The boys ate the inside and we have the shell.

Your loving uncle Alex

B.M.S.
Yalikina
11/4/30

My Dear Clara Yours was a very careful and pretty little letter to me. I think you must be getting on well at school. Do you like working in the house too? My black cook forgot the loaf which was baking in the oven & it came out as black as himself. He was very sorry about it & I remembered a famous king who once burned some cakes so I forgave him.
Your little electric stove would not do that would it.

Your loving uncle Alex

My Dear Clara / What a nice letter you sent me with the picture of the dress which Mamma made for you. I think it will look very nice indeed.

Barbara will be going to the seaside in 3 weeks + she has a [bucket] and a [spade]

12/?/79.

My dear Clara / I always remember you singing "Daffodilly" and I hope you are now able to learn a great many more things at school. Barbara bought her Auntie Florrie a nice plant in a pot for Christmas. I was like this. I forget the name of it. It had red flowers. I wonder what you gave to Mummy + Daddy. Your loving Uncle ALEX.

Can Mr & Mrs Mill please see the Secretary?

APPENDIX F
MEMORIAL RESOLUTION
July, 1956
Mrs. A.G. Mill
(Ethel Clara Starte—died 9/5/56 aged 76)
Presented by Gladys C. Ennals

It is with thanksgiving for a life of rare devotion of service for the Master that we record the passing of Mrs. A.G. Mill (nee Ethel Clara Starte) on June 9, 1956 at Cambridge.

Mrs. Mill joined her husband as a member of the Baptist Missionary Society staff in the Congo at the time of their marriage in 1918. From then until their retirement in 1945, "Mama Bandombele", as she was known to thousands of Africans, gave unstintingly of her time, her strength and her gifts in the service of Jesus Christ, for the salvation of African men, women and children.

Mr. And Mrs. Mill were responsible for an immense section of the Yakusu District, and lived first at Yakusu, then at Yalikina and later at Irema, one hundred and fifty miles up the Lomami River, and the sub-station farthest from Yakusu.

They were "in journeyings oft", on foot, by cycle, by Mission steamer, and later by motor boat, visiting the young and growing Christian community in the Esoo and Bambole forests and in the countless villages from Yanjali on the main river to Opala on the Lomami.

Mr. and Mrs. Mill had the spirit of the early pioneers, and the call of the "unreached" was ever with them. Unwearyingly they served, never once putting self first. Mrs. Mill as a nurse was always on call for the sick and suffering ones by night and day. Her medicine chest was the last load to be packed when moving camp, and the first to be unpacked, and though tired, and in need of refreshment after a hard day's journey, if a sick person needed care then the much needed cup of tea could wait.

Whether examining a village school, or a candidate for baptism and church membership, or in personal interview with church members, or assisting in teacher training courses, or tending the sick, Mama Bandombele was always ready to do "whatsoever my Lord and King shall appoint". The verse:

"Go, labour on, spend and be spent, Thy joy to do the Father's will.
It is the way the Master went, should not the servant tread it still?"

sums up her life of self-sacrificial service for the advancement of His Kingdom in the Yakusu District of the Belgian Congo. Now she has heard the Master's "Well done, good and faithful service, enter thou into the joy of Thy Lord".

Her last months of increasing weakness have been patiently borne, and our deep sympathy is extended to her husband and invalid daughter, Barbara.

APPENDIX G
A FUNERAL MESSAGE
upon the death of
The Reverend Alexander G. Mill
St. Andrew's Street Baptist Church, Cambridge, England
December 5, 1969

"With mercy and with judgment, my web of time He wove; And aye the dew of sorrow was lustered by His love.
I'll bless the hand that guided; I'll bless the heart that planned.
When throned where glory dwelleth in Emmanuel Land."
This hymn was a favorite of both my Grandfather Mill and my Uncle Alex. For Uncle Alex believed that God wove the web of his years which spanned nearly 85 years.

It was fitting that God called his servant Home on the eve of the First Sunday in Advent. In this joyful season, we unite our voices with all creation to praise God's Son. My uncle would have wished that the first words spoken in this message be words of praise to Jesus Christ. As St. Paul wrote:

"He that glories, let him glory in the Lord." (II Cor.10:17)
As a small boy, he came to know the One whom to know is Life Eternal. Across the years he never doubted the Companion of his ways. With Count Zinzendorf, founder of the Moravian movement, Alex Mill could affirm:
"I have but one passion. . .it is He."

Godly parents left indelible imprints on his life. The bairns were often bedded down with the hymn "Loved with Everlasting Love":
"Heaven above is softer blue; earth around is sweeter green,
Something lives in every hue Christless eyes have never seen.
Birds with gladder songs oe'r flow; earth with deeper beauties shine;
Since I know as I am known, I am His and He is mine."

Alexander Mill loved both nature and the works of men because he saw in everything the power and mercy of God. He tried to observe all life through the eyes of Christ. He was sensitive toward everything that God and man had made.

He spoke to all unashamedly and forthrightly about Jesus Christ, yet he avoided an artificial and sanctimonious air in his simple, clear-cut testimony. He wanted to introduce everyone to his Best Friend, Jesus of Nazareth, whose life had given deep meaning to his own life.

St. Paul wrote:

"Be followers of me, even as I am a follower of Christ." (I Cor. 11:1)

Only in these terms would Uncle Alex have permitted me to speak a word of tribute about him. He was fully aware, as was St. Paul, of his human frailties. Any virtues he had were those which he had received by the Grace of God. Alexander of Glasgow could say with Paul of Tarsus:

"Follow me only in so far as you have seen me follow Christ".

Alex Mill was interested in people—one by one. Some like people, but not in batches! My uncle loved people better in small groups. He seemed to be able to accept people as they were and to communicate this acceptance to both young and old. His humble ways endeared him to many.

He was first of all a missionary, a person who seeks to cross the barriers of language, culture and class and there make known by word and deed the love of God. Early in his teens, Alex Mill wanted to be an overseas missionary. On Livingstone Sunday in 1900 he signed a covenant card as did many Scottish youth of his day. The following life purpose of David Livingstone became his goal in life:

"I will place no value on anything I have or may possess, except in relation to the Kingdom of Christ. If anything I have will advance the interest of that Kingdom, it shall be given up or kept, as by keeping or giving it up I shall most promote the glory of Him to whom I owe all my hopes, both in time and eternity. May grace be given me to adhere to this."

The grace to fulfill such a lofty life purpose was granted to Alexander Mill. He sailed for the Belgian Congo alone in 1911. It was only after his second furlough in 1918 that he was married to Ethel Starte, a nurse, and a person equally dedicated to the missionary task.

Across more than three decades this team of stalwart pioneers—Ethel a nurse and Alex an evangelist and teacher—trekked through the jungles and criss-crossed the rivers of the Central Congo. They stood together amid deprivation, disenchantment and even deep despair. In 1920 he wrote:

"Three men have died and their wives have gone back to England. So we are dreadfully understaffed, having lost six workers."

My uncle was a restless soul—both in his gait and in his "wait". Part of this restlessness grew out of living in the Presence of the One who said:

"Other sheep I have which are not of this fold. Them also I must bring. . ." (John 10:16)

He was happiest on the farthest frontier. Perhaps he was too much of an individualist. He might have been a headache on certain occasions to the mission board secretary in London. He seemed to hear the Macedonian call just when the board policy was "consolidate". As both a former missionary and now a mission board secretary, I know that the Macedonian call comes to different people at differing levels of audibility!

He was known among the Africans as "Bandombele" ("tall white man"). Uncle Alex loved Africa and all that was African with his whole being. In a eulogy given on the passing of an African pastor called Abraham, he used these words in a tribute entitled "Black Shepherd":

"I will not call him black. Black is for death.
This man is living, and God's vital breath moves in the fleeting
      change of his face.
A ready wit moves him to facile speech. Keen sympathy commands
      a kind outreach.
Beneath the black skin, blood cells, red like mine, impart a vivid
      glow to features fine
In which love, loyalty and laughter blends.
I will not call him black—he was my friend".

Alex Mill not only loved the African, but he believed in African leadership. In the early spring of 1961 I spent an Easter weekend with my uncle in London. The Republic of Congo was then less than a year old and this new nation was agonizing in the throes of civil war. Yet Uncle Alex was serene in his faith in Congolese leadership, both in the government and in the church.

Uncle Alex had an eagle's vision of the world, not a frog's view which affects some missionaries who are long isolated from the current of world affairs. Alex Mill kept in mind the broad dimensions of the mission of Christ throughout the entire world. The hymn which we sing at this service was a favorite of his because it spoke to him of the Family of God around the globe:

"We thank Thee that Thy Church, unsleeping
While earth rolls onward into light,
Through all the world her watch is keeping
And rests not now by day or night."

He had his low moments, too. He wrote these words in the early years in the Congo:

> "I'm in no mood to extoll my missionary life. . .I feel my existence circumscribed, monotonous and poor although I am in a land full of wonder and in a work large with outlet for effort."

Again in the dark days of the early 1940s, Alex wrote to my father:

> "We seem to run the risk in Africa of being the backwash of the mission's concerns. I'm a bit despondent yet I remember that the Baptist Missionary Society will soon be 150 years old. Our founder said: 'Expect great things from God; attempt great things for God'. . .and he penned those words during the period of the bitter Napoleonic wars. . ."

He would want me to lift up before the Church today the needs of modern Africa—different from his or Livingstone's Africa, but still in need of the understanding heart and the reconciling, forgiving Word. It was significant that as I received the news of Uncle Alex's death over the telephone from the cable office, we had a Tanzanian visitor at our family table, a college friend of our eldest son, David Mill Sinclair. His name was Dinish from Zanzibar, the great grandson of a Hindu trader who came to Zanzibar in 1849. So it was with a young African that we first shared the news of Uncle Alex's entry into his heavenly home.

LET US FOLLOW ALEXANDER MILL IN HIS QUEST FOR WORLD PEACE. From his early years he believed in the power of love to overcome evil. He affirmed in his gentle, mild way an absolute trust in the effective use of non-violence as an alternative to armed conflict. His commitment to peace grew out of more than humanitarian motivation. It arose from a deep faith in the power of love and right to overcome finally the forces of hate and injustice. Uncle Alex wore with conviction a "Ban the Bomb" button across Britain and the United States. He tramped long miles in peace marches. He would have been saddened by the recent disclosure of the sordid Songmy massacres in Vietnam. Yet his heart would have been set singing at the order of President Nixon to destroy material for bacteriological warfare. He believed that "there never was a good war, nor a bad peace".

Yet he was also quite pragmatic in his peace crusade. In 1941 when the United States entered World War II, he wrote my parents:

"Perhaps one advantage of the U.S. entry in the war will be that the idealism of your country will be present at the peace table".

ALEXANDER MILL WAS DEVOTED TO HIS IMMEDIATE FAMILY AND FRIENDS.

My father and Uncle Alex were close friends from boyhood days. Their correspondence across the years was mutually stimulating. He and my father would disagree at times, but listened to each other at least. When Harry Emerson Fosdick was a controversial religious figure in the United States, my father sent Uncle Alex a copy of "The Modern Use of the Bible". My uncle responded:

"I'm reading this book although I will admit naething, yet I'm willin' tae argye the pynt".

Alex Mill was generous and thoughtful of his brother, Gladstone, and his sister, Clara. During the long years of his daughter Barbara's incapacity, he was all that a father should be to his only child. He has nine nephews and nieces in Scotland and America. He has influenced each of our lives despite the thousands of miles which separated us from him. He penned carefully individual letters for us. In these letters, often illustrated with sketches from African life, he responded to each of our interests. He encouraged a niece in her poetry, another in her business skills and another in scientific pursuits. He told us about an orphaned baby monkey, a family of kittens in his bookshelves and a hen which always laid her egg in the wood bin.

His habitual generosity was gratefully received by a minister's family of six children during the depression years of the 1930s. From his meager stipend he remembered each of us. I especially remember the 10 pounds he sent me during my first year in college which tided me over several weeks to pay for my room and board.

In closing let me share two brief extracts from letters, one from Aunt Ethel and the other from an African chief. In the early 1920s Aunt Ethel wrote us after they had moved into the new house which Alex had built for his bride and baby daughter:

"Uncle Alex is so tired. I have just looked up and his eyes are shut and his head is nodding. So we had better soon go to bed. He is making the house look so nice. I like it better than any I have been in the Congo. The arches in the room are so pretty. . .I'm teaching fifty black children the hymn 'Hushed Was the Evening Hymn'. At the same time they look at the picture of the boy Samuel telling Eli that he heard him call. . ."

Alex Mill has now heard the last Heavenly Call and willingly answered, "Here am I". The eyes of both Alex and Ethel Mill now gaze on Him whom to behold is true life.

A second letter was scrawled in the Lokele dialect with a translation penned between the lines:

"O Bandombele. Listen, the chief Fatafata prays you. He wants you to come sleep in his village because of the magic lantern. He has great desire that you come."

And now another Chief—the King of Kings—has called his servant, Alexander Mill, to come and live in His Celestial village forever. "Even so. Come, Lord Jesus."

Let us pray.

"Thanks be to Thee, O God, that Thy Son, Jesus Christ our Lord, conquered death and brought life and immortality to light through the Gospel. We praise Thee for His assurance of That House with many rooms where He has prepared a place for each of us, that where He is, there we may be also.

"We bless Thee above all for our Lord's glorious resurrection from the death and for the sure hope of life with Him forever. We would therefore rejoice in the hope that the one whom we have lost on earth is now with Thee. Though we sorrow in our loss, we bless Thee for his gain, knowing that for him to be with Christ is far better. By Thy grace comfort our hearts with the assurance of his perfect safety and complete joy. Help us so to walk before Thee in faith and love, that in Thy good time, we may be joined with him and with Thee in Thy Heavenly Presence for evermore. Through Jesus Christ, our Lord. Amen."

John H. Sinclair

"THE NURSES" MEMORIAL CHAPEL in Westminster Abbey

There is a tiny chapel which scarcely seats sixteen people. In a casket in the room are the names of 3,076—men and women—who served as nurses in World War II and lost their lives.

The stained glass window depicts Mary, the baby Jesus and St. Luke, the physician. A nurse is kneeling in worship. At the bottom of the window are the different kinds of badges of the British Nurses' Service of World War II.

The "tracery" above the main panel of the window has a lovely Florence Nightingale lamp, a red crown and a crown of thorns. On the wall is a plaque with the Florence Nightingale pledge.

APPENDIX H

CONGO: LEOPOLD II AND MOBUTU

I have recently read a book by Adam Hochschild, KING LEOPOLD'S GHOST: a story of greed, terror and heroism in Colonial Africa. (1999) This book put into perspective the extended tragedy of the Congo, both in the times of Leopoldo and of Mobutu.
This book gave me insights into the following:

1. The impact that the revelations about the atrocities in the Congo certainly had on my parents and Uncle Alex in the period, 1895–1905, when they were children and young people in Scotland. The Baptist church magazines and the literature sent out by the Baptist Missionary Society were widely available to them. They drank it all in, heard missionary speakers and saw stereopticon slides of missionary work in the Congo.
2. The role of the Baptist Missionary Society had a very visible and public role in Great Britain and Europe at that time in informing the churches and society in general. They were involved deeply in the human rights struggle of the Congo Reform Association, led by Dene, Morel and Casement.
3. The tragic legacy of the Belgian colonial administration of the Congo Free State on the people of the Congo left a deep negative impression on the minds and hearts of the native population. White missionaries who arrived in the 1910s had to redeem themselves!

The legacy of Leopold II was certainly a factor in producing a Congolese dictator like Joseph Mobutu Sese Seko. The philosopher Ibn Khaldun had written in the 14th century:
"Those who are conquered always want to imitate the conqueror in their main characteristics—in his clothing, his crafts, and in all his distinctive traits and customs. . ." (p. 303)

"Mobutu's luxurious Villa de Mar on the French Riviera, complete with indoor and outdoor swimming pools, gold-fitted bathrooms and heliport, lay a dozen miles down the coast from the estate Leopold once owned at Cap Ferrat. From one cape you can see the other. . ." (p. 304) ". . .Aside from the color of his skin, there are few ways in which he did not resemble the monarch who governed the same territory a hundred years earlier. His one-man rule, his great wealth taken from the land, his naming a lake after himself—all the same. His yacht; his appropriation of state possessions as his own; his huge shareholdings in private corporations doing business in his territory. Just as Leopold, using his privately controlled state, shared most of his rubber profits with no one, so Mobuto acquired mines and rubber plantations for his own purposes. Mobutu's habit of printing money when he needed it resembled nothing as much as Leopold's printing of Congo bonds. . ." (p. 304)

Before Mobutu was overthrown, his thirty-two years in power had made him one of the richest men in the world. His personal wealth at its peak was estimated at four billion dollars.

As to the deaths he caused through murder, starvation, disease and the plummeting birth rate, the exact number is difficult to determine. No territory-wide census was taken in the Congo until long after the rubber terror was over. However the general consensus is that by 1924 the population of the Congo during the Leopold II period and its immediate aftermath had caused the population to drop by approximately ten million people. (Cf. pp. 232–233)

APPENDIX I
BIBLIOGRAPHY

I. Books, journals and pamphlets

Baptists in Scotland, Glasgow, Baptist Union of Scotland, 1991.

Baptist Historical Materials, Microfilm catalogue of, Historical Commission of Southern Baptist Convention, Nashville, 1985.

Baptist Mission Society Atlas, London, BMS, 1904.

Butterworth, Jane, *Mokili of the Congo*, the story of the Millmans by a granddaughter. Mss, Angus Library, Oxford, nd.

Carrington, John, *Talking drums of Africa*, London, Carey Kingsgate Press, 1949.

Carpenter, George W., *Highways for God in Congo,* Leopoldville, LECO Press, 1952.

Crawford, Dan, *Thinking Black*, 1912.

Crawford, John R., *Protestant Missions in Congo: 1876–1969,* Kinshasa, LECO Press, nd, p. 26.

Duffy, James, *Portuguese Africa*, Cambridge/Harvard University Press, 1959.

Forbath, Peter, *The River Congo: The discovery, exploration and exploitation of the world's most dramatic river.* Boston, Houghton Mifflin, 1977.

Fullerton, W.Y., *The Christ of the Congo River.* London, The Carey Press, 1928. With an introduction by His Majesty, Albert, the King of the Belgians. Includes a list of Congo missionaries from 1978–1928.

Guiness, Mrs. H. Gratton, *The First Christian Mission in the Congo*: *The Livingston Inland Mission, its sphere, nature, history, present position and prospects.* nd circa 1882, Harley House, Bow, London E.

Hemmens, H.L., *George Grenfell, Pioneer in Congo*, London. SCM, 1927.

Myers, J.B., *Congo for Christ: The story of the Congo Mission*, London, S.W. Partridge and Co., 1895. By a pioneer of the Swedish Missionary Alliance.

McGavran, Donald A. and Norman Riddle, *Zaire: Midday in Mission*. Valley Forge, Pa., Judson Press, 1979.

McVeigh, Malcolm J., "The Early Congo Mission", MISSIOLOGY, Vol. III, No. 4, October, 1975. pp. 501–518.

Kimbangista Movement, The

Irvine, Cecilia, *The Birth of the Kimbangista Movement in the Bas-Zaire, 1921*. In the JOURNAL OF RELIGION IN AFRICA, Vol. VI, fasc. 1, December, 1978. Published by the University of Aberdeen. A day-to-day story of the events in 1921.

Hochschild, Adam., *King Leopold's Ghost*, Houghton Mifflin, Boston, 1998.

The National Geographic, Sept. 2013, Article on "Kinshasa, the Chaotic Capital"

Neil, Stephen, "The Belgians in Africa" in *Colonialism in Christian Mission*, New York, McGraw-Hill, 1966. pp. 359–385.

Pakenham, Thomas, *The Scramble for Africa*, New York, Random House, 1991.

Slade, Ruth M., *English-speaking Mission in the Congo Independent State, 1878–1908*. Academie Royale de Sciences coloniales. Rue de Livourne, 80 A, Bruxelles, 1959. Ph.D. thesis, London. p. 432.

Slade, Ruth M., *The Belgian Congo,* second ed. London, Oxford University Press, 1961.

Smith, H. Sutton, *Yakusu: The very heart of Africa*, London/Edinburgh, Marshall Brothers, c. 1912.

Wilson, C.E. et. al., *After Forty Years: A missionary embassy to Congo, May–November, 1919*. London, BMS, nd.

Vansima, Jan, *Paths through the Rainforest*, Department of History, University of Wisconsin, Madison. 1990.

II. Correspondence (*)

Letters from A.G. Mill and Ethel C. Mill to John P. Sinclair, Clara A. Sinclair and John H. Sinclair from 1907–1969. Letters of A.G. Mill to Ethel C. Starte, 1914–1918. Letters of Barbara M. Mill to her parents,

1930–36. Letters of A.G. Mill and Ethel C. Mill to her Sinclair nieces and nephew, 1920–1936.

Selected letters from African colleagues to A.G. Mill, 1912–1960.

Selected letters from John F. Carrington to John H. Sinclair and A.G. Mill, 1960–1975.

Selected letters of the Baptist Missionary Society and related missionaries in the former Belgian Congo, 1882–1946. Angus Library, Oxford.

Selected letters from former colleagues of the Mills in retirement in England to John H. Sinclair, 1990–92.

(*) This correspondence now in the possession of John H. Sinclair will eventually be deposited with the Angus Library, Regent's Park College, Oxford.

III. Interviews

John H. Sinclair with the Frederick Drakes and Nora Carrington, colleagues of the Mills. June, 1991.

John H. Sinclair with Robin and Muriel Starte, Michael Nurse, Geoffrey Smart, Esq., and other members of St. Andrew's Street Baptist Church, Cambridge. June, 1991.

John H. Sinclair with Nancy Hunt, graduate researcher on Baptist medical services in Zaire. Oxford, May, 1991.

John H. Sinclair with his sisters: Grace Robertson, Mona Knapp, Martha Koenigsdorf, Clara Sinclair and Edith Downing. 1991–92.

IV. Magazines and pamphets

YAKUSU NOTES, 1911–1946.

THE MISSIONARY HERALD, 1911–1946.

THE BAPTIST

V. Other documents

Missionary application papers of A.G. Mill to the Baptist Missionary Society, 1910. Angus Library, Oxford. UK.

Personal daybooks and records of A.G. Mill, 1946–1969.

APPENDIX J
YALIKINA
(1930s)
By A. G. Mill

This is the statistics number, but I never remembered any statistics I ever heard except when once Dr. Pearce Gould likened the B.M.S. to a boy who had 6d to spend and had so many things he wanted to buy with it.

The *Statistics for Yalikina Sub-Station have* nothing to *compare with in your mind except perhaps the size of Wales.*

The number of things which are not there are remarkable!

No. of Libraries		0
" " Almshouses		0
" " Orphanages		0
" " Welfare centres		0
" " Govt. Medical men		1
" " Commercial Medical men		1
" " Dispensaries		4
" " Witch doctors		Legion

This is all the philanthropic work which is going on *apart from the B.M.S.*

From Yalikina Sub-Station we have re-explored all the riverine work on the Lomami as far as Opala, all the forest district on the left bank of the Lomami and both banks of the main river below Isangi.

This meant five journeys of from two to eight weeks duration and all the work which Mr. Parris had so splendidly kept together was a considerable encouragement to us. But we could not fail to be conscious of a considerable falling off of the interest of the chiefs and headmen. This is due partly to the way in which commercial enterprise has captured the labour market of even the far interior and so stirred up the cupidity of the black heart for trade goods which don't include Bibles and Hymnbooks.

The influence too of some unsympathetic and cynical Government officials has discouraged many of our native workers.

Nevertheless, mud and thatch school-chapels are still the Town Halls of many a hamlet and many black children are learning their letters on their log seats.

The two villages of Yanjali and Yalosambo have each accomplished this year a brick school-chapel of which they are justly proud. 250 bush schools are functioning which represents about 7,500 school-children, each with knowledge of the facts of religious belief from the Catechism and at some stage of reading. *About 750 of them are doing a little writing and Arithmetic. This year alone 562 passed from the Primer to a reader.*

These are not the only adherents we have in the district. There are lots of old boys who are now working for traders and some for the Government, even although they have lost touch with the work they are still friendly to us.

The native Church although it numbers 846 and is very scattered has backslidden greatly. On the visit of a Missionary some wear their better clothes and come to a service but in his absence they neglect to feed their spiritual life on the Word and are overborne by the common cares of life. It must however be admitted that the faithful little group of church members who act as Teachers on a meager honorarium, are an ornament to their calling and the salt of the native Church.

These are all the Statistics, but we don't know. (Shall we ever know?)

How many children grow up in a world of darkness and fear?
How many dying heads writhe in fear into the grave?
How many victims of cruel beliefs suffer through life?

We don't know because they are in the unoccupied territory next to us on the Upper Lomami.

THROUGH A GLASS DARKLY

Thinking back is going on all the time but people do not show their thoughts every day. Today was a wet Sunday and as there was no service I had the Royal Scroll of pictures out for the house boys to look at.

At the same time up came a crowd of raw natives from the forest.

There was the chief with his necklace of leopard teeth, and his headmen, one wearing a monkey skin cap, and I had a fine opportunity of engaging them in conversation as I explained the pictures.

On Hoffman's picture of Christ preaching by the lake there are some children paddling at the water's edge and the chief remarked "See there are Christ's children". I corrected and explained.

The next interruption was from one of the headmen who asked "What is this thing called Death?" The question was asked with sad anxiety. I told him of the comforting picture of a child asleep in his father's arms and told them that if they would trust His arms in life, they would not fear death. "And in Europe if one of your friends dies do you not wail?" Yes, I said, if our child should die I should cry but second thoughts would bring the joy of reunion afterwards in the world above.

Then the talk drifted on to the common idea that the spirit and body go together into the underworld and one asked *"Who is the stronger, the power in the grave or the power in heaven? I answered by another question, Which is the more valuable, the oil of the palm not or the waste-fibre?*

When we came to the picture of the death of Christ they said simply: "What a pity."

Then, they asked *"In which country on earth did these things happen?"* And when they heard that it was near Europe they asked *"Does the sky sink down and join on to the Earth away there?"* I answered "No man hath ascended into Heaven save He who came down from Heaven even the Son of Man who is in Heaven," and I told them of the Revelation of John which he had of Jesus Christ.

They gave the conversation a solemn turn when one asked *"What does God do when a man who has done wrong goes before Him?"* I had no difficulty in answering that He would by no means clear the guilty but also added that the long-suffering of God is salvation.

Then they pointed to the pictures themselves and asked *How are these things made? Is it spirits who make them?*

I then had to explain painting and brushes which I likened to little bundles of monkey's fur.

As the *conversation flagged the chief drew out a franc* and *asked to buy a writing book. I declined as it was Sunday.* But, objected one mildly, is not Sunday a day, how is it different from a day? In no way I said, except that we make it different by obeying God's command to remember in it Him who has made all other days.

As they had it on their minds they asked about the Devil. Are he and God equally powerful? Are they allied? I told them there was not much difference between the Devil and themselves. That his reign was conditional on their supporting him but that he had been deposed by God.

Then as time had passed they said they were going.

As I remembered that these very natives had been visited by us annually for ten years and had heard the Gospel story by Lantern and Preaching and that some have left off certain evil practices although they have not joined the Church; I thought again of the meaning of the words "Now we see through a glass darkly".

And Paul said "We." *Had I firmly believed everything I had myself said?* I thought again and could not think of any other I could have said, but the words of Jesus. *I am glad I am a Preacher and not an originator.* I am glad that I can see even though darkly into the great mysteries of the beyond, through Christ, since there are so many who have not yet even looked to see "The light of the knowledge of the glory of God in the face of Jesus Christ."

A. G. MILL

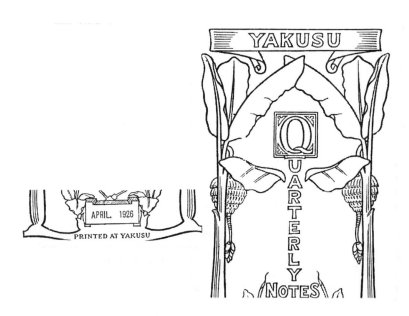

A CONGO OUTPOST
By A. G. MILL, Irema, Congo

Irema is a sub-station in the wide Yakusu area which is situated on the Lomami river, a tributary of the Congo. Mr. and Mrs. Mill make it the centre of their work, which is described in this article.

We returned here about a year ago after furlough. It was with some difficulty that we got our possessions past the rapids. Now we are comfortably installed in our own house around which flowers brought from Yakusu bloom. The sick were brought to us on the morning after our arrival, and since then medicines have been distributed to large numbers of people and every morning the Gospel has been preached to those who come. We have now nearly completed the dispensary building.

We have had many gatherings for worship and prayer in the mud hall, which the native pastor built before we arrived. Best of all, this simple building, with an earth floor and fitted with rude benches, has served for *two conferences—refresher courses for study, fellowship and training for the one hundred and forty native teacher-evangelists whom we have in the Irema area.* For a month at a time, living together and on the simplest fare, they have had classes daily from 5 a.m. to 5 p.m. They have also worked on the plantation and have attended a practice school. The first of these courses was for *seventy Bambole teachers in the Lingala language*, and *the second was for a similar number of men speaking the Lokele language.* As a result these men are thus better fitted to lead forward their scholars and inquirers in the villages in the knowledge and love of God.

(From *THE MISSIONARY HERALD*, 1940)

I owe a great debt to my native superintendents and the pastor. I often have merely to stand by and let them bear their own testimony which so well suits their native brethren. They are with me in these refresher courses, and each has his own class in the different subjects. The pastor—who is the equivalent of a General Superintendent at home—has often surprised me with his earnest and apt injunctions or corrections. They are out in the district for the rest of the time visiting the village teachers in their own villages and gathering the monthly collections.

We have not gathered many in by baptism, but had ten baptized during the first conference and forty-six during a month's journey which we took in the Esoo forest area. *There are about five hundred inquirers in the district.* Here at the centre we hold a school daily for *twenty self-supporting boarders*, in addition to a school for women.

Calls come persistently from the untouched parts of the Bambole tribe which adjoin us, and which we dare not visit lest we involve the Society in additional work and expense. The Boyela tribe on the west of this area is receiving instruction in its border villages. Here or at home our work is still directed by our invisible Head towards the consummation of His appearing and His Kingdom.

FROM THE NATIVE CHURCH MAGAZINE.

A NATIVE MEDICINE MAN AND A FISHERMAN

Medicine:	O Fisherman I have a charm which will bring fish to your net without fail. If you have a net which does not catch fish buy this charm and your net will speedily enrich you.
Fisherman:	Eh! Mr. Medicine-man this is good news. Where did you get this charm from? Has it the power of God?
M.	No! It is a twig from a rare tree. I had it from the spirit of my grandfather who died long ago. He appeared to me one day in the forest and gave me this sacred twig. It has nothing to do with God.
F.	But, Kanga, who made the tree from which the twig was plucked? Was it not God?
M.	Don't talk that stuff to me. Trees grow of themselves.
F.	The same to you Kanga. But things do not come up from the ground without someone being responsible and knowing all about it.
M.	Not so fast, my son. Do not the birds carry fruits away, and leave the seeds in other places; and do not these grow up into trees?
F.	True, O Kanga That certainly is no lie. And who planted the tree from which the bird took the seed?
M.	It came from a seed left by a previous bird, of course.
F.	And who planted the tree that gave the first bird a seed when as yet no other tree had borne fruit that had been eaten by any bird?
M.	Seeing you are so clever, Fisherman, perhaps; you can answer that question yourself.
F.	Well, is not God the Lord and maker of all things?
M.	Perhaps! But what do you say about buying the charm?
F.	Your charm is just a worthless twig. See, I am a grown man. Well, if I had not eaten food I should have died long age. I did not get this food by a charm but by the help of God, the God of life who made the food grow.
M.	What, about it?
F.	Why what the proverb says. A man who gets his living by catching fish in a net will not forsake the use of floats and weights. And I am not going to forsake Him who has hitherto given me my food.

Joseph Baelongandi

Her Majesty Queen Astrid of Belgium

Queen Astrid—then Princess—in the Congo at Yalikina, 1933

IMPRESSIONS OF NICHOLAS NOTEWELL
GEORGE GRENFELL

When George Grenfell died at Basoko two years ago, the Belgian doctor who had attended him during the last days of his suffering bowed his head and said with emotion, "It is vast trouble when a great man dies like this." There were probably few, even among his friends, at that time, who realised how great was the man who had entered into the rest for which in his weariness he often longed. Grenfell's magnitude was veiled by his modesty, and one is moved to regret that in his lifetime the greatness of his services to science, to humanity, and to the Kingdom of God were not more adequately recognised. Happily, he never coveted fame or applause, and probably never dreamed of himself as great. It was his passion to fill his life's day with faithful work, work for God, work done in obedience to the will of God. Often the bit of work that occupied him was not the work he would have chosen; but as soon as it was clear to him that God required the task at his hands, he gave himself to it with no sentimental lagging and no vain regrets. At the time of Grenfell's death Dr. Keltie, Secretary of the Royal Geographical Society, in eulogising his work, remarked that Grenfell might have written a score of books and made a fortune. This striking statement is according to fact. He might have done. Two-and-twenty years ago Messrs. Hodder and Stoughton showed their prescience by requesting him to write a book upon his travels, which they would be prepared to publish upon generous terms. The suggestion pleased him, and was entertained for the hour, but stress of mission business, much of it laborious drudgery, however, upon which the continuity of the campaign and the health and life of his colleagues depended, occupied his time, and the book was never written.

Regret is mitigated by the issue of Sir Harry Johnston's monumental volumes on "George Grenfell and the Congo," in which he secures the explorer's fame and augments his own. This noble work was skillfully and sympathetically reviewed in the leading article of THE BAPTIST TIMES last week, and it is due to the editor and myself to say that it is only by his express request that these supplementary paragraphs are written.

As Baptists, we may well rejoice that a man of Sir Harry Johnston's distinction, experience, learning and literary skill has undertaken, with enthusiasm, to write such an appreciation of our mission work upon the Congo. Here is a witness, the adequacy of whose knowledge cannot be impugned, and who is beyond suspicion of party bias. Travelers of sorts have been accustomed to sniff at evangelical missions to the heathen, and have sometimes hinted that missionaries were for the most part feeble and fanatical folk, spending large money in futile interference with heathen customs and beliefs, money which might be more profitably employed in practical patriotic or humanitarian interests. Sir Harry Johnston's authoritative review of the gains to science and civilisation, accruing from the work of our missionaries on the Congo, will go far to silence such ignorant and libellous criticism.

One of Sir Harry Johnston's reviewers complains that he has marred the homogeneity of his work by his somewhat elaborate history of our earlier African missions at Fernando Po and the Cameroons. But as Grenfell and Comber were both at the Cameroons, and did notable work there, involving singular preparation for their wider labours on the Congo, the criticism seems scarcely fair. In any case students of missions, and Baptists in particular, will be grateful for these luminous and informing chapters. The following extract from Winwood Reade, quoted by Sir Harry Johnston, will be read with special interest:

"I do not at all understand how the changes at the Cameroons and Victoria have been brought about. Old sanguinary customs have to a large extent been abolished; witchcraft hides itself in the forest; the fetish superstition of the people is derided by old and young, and well-built houses are springing up on every hand. It is really marvellous to mark the change that has taken place in the natives in a few years only. From actual cannibals, many have become honest, intelligent, well-skilled artisans. An elementary literature has been established, and the whole Bible translated into their own tongue, hitherto an unwritten one. There must be, surely, something abnormal about this."

There was something abnormal, and the explanation dates back to the giving of the Holy Spirit on the day of Pentecost. As Alfred Baker was the father, in missionary enterprise, of Grenfell and Comber, the pioneers of the Congo Mission, it seems fitting that a generous account of him and his work should find place in "George Grenfell and the Congo."

I fear the suggestion made in THE BAPTIST TIMES last week, that the story of Grenfell's pioneering work should be told in another column, may have had reference to this column. But in the space at my disposal it would be possible to do more in the way of telling that story than to repeat the brief statement already made. While waiting the arrival of an engineer at Stanley Pool to superintend the reconstruction of the *Peace,* Grenfell made a prospecting voyage to the Equator in a whaleboat 26 ft. long, and observed some hundreds of miles of the great Upper River upon which his life's work was to be done. The account of that journey, together with the narrative of the first three voyages of the *Peace,* would fill a modest-sized volume. Condensation into a paragraph exceeds the possible, and the reader must be referred to Sir Harry Johnston's "condensation," which occupies two or three chapters of vivid interest. In these voyages Grenfell had often to record kindliest receptions, but there were many hours of peril—peril of the river and of storms, and peril of ignorant human enmity, when poisoned arrows were flying, and war canoes threatening the little steamer and her crew.

The hideous cruelties and abominations of savage heathenism were well in evidence. "The people on both banks of the Juapa were cannibals. On the 15th of September, 1885, Grenfell came upon a group who were just about to kill a man and eat him. He tried, without success, to redeem him for a cash payment. In another place they offered him a fine-looking woman as a wife in exchange for a plump boatman whom they wanted to eat! Yet there are plenty of oil-palms up the Juapa, also sugar-cane and cassava." In yet another place Grenfell came upon a chief's son who was so appreciative of human flesh that he would "like to eat everybody on earth." Sir Harry Johnston's calm and judicial review of the history of the Congo Free State will be of peculiar value in the present political exigency, and the scientific chapters of his second volume, packed with information, lucidly and most readably arranged, will be of lasting interest and importance. It is a great book, and a not unworthy memorial of one whom *The Times* reviewer characterises as "an Englishman of almost incredible industry, of unblemished reputation, and of imperishable fame."

HELD UP!
REFLECTIONS OF A MISSIONARY

Locked away in the primeval forest of Congo the missionary looked after a retreating file of figures as they disappeared on the path into the forest. *"Who are these people?"* he asked his native Christian helper. *"They are of another tribe which inhabits the regions beyond."* "A big tribe?" "Very big but very wild." "Have they ever heard the Gospel?" "No, but some of the villages which border on this tribe would gladly welcome you if you would go to them. They have asked for the teaching."

The missionary looked at his provision boxes. They were nearly empty. He thought of his weary carriers, and remembered that he had a fortnight's journey to get back to his base at Yalikina. *His heart went out to these lost sheep, but he had trouble enough with the 220 village schools already under his supervision*, and he was now on the fringe of his district. It seemed impossible.

He thought of the will of God in this case, he thought of the recompense of the reward, but he was "held up."

II

The missionary and his colleagues sat with paper blocks on their knees and plans in their minds around the table in the home of the senior missionary.

There were plans for the Station School and its filling of the empty vessel of the African's mind.

There were plans for the Girls' School and the creation of the future African mother and home.

There were wrestlings of mind to condense and harness the springtide enthusiasms of African Church life into fruit-bearing usefulness, and to create for them a Native Pastorate when the autumn harvest of souls shall have come.

Medical work, too, was represented.

There were glances out of the window which passed into space as the plans were made for our journeys of preaching and teaching and healing.

The missionary of the Lomami told how he had been held up. . . . We prayed, and thought we had found a way. We were on the point of deciding it when a typewritten paper was brought to our notice. The Field Secretary had received it from the B.M.S. Committee:

> *CONGO GRANT FOR THE YEAR IS £5,200.*
> *N.B.—A Reduction of £200 on last year.*
> And the Field Committee was "held up."

III

The members of the B.M.S. Committee were in the library of the Mission House in London. Letters of appeal and the voices of visiting missionaries brought before them the teeming millions of Asia, distracted by false teaching, and the millions of Africa, dark and untaught. They represented people in the Baptist Churches whose hearts and voices throbbed with the desire to spend and be spent that the Gospel might be shared. But—

"We have neither the men nor the money to answer the appeal of the man from the Lomami and the other urgent pleas." "Held up" again!

IV

Yes, but let us know the strength of the bars of our cage. Six men are required for the Congo field alone. Last year only one recruit went out from a Denominational College in England.

But are there not men, ministers in successful churches at home, unattached young men in the teaching profession, groupers who hear the voice of God in the silence clearly and want to know where they might serve? Perhaps! It has happened before.

But even if we had the men, could we send them, and support them when we had sent them? Is not the denomination overburdened and overtaxed?

Not so. What does the sending out of these men involve? First, that every church contributing keeps up its present contribution, and, second, that every member who does not yet give shall give at least two pence per week, or ten shillings per year.

No sane person can say that the Baptist Church does not hold the key to this "hold-up." *What if the key should be in your pocket?* God touch our pockets since they lie so near our hearts!

A. G. M.

MISSIONARY HERALD, 1934

THE STRUGGLE FOR RIGHT LIVING
MRS MILL

Abraham and his wife finished their trip in the forest and joined us at Loya. They now live in the canoe by the side of the *Grenfell*. Malia has been most useful. She preaches either in Lokele or in Bangala to the women in every village, and I call up her little daughter Balabala to show that little children can learn to read. Yesterday we stayed for a few hours at a Company's place. Mr Mill and Abraham had a good crowd of workmen and I went off to find their wives. Malia spoke to them from the picture of the Woman of Samaria.

The women gazed at her in astonishment as she read out the hymns. I am sure God gave her the idea and wish to come. Several women came afterwards to buy primers for their children.

The *steamer crew* have been a great help in the Sunday services. Last Sunday in one village they got a small native drum and an empty flour tin and some iron bars and forming a band went round the town and brought the whole population to the service. They played for every hymn.

To see the people come running after that band made one think of the Pied Piper of Hamlin.

One day I received an urgent call to help a white woman who was expecting her baby. Her husband was an agent of the Lomami Company. While waiting for the new arrival I used to attend the services at the B.M.S. village school on Sundays and the prayer meetings there on Tuesdays. On other weekdays I used to take a walk in the same direction and have a little time with the children in the school just before evening came on.

One morning the teacher called on me and said that nearly every body in the village had been at a Kwaya dance. As soon as I could I went to the village and visited each square making my protest against the disgracefulness of these indecent dances.

They all averred that they would not do such a thing and I said "No, it must have been the trees, not you."

There are two chiefs. One said he never allowed the dances mentioned and the other said it should never occur again. But the teacher had given me the names of some he had seen there and these I visited at their homes. Some of them were Church Members and I sent their names to Mr Mill for Church discipline. If after six months they will stand up before the Church and say they are sorry and that it shall not happen again they will be received back again.

The following Sunday Mr. Mill made a journey of twenty miles to get here. He started early on his bicycle, crossed the river by canoe, cycled another eight miles and arrived at mid-day having assisted at two Church services.

Five minutes after dinner an old boy of ours, now working for the Company, told us that the immoral dancing was actually going on not two hundred yards from where we were, in the quarters of the Company's workmen.

They had put a man to watch the path approaching and as soon as we were sighted a signal was given and the dancers dispersed leaving only a few spectators seated around.

These admitted that others has been dancing indecent dances and when we asked them why they had not tried to stop them they simply shrugged their shoulders as if to say "Am I my brother's keeper." They had evidently found pleasure in the disgusting spectacle.

Soon afterwards we met an Administrator from a territory farther up river. He was travelling to consult a Doctor dispensary. Luta said, "We want them, to be trained and be happy and not spoiled by the influences of the village. We know you will take care of them and train them". These little grand-children of the Boarding-school have a fine start in life and many are the high hopes which we, with their parents, have for them both.

Lofonga is another motherless bairn, brought up by Mr. and Mrs. Mill at Yalikina until their furlough when she joined us. Love and care have done much for her and she is now a very happy little member of this group. She was delighted to be able to read to Mr. and Mrs. Mill recently and shows promise of being bright but she does find it hard to be neat and tidy! She, like Luta, has pluck and grit won from the very squalid nature of the family background and both have the makings of fine Little Folk.

Lituka and Lisungi, both about eight years old are slight and fairylike; dainty in all they do and gentle and kind. They are two charming Little Folk willing to help with their smaller sisters or indeed, in any way. Lituka was sent here with her sister Miriama by their father who is a church overseer and often far away from their own village. He wanted to be sure they were trained and could go to school.

Lisungi is the child of "Salt" and has always lived at Yakusu, but when her mother died and "Salt" went with Mr. Young to Yalikina, she came to live in the Boarding-school. Her father is noted for his gratitude a pleasant manner and she has the same charming manner and is such a willing little girl. She, with Lituka, also has that Christian background which just makes all the difference in the world.

I could write so much about the many fascinating, childish things they say and do, I could tell you of anxious moments, days and nights where they have had their share of the whooping-cough, measles and mumps epidemics.

School has been closed and it has been an anxious and sad time, but we have now started again. As I look at these Little Folk with their bright eyes and shining white teeth I think, "Must you grow up? I would much rather keep you as you are, free, happy and unspoiled, with your simple trust in your Friend Jesus, Who hears your lisping prayers and takes care of you. But we must let you go on, loving you more and more every day, laughing with you, often fearing for you as we do for your older sisters, but always working, hoping and praying for you. May God bless you! You are very precious to Him and to us".

Note:

One of the few published articles by my aunt (Mrs. Mill). Aunt Ethel wrote little and was much more of "a doer" than a speaker or writer. This article reveals her deep affection for the children of the Congo.

JHS

The Lokele World

The Lokele world is a section of river seventy-five miles long, called by them "liyande," called by us the Congo. It is unusual to find a Lokele who has travelled twenty-five miles inland from the river on the north or south bank, or beyond Stanley Falls on the east or Basoko on the west. We have frequently taken our boys to places in the immediate neighbourhood that they had never visited before. On my first journey to Chopa Falls, Lindi River, I was surprised to find that several of my Lokele boys had never seen them.

In the unrecorded past there was a split in the tribe which accounts for a slight variation in dialect today, and for the division of districts. The Yawembe district centring in Isangi at the embouchure of the Lomami tributary, and reaching almost to Yalemba, is the most western. It has some thirteen villages, with a minimum population of 10,000. The Yaokanja district is next in importance, stretching from the Lomami to the Ile Bertha with its sixteen villages and a minimum population of 13,000; and then there is the "liyande likolo" (upper reach of the river) which includes the three parts of Yakusu and the broken village of Yatumbu, in all perhaps 2,500 souls.

Until the white man's road was made, the only means of communication between village and village was by canoe, and the river is still the favoured route of the natives. The Lokele have finely-formed, muscular legs, but they are not good walkers. An English boy could soon tire the most stalwart Lokele on the road.

Yakusu

Put him in his canoe, however, with his loved paddle, and he will astonish you with his feats of endurance. So the highway for long years has been the river, and will be yet while there are trees to be carved out for canoes.

This little world of riverine villages is a world without a history. Stanley was the first man to write of it, and the first white man the Lokele saw. Now and then we come across an old native who remembers seeing him.

After Mr. Stanley had negotiated the fifty-six miles of broken water, which constitute the Stanley Falls, he had a most trying and difficult passage for 150 miles. Multitudes of the people flocked down to the beach as he passed, and each mile of the journey his party were in constant jeopardy of their lives from the excited savages, who paddled out in their huge canoes to obstruct their passage with menace of spear and arrow. It was a marvel that they escaped. The tribes were undoubtedly numerous, active and hostile. This was in the year 1877.

Six years later Mr. Stanley passed up river again on the journey which resulted in the founding of the Congo Free State, and the assumption of authority over it by King Leopold II of the Belgians. I give the words of Mr. Stanley descriptive of the condition in which he found this same district after passing the mouth of the Aruwimi: "The next morning we continued our journey. Two hours later we saw a break in the solid wall of forest trees along which we had travelled, and I remembered its position very clearly. On my old map it is marked Mawembi, and was strongly palisaded; but now, though I looked closely through my glass, I could detect no sign of palisade or hut. The clearing was there, it was true, the site of the palisaded village was also there, and, notwithstanding its emptiness, it was recognised. As we advanced we could see poor remnants of banana groves, we could also trace the whitened paths from the water's edge leading up the steep bank, but not a house nor a living thing could be seen. When we came abreast of the locality we perceived that there had been a late fire. The heat had scorched the foliage of the tallest trees, and their silver stems had been browned by it. The banana plants looked meagre, their ragged fronds waved mournfully their tatters as if imploring pity. We slackened the speed to contemplate the scene.

"Six years before we had rushed by this very place without stopping, endeavouring by our haste to thwart the intentions of our foes, since which time the history of this land had been a blank to us. Surely there had been a great change. As we moved up the stream slowly another singular sight attracted our gaze. This was two or three long canoes standing on their ends like split hollow columns, upright on the verge of the bank. What freak was this, and what did the sight signify? Each canoe must have weighed at least a ton. This could not have been done by a herd of chattering savages. As they stand they are a tacit revelation of the effect of energy and cohesion. They are Arabs who have done this."

Later he came upon the Arab camp and described its gruesome details: "Line upon line of dark nakedness, relieved here and there by the white dresses of their captors. Rows or groups of naked forms, upright, standing or moving about listlessly, naked bodies stretched under the sheds in all positions; naked legs innumerable are seen in the perspective of prostrate sleepers; there are countless naked children, many mere infants. Mostly all are fettered."

"I walked about," continues Mr. Stanley, "as in a kind of dream, wherein I saw through the darkness of the night the stealthy forms of the murderers creeping towards the doomed town, its inmates all asleep, and no sounds issuing from the gloom but the drowsy hum of chirping insects or distant frogs, when suddenly flash the light of brandished torches, the sleeping town is involved in flames, while volleys of musketry lay low the frightened and astonished people, sending many through a short minute of agony to their soundless sleep. I wished to be alone somewhere where I could reflect upon the doom that has overtaken Bandu, Yomburri, Yangambi, Yaporo, Yakusu, Ukanga, Yangonde, Ituka, Yaryembe, Yaloche, populous Isanghi and probably thirty score of other villages and towns."

The state of things was, happily, not so bad as Mr. Stanley had imagined. The Arabs had not had time to do their worst in that district; and as but a few months elapsed before their power was forever broken, the natives came out of their hiding-places and rapidly reformed their towns and villages. Had he visited it again ten years later, Mr. Stanley would hardly have recognised it, so populous had it once more become.

The point must remain in doubt as to whether there was ever one chief over all the Lokele. It seems extremely probable that the paramount authority was in the hands of one family perhaps not more than a century and a half ago. As a people they are exceedingly clannish, and in our thirteen years' experience of them we have not known a serious fight between two Lokele villages. Jealousies there are, of course; and these have led to splits. Various forces have been at work breaking up the village chief's authority and alienating his people from him. But this disintegrating process has been going on longer than the presence of the white man in his district. It is the Arab, I think, who is primarily responsible for beginning it. It is certainly true that the corporate life of the tribe has not gained by this waning authority of her chiefs. The villages where the chief's voice is still a power contain young people who are much more amenable to discipline than the average Lokele.

There is no other section of the river that has so successfully withstood the effect of the many changes that the advent of the white man has introduced as the Lokele world has done. Today the tribal influence is almost as strong as ever over seventy-five miles of river. Native industries are maintained almost as they were thirty years ago before the blue flag with its yellow star was seen. Most fortunate of all the wide districts of the Congo basin, it has hitherto escaped the scourge of sleeping sickness, and probably the official census would show little, if any, diminution of the population during the last decade. But there are signs that this will not long remain the case unless very strict measures of segregation are enforced.

The freely-moving, freedom-loving Lokele have regarded with very little pleasure the assumption of supreme authority by the white man; but he soon learned that he had no need to fear it as he feared the Arab. He stood in awe, and had the wisdom to make obeisance. That act secured him his continued freedom amid the conditions he loved so well, and he has not known trouble so long as he has paid his taxes in fish or iron (the currency of the district) to the central authority. While not well-off, he has generally found the Government demands not above his means to pay. In any case, whatever taxes he had to pay he knew that he was a hundred times better off than under the Arab.

A Lokele village is self-contained. Each man is a member of a little community called a "bokulu" or square; there will be from eight to fifteen or more squares in a village. Each "bokulu" has its headman, who maintains order in the square, arranges the work of the members, and settles the disputes, except such as are of more general importance, when the chief's presence is requested, or the matter comes up before a gathering of the general council of headmen that meets from time to time with the chief. Perchance the parties are too cantankerous for the chief to manage them, or the matter in dispute is too involved for them to come to a conclusion, and they then seek some outside authority, as that of the nearest white man.

Each square has its name, and when the missionary knows these he can describe exactly the part of the village he wishes to send to. Or if he knows the name of the headman of the square, it answers the same purpose as knowing the name of the street to which you wish to post a letter.

The chief's square is the centre of the village, the "liso lia bokenge"— "the eye of the town," and usually contains the neatest huts, the most cleanly exteriors, and the largest "ngwaka," or council-house. But the ngwaka is oftenest built on the cliff front, and the chief's drum placed on a platform at one end of it. This building is of the simplest construction, being like a long, low shed, with open ends. Purposely built in this fashion, and placed parallel with the river, the deep notes of the drum are carried far over the water in both directions. The range of communication possible with such a drum can be scarcely less than ten miles, for villages at four and five miles distance east and west easily catch and interpret the notes in the dead of night. Its range in the daytime is obviously more restricted owing to the persistent hum of village life.

By it the chief communicates his wishes, calls a town council, or announces a market. With it he vents his wrath in a harmless way on a neighbouring village that has given him cause for offence. Cursing is liberally indulged in at such times, and while it may appear harmless enough, its aftermath of bitterness and open hostility make it a dangerous weapon. It is a wireless telephone which can only be operated by a few. The chief and his near relatives hold this privilege almost exclusively. Those who can interpret the drum are a much larger number.

Late in the evening, when the meal and the fireside talk are over, and the smouldering sticks have been gathered up and taken into the hut; when the little children are asleep, and the murmur of their elders' voices is dying down, a voice startles the night air. Distinctly every word comes to the ears of the listening villagers, and the drowsy ones rouse themselves, as the chief or one of his headmen imparts some news or tells his wishes in regard to some event of the day. Sometimes the chief will leave his bamboo couch in the very dim light of earliest morning, and, standing in the town, raise his voice to awaken the sleepers and make known to them his intentions for the day. Something of importance is to take place when this happens. I shall never forget lying in my tent one morning in one of the largest Lokele villages and hearing my name again and again repeated by the chief in a long harangue.

There are many drums in a village. Several of the headmen will have one of their own. They almost venerate them, and would as soon think of parting with them as of selling their hut. The village drum would never be put on the market for sale; it is a village institution.

To communicate with the forest villages a smaller drum of a much shriller *timbre* is used. This can, as a rule, be well heard over two or three miles of intervening bush.

In the Lokele institutions there is all the organisation necessary for good government, for the exercise of justice, and for the freedom and happiness of the individual, if the moral integrity of the people could be assumed as even partially existing. That is the weak spot. On the whole, the verdicts of the chief may be said to be impartial when his own interests are not at stake.

The Lokele world has wider boundaries than we may have thought from the above descriptions. There are four tribes on its borders, with whom the Lokele live on most intimate terms, encouraged by daily commercial and domestic relations. A description of the interesting peoples who are privileged to be on intermarrying terms with the Lokele must be reserved for another page. Let it suffice here to say that the south bank Lokele villages have frequent intercourse with the very numerous Tovoke, or Foma, people of the bush villages, running parallel with the river, and at only short distances from its banks; the Ba-Olumbu bush people of the north bank are likewise in constant touch with their nearest Lokele neighbours; at Stanley Falls exist 3,000 Ba-Genya folk, who also have been looked upon and chosen by the Lokele as close friends; lastly, and least, the Lindi tribe of Bamanga people have sometimes intermarried, but more often squabbled, with Lokele traders. However, their ingenuity at wood-carving is seen in every Lokele village in the shape of drums, canoes, wood-salvers, spoons, stools, water-scoops, etc. The language of each of these tribes is distinct, but among the two most numerous the Lokele language is well understood.

Into this world of five tribes a semi-nomadic race of people has entered who have scarcely any points in common with any one of their neighbours. Wild and wiry, the Bakumu are great hunters and agriculturists. With the same cool daring they attack the elephant's swaying mass with spears and poisoned arrows, or two pigmy-sized men will look up the towering hundred feet of a giant tree, and with their tiny axes lay it level with the ground in a few hours. Such forest levellers are they that they supply the world with plantain from their extensive plantations. But intercourse with them is purely commercial. The Lokele is shy of their wildness their medicine, their fierce moods and treacherous ways. Their code of morals is looser than that of any of their neighbours; their dances more frequently obscene.

Into this Lokele world the Arab came to stay, not as the ruthless destroyer he intended to be, but as a peaceful cultivator and unrivalled trader. The power that changed his purpose is firmly established at Stanley Falls, at Romée, twenty miles down river, at Yanongi, at Isangi, and at Basoko. Every Lokele knows these, and many other places, too, as the towns of Bula Matale.

The Arabs and their miscellaneous following of domestic slaves, gathered from many tribes in past raids, congregate round Romée and the Falls. Rice, tobacco and vegetables are raised in great quantities, while the ever-increasing demand for ducks, fowls, eggs, sheep, and goats is probably better supplied round Stanley Falls than anywhere else between that place and Matadi. A moderate estimate of the number of the Arabs is, I believe, that there are 10,000 at Romée and 3,000 at Stanley Falls.

Protestant missions are represented solely by the Yakusu staff of the Baptist Missionary Society.

The Roman Catholic Church is represented by "La Mission du Sacre Cœur de Jesus" with their headquarters at Ste. Gabrielle, about three miles west of the Falls, and more recently at the Falls itself. At the latter place a large cathedral has been built and recently dedicated. This mission has several outposts throughout the district. Under the devoted and able direction of Msgr. G. Grisson it has made remarkable progress. Amongst the Lokele the Catholics have never gained much ground, but at the Falls, and amongst the Bakumu tribe their efforts have apparently been more successful. I cannot say whether they have gained any Mohammedan converts.

The Congo Free State Government has been fortunate on the whole in the choice of its officers who have held high authority at the Falls. In consequence the district has suffered much less from the Belgian *regime* imposed upon the Congolese than other places in the vast watershed.

COLLARS IN UPPER . . . CONGO
By the Rev. JOHN WHITEHEAD

THE CONGO COLLAR (1911)

For the collars worn by the natives on the Upper Congo the seamstress and laundress are not needed; but the blacksmith with his adaptability for working brass is essential. He takes the brass wire used as currency, and melts it down in crucibles which are prepared by women from old body completely covered with camwood paste (camwood rubbed down with palm oil), they look "lovely"! The collar in the photograph weighs 23 lbs., and would cost about £2 in comparative currency. *The collar worn by the photographed* woman *weighed 21 lbs.* When the ornament was placed around the neck, she had to lie down on her side, with the underside of the collar resting on a block of hard wood, and the blacksmith, with his heavy wooden club, closed the collar opening to about half an inch; this opening is worn at the back of the neck and is filled up with fibre and clay and camwood dressing, and frequently adorned with brass chair nails.

REMOVING THE COLLAR

Both the woman in the collar and the one upon the anvil came to the mission had cooking pots broken up, ground to powder, and moulded up again for the new purpose. He prepares a long open mould as straight as guessing can judge. When the brass is molten he attacks the crucible with tongs formed of the singed midriffs of bananas (a disastrous proceeding sometimes), and pours the contents into the open mould.

When the casting is removed there are, of course, innumerable flaws, but considerable attention with the handleless hammer covers up the multitude of faults. *Then the bar is bent with heavy wooden clubs into collar shape, leaving the ends apart merely enough to permit the honoured wearer to wriggle her neck between, as in the photograph. It is easier to wriggle in than to wriggle out, and only the ladies delight to wear these collars.*

The man who becomes enamoured of his only or selected wife desires her to be distinguished above the rest of her sex by the splendour of her jewels. Some are presented with anklets, some with spiral leglets of immense weight, others with wristlets of various sizes and metals, while others are adorned with these collars; and when they are duly hair-dressed, eye-dressed, skin-dressed, *i.e.,* hair well plaited and oiled, eyelashes pulled out, eyebrows shaved off, the whole Lukolela to be relieved of their jewels. The favour of the husbands had either come to an end or it was no longer esteemed, and they wished to return the "ring." *Sometimes they have* come because the *weight of glory* is no longer physically *bearable, or because sores* have been *created by the collar on* the neck and shoulders. But for some time past at Lukolela there has been a great difficulty in finding a blacksmith able to remove these collars, hence the appeal to the missionary, who is glad to assist the desire to be rid of such ornaments, whatever the reason may be for their removal.

The other photograph shows how the collar is removed on the anvil with sledge hammer and steel wedges.

S. OUT-STATION AT IREMA, NEAR YAKUSU
[Photo by Rev. A. G. Mill]

STILL PIONEERING
FORWARD ON THE LOMAMI
By the Rev. A. G. MILL, of Yakusu

The Mission outpost in the above picture is fourteen hundred miles up country on the Lomami river. Just out of sight, round the bend is the native village of Irema, in which stand two trees, gaunt and gigantic, under which the Arab slave-raiders in the last generation sold their human merchandise. It was from this region that the little slave girl Salamu was captured, who was saved by the missionaries from the slave gang on its way to the coast at Monsembe. Although, when Mr. Stapleton took her to Yakusu in 1895, Salamu was recognised as a native of those parts, and became the first evangelist in the native language at Yakusu, yet her old home on the Lomami remained long unevangelised.

It was in 1915 that I was privileged to take, with Mr. Millman, the first long itineration on the Grenfell up the Lomami, which disclosed to us our responsibility for the Esoo and Bambole tribes which live on its banks and in the forest hinterlands. *We made friends with many chiefs for two-hundred miles up the river to Irema and on our return started at the mouth to work up and establish the Gospel wherever we found a response.*

From the sub-station of Yalikina in 1916, at the mouth of the Lomami, the work was supervised and preaching stations were opened not only on the lower reaches of the Lomami but also in the Esoo forest on the western bank. No sooner were we able to train or enlist intelligent young Christian natives to fill these posts than they were eagerly received and installed in the villages. On the Lomami river itself, myself and my colleagues were constantly called on to supply the earnest appeals for teachers and in 1926 it was realised at the Field Committee, that the work had outgrown the reach of Yalikina and needed a white missionary to make the Upper Lomami his special care. All the same our missionary duty was not along the river alone, but also in the vast forest hinterland, so while we held on to our schools on the Lomami, we spread the Gospel in the Esoo tribe to its furthest limits up the west bank of the Lomami. By God's blessing, and by enthusiastic labour by as many native Christian teachers, two-hundred and fifty Esoo villages had been occupied by 1928.

This brought us to the Bambole tribe. Mr. Parris had already worked among a branch of this tribe on the east bank, and when, in 1928, he crossed to Opala, which is the Belgian Administrative outpost of the Bambole tribe, he was told that probably eighty thousand of that tribe were untouched by any Christian mission. The native Christians from the east bank made earnest efforts to start schools in the needy area, and one devoted evangelist, Filipo Kewaita, died while endeavouring to push forward the boundaries of the Kingdom. The work, however, had to wait for funds and the financial crisis of 1931 made it impossible to start an outpost near Opala to coordinate the work.

I have to tell the unpleasant truth that the evangelisation of the natives was displeasing to the Roman Catholic priests, and through their National Catholic organisation they installed themselves in 1933, first at Yalikina and later at Opala, avowedly to make Christian Protestants into superstitious Roman Catholics. We are now outnumbered by them three to one, but with our open Bible and the record of Yakusu's work, we have three times the effectiveness in our appeal.

It is strange, but true, that not ten miles from these lovely palms, and among primitive people, unclothed to an almost shocking extent, the whirr and clank of industrial machinery is constantly sounding. Three thousand are employed in exploiting the palm oil and coffee at Ekoli and two thousand are exploiting palm oil and coffee and rice in the mills at Yaluwe.

And what is the B.M.S. doing? Responding to the appeal of bewildered lives, disputing the dominance of religious bigotry, calling out from the heathen a people for the glory of Christ's name!

Irema was once a slave post, but since 1920 a native teacher has been there, and in 1937 the missionaries were welcomed by the natives to the site shown here, and in the mud-house with the corrugated iron roof seen in the picture a symbol of liberty has been erected.

Was not *1938* the Diamond Jubilee year of Congo Missions? The loving gifts of supporters have made possible the building of the house and we have faith to believe that the support needed for its running will be forthcoming as an addition to Yakusu's work for Salamu's sake, and that, there, sin's slaves may find their Saviour.

SOUTHWARD HO!

By Rev. A. G. MILL, of Yakusu, who for many years has
been engaged in pioneering work on the Upper Lomami

We steamed out from Yalikina bent on avenging the centuries of hate and darkness which the Devil has contrived in the remoter fringes of Yakusu's area.

Armed with books and Scriptures, pictures and medicines, we went from village to village, up and up the Lomami river, across the Equator, a hundred miles, a hundred and fifty miles, to the borders of the ramparts of pride and ignorance surrounding the Bambole tribe. Then we disembarked, and, sending back the *Grenfell* with Mr. Chesterton to guard the base at Yalikina, my wife and I entered the forest, and immediately found that Satan hindered us, for we had to fight not only personal feelings in the villages but the blatant godlessness which had said in its heart: "Because the missionary only comes here for one visit a year, there is no God."

People had found that the trader with his demands for produce and his attractive goods was a force in their lives, and palm-wine drinking and laziness filled up their minds between his visits. But our presence once more made them remember God, and they were troubled.

BAPTISM OF CONVERTS IN THE LOMAMI RIVER, 100 MILES BEYOND
THE EQUATOR, BY THE REV. DOUGLAS CHESTERTON [Photo by Rev.
William Millman] (c. 1943)

New school frames of poles were erected in the villages and the precious
lives of little children filled them like flowers turning their faces towards
the light. As the parents protested that the Government's work prevented
them from helping the children, the children themselves threw themselves
into the work. I remember the sad look on the face of one unfaithful teacher when he saw all the little boys and girls replastering the walls of the
House of God and patching the thatch of the roof, which he had allowed to
fall into disrepair. More faithful teachers are what we need.

Again we plunged into the forest and reached a group of villages which
we have not visited for two years or more, and found the two Church
members halting, but hoping, on their heavenward road. The paramount
chief of this area, a young man, promised to build the school house again,
and asked for a teacher. From here the road diverged in three directions,
all of which led to unevangelized territory, but we were only able to follow
one, and it led to where, last year, a white missionary's face had been seen
for the first time.

We found that since our last visit faithful work had been done by some
local seekers after God whom we had left to help the children of each village. Three of the larger villages had aimed at placing some of their children as boarders at their own expense near the village school house, but

one of these villages excelled the others. The paramount chief here, again a young man, had welcomed the teacher from Yakusu Training Centre, and in the part of the village where his own quarters were he had cleared a space fifty yards wide and built a school chapel in the centre. Around this the boys who wished to be boarders had built a quadrangle of living houses facing on to it, one of which was for the teacher himself. Being advised of his tastes I gave the chief a present—not cloth, nor a mirror, nor beads—but a fountain pen which, thanks to our teacher, he can now use.

With the citadel thus captured, we marched south-west again to a post near the river where our native pastor, Bofululu, has his centre. Fifty-five teachers gathered for a fortnight's classes each day from dawn till dusk. Toward the end we sifted our inquirers and baptized nine men and three women, who rejoiced in the privilege. Then they dispersed into the dark forests.

Two days later, when we were about to slip our cables for the homeward trip, one of the leading teachers returned bruised and bleeding from a ruffianly assault which he had suffered on his way to his outpost. Did not Jesus say: "Behold I send you forth as sheep in the midst of wolves"?

He returned again to seek his people and to continue his work. I felt somewhat ashamed to come away and leave the place after that, especially as fifty miles farther up river a powerful Roman Catholic Mission have placed two priests who have established themselves there, with the help of the Government, as the "National" Mission of these people.

Does not Jesus say "Feed my sheep"? Do not let us say, "We can't do it."

"This is me baptizing in a pool in the Esso Forest. One of the seven baptized was a leper." A.G. Mill

THE COST OF KONDIMANA NA SIKA
THE LINGALA NEW TESTAMENT—AN
APPRECIATION

By A. G. MILL, Irema, Yakusu, Congo

The packet arrived at our post 200 kilometres up the Lomami river by the little Company steamer and had written on it "Advance copy of Lingala New Testament." We were just coming out of the prayer meeting. I opened it at once and savoured the pleasure of handling the shapely volume in black and red, and dipped at once into its contents.

I called in my two chief native helpers and *we looked up some well-known passages, John xiv., 1 Cor. xi., the birth and death of Christ, and some others.* Then we prayed together and gave thanks that our many prayers had been answered. In the note which my colleague sent with the book, she said: "I cannot tell you the price, for in the invoice there is only a '?' in the price column." That set in motion a train of thought most appropriate. Did I know what it had cost the men who go down to the sea (and even in it) in ships these days? *Did I know what it had cost the strenuous workers of the British and Foreign Bible Society who work under a shell-filled sky and with innumerable handicaps and oppositions?* Did I know what it had cost in care and concentration to the translator and collator? No, I did not know what it had cost, and I handled it the more lovingly for that.

Now I hope that those concerned will feel that it has been worth their efforts to produce it and get it here. I am sure they will when they get by return of post (if there is such a thing these days) a letter which reads that the edition is sold out and "Oliver asks for more." I have 100 native teachers awaiting their copies and I am only one of scores of other missionaries. There are two large Company Plantations near to us where the music of its message among the employees will cheer heart and soul, and there is a whole hinterland of unreached heathen whom we can teach only through this Bula-Matadi language. Their thanks will come later.

But the printed word is not the full cost. The Christ and Spirit speak and speak at cost. Some words bear marks of sweat and others spring up with blood shedding, that they might speak the peace of sins forgiven. May we who use it see in the red edges of the pages we turn over some of the cost and be faithful proclaimers of a word so rare.

(c. 1942)

14. 8   YOANE   14. 22

longwa na sasaipi bojali koyeba ye mpe bosili komɔna ye.

8 Filipo aloba na ye ete: Motei, mɔnisa biso Tata,
9 mpe ekokoka na biso. Yesu aloba na ye ete: Najali na bino ntango molai boye, Filipo, ¿mpe oyebi ngai tɛ? Oyo asili komɔna ngai, asili komɔna Tata.
10 ¿Yɔ olobi boni ete, Mɔnisa biso Tata? ¿Ojali kondima tɛ ete tojali, ngai kati na Tata, mpe Tata kati na ngai? Mpɔ na maloba makolobaka ngai,—nakosololaka yango na ngai mpenja tɛ; nde Tata, oyo ajali kati na ngai, akosalaka misala na ye.
11 Bóndima ngai ete ngai kati na Tata mpe Tata kati na ngai; sɔkɔ boye tɛ, bóndima ngai mpɔ na misala.
12 Najali koloba na bino sɔlɔ mpenja ete, mpɔ na oyo akondimelaka ngai, ye akosala misala mikosalaka ngai, akosala mpe misala mileki oyo, mpɔ ete ngai
13 nakei mboka na Tata. Nakosala mpɔ na mpɔ ekolɔmba bino na nkombo na ngai, ete Tata ákumama
14 mpɔ na Mwana. Sɔkɔ bokolɔmba likambo nini na nkombo na ngai, ngai nakosala yango.

Mpɔ na Mosungi

15 Sɔkɔ bolingi ngai, bótosa malako na ngai. Ngai
16 nakobɔndɛla Tata, mpe akopɛsa bino Mosungi mo,
17 susu ete ájala na bino elɔngɔ libela,—ye Molimo na sɔlɔ. Mokili ekoki konyangela ye tɛ, mpɔ mojali komɔna ye tɛ, mojali mpe koyeba ye tɛ; bino nde bojali koyeba ye, mpɔ ete ajali koumela epai na
18 bino, ajali mpe kati na bino. Nakotika bino bitike
19 tɛ, nakoya mboka na bino. Naino mwa ntango mokɛ mpe mokili ekomɔna ngai lisusu tɛ, nde bino bokomɔna ngai. Bino bokojala na bomɔi, mpɔ ete
20 ngai najali na bomɔi. Na mokɔlɔ yango bokoyeba. ete tojali, ngai kati na Tata na ngai, bino kati na
21 ngai, ngai kati na bino. Oyo ajali na malako na ngai mpe akotosaka yango,— ye ajali molingi na ngai. Molingi na ngai akolingama na Tata na ngai, ngai nakolinga ye mpe nakomimɔnisa na ye polele.
22 Yuda, ye Mokeliota tɛ, aloba na ye ete: ¿Ekojala boni, Motei, ete olingi komimɔnisa na biso polele

An article in the MISSIONARY HERALD, 1943 written by Uncle Alex in appreciation of the work of the British and Foreign Bible Society which "under a shell-filled sky. . ." worked to overcome handicaps and printed these copies during World War II.

A page from the translation of the NEW TESTAMENT into the Lingala language, a Bula-Matadi language used by Uncle Alex during his last years of service in the Congo at the Irema station. This page is copied from his personal copy and dated "Aout, 1943". The text on this page is St. John 14: 8–21.

KOSOLOLO BILANGA NA CONGO BELGE

OBELE kala kala ba-Portugais mpe ba-Putu mosusu babundaka poa na ko-kamata ese na monoko na Congo epai na Matadi.

Bankoko na ba-Portugais bakumaki kuna liboso 1482 na ba-Belge lokola.

Batu na masua mpe batu na Njambe-na-Mupe baku-maki na nsima poa na kosumbana libongo na Bakongo. Poa na bitumba mingi, ba-mindele na Mupe balongwaki. Batu na Congo balingaki koto te ba-Portugais poa nini bamoko bakamataki batu miombo.

Nsima na bilanga soko kama misato (300) batu basusu ba Putu bajon-gaki lisusu kotambola kati kati na biese bisusu na batu pipi.

Bakotaki mai na Congo paka na lota monene na mai, yango ekopekisa basua kopanda na likolo na Matadi. Mutu moko na Portugais akotaki ese na Congo epai na Katanga mpe mosusu akotaki ese na likolo na Kasai.

Nde mutu na liboso koleka mokili yonso na batu pipi *ajalaki Living-stone.* Ye akumaki na Zanzibar mpe Dar-es-Salaam na Tanganyika. Livingstone ajalaki Monganga kosunga batu na maladi mpe ajalaki mutu na Njambe. Motema na Livingstone na baninga na ye bayokaki kanda mingi esika na ba-Alabu poa nini baka-mataki miombo na makasi mabe. ba-Alabu yango basalaki boye. Bakamataki babalimakasi na bilenge-miasi-malamu miombo. Na nsima batiyaki mboka mŏtŏ mpe babomaki bango batikali. Djamba penja bakolaki kati na libongo na mboka na basenji nsi-ma na vita na ba-Alabu mpe bakalakala-na-djamba balalaki kati kati na mbele na batu.

Livingstone na baninga na ye bayebisaki batu na Putu boye na ba-Min-dele bakanisaki kobunda na ba-Alabu poa na yango.

Stanley moninga na Livingstone abilaki ye na batu na Zanzibar kama minei (400) poa na koluka ba-njila kati kati na Congo.

Tippon Tip abotami na mwasi-mombo na mu-Alabu moko na Zanzibar mpe akumaki mutu monene na akamataki batu mingi miombo. Alobaki ete ye mene mene ajalaki mokonji monene na ba Alabu yonso na mboka na Kasongo epai na mai na Lualaba.

Tippou Tip na Stanley bakutanaki; mpe Tippou Tip ayebaki kobunda na Stanley te. Nde ye amonisaki *Stanley njila na mai na Lualaba paka Kisangani* na bota monene na ebali bajali kuna. Tippou Tip ayebaki njila na Congo epai na Kinshassa te. Ye ajongaki likolo nde Stanley na batu na ye batambolaki obele ngele poa na koyeba mai monene na Congo yonso. Ayengaki na kotambola oyo mikolo kama libwa na tuku libwa na mikolo libwa (999).

Mondele *Stanley abimaki na Kinshasa na Boma* na nsima na kobunda bitumba mingi mpe koyoka matata mingi. Batu 285 na ye basilaki kokufa na njela. Roi Léopold II abiangaki ye na elanga 1878 mpe atunaki ye kosolela ye nsango na njela yango yonso na mai na Congo.

Amonaki ete Mai na Congo aleki kati kati na ese mingi mingi. Ese yango baleki yango na Congo emonaki ba-Portugais kalakala na monene. Ayokaki ete mai mingi mosusu asanganaki na mai na Congo, soko Lomami, soko Ruki, soko Kasai mpe batu mingi na biloko mingi bajalaki kuna. (Wana Stanley atambolaki, le Roi Léopold II des Belges abiangaki baMindele oyo basili kotambola na Afrique liboso na elanga na 1876 poa na kotuna bango nsango na ese yango.)

Stanley ayokisaki Roi na l'Angleterre lokola na Président na Amerique, nde *obele Roi Léopold* II ayokaki mposa kotinda batu na ye na Mai na Congo. Le Roi Léopold II asili kotinda ba-Belge na Zanzibar poa na kokota Afrique. Mingi bakufaki maladi mingi bakufaki libeela. Na elanga na 1879 ba Beige batongaki mboka na Karema na mai na Tanganyika. Bango na bato pipi na epai na Congo bakatanaki ndeko mpe ba Beige baleki Tanganyika mpe bakumaki na Mtoa mpe Mpala na elanga na 1881. Na nsima bayaki na Nyangwe

FIRST PAGES OF A PRIMER ON THE HISTORY OF THE BELGIAN CONGO (from a European perspective!) Note the references to "Portugais. . . 1482. . .Livingstone. . . Stanley. . . Kinsangi. . .Leopold II. . . ."

14. 6   **YOANE**   14. 21

6 Yesu loonga lande mbo:—Imi yende Mboka, la Wewe, la Loiko, angwene boto angomwito boke ende Sango, sakolo ko eke lami.

7 Boluwa Imi ani otoluwa nde Sango wami, kwɔno ino botoluwa
Inde, osoene Inde.

8 Filipo loonga lande mbo:—Eneseke to iso Sango, limo betema
beaeke se. 9 Yesu lomutola lande mbo:—Mbo ani asoumwa Imi
lanu mbile efi ongoma, mbo ae Filipo oitoluwa Imi? Inde oyasoene
Imi, asoene imo ko Sango wami. 10 Monito otofela Imi mbo:—
Eneseke iso Sango? Boitoimela mbo Imi yende nda Sango, la
Sango nda Imi? Njaso ebitokangesa Imi ekangesa ino batotina,
iitonga yao la isosha shami angene, nde Sango oyayali ndatiteni
yami Inde atokelakaka tomo yande. 11 Imelakai baoi bami mbo
Imi yende ndatiteni yande, ango ko eoka ya tomo ebitokela Imi.
12 Itoonga lanu wewe mbo, oyatolendelo Imi, ani tomo ebitokela
Imi, inde kokela imo ko yao, la inde kokela tomo ndolongela yao,
nyongo isamboke ende Sango. 13 Njaso bitotina ebitofela ino efela
Imi nda lina liami, itokela ngo ko yao, mbo Sango ataliomoko nde
tala, ko l'eoka ya Wana.

14 Eni yeka ekombeke ino womba Imi, ko la lina liami, yefaka nd'ino
yao. 15 Bosamai Imi ambo bolitesaka nde bikela yami. 16 La
yefelaka nde Sango, la Inde efaefaka nd'ino Mbate yasi ndoyala lanu
laya laya, ango ko *Bolimo* wa Wewe. 17 Eba bienda baitokokolo ndoaela
e *Bolimobo*, nyongo baitoene Inde, la baitoluwa Inde, ino ndasoluwa
Inde nyongo ale lanu, la atoyala ndatiteni yanu. 18 Iitomacha ino
kwa eba lotika, yeyaka nde ende ino. 19 Ko la sinyo sha mbile kongo,
lamao eba bienda bacheneke imo Imi liasi, nde ino weneke nde Imi.
Eoka Imi ile la liwawi, ko ongoma ino boyalaka nde la liwawi. 20
Nda mbile ena ino boluwaka mbo Imi ile ndatiteni ya Sango, la mbo
ino ole ndatiteni yami, la Imi ndatiteni yanu. 21 Inde oyale la bikela
yami, ndolitesa yao, ende inde oyatosama Imi, la inde oyatosama Imi,
esamomoko imo la Sango wami; yesamaka ngo ko inde, la yeneneke
ende inde fololo.

| 14. 8 | YOANE | 14. 22 |

longwa na sasaipi bojali koyeba ye mpe bosili ko mɔna ye.

8 Filipo aloba na ye ete: Motei, mɔnisa biso Tata

9 mpe ekokoka na biso. Yesu aloba na ye ete: Najal na bino ntango molai
boye, Filipo, ¿mpe oyebi nga tɛ? Oyo asili komɔna ngai, asili komɔna
Tata

10 ¿Yɔ olobi boni ete, Mɔnisa biso Tata? ¿Ojal kondima tɛ ete tojali,
ngai kati na Tata, mpe Tata kati na ngai? Mpɔ na maloba makolobaka

ngai,—nakosololaka yango na ngai mpenja tɛ; nde Tata oyo ajali kati na ngai, akosalaka misala na ye

11 Bóndima ngai ete ngai kati na Tata mpe Tata kat na ngai; sɔkɔ boye tɛ, bóndima ngai mpɔ na misala

12 Najali koloba na bino sɔlɔ mpenja ete, mpɔ na oyo akondimelaka ngai, ye akosala misala mikosalaka ngai, akosala mpe misala mileki oyo, mpɔ ete nga

13 nakei mboka na Tata. Nakosala mpɔ na mpɔ eko lɔmba bino na nkombo na ngai, ete Tata ákumama

14 mpɔ na Mwana. Sɔkɔ bokolɔmba likambo nini na nkombo na ngai, ngai nakosala yango.

Mpɔ na Mosungi

15 Sɔkɔ bolingi ngai, bótosa malako na ngai. Nga

16 nakobɔndɛla Tata, mpe akopɛsa bino Mosungi mo

17 susu ete ájala na bino elɔngɔ libela,— ye Molimo na sɔlɔ. Mokili ekoki konyangela ye tɛ, mpɔ mojal komɔna ye tɛ, mojali mpe koyeba ye tɛ; bino nda bojali koyeba ye, mpɔ ete ajali koumela epai na

18 bino, ajali mpe kati na bino. Nakotika bino bitike

19 tɛ, nakoya mboka na bino. Naino mwa ntango mokɛ mpe mokili ekomɔna ngai lisusu tɛ, nde bino bokomɔna ngai. Bino bokojala na bomɔi, mpɔ ete

20 ngai najali na bomɔi. Na mokɔlɔ yango bokoyebaa ete tojali, ngai kati na Tata na ngai, bino kati na

21 ngai, ngai kati na bino. Oyo ajali na malako na nagai mpe akotosaka yango,— ye ajali molingi na ngai. Molingi na ngai akolingama na Tata na ngai, ngai nakolinga ye mpe nakomimɔnisa na ye polele.

22 Yuda, ye Mokeliota tɛ, aloba na ye ete: ¿Ekojala boni, Motei, ete olingi komimɔnisa na biso polele

TRANSLATIONS OF THE NEW TESTAMENT in the Lokele and Lingala languages used by Alex and Ethel Mill. These translations were made in 1927 and 1943. These are the same passages from chapter fourteen of the Gospel of St. John.

Nkolo na Bilembo—Our Redeemer—Lingala, DRC

Oh, Lord God,
God of Great deeds   4x
God of wonders   4x

God of Great deeds   2x
You perform wonders that astonish people
God of great deeds

God of wonders   2x
You do things that are greater than what human beings can do.
God of wonders

Lead
It overwhelms me. It awes my heart. It awes my family. It awes my friends
It awes my children

Choir:
Jesus performer of miracles
You perform miracles each day
Ah, redeeming Lord

Lead:
He redeemed me. This is not hearsay. I've seen it with my own eyes. I was
nothing. He made me a worthy person. The whole world understands that
He is Jesus. He is the Redeeming Lord

He picked me up, He gave me reason to live
The world confesses that He is Jesus
You are the redeemer
You are the redeemer

A PAGE FROM "UN CATECHISME CHRETIAN" IN THE LOKELE LANGUAGE

4. YESU.

1 Mungu amachaka batɔ nda bofoka wa Satana? Mba. Mungu ale la
losamɔ ende batɔ ebakelaka Inde, atomaka Wana wande se litina lia
mbo ebatoimela Inde angoseesele, kongoko batɔɔlɔ loiko loa laya laya,
Yoane 3;16
2 Wana wa Mungu ako ndai?
Wana wa Mungu ako Masiya, Ngene wa liuwesi.

Ebele 5:9.

3 Wana wa Mungu akelaka nd'iye?
  Ayaka se kwa wana oli wa otomali ako Malia.

Luka 2:7

4 Yesu aotomoko nde anima?
  Yesu aotomoko nda yese ya Ba-Yuda, nda bokenge wa Betelehemu.

Luka 2:4.

5 Ndai yakotaka ndoola Wana Yesu?
  Bɔkɔta Heloti akotaka ndoola wana Yesu.   Matayo 2;16

6 Acholak'inde?
  Mba. Mungu loluwesa Yosefa, bolome wa Malia, nda saki, limɔ iyo
  lotangwa la ocho la nyango la wana amamwito.   Matayo 2;13

7 Iyo lɔke to anima?
  Iyo lɔke nda yese yasi eko Ejipeto, awaka Bokota Helodi iyo loinwa
  nda Nasaleta.   Matayo 2;14

8 Yesu nda wainenge ayalaka bɔfɔɔnɔ wiye? Inde lolitesa sango la
  nyango nda njasɔ bitotina la batɔ lomwaala welï wande. Luka 2;40–52

5. YESU.

1 Ayalaka Yësu otowange akelaka nde iye?
  Yesu alufiomoko la Yoane nda lilufi lia likalangani.   Matayo 3;11

2 Yesu ayalaka nde la obe?
  Mba, Yesu achayalaka la obe, Inde lotola bobe wasu.   2 Kolinto 5;21

3 Yesu lolufiomo to moni?
  Inde loonga mbo: Bolau ko mbo yenganeseke njasɔ bilau bitotina.

Matayo 3;15

TWO HYMNS IN THE LOKELE HYMNAL
"KETI YA BEELE" (translated by A.G. Mill, 1917)

136

"Let me come closer" C.E. 203 (June Changed)

1 KELAKA imi boekesi
  Ndokuwela Yesu
  Komiaka bekeeli'ami
  Ndokweela ko Yesu.

2 Faefaka imi isosha
  Shoima e babe.

Ko la bekela ndokufesa
Eba litefoli.

3 Losamo loac clotouwesa;
   Weleke 'mi Yesu
   Mbo iweleke imo basi
   Ndoluwesa iyo loao.

4 Weli wami boitolonga
   Baiyani bami.
   Kee osofa imi lokasa
   Loa weli wa use.

A. G. M., 1917.

110

"Christian walk carefully," SS 591.

1 KOKOMELEKE to nda mboka yae.
   Lokendo lole la tale ende ae,
   Yeme ya bobe bilimba nde ae
   Limo Satana kokwesa nde ae.
      Yesu Bouwesi
      Kokomeseke 'mi
      Yalakaka la'mi
      Mbo itakwa.
2 Tangwaka to imo la limengo.
   Ango biyani besungamel'ae,
   Ango bemusi bekanda nde ae,
   Unda loiko lofomu nda use.
3 Botema sambo to bole bolau,
   Inga lofolo nda mboka y'use.
   Yalakai to la liimeli
   Watemakaka la Bouwesi.

A.G.M., 1917.

A tribute to Pastor Abraham—"I will not call him black. . . He was my friend"

He was tall, I can see his stance now, six feet of him, solid and smiling, with his kind thick lips and earnest white-rimmed negro eyes. And he stood ready to enter into any Christian service which he might be led to do for his fellows.

What were his origins? Though he himself had not been a cannibal he was born in the village of Yalikina, at the mouth of the Lomami river, whose chief Bonjoma gloried in the number of his Esoo enemies whom he had eaten.

He chased hippos with his father in his youth, and in his boyhood the first young Yakusu teacher came into his village. The youths were drawn together by the new message of the young Man of Galilee, and by grace through faith the young man *Akilabana* saw himself and saw in the waters of Congo the symbol of the outpoured life of Christ and dared to be baptised into Him and called Abraham. This began the adventure of the life of separation from the world and devotion to God in which every good work had a place. But he was challenged too with the call to preach for Christ to the erstwhile enemies of his tribe. In a prayer meeting in a little mud chapel lit with palm oil flares he responded to the call and went out to live in a village of the Esoo forest to begin his lifework.

He had not thought of marriage as yet, but with prudent African foresight his parents had, and God had provided in the young Christian girl Bolaya a fine wife of whom he might have said with R. L. Stevenson:

"Trusty, dusky, vivid, true.
With eyed of gold and bramble dew
Steel true, and blade straight,
The great Artificer made my mate".

This young Christian pair did not fit into native life but were drawn into service with the white missionary who was beginning to build the Yalikina Substation beside his village.

Abraham built in brick, and he built in men. His straight-forward manliness commanded obedience among employees but he did not dominate and could forgive even personal injury with Christian self-control. But the bases of our work were over a hundred square miles of forest and he became a pilgrim with me in staking out claim for Christ in hundreds of villages. Even ahead of the white missionary he went up to possess the land, and many a man in the Esoo church looks upon him as spiritual father. He gave himself up to become an efficient teacher and in the dining conferences at Yakusu, at which he was taught periodically he advanced wisdom.

In cooperation with the white missionary in the organization of junior ichors and in keeping records and reports he was an invaluable kindred spirit. every difficulty he went to God's word and, once he found direction in the New Testament he submitted to God's will.

In his own home, which was first graced with twins, and since by three other children, he showed an example of Christian love and care and kept the altar family worship burning.

God blessed his work but claimed his whole hearted faithfulness. Once on he had promised to follow me on a fixed date into the district when his child fell ill. He left the child with prayers, and instruction, in the arms of the mother, assured as he told me, that he would not expect God to hear his prayer if he failed in faithfulness to his work.

After ten years of faithful service by him and his wife he was appointed as Native Pastor, and after another ten years of faithful and energetic shepherding he was given the independent care of the most difficult part of the latest work behind Yalikina, and went to live at Yabahondo, twenty miles inland.

His eldest son had been trained at the Yakusu school and was now able to be a teacher in the school, Malia, his wife with a zeal God for her ignorant forest sisters, was seeing a revival and an unusual ingathering and all seemed well.

But it was at this juncture that the shadow of the cloud of death began to hover over him and the brightness of his face was dulled and the solid frame wasted with painful muscle swellings. In March he wrote when he sent in his reports that each was encouraging but his one regret was that the pain prevented him from and getting about. A little improvement took place and the local B.M.S infirmier did what he could for him, but again at the beginning of April he was incapable of moving both legs and one arm. All the same he gave instructions concerning the work, and wrote with his own hand the report. He also wrote to his son, who was taking the Teacher Training course at Yakusu, a letter in which he simply said it was going worse with him, but added, "My son, be established, by God's help, in His work."

The missionaries then sent for him to be brought to Yakusu hospital and by the 23rd of April he was in the most expert care, but too weak to recover.

His last message to the teachers under his care was: "Do God's work courageously. I am going ahead to be with the Father in heaven, and we shall meet again as Jesus said in John 14-one and two". He passed away unconscious on April 26th.

When his native brethren and the missionaries met at the funeral the uppermost thought in the minds of all were expressed by *Mr. Ennels* when he said, "The rich legacy of Abraham's work has been left to us, let us rise up and see to it that we honor his memory by continuing it". He has only left the church militant to join the Church Triumphant. I *was on my way back to Yakusu* when I heard of his death, and would add my tribute.

"I will not call him black
Black is for death,
This man is living, and God's vital breath
Moves in the fleeting changes of his face.
A ready wit moves him to facile speech
Keen sympathy commands a kind outreach.
Beneath the black skin, blood cells red like mine,
Impart a vivid glow to features fine
In which love, loyalty and laughter blend,
I will not call him black—he was my friend."

The Upper Congo Mission Areas (c. 1940)

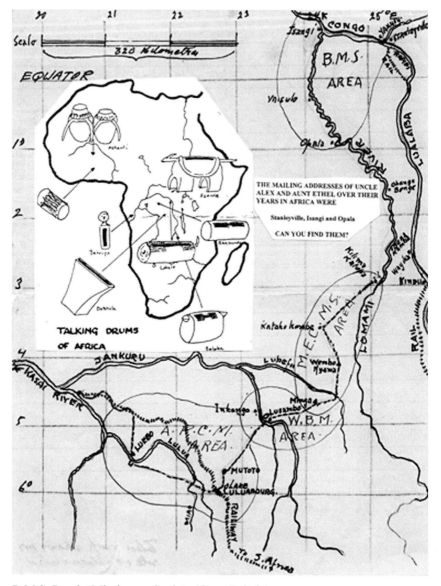

B.M.S. Baptist Missionary Society (Great Britain)
M.E.C.M.S. Methodist Episcopal Congo Mission South (U.S.A.)
A.P.C.M. American Presbyterian Congo Mission (U.S.A.)
W.B.M. World Baptist Mission (U.S.A.)

THE TONAL STRUCTURE OF KELE (LOKELE)
By J. F. CARRINGTON

(1) The Kele tribe comprises a riverine people living on the North and South banks of the Congo river between the mouths of the Lindi (some ten miles below Stanleyville) and the Lomami. Their villages extend also for a considerable distance up the Lomani river. From the main portion of the tribe, which numbers about 26,000 people, small groups have broken away from time to time and have taken up permanent residence as traders or fishers at points as far away as Kongolo (up-river) and Léopoldville (down-river).[1]

Three main divisions in the tribe are recognised:

(*a*) The most westerly group, around the mouth of the Lomami and extending up-stream on both banks of that river. This group is called Yawɛmbɛ.

(*b*) A central portion inhabiting both banks of the Congo, this group being called Yaokanja.

(*c*) The most easterly group, sometimes called Yuani, and also spoken of as the " river of upstream" . . . *liande lia likolo.*[2]

(2) Little is known of the history of the tribe. But, of recent events we may note that Stanley passed through Kele territory in 1877 while on his journey across Africa. He notes[3] the warlike habits of this riverine people and their use of large signal drums. Stanley returned in 1883 to Kele country and found the tribe scattered by Arab slave-traders.[4] Twelve years later missionaries of the English Baptist Missionary Society prospected for a site among the Kele people and finally chose a position at the extreme corner of the Kele territory, near the village of Yakusu (more accurately written *Yakoso*). The early Yakusu missionaries reduced the Kele language to writing and began to use this tongue as a medium for evangelistic and educational work.

(3) "Standard Lokele" as used by the Yakusu printing press is taken as the language spoken by the central portion of the tribe (i.e.,

---

[1] Maes et Boone: *Les peuplades du Congo Belge.* Bruxelles; 1935.

[2] The Kele language has become the "market language" etc. for a district far greater than that occupied by the Kele tribe alone.

[3] Stanley, H. M: *Through the Dark Continent.* London, 1878. Vol. ii, p. 257.

[4] Stanley, H. M: *The founding of the Congo Free State.* London, 1885. Vol. ii.

Yaokanja). There are some phonetic differences in the dialects spoken at different villages throughout the Kele area, but tone patterns remain very constant.[5]

(4) Published information on Kele is available in the following works:

(*a*) Stapleton, W. H.: *Comparative handbook of Congo languages.* Yakusu 1903.

(*b*) Sutton-Smith, E.: *Yakusu, the very heart of Africa.* London, 1910.

(*c*) Millman, W.: *An outline of Lokele grammar.* Yakusu, 1926.

(*d*) Millman, W.: *English-Lokele vocabulary.* Yakusu, 1926.

(*e*) Ford, W. H.: *A Lokele grammar.* Yakusu, 1936.

(*f*) Carrington, J. F.: *The Tonetics of Lokele.* Yakusu, 1940.

Tonal structure is referred to in detail only by Ford and Carrington, although it is of interest to note that Stapleton mentions what is really the semantic function of tones when he describes under the heading of "accent" the method of differentiating subjunctive positive and negative forms which are orthographically indistinguishable[6] (see section 49).

The following study of Kele tone patterns is essentially a revision of (f) above, undertaken after further investigations into the tones of Kele itself and those of other languages spoken near Yakusu, and after a perusal of the literature relating to tones in Central African and other languages.

Technique of study:

(5) (*a*) The main method of study has been to ask literate Kele youths and men to read slowly portions of our printed books. At the same time the author wrote down over the printed words the tones of the spoken syllables, using the system of notation described in section 8. In this way have been annotated for tones in the Gospels of Matthew and Mark, together with large portions of those of Luke and John, the whole of the Acts of the Apostles and a good deal of the Epistles. In addition some secular books used in our Yakusu school work have been noted for tones. These tone marks have since been checked repeatedly and carefully against the tones used in public readings, sermons, school lessons, "palavers" and ordinary conversation by Kele folk of both sexes and varying ages.

(6) (*b*) The tones worked out by method (a) have been compared with the tones of the same words appearing in the drum language of the Kele

---

[5] This has been observed for other tone languages, cf. Ward, I. C: *An introduction to the Ibo language,* Cambridge, 1936: p 14.

[6] Stapleton, W. H.; see (a) in the above list: pp. 5 and 184.

tribe and also in the related "shouting-at-a-distance" language, whistling and horn languages. It has been shown[7] that all these "signalling" languages are essentially the same as the spoken language. Whistling, horn-blowing or drumming on the two-toned slit-drum have been resorted to in order to clarify the tone pattern of words not properly obtained by ear. The author fully endorses the suggestion made by Burssens[8] working on the tones of Luba as to the value of the two-toned slit-drum ("seintrommel") in investigating the tone patterns in a Central African language (see Appendix I).

(7) (*c*) Tone patterns annotated as in (a) have also been checked against the patterns occurring in the words of some old tribal songs. It has been pointed out for Kele[9] and for some other songs[10] that the sung melody follows closely the tone patterns of the spoken words; indeed, the melody can be regarded as essentially the sung tone patterns of corresponding words in the spoken language (see Appendix II).

Notation employed:

(8) Five tone elements can be distinguished in the Kele language, viz.: a high-level tone, a low-level tone, a mid-level tone, a rising tone and a falling tone. These have been represented for the purposes of this study by a system of dots or lines placed between two parallel straight lines. In the representation of single tones or the tone pattern of single words, square brackets replace the parallel lines.[11]

---

[7] Carrington, J. F.: unpublished.

[8] Burssens, A.: (i) *Tonologische schets van het Tshiluba.* Antwerp, 1939. p. ix. (ii) *Le Luba, langue à intonation, et le tambour signal.* "Proc. 3rd. Internat. Cong. Phonetic Sci." Ghent 1938.

[9] Carrington, J. F.: *Tonetics of Lokele.* Yakusu, 1940.

[10] Westermann, D.: *Zeichensprache des Ewevolkes in Deutsch-Togo.* "Mitteil. d. Semin. f. Orientalische Sprachen." Berlin 1907. Bd. X: S. 8, 9.

[11] This is the system recommended by Westermann and Ward: *Practical Phonetics for students of African Languages.* Oxford, 1933. p. 133.

The Kele text is written in the symbols approved in Memorandum I of the International Institute of African Languages and Cultures. Since these symbols are not used entirely in present-day printed books produced at Yakusu, some changes in the existing orthography have had to be made when using material from Scriptural and other passages. In grammatical classification and nomenclature the writer has attempted to follow the scheme put forward and used by Doke.[12]

The Number of Tonemes in Kele:

(9) Kele has two tonemes only: a high toneme and a low toneme.[13]

(10) The mid-level tone which is heard frequently in conversation may belong to either the high or the low toneme but the fact that this mid-tone is not a separate toneme may be determined by applying the test of significance: i.e., no two words are known in Kele which, differing in a single mid-tone of one replacing a high or low tone of the other, differ also in meaning. With regard to the non-significance of the mid-level tone of Kele it may also be noted that the drum and horn languages are produced on two notes only.

(11) The mid-level tone is produced in two main ways:

(*a*) By the influence on an essentially low tone of a preceding high tone. Thus: *baaŋa?* `· · ·` (how many—men) may be regarded as *ba-* [`·`] *-aŋa* [`.·`].

Here the low-toned *-a* is raised to a mid-level tone. This is an example of a mid-level tone belonging to the low toneme.

(*b*) By the influence of what is described in this study as the "end-fall effect" (see section 14), under which the terminal high tones of a word, occurring after a preceding low tone, are thereby lowered to mid-levels. Thus:

   imbale `·.·` (two)   *itikele* `·..·` (I did not do)

   likundo `·.·` (revenge)   *atilɛmbɛ* `·..·` (he does not want).

---

[12] Doke, C. M: (i) *Bantu Linguistic Terminology*. London, 1935. (ii) *Textbook of Lamba Grammar*. Johannesburg, 1938.

[13] In normal conversation the interval between the highest tone of the high toneme and the lowest tone of the low toneme is about a musical major 1/3.

In these examples the terminal mid-level tones all belong to the high toneme. It is of interest to note that the drum, which can only produce two notes, gives the true tonemal character of these mid-level tones: *imbale* ‾•‿•‾, *atilɛmbɛ* ‾•‿•‿•‾, *likundo* ‾•‿•‾, all of which words are used in the drum language.

(12) Falling and rising tones, together with lengthened tones, are regarded in this study as in most cases due to the juxtaposition of two like vowels which have a high-low, a low-high, a low-low or a high-high tone sequence respectively, i.e., $o = [\smallfrown] = oo$ [•‿•]; o [⟋] $= oo$ [•‿•] ; a [—] $= aa$ [• •] ; a [—] $= aa$ [• •].

A falling-rising tone, referred to by some students of tone in Central African languages, would in this way be represented by three juxtaposed like vowels. Thus; O [$\sim\!\!\frown$] $= ooo$ [•‿•].

This possible representation of rising and falling tones, already envisaged by some writers[14] is rendered a probability for Lokele and the languages of surrounding tribes for the following reasons:

(*a*) Two juxtaposed vowels which could be called single vowels with rising or falling or lengthened tones may be separated in the corresponding words of cognate languages by a vowel. Thus:

Kele: *bɔɔmwi* ‿•‿•‿ (five); Mbɔlɛ: *ɔhɔmɔi* ‿•‿•‿•‿

(*b*) A rising or falling tone may be synthesised by the placing together in a word of infixes so arranged that two similar vowels, but with different essential tones, are juxtaposed. Thus: *atokela* ‿•‿•‿• (he will do), plus the infix -*oka*- ‿•‿ (to go) give together: *atookakela* ‿•‿•‿•‿•‿• (he will go to do). This could be written *atokakela* ‿•‿\‿•‿•‿, but the analytic method is preferred in this study.

(*c*) The signalling drum analyses what might otherwise be written as falling or rising or lengthened tones into their component vowels, each with a distinct tone. There are reasons for believing the drum language to be more primitive than the present-day spoken language.[15] Thus:

orally: *bɔmwi* ‾⌒•‾ (five). Drum gives

" *bɔɔmwi* ‾•‿•‿•‾ or ⋮•⋮• [16]

" *asoya* ‾•‿\•‾ (he has come). Drum:

---

[14] Meinhof, C.: *Grundriss einer Lautlehre der Bantusprachen.* Berlin 1910. S.10.

[15] Carrington, J. F.: unpublished.

[16] The notation ⋮ indicates that the high-toned and low-toned drum lips are beaten simultaneously.

asooya ⎯⎯⎯⎯
asota ⎯⎯⎯⎯ (she has borne).
Drum: *asooota* ⎯⎯⎯⎯
baololo ⎯⎯⎯⎯ (elders).
Drum: *baoloolo.*

The "end-fall" effect:

(14) When noting the general tone level of a Kele sentence or clause, it is evident that there is a marked falling in pitch from the beginning to the end of the sentence. A secondary rise in pitch occurs at the beginning of each new clause in a sentence containing a number of clauses.

Brown Street Guild Meeting.

AFRICAN TRADITIONAL LITERATURE.

Intro: "Literature?" of English literature: Shakespeare, Chaucer, Bacon, Scott, Thackeray, Dickens. . .Palgrave. . . *Books* But our ancestors had their stories before they could write. . .oral literature (Literature didn't begin with printing any more than beautiful scenery began with photography!). Africans had *oral* literature long ago and still have it today.

I. Its *beauty*   depends partly on the beautiful language—open syllables,
- tonal structure: garaka haraka haina baraka!
- use of completive adverbs: asweta *fwa*, asookwa se *kpuu* toumbakeli teee. . . najali bobɛlɛ ngonga ekolobaka ngbaa ngbaa to elonga ekolobaka ngbengbele ngbengbele

II. But also on the ideas expressed. Main examples of literature:

A - riddles: no time of asking and replying
my house has no windows nor doors / has only one pillar
you cut me all the time but I never murmur
I walk on 4 legs in the morning, 2 at mid-day and 3 at night.
Likonga konda lokonda

B - proverbs.   Some very similar to our own but with African content -
Lokele fishermen: Oineleke lifonja likoyali ose ya alia (chickens)
Olombo farmers: Okalielanga yal otangeke mbo ela
Isese nd'akinjwi lis wa (stitch in time?)
Olola ngai ko linɛnɛ (crying for the moon)
Owala ngonda otete walaka likama (hung for a sheep)
Bosokola ngwa nda liulu (biting the hand that feeds)
Others are local -but very apt:
Ifimbilimbi angowanga kito ya ɔkɔta (a cat and a king?)
oféke longa bakolo
bolome wa loo angoeno lisoo
bosokola wali la nɔngɔ, likɔkɔ liyaka
faka oto yeka, likaɔ lyende boise

totangi nde mbo bosenge ende kumbo nde bosenge
ati kumbo
kɛmbɛ ati la ngɛnɛ
ngwa atite lokoka, mbuli angosoola ɔnɔkɔ
One I don't agree with: okakeli, okeleke, otat n la bokelakela
Use by pastors in our churches. Note the need to know them well:
Oluwa baoi, koosala nda mbile ya osho!

C - myths about origins - Yebisa and the pot from heaven
        - Lilwaakoi myth

D - Conundrums - in initiation ceremonies, etc.
        The man with the goat, the leopard and the spinach
        The village with famine (sick man), pertilence (old
        man) and war (man with 2 wives)
        cf Daniel and the dreams

E - fables about animals and Brier Rabbit—cf hare Kabundi.
        Eulu stories—tortoise and hare, African fashion
        - tortoise and jackal (flute)

F - Poetry - Swahili epic poems and love-songs (Mgeni/Praises of my
        beloved)

G - Court-room cases: man with 2 wives who caught a runaway slave
        the 3 brothers with their wedding presents.

Ending: note the human values on peoples all over the world. . . what a lot
we have to learn from other cultures.

APPENDIX K

THE CONGO ATROCITIES; A SUMMARY OF THREE ARTICLES IN THE BAPTIST (1906) AND THE MISSIONARY HERALD (1911)

"Pure religion and undefiled before the Father is to visit the orphan and the widow in their affliction. . .", yet there are those who become so spiritual that they forget "the Word made flesh". The true measure of our heavenly creed is our earthly character. Our interest in God should correspond to our interest in the welfare of man.

THE SITUATION IN THE BELGIAN CONGO IN 1911

Our missionaries, Messers D.C. Davies and A.B. Palmer have recently made a visit to the area between the Aruwimi and Lulu Rivers to introduce the Gospel to those villages. Much to their distress they found that the State taxes were still being paid in rubber and that its collection involved oppression and misery to an intolerable degree. And if Jesus were here today, King Leopold would be seen as the strongest enemy of Jesus and Jesus hailed as the dearest friend of the people of the Congo. Will the Christian Church fail to raise their voice on behalf of those enslaved by the tyrant and become their savior?

The missionary observers noted in the larger towns the complete absence of males except small boys. They saw hundreds of well-built huts neglected and abandoned. The men who owned them were out rubber gathering and the women had to cultivate the gardens, cook the food and then carry the food long distances to where the men were working. In some cases this involved three days of travel to reach the rubber camps. The people of a large town have to spend as much as three months each year in the rubber camps which were five days march distant.

Outrages have been perpetuated on women by the sentries and soldiers (estimated at more than 30,000) and the plight of the natives is worse than that of the native chimpanzee. Mutilation is being practiced without mercy, except the mercy which comes by death. A young woman, because her husband did not bring in "the sufficient amount" of rubber, was fastened to a tree and chopped in halves with a hatchet. Other publications have shown buckets of severed hands and feet as punishment for not bringing in "the quota" of rubber. It is living hell as floggings are given under the guise of "administration". This is forced labor in a state called "Free Congo"! King Leopold's "philanthropic enterprise" has become a regime of poverty and ugliness.

Cf. Fullerton, M.V. THE CHRIST OF THE CONGO RIVER with an introduction by His Majesty, the King of the Belgians. London, William Carey Press. 1928, page 216.

A LIST OF CONGO MISSIONARIES
MEN
Date of Acceptance

1. Grenfell, G. (Cameroons, 1874).	– 1878	Died at Basoko, 1906.
2. Comber, T. J. (Cameroons, 1876).	– 1878	Died at sea, 1887.
3. Bentley, W. Holman	– 1879	Died at Bristol, 1905.
4. Crudgington, H. E.	– 1879	Transferred to India, 1885.
5. Hartland, J. S.	– 1879	Died at Bayneston, 1883.
6. Dixon, H.	– 1880	Transferred to China, 1884. Martyred in 1900.
7. Weeks, J. H.	– 1881	Died in London, 1924.
8. Butcher, H. W.	– 1882	Died at Manyanga, 1883.
9. Doke, W. H.	– 1882	Died at Underhill, 1883.
10. Hughes, W.	– 1882	Returned, 1885.
11. Moolenaar, H. K.	– 1882	Returned, 1890.
12. Ross, W.	– 1882	Returned, 1884.
13. Comber, S., M.B.	– 1882	Died at Wathen, 1884.
14. Whitley, H. G.	– 1882	Died at Lukunga, 1887.

Date of Acceptance

15. Hartley, J. W.	–	1882	Died at Manyanga, 1884.
16. Cruickshank, A. H.	–	1884	Died at Wathen, 1885.
17. Darling, F. C.	–	1884	Died at Underhill, 1887.
18. Cameron, G. R. R.	–	1884	Returned, 1913.
19. Macmillan, D.	–	1884	Died at Underhill, 1885.
20. Cowe, A.	–	1884	Died at San Salvador, 1885.
21. Charters, D.	–	1885	Returned, 1887.
22. Cottingham, W. F.	–	1885	Died at Underhill, 1885.
23. Biggs, J. E.	–	1885	Died at Stanley Pool, 1887.
24. Comber, P. E.	–	1885	Died at Wathen, 1892.
25. Davies, P., B.A.	–	1885	Died at Wathen, 1895.
26. Maynard, J.	–	1885	Died at Underhill, 1886.
27. Richards, M.	–	1885	Died at Banana, 1888.
28. Scrivener, A. E.	–	1885	Died at Southampton, 1916.
29. Seright, W., M.B.	–	1886	Returned, 1886.
30. Darby, R. D.	–	1886	Returned, 1894.
31. Silvey, S. (Cameroons, 1882).	–	1886	Died at sea, 1889.
32. Graham, R. H. C.	–	1886	Retired, 1924.
33. Phillips, H. Ross	–	1886	
34. Shindler, J. H.	–	1886	Died at Underhill, 1887.
35. Lewis, T. (Cameroons, 1882).	–	1887	Now Welsh Representative of the B.M.S.
36. Brown, J. G.	–	1887	Died at sea, 1889.
37. Harrison, F. G.	–	1887	Returned, 1895.
38. Pinnock, J.	–	1887	Returned, 1909.
39. Slade, A. D.	–	1888	Died at Wathen, 1888.
40. Oram, F. R.	–	1888	Died at Upoto, 1894.
41. Clark, J. A.	–	1888	
42. Roger, J. L.	–	1888	Died at Kinshasa, 1901.
43. Forfeitt, W. L.	–	1889	Retired, 1924.
44. White, W. H.	–	1889	Died at sea, 1897.

Date of Acceptance

45. Forfeitt, J. Lawson	– 1889	Returned, 1906.
46. Glennie, R.	– 1889	Returned, 1896.
47. Wilkinson, W. F.	– 1889	Died at San Salvador, 1889.
48. Stapleton, W. H.	– 1889	Died in London, 1906.
49. Gordon, S. C.	– 1890	Retired, 1926.
50. Whitehead, J.	– 1890	
51. Balfern, W. P.	– 1890	Died at Madeira, 1894.
52. Hughes, E.	– 1891	Returned, 1894.
53. Jefferd, F. A.	– 1891	Returned, 1894.
54. Brown, G. D.	– 1892	Returned, 1896.
55. Webb, S. R., M.D.	– 1892	Died at sea, 1896.
56. Pople, G. R.	– 1892	Died at Tumba, 1897.
57. Kirkland, R. H.	– 1893	Retired, 1927.
58. Stonelake, H. T.	– 1894	Transferred to China, 1907.
59. Field, S. M.	– 1894	Returned, 1898.
60. Stephens, J. R. M.	– 1894	Returned, 1906.
61. Bell, J., A.T.S.	– 1895	Transferred to China, 1905.
62. Smith, Kenred	– 1895	Resigned, 1918.
63. Dodds, C. J.	– 1895	Returned, 1911.
64. Beedham, R.	– 1895	Died at Matadi, 1900.
65. Howell, J.	– 1896	Retired, 1922.
66. Wherrett, A. E.	– 1896	Died at Yakusu, 1896.
67. Frame, W. B.	– 1896	
68. Millman, W.	– 1897	
69. Jeffery, J.	– 1897	Died in England, 1900.
70. Adams, A. G.	– 1897	Returned, 1900.
71. Smith, H. Sutton	– 1899	Transferred to China, 1910. Died, 1917.
72. Bowskill, J. S.	– 1899	
73. Wooding, W.	– 1899	Resigned, 1925.
74. Stonelake, A. R.	– 1899	
75. Hooper, G.	– 1899	

Date of Acceptance

76. Kempton, S. O.	–	1899	Died at Yakusu, 1908.
77. Williams, C. T.	–	1899	Returned, 1907.
78. Jennings, R. L.	–	1899	
79. Kirby, W. R.	–	1901	Resigned, 1922.
80. Moore, G. E.	–	1901	Died at Yakusu, 1903.
81. Mayo, A.	–	1901	Died at San Salvador, 1904.
82. Dron, D.	–	1902	Transferred to India, 1905.
83. Wilford, E. E.	–	1902	Died at Yakusu, 1914.
84. Murdoch, W. C.	–	1904	Returned, 1909.
85. Lowrie, P. R.	–	1904	Died at Mabaya, 1911.
86. Oldrieve, F.	–	1905	Transferred to India, 1909.
87. Davies, D. C.	–	1906	
88. Knight, P.	–	1906	Transferred to India, 1909.
89. Thomas, G.	–	1906	
90. Longland, F.	–	1905	Resigned, 1921.
91. Marker, J. H.	–	1906	
92. Gamble, M., M.D., Ch.B.	–	1907	Resigned, 1921.
93. Girling, E. C., M.D., Ch.B.	–	1907	Resigned, 1923.
94. Busfield, E.	–	1908	Returned, 1910.
95. Norman, P. G.	–	1908	Returned, 1910.
96. Beale, F.	–	1908	Resigned, 1926.
97. Pugh, C. E.	–	1909	
98. Jones, David	–	1909	Resigned, 1918.
99. Palmer, A. B., B.A.	–	1909	
100. Lambotte, Henri J.	–	1909	Died at Yakusu, 1918.
101. Exell, F. G.	–	1909	
102. Thompson, S. F.	–	1909	Resigned, 1925.
103. Burrett, G.	–	1909	Returned, 1914.
104. Claridge, G. C.	–	1909	Resigned, 1921.
105. Jones, E. R., M.R.C.S., L.R.C.P.	–	1910	Resigned, 1921.

Date of Acceptance

106. Allen, A. E.	–	1910	
107. Holmes, E.	–	1911	Resigned, 1920; Reappointed, 1922.
108. Powell, T., B.A., B.D.	–	1911	Resigned, 1919.
109. Cook, J. L.	–	1911	Resigned, 1923.
110. Clark, J. N.	–	1911	
111. Mill, A. G.	–	1911	
112. Hynes, W.	–	1912	Resigned, 1921.
113. Reynolds, W. D., B.A., B.D.	–	1912	
114. Lambourne, A. A.	–	1912	
115. Wilkerson, G. J.	–	1912	
116. Gilmore, H. C., L.R.C.P., L.R.C.S.	–	1913–1914	*Locum tenens.*
117. Starte, J.H.	–	1914	
118. Guest, A. E.	–	1916	
119. Hillard, A. W.	–	1917	
120. Jackson, W. M.	–	1917	Resigned, 1921.
121. Chesterman, C. C., O.B.E., M.R.C.S., M.R.C.P., M.D., B.S., D.T.M. & H.	–	1919	
122. Gilmore, H. C., L.R.C.P., L.R.C.S.	–	1919	Resigned, 1926.
123. Austin, P. H.	–	1920	
124. Guyton, E. D. F.	–	1920	
125. Weeks, L. J.	–	1920	
126. Davidson, J.	–	1921	
127. Osborne, S. H.	–	1921	Resigned, 1925.
128. Ennals, W. H.	–	1921	
129. Ford, W. H.	–	1921	
130. Joy, H. C. V., M.D., B.S., M.R.C.S., L.R.C.P., D.T.M. & H.	–	1921	

Date of Acceptance

131. Spear, F. G., M.A.,   –   1921–1923   *Locum tenens.*
     M.B., Ch.B.,
     D.P.H., D.T.M.
     & H., M.R.C.S.,
     L.R.C.P.
132. Glenesk, A. W.   –   1921
133. Wallace, W.   –   1921   Resigned, 1925.
134. Parris, H. B.   –   1922
135. Simpson, A. R. D. –   1922
136. Morrish, E. H.   –   1922
137. Thompson, R. V.   –   1923
     de C.
138. Tyrrell, R. T.   –   1923
139. Chesterman, A.   –   1923
     de M.
140. Wooster, C. H.   –   1923
141. Fox, F. W. W., M.B., – 1923
142. Wilson, W., M.B., –   1923
     Ch.B.
143. Hancock, M. W.   –   1924
144. MacBeath, A. G. W., – 1924
     M.A., B.D.
145. Newbery, S. J.   –   1924
146. Tweedley, J.   –   1924
147. Neal, A. R.   –   1925
148. Todd, K. W.,   –   1926
     M.R.C.S., L.R.C.P.
149. Hern, J. P.   –   1926
     (Associate).
150. Russell, J., M.A. –   1927
151. Parkinson, K. C., –   1927
     M.A.
152. Frost, Donald,   –   1928
     M.B., B.S.,
     M.R.C.S., L.R.C.P.

WOMEN

Date of Marriage or Acceptance

1. Comber, Mrs. T. J.	–	1879	Died at San Salvador, 1879.
2. Grenfell, Mrs.	–	1880	Returned a widow, 1906.
3. Crudgington, Mrs.	–	1883	Transferred to India, 1885.
4. Weeks, Mrs. (*née* Reddall).	–	1886	Died at Monsembi, 1899.
5. Spearing, Miss M. S.	–	1886	Died at Stanley Pool, 1887.
6. Bentley, Mrs.	–	1886	Returned, 1904.
7. Darling, Mrs.	–	1886	Returned a widow, 1887.
8. Lewis, Mrs. (*née* Thomas). (Cameroons, 1884–6).	–	1887	Died at sea, 1909.
9. Moolenaar, Mrs.	–	1887	Returned, 1890.
10. Pinnock, Mrs.	–	1887	Died at Eastbourne, 1895.
11. Phillips, Mrs. (*née* Phillips).	–	1888	Died at San Salvador, 1899.
12. Butcher, Miss (Mrs. J. G. Brown).	–	1888	Returned a widow, 1889.
13. Silvey, Miss (Mrs. Cameron).	–	1888	Died at Wathen, 1893.
14. Graham, Mrs.	–	1888	Returned, 1924.
15. Harrison, Mrs.	–	1890	Returned, 1895.
16. Comber, Mrs. Percy	–	1890	Died at Banana, 1890.
17. Darby, Mrs.	–	1891	Returned, 1894.
18. Webb, Mrs.	–	1893	Returned a widow, 1895.
19. Roger, Mrs.	–	1893	Returned a widow, 1901.
20. Glennic, Mrs.	–	1893	Returned, 1896.
21. Stapleton, Mrs. (1908, Mrs. Millman).	–	1893	
22. Whitehead, Mrs.	–	1893	

Date of Marriage or Acceptance

23. Forfeitt, Mrs. W. L.	– 1893	Returned, 1924.
24. Forfeitt, Mrs. Lawson.	– 1894	Returned, 1906.
25. Scrivener, Mrs. (*née* Baker).	– 1895	Died at Bolobo, 1898.
26. De Hailes, Miss L. M.	– 1895	
27. Gordon, Mrs. (*née* N. Gordon).	– 1896	Died at Atlanta, U.S.A., 1901.
28. Pople, Mrs.	– 1896	Died at Tumba, 1897.
29. Howell, Mrs.	– 1896	Returned, 1922.
30. Bell, Mrs. (*née* Feisser).	– 1896	Died at Wathen, 1901.
31. White, Mrs.	– 1896	Returned a widow, 1897.
32. Clark, Mrs. J. A.	– 1896	
33. Kirkland, Mrs.	– 1896	Died at Bolobo, 1901.
34. Stephens, Mrs.	– 1898	Returned, 1905; died in England, 1923.
35. Brindal, Miss L. A.	– 1898	Returned, 1900.
36. Dodds, Mrs. (*née* Carr).	– 1898	Died at sea, 1903.
37. Beedham, Mrs.	– 1899	Returned a widow, 1900.
38. Wooding, Mrs.	– 1899	Returned, 1925.
39. Stonelake, Mrs. A. R.	– 1899	
40. Smith, Mrs. Kenred (*née* Gregg).	– 1899	Died at Yakusu, 1901.
41. Stonelake, Mrs. H. T.	– 1900	Died in England, 1903.
42. Cameron, Mrs. (*née* Glover).	– 1901	Returned, 1913; died in Canada, 1927.
43. Millman, Mrs. (*née* Langley).	– 1901	Died at Monsembi, 1902.
44. Scrivener, Mrs. (*née* Gillman).	– 1902	Died at Bolobo, 1903.
45. Gordon, Mrs. (*née* Jackson).	– 1902	Died at sea, 1910.
46. Bowskill, Mrs.	– 1903	

Date of Marriage or Acceptance

47. Kirby, Mrs.	–	1903	Returned, 1922.
48. Pinnock, Mrs. (*née* Brown).	–	1903	Returned, 1909.
49. Weeks, Mrs. (*née* Wadlow).	–	1903	Returned, 1906; died in England, 1926.
50. Denton, Miss	–	1903	Returned, 1904.
51. Hooper, Mrs.	–	1904	
52. Jennings, Mrs.	–	1904	
53. Mayo, Mrs. (1905, Mrs. Kirkland).	–	1904	Returned, 1927.
54. Dodds, Mrs. (*née* Mann).	–	1906	Returned, 1911.
55. Frame, Mrs.	–	1906	
56. Wilford, Mrs.	–	1906	Returned a widow, 1914.
57. Phillips, Mrs. (formerly Mrs. Bauer, S.M.S.).	–	1906	
58. Gamble, Mrs.	–	1908	Returned, 1921.
59. Coppin, Miss H. G.	–	1908	
60. Shead, Miss M.	–	1908	Returned, 1914.
61. Beale, Mrs.	–	1909	Returned, 1926.
62. Cotter, Miss B.	–	1909	Died at San Salvador, 1910.
63. Smith, Mrs. H. Sutton.	–	1909	Transferred to China, 1912.
64. Lowrie, Mrs.	–	1909	Returned, 1910.
65. Collett, Miss L. A. W.	–	1909	Resigned, 1921.
66. Paterson, Miss H. A. (1916, Mrs. Claridge).	–	1909	Returned, 1921.
67. Jackson, Miss A.	–	1909	Returned, 1916.
68. Bell, Miss A. H.	–	1909	
69. Smith, Mrs. Kenred (*née* Walker).	–	1910	Returned, 1918.
70. Longland, Mrs.	–	1910	Returned, 1921.
71. Girling, Mrs.	–	1910	Returned, 1923.

Date of Marriage or Acceptance

72. Marker, Mrs.	– 1910	
73. Whitmore, Miss E. N. (1914, Mrs. Lambotte).	– 1910	Returned a widow, 1918.
74. Lewis, Mrs. (*née* Bean).	– 1911	Died in England, 1923.
75. Thomas, Mrs.	– 1911	
76. Holmes, Mrs.	– 1911	
77. Gee, Miss (1915, Mrs. Hynes).	– 1911	Returned, 1921.
78. James, Miss D. H.	– 1911	
79. Pugh, Mrs.	– 1912	
80. Hickson, Miss G. M.	– 1912	Resigned, 1921.
81. Moss, Miss M. M. (1913, Mrs. Powell).	– 1912	Returned, 1919.
82. Wilson, Miss A. M.	– 1912	
83. Wilkerson, Mrs.	– 1912	
84. Exell, Mrs.	– 1913	
85. Thompson, Mrs. S. F.	– 1913	Returned, 1925.
86. Palmer, Mrs.	– 1913	
87. Clappen, Miss S. K.	– 1913	Resigned, 1921.
88. Claridge, Mrs. (*née* Darcy).	– 1914	Died at San Salvador, 1914.
89. Allen, Mrs.	– 1914	
90. Cook, Mrs.	– 1914	Returned, 1923.
91. Davies, Mrs.	– 1914	
92. Clark, Mrs. J. N.	– 1914	
93. Jones, Mrs. E. R.	– 1914	Returned, 1921.
94. Brooks, Miss Mary O'K. (1921, Mrs. Gilmore).	– 1916	Returned, 1927.
95. Ingram, Miss E. E.	– 1917	Resigned, 1921.
96. Lambourne, Miss J.	– 1917	
97. Reynolds, Mrs.	– 1917	

Date of Marriage or Acceptance

98. Hughes, Miss H. (1923, Mrs. Hillard).	–	1918	
99. Smith, Miss F. J.	–	1918	Resigned, 1921.
100. Mill, Mrs. A.G. Mill	–	1918	
101. Chesterman, Mrs. C. C.	–	1919	
102. Peacop, Miss D. (1924, Mrs. Wooster).	–	1919	
103. Barter, Miss E. W.	–	1919	Resigned, 1922.
104. Birrell, Miss C.	–	1920	Transferred to China, 1924
105. Bull, Miss B.	–	1920	Resigned, 1924.
106. Bliss, Miss G.	–	1920	
107. Austin, Mrs.	–	1920	
108. Starte, Mrs. Wife of Harold Starte	–	1920	
109. Hammond, Miss M.	–	1920	
110. Milledge, Miss E. K.	–	1921	
111. Joy, Mrs.	–	1921	
112. Head, Miss L. E.	–	1921	
113. Harper, Miss F. M., M.B., Ch.B., D.P.H., D.T.M.	–	1921–1923	*Locum tenens.*
114. Scruton, Miss E.	–	1921	Resigned, 1923.
115. Petrie, Miss N. F.	–	1922	
116. Reiling, Miss G.	–	1923	
117. Wilkinson, Miss A.	–	1923	
118. Davidson, Mrs.	–	1923	
119. Morrish, Mrs.	–	1923	Died in England, 1926.
120. Simpson, Mrs.	–	1923	
121. Weeks, Mrs. L. J.	–	1923	
122. Wilson, Mrs.	–	1925	
123. Ennals, Mrs.	–	1925	

Date of Marriage or Acceptance

124. Ford, Mrs.	– 1926	Died at Yakusu, 1927.
125. Lofts, Miss P.	– 1926	
126. Hern, Mrs. J. P. (Associate).	– 1926	
127. Coles, Miss M.	– 1927	
128. Tyrrell, Mrs.	– 1927	
129. Thompson, Mrs. R. V. de C.	– 1927	
130. Tweedley, Mrs.	– 1927	
131. Guest, Mrs.	– 1928	

APPENDIX L
INDEX TO PHOTOS AND MAPS

Uncle Alex's birth family
Alex and Ethel (c. 1950)
Alex and Barbara (c. 1960)
A pen drawing of the "Grenfell"; marriage of Mons. Lambotte and Ms. Whitemore, 1914
Aunt Ethel's graduation photo; On the field in the 1930s
Life in the Belgian Congo (1925–1940)
Childhood photos of Barbara Mill and her parents
Uncle Alex, Barbara, and Glasgow cousins
The Upper Congo Mission Areas (c. 1940)
Congo Independent State: Roman Catholic and Protestant Missions (1878–1908)
Diploma from the Ecole de Médecine Tropicale, Bruxelles
Photos of Uncle Alex with some of the American relatives
Photos of visit of John, Maxine and David to Cambridge, 1956
Record of service as chaplain with the Belgian Congo Army—1916

THE BIRTH FAMILY OF REV. ALEXANDER G. MILL

Father, Frederick George Stuart Mill; Mother, Catherine
Goudie Mill; Gladstone Stuart, Alexander George and
Clara Anna (my mother)
  Glasgow. c. 1900

Rev. and Mrs. Alexander G. Mill
Baptist Missionary Society
Haut Congo Belge
West Central Africa

UNCLE ALEX & AUNT
ETHEL
In their garden, 40 Blinco
Grove, Cambridge c. 1950

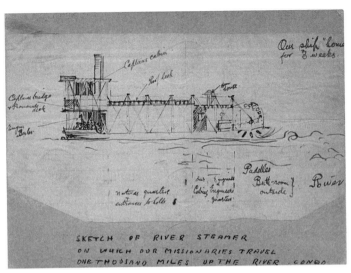

A DRAWING BY A.G. MILL of the river steamer "Grenfell".
(Note: I saw the rusting boiler and engine on the banks of Stanley
Pool, Kinshasha in Zaire in December, 1975.)

THE WEDDING OF HENRI
LAMBOTTE AND E.N.
WHITEMORE in 1914 in
Yakusu. He was the first
Belgian missionary to be sent
to the Congo in 1908. He met
and married Ms. Whitemore,
a fellow missionary, in 1914.
A daughter, Yvonne, was
born to them in 1917. M.
Lambotte died suddenly at
the age of 34 years in 1918.
He and Uncle Alex were fast
colleagues and housemates
during Alex's first years in
the Congo, 1909–1911.

ETHEL CLARA STARTE
Graduation photo, Guy's Hospital
London c. 1915

AUNT ETHEL at Okuru, Upper Lomami greeting the Chief's wife, 1930s

LIFE IN THE BELGIAN CONGO (1925–1940)

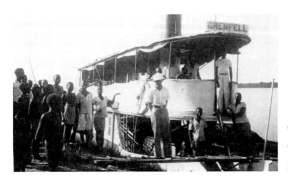

The mission river boat "Grenfell" on the Congo River c. 1930

Aunt Ethel boarding a river raft on the Lomami River, Belgian Congo c. 1940

Aunt Ethel and her bicycle in front of the Yalikina church in construction c. 1930

The lovely Yalikina missionary residence built by Uncle Alex around 1930. This was the mission station which they built in the early 1930s. It was strategically located at the confluence of the Congo and Lomami Rivers.

BARBARA MARY MILL—c. 1920–1930

As a baby in Yakusu, Belgian Congo

At age three in Belen, New Mexico with her parents. They were visiting my parents on their first and only trip to the U.S.A. as a family. 1923

At home in Yakusu. Uncle Alex, Aunt Ethel and baby Barbara on the veranda. c. 1921

On vacation in France, 1929

MAXINE AND
UNCLE ALEX
At King's College
Chapel Cambridge,
England 1969

UNCLE ALEX IN THE U.S.A. 1967
with his great nieces Kay and Andrea

OUR VISIT WITH UNCLE
ALEX IN CAMBRIDGE
1956

JOHN, PAUL, UNCLE
ALEX AND MAXINE
Cambridge, England 1969

UNCLE ALEX,
DAVID AND
MAXINE 1956

UNCLE ALEX, DAVID AND MAXINE
Boating on the Cam River, Cambridge 1956

UNCLE ALEX AND DORIE
MILL Glasgow 1968

THE UPPER CONGO MISSION AREAS (C. 1940)

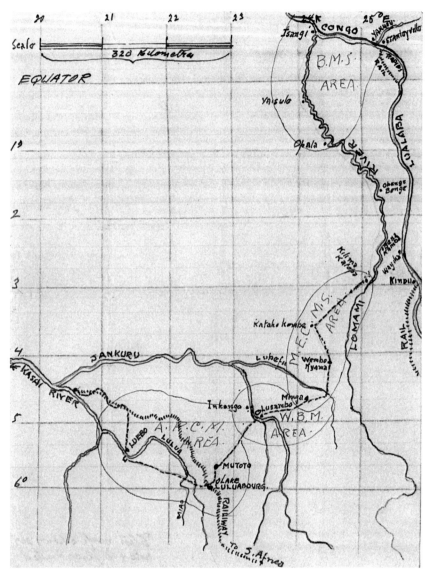

B.M.S. Baptist Missionary Society (Great Britain)
M.E.C.M.S. Methodist Episcopal Congo Mission South (U.S.A.)
A.P.C.M. American Presbyterian Congo Mission (U.S.A.)
W.B.M. World Baptist Mission (U.S.A.)

MAP 2. – Protestant Missionary settlement in the Congo (with a location of the areas of Catholic settlement).

Source: Slade, Robert N., editor, ENGLISH-SPEAKING MISSIONS IN THE CONGO INDEPENDENT STATE: 1878–1908, published in 1959.

ROYAUME DE BELGIQUE

MINISTÈRE DES COLONIES

ECOLE DE MÉDECINE TROPICALE

BRUXELLES

Le présent certificat est délivré à M. Mull. Alexander George, né à Glasgow, qui, pour satisfaire qu'il a pris part régulièrement du 1er Mai au 1er Juillet 1914 les cours suivants de l'École de Médecine Tropicale de Bruxelles: éléments de petit chimurgie et de pharmacologie, Hygiène coloniale, Zoologie médicale, Pathologie exotique, Bactériologie et helminthologie, Pathologie pathogène, Pathologie animale exotique.

Etc., et a subi, obtenu soixante trois points sur cent à l'examen sur les dits matières.

Bruxelles, le 8 Juillet 1914.

Le Ministre

Les Professeurs.

Signature du Porteur du Certificat.

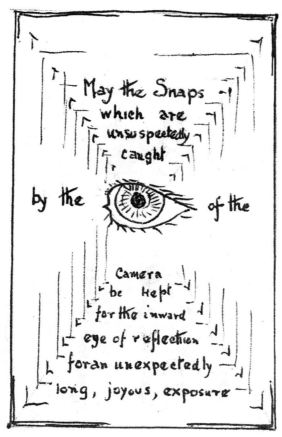

A PEN DRAWING BY UNCLE ALEX found on the inside cover of his photo album. This is one example of his artistic and romantic sense in much that he did.

APPENDIX M

Candidate papers of A.G. Mill to the Baptist Missionary Society.

Rev. Princ. A. M'Craig.

Name of Candidate.

Alexander George Mill.

How long have you been personally acquainted with the Candidate?

About four years

What has been the nature of
the home training and discipline?

Good Christian - His father is a ...

What is your impression as to
general mental power, education, and
aptitude for learning?

He has considerable mental power, & good ...

Is the Candidate likely, in
your judgment, to thoroughly
acquire a foreign language?

Is there reason to think that
the Candidate is well able to secure
success at home, and that the offer
of missionary service is made from
pure and good motives?

Has the Candidate ever been
engaged to be married?

I do not know

If the Candidate is at present
engaged to be married, are you able
to state that, in your judgment,
the engagement is entirely suitable
in view of the prospect of foreign
missionary service?

do

What testimony can you give as
to personal habits, temper and
general deportment?

343

Is the Candidate possessed
of good judgment and resourcefulness?   *[handwritten]*

Is the Candidate thoroughly
practical, orderly, and diligent
in every-day matters?   *[handwritten]*

Is the Candidate, as far as
you know, disposed to be quarrelsome
or difficult to work with?   *[handwritten]*

As far as you are able to judge
has the Candidate a good physical
constitution.   *[handwritten]*

Do you know of any serious illness in the past, or any matter which
is liable to render the Candidate
unable to stand life and work in a
tropical climate?   *[handwritten]*

Can you testify to the personal
piety and religious earnestness of
the Candidate?   *[handwritten]*

Do you know of any instances in
which the Candidate has been the
means of the conversion of souls?   *[handwritten]*

In what kind of Christian work
have you known the Candidate to engage?   *[handwritten]*

Have you ever heard the Candidate
speak in Public?   *[handwritten]*

What is your judgment as to
the Candidate's ability to convey the
teaching of the Gospel to non-Christians
in a clear and forcible manner?

[handwritten] At first there was some lack of clearness in his presentation of the truth, but he has developed excellent readiness ... his preaching in the churches.

Does the Candidate hold a
place of honour and respect among
friends in the Church, and outside
the Church?

[handwritten] Yes, undoubtedly.

Can the Candidate get on
well with children?

[handwritten] I think he can.

Can you heartily recommend
that the Candidate be accepted as a
Missionary of the Baptist Missionary
Society?

[handwritten] I can

Signed *[handwritten] A. McCbay*

[handwritten paragraph] I really believe Mr Mill will make a good missionary. He has the missionary spirit ... enthusiasm, although his natural disposition might incline to ... and deliberation. He is not an ordinary every man. His powers are something special ... of a high order, and believe he is fully consecrated to the great work. He will never be a mere echo of other voices, or a ... imitator of other men, but in his own personality he will be ... to the great Master.

[handwritten] A. Mc

Rev. R. A. Edgar Anderton.

Name of Candidate.

Alexander George Mill.

How long have you been personally acquainted with the Candidate?

Since June, 1902.

What has been the nature of
the home training and discipline?

His mother was an earnest Christian
& trained her children well; the father
tho' a professing Christian, is a strange man &
has little influence over his family.

What is your impression as to
general mental power, education, and
aptitude for learning?

I should say that the mental power is
above the average, education moderate; aptitude
for learning good.

Is the Candidate likely, in
your judgment, to thoroughly
acquire a foreign language?

Yes, I can speak from first hand
knowledge.

Is there reason to think that
the Candidate is well able to secure
success at home, and that the offer
of missionary service is made from
pure and good motives?

Yes.

Has the Candidate ever been
engaged to be married?

Not as far as I know. He has not
yet told me of a definite engagement,
but he is on the way.

If the Candidate is at present
engaged to be married, are you able
to state that, in your judgment,
the engagement is entirely suitable
in view of the prospect of foreign
missionary service?

What testimony can you give as
to personal habits, temper and
general deportment?

A very favourable one; candidate's
habits have always been those of a
Christian, he has great command of
his temper.

Is the Candidate possessed
of good judgment and resourcefulness?

I think so.

Is the Candidate thoroughly
practical, orderly, and diligent
in every-day matters?

As far as I have been able to judge.

Is the Candidate, as far as
you know, disposed to be quarrelsome
or difficult to work with?

No.

As far as you are able to judge
has the Candidate a good physical
constitution.

Yes.

Do you know of any serious illness in the past, or any matter which
is liable to render the Candidate
unable to stand life and work in a
tropical climate?

*No, in his early college days he was
for a time rather unwell, but seems
to have quite recovered.*

Can you testify to the personal
piety and religious earnestness of
the Candidate?

Most certainly & gladly.

Do you know of any instances in
which the Candidate has been the
means of the conversion of souls?

Yes.

In what kind of Christian work
have you known the Candidate to engage?

*Sunday Sch., C.E. (junior & senior), open
-air speaking, visitation, preaching.*

Have you ever heard the Candidate
speak in Public?

Frequently.

What is your judgment as to the Candidate's ability to convey the teaching of the Gospel to non-Christians in a clear and forcible manner?

clearness & force
In this respect he has shown a marked improvement during the last two or three years.

Does the Candidate hold a place of honour and respect among friends in the Church, and outside the Church?

Undoubtedly.

Can the Candidate get on well with children?

Rather.

Can you heartily recommend that the Candidate be accepted as a Missionary of the Baptist Missionary Society?

With a solemn sense of responsibility, I can answer "yes."

Signed *R. A. Edgar Anderton*

B. M. S.

APPLICATION FOR MISSION SERVICE.

No. in Candidate Register *520*　Date of Application *12th March 1908*

For what Mission *Congo?*

NAME *MILL, Alexander George*　AGE *25*

ADDRESS *92 Stratford Street*
Maryhill Glasgow

COLLEGES *Pastors' and Livingstone*

Questions Sent *9th Feb 1911*　Answers Rec'd *9th March 1911*

REFEREES.

Rev R. A. Edgar Anderton	Letters
Mr G. A. Saunders ✓	sent
Mr W. Olney ✓	4th
Princ. A. M'Caig ✓	May
Dr. C. F. Harford ✓	

CANDIDATE COMMITTEE *15th May 1911*

GENERAL COMMITTEE *16th May 1911*

MEDICAL OPINION (self) *Bars Congo suggests India.*

(fiancée) *To see Dr again after Xmas holidays*

RESULT *Accepted.*
SIGNED AGREEMENT

PASTOR,
R. A. E. ANDERTON,
34 GOWER STREET, KELVINSIDE, N.

SECRETARY,
W. FORSYTH,
ROMAN ROAD, BEARSDEN.

TREASURER.
A. A. KENNEDY,
26 PERCY STREET, KELVINSIDE, N.

Kelvinside Baptist Church,
Queen Margaret Drive,
Glasgow.

July 1st 1907

Dear Mr Wilson,

I should have answered your circular before this.

Owing to another Anniversary on June 23rd & 24th we were unable to arrange for any Missionary service or meeting on those dates. But we had an extra Missionary meeting on June 18th.

We are a small Church and are struggling with a building scheme, but you may notice that

I Remain,
Yours Faithfully
R. A. Edgar Anderton

though our offerings to the B.M.S. and S.S. &c. have not largely yet each year they are steadily increasing, especially is this the case with the Medical Auxiliary.

During the year closing this March, our Sunday contributions came to within a few pence of £35, fine offerings they were under £6.

One of our finest young members, Mr. Alec. G. Brill, is this August entering the Pastors' College, and it is his earnest desire to offer himself to the B.M.S. Committee for service at the close of this course.

Generally, there is a fine missionary spirit in our Church and we never miss the monthly prayer meeting, besides having study classes for the young men in the winter.

"One personal word. I wish you abundant blessing in your great work as the General Secretary of our Society.

Often when you were a student at Regents Park, I heard you preach at Gaze Pond,—before and during Mr. Kettle's ministry. I was brought up at Gaze Pond, and had my first experience of Christian work there, being eventually S.S. Secretary.

With apologies for trespassing so much on your time,

MILL,

a G { 148. Stockwell Park
Road
Brixton. S.W.

c/o Saunders

15 Warner Street,
SW.

AGE.

Student at { Livingstone
Pastors } Colleges

Questions A. sent ... 9. 2. 11.

Interview with Mr Wilson

13th March 2.30 pm.

- Preliminary Medical Inquiry
started - Nov: '10.
- To see C.E.W. when calling
to see Dr Moorshead
- Free to leave Coll:
- Profr: Hackney urges course
at Livingstone Coll:, &
asks re financial help.
- Medical testimony bars Congo.
but suggests India.
- Wrote suggesting interview
for 4 Jany. 24:12:10.
✱ Entering Livingstone Coll: Jan: 9
for 6 months' course.
£25 P. Coll, £25 C.I. Foster.

Form. A.

Question N8 1. Alexander George Mill

2. 92 Stratford St, Maryhill, Glasgow (after June 1911)

3. 25 Years.

4. No.

5. Belmonside Baptist Ch. Glasgow. 1898

6. " " " "

7. General Education in Connal School,
Evening Classes in. Art, Building Construction, Architecture
(apprenticeship for 7 years): Engineering & Surveying

8. Commercial & Engineering Office work.

9. The Theological course at Pastors College, Newington S.F.
any the 6 Months course at Livingstone Coll.

10. (Public) Evening Class Examinations. I have no failures to
record and I have obtained Certificates in, Building Construction,
and Engineering & General Drawing.

11. It formed in my mind vaguely when a child of
seven years of age through the influence of a
Missionary Meeting and was expressed as a desire
at that time. When at the age of thirteen, my
parents allowed me to take up Architectural work
as a probable equipment for Pioneer work.
"When fourteen years of age I formed my own
definite resolve under strong inward conviction.
The purpose" was not arrived at by reasoning
but by the combined feelings of anxiety for the fate of
the Heathen and a desire to glorify Christ in their
Salvation.

Question 11^con The reasons why I personally offer myself are that I have had the honour of serving Christ here and I feel that my talents may be put out to the best interest in a Heathen land.

12. The Congo has been my objective and the work on the upper river at Yalemba is that to which my mind especially turns

13. Sunday School (Teaching)
Bible Class. (Essays &c)
Junior Christian Endeavour Society (Superintendency)
Senior " " " (Secretaryship)
Local Preaching
Open Air "
Sick Visiting

14 Wherever the glad tidings have not been known or are imperfectly understood I consider it my prime business to proclaim the Evangel and afterwards to guide the converts in its practical developments.
I have had considerable dealings with individuals in connection with open air work but most of these have been intoxicated, indifferent or disputatious. Very few have been enquirers. I have visited a number of cases in their homes but have not had a stated post as "district visitor."

15 In the Classical Languages my examination results have been 90% but I have not acquired the ability to converse in any modern language and I have not travelled abroad.

Question 16. I have not made reading a pastime and most of my time has been given to prescribed College studies.

History, Green's Short History of Eng; people (Part): Annals of Tacitus (Extract): Gibbon's Decline & fall of Roman Empire (Extract): Prescott's Conquest of Mexico & Peru (Extracts).

Poetry. Tennyson:-
In Memoriam (Part)
Palace of Art.
Maud
Idyls of the King
Lockesley Hall
The Lotos eaters
Œnone &c

Longfellow
Golden Legend
Hiawatha
Evangeline
The Ship &c

Cowper.

Milton
Paradise Lost (part)
" Regained
Samson Agonistes &c

Shakespere
Miscellaneous.

Scott.
Lady of the Lake

Lay of the Last Minstrel
Rokeby.

Macaulay

Fiction. Boys stories: Tale of Two Cities, Dickens: Lorna Doone, Blackmore: Sesame & Lillies, Ruskin.

Travel. Through Darkest Africa, Stanley:
Geographical works:- Reclus:

Biography. Wm Carey: Jas Chalmers of New Guinea: David Livingstone: James Gilmour of Mongolia: McKay of Uganda.

Missionary Work. Missionary Herald: Social Evils of the Non Christian World: Uplift of China; Desire of India: Daybreak in the Dark Continent Reproach of Islam, Decisive Hour of Christian Missions: Congo for Christ. Pioneering on the Congo (Vol 1): Things as they are.

Theology. Christian Doctrine, Dr Dale: Life of Christ, Dr Stalker: Trial & Death of Jesus Christ, Imago Christi, Ethic of Jesus, The Four Men, Ibid:

17. I have only made a general survey of Non Christian religions through the Mission Study Textbooks. The

Question 17. The subject of Animism and Fetichism as the superstition of the Congo I have only considered in Daybreak on the Dark Continent, The Congo for Christ and Pioneering on the Congo.

Question 18. The Salient truths of Christianity first of all with regard to God are these in my judgement. That knowledge of Him comes through a moral revelation given through men by the Holy Spirit and centralised in the Incarnation of Jesus Christ. That access to this knowledge is obtained by reverent obedience to the teaching of Jesus as recorded in the Gospels. That His nature is that of an Invisible, Holy, Loving Person without equal, who does not seek the sacrifice of man but sacrifices for him in the Person of the Lamb of God. That His purpose is to gather together all things in Christ as the federal head of a new race and to glorify all believers with Him in a future life.

That He claims to govern men by the Law of Virtue: blessing the willing and punishing the stubborn. That He claims the right to forgive and to exercise on the ground of His own sacrifice boundless mercy to the penitent. That He claims the power to destroy everyone hostile to Him and to glorify every one serving Him in a future life.

The outstanding truths of Christianity with

Question 18 Ans — with regard to man, in my judgement, are these
That his sin consists in a turning away of the Soul
from God: manifested in dishonouring thoughts and
disobedient actions and issuing in a persistent
course of wandering, perverse, desires which are
controled by the Devil.   That man's soul
is the part which recognises God since it was
made in His image. That man should live all
this life for the development of his soul for
if he neglects and looses this he is condemned
to Eternal death.   That it is mans duty
to submit to all the dictates of conscience;
to exercise kindness to all his fellow men and
to try to achieve Gods glory. That Mans
destiny in this life is to develop character..
It can only be fully done when he has accepted
Christ and becomes like Him.   That mans
destiny in the future life is to enter into the
true possession and full exercise of all his
faculties in a ressurection body fit to enjoy
pleasures apart from sin, and which centre in
Christ.   This is only possible if he is redeemed.
If he is not redeemed he is condemned, (if
impenitent) to be deprived of his abused faculties
and to be confined in a ressurection body unfit to
achieve its desires and deprived of the opportunities
for sinful enjoyments and to be associated with the
                                                    Devil.

Question 18 ᶜᵒⁿ Communication between God and man is possible entirely through the Spirit in the most intimate manner. Such communion is possible only for pure souls since "they walk in the light as He is in the light ..... and the blood of Jesus Christ, His Son, cleanses them from all sin."

This purity is possessed in the act of Faith which continues through a life of Faith.

My message is :-

"That repentance is the attitude we must take up respecting our sins and that implicit faith, for full deliverance from guilt incurred and for blessing in this life and immortality and glory in the next, is to be placed only in the Lord Jesus Christ; who accomplished, on Calvary the Redemption from Sin and the Atonement.

"Herein is Love, not that we loved God, but that He loved us and sent His Son to be the propitiation for our sins."

19. Yes.
20   (a) Mr Wilson. Havington Causeway. S.E.
     (b) No
     (c) Yes (but with slight indigestion)
     (d) Yes.

Question 21.   Rev. P. A. Edgar Anderton
                84 Gower St. Kelvinside N. Glasgow
Mr G A Saunders
                15 Warner St. New Kent Rd. S.E.
Mr William Ilney,
                Haddon Hall. Tower Br Rd. S.E.
Principal A. M'Caig.
                Signature :- A. G. Mill
                        Date :-   7/ May 1911.

TELEPHONE,
STREATHAM 967.

GRESHAM LODGE,
STREATHAM COMMON NORTH,
S.W.

Dec 5th 1910
Dear Mr Wilson

Mr Mill of Rawdon College is coming to see you.
He is a man of somewhat remarkable quality.
a strong personality. taking his own way: resolute
almost to a fault. when he is convinced, very thoughtful.
a first class student + worker: earnest + devoted
in his own piety. a character: with some Scotch
drawbacks. which will be rubbed off. + have a
vigorous. dependable. brainy. and fruitful nature.
I believe. His health is a care. as to whether it
is firm enough for what he wants. If he can have

APPENDIX N

Article "The Severed Hands" pp. 585–601

PART FOUR RESISTANCE AND REFORM

IN THE RUBBER COILS

CHAPTER 32
The Severed Hands
Brussels, London, Paris and the Congo
16 May 1902–February 1904

> Wild beasts—the leopards—killed some of us while
> we were working away in the forest and others got
> lost or died from exposure or starvation and we
> begged the white men to leave us alone, saying we
> could get no more rubber, but the white men and
> the soldiers said: Go. You are only beasts
> yourselves. You are only Nyama [meat].

> Testimony of Congo villagers interviewed by Consul
> Casement, 1893

Early on the morning of 16 May 1902, a fortnight before the peace treaty between the British and the Boers was signed at Vereeniging, when stray shots from the veld still echoed through the columns of the European papers, the canister containing *The Times* arrived with its usual thump in the royal siding at Laeken, outside Brussels.

No doubt King Leopold read page eleven with attention, after enjoying his early morning ride round the park at Laeken, mounted on what he called *"mon animal"*[1]—a large new tricycle. That morning's *Times* devoted a half column to a protest meeting held in the Mansion House, London, the evening before, to condemn "grievous wrongs" against the natives of the Congo. Two resolutions were solemnly adopted: to call on all the Powers which had signed the Berlin and Brussels Acts to "co-operate in procuring the necessary reforms"; and to call on the British government to take the initiative.[2] But the hall at the Mansion House was half empty, and there seemed nothing to alarm the King.

The driving force behind this protest meeting was a couple of English do-gooders who had been yapping at the King's heels for many years— Richard Fox Bourne, secretary of the old-style emancipationist society, the Aborigines Protection Society, and Sir Charles Dilke, the Radical MP for the Forest of Dean. Clearly their aim was to poison international opinion against Leopold, but their efforts were only sporadically successful. Neither of these self-styled humanitarians was the man to turn Congo agitation into a movement—even in England. Fox Bourne enjoyed a wide circle of enemies, as he dutifully denounced European administration all over Africa. Dilke had been considered a pariah by many of his old friends ever since his appearance in Mrs. Crawford's lurid divorce case, seventeen years before.

What was new was that these humanitarians had now joined hands with the men of commerce, God with Mammon. John Holt, Vice-President of the Liverpool Chamber of Commerce, claimed that he had a commercial grievance against the Congo Free State for breaking the rules of free trade laid down in the General Act of Berlin. Leopold seized upon this pact with Liverpool eagerly. For ten years Fox Bourne and Dilke had been shaking their fists at him and their motives had puzzled him. Had they been duped by disgruntled ex-employees of the Free State? It seemed clear to him now that their concern was a sham—a cloak beneath which the Liverpool merchants, jealous of his own commercial success, were trying to steal the Congo from him. (The King, so skilful at concealing his own motives, was all the more ready to detect the same talent in others.)

Leopold, however, did not have to muddy his hands exposing the plot against him. He left that to his official diplomatic network, and to the hidden ring of admirers he continued to recruit in Europe and America. The Free State delegates he sent to the Mansion House meeting in London (of which the organizers had forewarned him) had been instructed to be bland and reassuring. Let the evidence of wrongdoing, if such evidence existed, be conveyed to the government of the Free State. In other words, the world could trust the King-Sovereign. He would see justice was done.

It was this majestic self-confidence that had kept the shine on Leopold's armour throughout the last, dangerous phase of the Scramble. Only once, in 1895–6, had the armour shown a conspicuous dent. There was the unfortunate business of the British trader, Charlie Stokes, who had insisted on selling Congolese ivory to German East Africa, and German guns to the Congolese. (Stokes was the ex-missionary and ivory trader who had played the crucial part in supplying arms to Lugard in Uganda.) In January 1895 he was caught gunrunning in the Congo, then tried and hanged by a Belgian officer, Captain Lothaire.

The story of the hanging had somehow slipped into the English newspapers, and there had been a fine hullabaloo. Salisbury's government protested about legal irregularities. As a result, Captain Lothaire had to endure three trials himself. He was conveniently acquitted, through lack of State evidence, and promoted director of the main concessionary company in the Congo. Leopold found the whole business distasteful. He had no wish to publicize the rough-and-ready way in which justice was dispensed on the Congo's eastern frontier, and he took steps to protect the good name of the Congo.

In 1896 Leopold appointed a six-man commission—the Native Protection Commission—to notify the judicial authorities of any "acts of violence of which natives may be victims".[3] Its members were all churchmen of unimpeachable rectitude: three Belgian Catholic priests, two British Baptist missionaries and one American Baptist. In the Congo their work never came to anything, of course. Their posts were too scattered for them to hold meetings, and they all lived far from the rubber-producing districts where the alleged atrocities took place. But in Europe the Commission worked wonders for Leopold. Who could now doubt his lofty motives—or deny that he was going to continue to put his personal fortune at the disposal of this great humanitarian venture in Africa to "regenerate" the black man and make the Congo (as he put it) a "model state"?[4]

This was the height of his ambition, Leopold repeated with arresting sincerity to the influential British visitors he counted on recruiting as admirers, after they enjoyed his hospitality at Laeken. Among them were diplomats, like the obsequious British minister, Sir Constantine Phipps, and the earnest young Consul, Roger Casement (whom Leopold entertained twice before he left to serve in the Congo as British Consul in 1900); timid missionaries, like Grattan Guinness and A.H. Baynes, the heads of the Congo Bolobo Mission and the Baptist Missionary Society; pushy capitalists like Alfred Jones, whose worldwide shipping interests included control of the Elder Dempster Shipping Line, which enjoyed the lucrative monopoly of the shipping service between Antwerp and the Congo.

Despite the lingering after-taste of the Stokes affair, the Native Commission took the sting out of the sporadic reports of abuses by the Congo State. As the years passed, the yelps of the British humanitarians began to seem faintly absurd. At the same time, the King savoured the new sensation of being honoured in Belgium.

Few constitutional monarchs have despised their subjects more cordially, yet yearned so much to win their affection. Leopold had long been fascinated by town planning. It symbolized autocracy, and suited his acquisitive tastes. He bought up land wherever he could find it—in the sand dunes of Ostend, the green fields outside Brussels, and the slums within it. In 1900, with the help of a French architect, he began to create public monuments of Napoleonic grandeur. He sliced avenues through Brussels, threw up a triumphal arch to celebrate, belatedly, the fiftieth anniversary of the Belgian State, built a Congo museum at Tervuren, enlarged Laeken, and laid out public parks in Ostend. Then he astonished everyone by presenting these splendid monuments to his people, together with Laeken and other royal domains he had inherited, in the form of a *donation royale.* Naturally his subjects were flattered to be invited to garden fêtes in the newly-donated property, though the King continued to occupy the palaces just as before. The point was symbolic. The monarch was prepared to be loved by his subjects—and love him some of them did. Once, when he came to lay the foundation stone of a new building, he was left speechless and almost in tears, so rapturous was the applause.

Less well advertised to his people were Leopold's ardent feelings for a buxom young French girl called Blanche Delacroix. The affair began in Paris some time in 1900 when Blanche was about sixteen. Leopold was sixty-five. For years he had enjoyed discreet diversions in the back streets of Paris. He was estranged from the Queen, Marie-Henriette, and from his tiresome daughters who insisted on marrying beneath them, after the collapse of the dynastic marriages he had provided. In 1902 the unfortunate Queen died at Spa. Leopold celebrated his release by installing Blanche in a villa discreetly linked to Laeken by a footbridge.

The affair with "Baronne de Vaughan" (a sham title conferred on the girl) had its ludicrous side. Who would have dreamt that this imperious old man, pedalling in the palace grounds at Laeken on a large tricycle, had a mistress of eighteen from whom he would meekly accept instructions? Sometimes he protested when Blanche ordered him around. Then she would laugh and light a cigar. It seemed that Leopold had finally discovered himself. Forgotten were the lonely years of childhood and the loveless years of marriage. Domestic happiness was a revelation. No matter that the liaison—and the two strapping boys, Lucien and Philippe, it was to produce in 1906 and 1907—had to be discreetly managed, so that even his personal secretary never set eyes on the voluptuous baroness during Leopold's lifetime.

With his private fund of happiness came another source of pride for the King, no less intense and private. In the Congo he was making money hand over fist. In public the emphasis remained on the success of private Belgian companies and of the King's own philanthropy. He had enough trouble from busy-bodies like Dilke and Fox Bourne to wish to reveal his unusual skills as a financier. Part of his own profits came from the Congo State's 50 per cent holding in these private companies. At the same time, its trade statistics were doctored to suggest that, like successful colonies in other parts of Africa, the Congo balanced its books, imports against exports, expenditure against revenue.

The true figures, as far as they can be disinterred, prove that the Congo was not like any other colony. Of course, it was not a colony. It was a personal state, the property of one capitalist of genius, the King-Sovereign. Leopold had ridden the world's rubber boom like a man on a trapeze. Before the boom, the Congo's exports had consisted of a trickle of oil and ivory. By 1902, rubber sales had risen fifteen times in eight years, and constituted over 80 per cent of exports, worth over forty-one million francs (£1.64 million). The rubber grew wild and the Free State method of harvesting, if rough-and-ready, was cheap. So exports came to twice as much as imports, and the State secretly amassed a huge surplus of income over expenditure.

Should Leopold re-invest this profit in the Congo, according to the unwritten code practised in colonies elsewhere, to benefit both the natives and European investors? Leopold saw no reason why he should. He flouted convention when he found it convenient, and this was his own money, not the Belgian taxpayers' (if one ignored interest-free loans). His own patrimony, fifteen million francs (£600,000), had been lavished on the Congo in those grim years when everyone except Leopold thought the State would go bankrupt.

He had put his fortune in the Congo. Now he intended to reap the benefit, repaying himself and enjoying the profits. It was these secret profits from the Congo, many times the size of the original investment, that supported the King's lavish spending in Belgium—for the arches and avenues, the parks and the palaces, which made up the *donation royale*—as well as a private paradise at Cap Ferrat in the French Riviera, to which he would slip away with Blanche, whenever the cares of the Belgian state and of his own African empire allowed.

How strange to think that in 1895, seven years before, Leopold had almost thrown in the sponge and handed over the Congo voluntarily to Belgium. On paper, the danger of a Belgian takeover had persisted. In March 1901 came Belgium's chance to exercise her ten-year option over the Congo, acquired in exchange for an interest-free loan of twenty-five million francs. Fortunately for Leopold, the Belgian government and people proved to have even less appetite for the Congo State when financially sound than in 1895 when it appeared on the verge of bankruptcy. The option to make the Congo a Belgian colony was allowed to evaporate. Fortune smiled on Leopold in other ways. He made a bold investment in Chinese railways, which was to net him a profit of about a quarter of a million pounds. But the Congo remained the source of his golden profits, and of his golden name as a philanthropist.

It was natural for English admirers to be dazzled by his talk of Livingstone, of the "3 Cs", and of the sacred task of opening Africa to civilization. Of course, that was not the way His Majesty spoke to his Belgian associates who directed the concessionary companies and their business partner, the Congo State. The employer they knew talked like an absentee landlord, eager for profit and determined not to know too much about how it was made.

In the 1890s, it is true, he had seemed to suffer from periodic twinges of conscience. Did the system of forced labour to extract rubber lend itself to abuse? When foreign missionaries first complained to him, he had accepted that at least some of these stories were true. "It is necessary to put down the horrible abuses," he told Liebrechts, one of the senior officials of the Free State. "These horrors must end or I will retire from the Congo. I will not allow myself to be splattered with blood or mud; it is necessary that these villainies cease."[5] Liebrechts and the others did nothing to check the abuses. They knew that the King's mood would soon pass, and they were right.

By now, in 1902, Leopold had written off his English critics as humbugs, and he was no longer troubled by his conscience. All he was concerned with was profit; and he saw no reason to be alarmed by the yapping of cranks like Fox Bourne or perverts like Dilke.

He had not reckoned with the earnest young man, a twenty-eight-year-old ex-shipping clerk, called Edmond Morel, who was about to change the faltering agitation for reform into one of the greatest of British crusades.

* * *

Georges Edmond Pierre Achille Dene Morel de Ville, to give him his Anglo-French drum-roll of names, was born in a seedy suburb of Paris, the son of a brilliant, feckless, French civil servant and a shy, prim, proud Englishwoman of Quaker stock. His tall, aristocratic good looks came from his father; his temperament from his mother. His father died, almost penniless, when Edmond was four, leaving his mother to scrape a living as a music teacher in Paris. Edmond was sent to England, to Bedford Modern, a public school whose no-nonsense teaching and modest fees appealed to expatriate parents. He left school at fifteen, a confirmed outsider. He identified with England, but with the England of Bunyan and his Quaker ancestors, the men who had launched the movement to abolish slavery.

When he was seventeen, in 1890, his mother wangled him a job as a clerk at Elder Dempster, the Liverpool shipping line controlled by Leopold's admirer, Alfred Jones. Liverpool was the centre of the West African trade and its sinister traditions. Morel soon came under the spell of the mysterious port. "To watch a steamer unload her cargo of palm oil," he wrote later, "bags of kernels, bags and casks of rubber, elephant tusks, huge mahogany logs and so on, always sent a shiver of excitement down my back."[6] To eke out his wages, he began to study Blue Books and write freelance articles on West Africa. In his early twenties he was already an expert on this obscure subject. At first his views on imperialism were conventional. He was a naturalized Englishman; he knew the French, and he distrusted them. He admired Chamberlain's energy in pushing railways into the West African interior. His heroes were the men on the spot who were outwitting Britain's rivals: Goldie, Lugard, Rhodes.

For ten years Morel burnt the candle at both ends, working for Elder Dempster by day, and writing for newspapers by night. His work delighted both sets of employers. At this period (though he did not care to recall it later) he took a brisk line with the old-style humanitarians like Dilke and Fox Bourne who were denouncing the ill-treatment of natives in the Congo. He told the readers of the *Pall Mall Gazette* that he could give them the facts *as they were,* "not as disappointed adventurers, needy place-hunters and misinformed philanthropists would have us believe".[7] As for those stories of ill-treatment of natives, even if true, "What European nation which has undertaken the heavy responsibility of introducing the blessings and vices of civilization into the Dark Continent can claim immunity for its representatives in this respect?"

Were the atrocity stories true? In 1899, after ten years, Morel, the leading British authority on West Africa, found it hard to say. He was prepared to admit that when the King talked of the "blessings" of civilization in the Congo, he was thinking of his own profits. Morel's own work at Elder Dempster brought him into frequent contact with Free State officials in Brussels and Antwerp, and he had not been impressed by their business morality. Whatever it was, the Free State was not a philanthropic enterprise.

There were only a handful of Europeans who claimed to have witnessed atrocities (apart from the Belgian witnesses to the hanging of Stokes). One was Captain Sidney Hinde, the British army doctor who had published a sensational book on his service with Dhanis in the Arab war, including accounts of the atrocities practised by the cannibals fighting for the Free State. Was Hinde's testimony above suspicion? The other witnesses were more objective—a Swedish missionary, the Reverend Sjöblom, two American missionaries, J. B. Murphy and William Morrison, and an English explorer, Edward Glave. All four claimed that administrative abuses were sickening and widespread. But why were these reports not corroborated by other missionaries? There were something like 240 Catholic and 220 Protestant missionaries scattered all over the Congo. Why did they keep silent? In any case, most of these charges were by now many years out of date.

Morel's conclusion was that if outrages had occurred, they must have been the work of African soldiers who got out of hand, and the stories were exaggerated. As for the central government officials, he had eaten and drunk with these cheery Belgians on the quays of Antwerp, and found it hard to imagine them having a hand in atrocities. If things had gone wrong, it must be due to ignorance and inexperience. Even British administrators would have had their work cut out dealing with savages like the Congolese.

But by 1900, Morel was prepared to eat his words. He had been duped by Leopold, after all.

While labouring over the desiccated statistics of the Free State, he suddenly stumbled on an amazing discovery. He saw what the humanitarians had never guessed—that the King had had the trade figures doctored. Morel compared the official figures with the Elder Dempster shipping returns and the sale of rubber by the Free State and its concessionary companies on the Antwerp market. The real figure for exports must be much higher than the figure given—and much higher than the figure for imports. (The so-called "trade" included quantities of European arms imported for the army of the State. Thousands of tons of tropical products, mainly rubber, were reaching Europe without any corresponding trade in exchange.) Clearly the Free State officials were not paying the natives to bring the rubber from the jungle, nor were the natives doing it for love. The officials must be using forced labour, beating and shooting the rubber out of them. This meant that, if anything, the humanitarians had underestimated the abuses. These were not haphazard, but *systematic.* In short, the King's philanthropy was founded on "legalized robbery enforced by violence". But who would ever believe this?

His discoveries left Morel "giddy and appalled". "It must be bad enough", he wrote later, "to stumble upon a murder. I had stumbled upon a secret society of murderers with a King for a croniman."[8] As soon as he could obtain a hearing, Morel went along to warn his chief, Alfred Jones. He found Jones curiously uninterested. It was absurd, Jones said, to imagine that the King would tolerate systematic abuse of the natives. Morel should remember that the Free State was one of Elder Dempster's best customers and had appointed Jones Honorary Consul at Liverpool. He told Morel to put his confidence in the King.

Morel found this impossible. His old colleagues at Elder Dempster now seemed to him to inhabit an "atmosphere of foul and filthy talk, of gross ideals and grosser methods".[9] He launched a series of expert articles in *The Speaker,* exposing the "Congo scandal". Then he decided to abandon ship at Elder Dempster, and take up his pen as a full-time writer on West Africa, before Jones threw him overboard.

Morel's articles in *The Speaker* during the summer of 1900, though anonymous, caught the eye of Dilke and Fox Bourne. Soon he was advising them on how to run their campaign. The Mansion House meeting of 15 May 1902, though not well attended, was their first joint project to arouse public opinion. It was not easy to proceed against the "royal megalomaniac", as Morel called Leopold, and strip the mask from him; Leopold was equally adept at threats and flattery. His was the "cleverest brain in Europe", and his arm had "a long reach",[10] Morel recognized with a shiver. They might never persuade the British missionaries in the Congo to end their craven silence.

Go for Mammon, was Morel's blunt advice to Dilke and Fox Bourne. For ten years they had been campaigning on too narrow a ground. They had appealed to the brotherhood of man, the good name of Britain, and the moral responsibility of Empire. It was the damage to British trade that would prod the imperialist public and stir Parliament to action. They had forgotten commercial self-interest. Commerce was, after all, the first of Livingstone's "3 Cs", and in the Congo economics were the crux of the matter. At a stroke Leopold had abolished not only the African's right to his own land but his right to trade with whom he pleased. He had also abolished the rights of free trade in the Congo, guaranteed to the international business community by the Berlin Act of 1885. In its place he had created an illegal monopoly for the State and its concessionary companies. The Congo Free State was robbing British merchants as well as African peasants.

At first Morel found that his argument had strangely little appeal for British businessmen. Some, like Alfred Jones, were dependent on a lucrative contract with the Congo; others did business with Belgians who were proud of the King's African work. Most British businessmen seemed more anxious to protect their existing markets than to expand them.

Then, in November 1901, a legal bombshell in the French colonial court at Libreville, capital of Gabon, and the administrative base for the French Congo, gave Morel the opportunity he needed to bully Mammon into joining his crusade.

The French Congo, despite the heady predictions of its founder, Brazza, had remained a fever-ridden backwater. It lacked most of the infrastructure needed for a viable colony, especially a railway to bypass the rapids and open up the interior. Brazza had tried to persuade Paris to assist. He had been recalled instead. Paris had been persuaded by some of Leopold's associates to adopt a much more profitable policy. Like Leopold's Congo State, the French Congo now gave concessions to private companies, and exploited the power (and guns) of the State to enforce a legal monopoly. It was the confirmation of the legality of this State monopoly, and the abolition of free trade, that constituted the legal bombshell at Libreville.

The spread of this economic plague—Leopold's monopolistic system—to the French Congo, and the eviction of British trading firms, rallied at least one large trader, John Holt, to Morel's side. Holt protested that he felt utterly unequal to the task. He loathed publicity and he loathed politics. But he was a genuine humanitarian, and Morel convinced him where his duty lay.

The first step, to fire British public opinion, by prodding the British press, proved successful. The Mansion House meeting the following May, even if ill attended, created a consensus among editors that something must be done about the Congo. Britain bore part of the responsibility for creating the Congo State at Berlin, based on free trade and philanthropy. Britain must now take the lead in persuading the Powers to institute reforms. This was the view of both imperial stalwarts, like the *Morning Post,* and Liberal free traders, like the *Daily News* and the *Manchester Guardian.* Already the press had been united by the failure of Belgium to end the anomaly by annexing the Congo in 1901, instead of allowing the option to lapse.

The second step, to persuade the Foreign Office to enforce both the free trade and the humanitarian provisions of the Berlin Act, was a flop. Vital to this plan were the business connections of John Holt, for he was Vice-President of the Liverpool Chamber of Commerce. Unfortunately, Alfred Jones, his rival, was the President. Holt and his supporters received sympathy and nothing else from the Foreign Office. Lord Lansdowne, Foreign Secretary since 1900, did not wish to advertise Britain's isolation in Europe and shrank from trying to involve France or Germany. The story of the Congo was lamentable, he was the first to admit, but even if it had been practical to reconvene the Powers who had signed the Berlin Act, it would re-open the whole question of the partition of Africa. He had already explained this to Dilke. It would not be "desirable in our own interests".[11]

So the reformers turned back to educating the British public. Again and again the terms of the equation were hammered home. Internal reform was impossible. State monopoly depended on a system of forced labour. This in turn made atrocities inevitable. If enough of the public grasped this equation, Parliament itself might force the hand of Lansdowne and the FO to enforce the Berlin Act. Early in 1903 Morel published *Affairs of West Africa,* with a chapter exposing the extortionate economics of the Congo. This was followed by Fox Bourne's *Civilisation in Congoland,* reworking the old revelations of the 1890s, including the story of Stokes's illegal hanging. Independently of the reformers, a British officer who had served with the Free State, Captain Guy Burrows, published *The Curse of Central Africa,* with lurid illustrations confirming the allegations that for some Belgian officials torture and murder were all in a day's work.

As press reviews of these sensational books generated further momentum for the campaign, the reformers organized public meetings and lobbied MPS to ask questions in the House. One firm obstacle remained: the failure to persuade the craven British missionaries to break silence. However, in April 1903, the Aborigines Protection Society was able to manoeuvre the Baptist Union into calling for a joint appeal to the Belgian government to institute an inquiry into the atrocities; and in May the American Presbyterian missionary, William Morrison, whose earlier revelations had been so influential, returned from the Congo with an updated report.

The King's answer was predictably underhand—and well-financed. Early in 1903 the Free State announced that Captain Guy Burrows would be sued in a British court for criminal libel against certain Free State officers. If Burrows were proved guilty, it would be a damaging blow for the reformers. Meanwhile, the allegations remained *sub judice.* At the same time the King, having lost the support of the Baptist Union, retained his hold over the other British Baptists by reducing their taxes in the Congo. A deputation from the Baptist Missionary Society was invited to meet the King in Brussels. They assured him how grateful they were for all his "wise efforts to instruct and elevate the conditions of the natives" in the Congo. Later they expressed "satisfaction" that the Burrows case would prove the real truth about the allegations against the Free State. By the end of March the affair had been turned into a propaganda coup for Leopold. Burrows failed to produce any witnesses from the Congo. The British judge assessed libel at £500 and ordered the book to be suppressed.

The King also launched a whispering campaign against Dilke. "The air was full of poisonous rumours," wrote Morel somewhat primly. "A public trial in which Sir Charles Dilke had formerly figured was revived."[12] And a Belgian official was sent to London to see what was Morel's price to call off the whole crusade.

This clumsy attempt to bribe him gave Morel some light relief in these harrowing weeks of the spring of 1903. The official, introduced by Alfred Jones, was politeness itself. He asked Morel if he expected to succeed against the power of His Majesty. "What did I stand to gain? My health would break down. I had done a great deal . . . Reforms would undoubtedly ensue. Serious reforms . . . I was a young man, I had a family—yes? I was running serious risks."[13] It was easy to tell this smiling Satan to get behind him, but harder to persuade the British public of the King's true character. Again and again, Morel met with the same baffled scepticism.

Then, on 20 May, the American missionary, William Morrison, gave grim details of atrocities to a meeting organized by the Aborigines Protection Society in London, including half a dozen MPS, and matters moved swiftly forward. A fortnight later the House of Commons debated the "evils" of the Congo for the first time since a motion had been proposed by Dilke in 1897. To Morel's delight and astonishment, the Commons accepted, without a division, the burden of the reformers' case. The government was now committed to conferring with the other Powers which had signed the General Act of Berlin "in order that measures may be adopted to abate the evils prevalent in that State".[14]

Lansdowne appeared to play for time. He was reluctant to have a row with Leopold and he still hoped to persuade him to abandon his dream of grabbing extra territory on the Nile beyond Lado. The FO announced that before Britain approached the other Powers about Congo abuses, the British Consul in the Congo Free State, Roger Casement, would be sent to make a full report.

* * *

Lord Lansdowne had good reason for his reluctance to be drawn into the crusade against Leopold in the summer of 1903—quite apart from the complications concerning Leopold's designs on the Nile. The FO itself had designs on Britain's other neighbour in Central Africa, France.

It was nearly three years since Lord Salisbury had been persuaded to promote Lansdowne from the War Office after winning the Khaki Election of 1900, and to hand him the glittering burden of the Foreign Office which he was too old to carry any longer himself. The promotion had raised many people's eyebrows. Lansdowne had proved feeble enough as War Minister. He had failed to prevent the war between the generals at the War Office which had crippled preparations to fight the Boers. He had failed to grasp that the Boers would prove a real enemy, able to exploit the power of modern weapons a good deal more successfully than the British.

Lansdowne's friends pointed to the reputation for prudence he had earned as a Viceroy, first in Canada and then in India. Despite his glamorous Whig background and armies of obsequious tenants spread over six counties of England and Scotland (with some less obsequious ones in Ireland), "Clan" Lansdowne was as diligent and serious-minded—and as unimaginative—as any civil servant in Whitehall.

As Foreign Secretary under Salisbury he had proved predictably modest. Now, in the summer of 1903, with the encouragement of the new Prime Minister, Arthur Balfour, he was contemplating the uncharacteristically radical step of ending Britain's isolation in Europe, which "splendid or otherwise" (in Rosebery's sarcastic phrase), had made Britain the Aunt Sally of Europe during the Boer War.

The FO's plan was for a *rapprochement* with France—for more, for an *entente cordiale,* a warm understanding. It would end, once and for all, those dangerous disputes about African territory which had bedevilled relations between the two countries ever since the British had taken Egypt in 1882. It would also help resolve the still more vital question of strategic defence. The British Admiralty were looking for a naval ally to help defend Britain and the Empire. France, Russia and Germany, in that order, were all pursuing Britain in a naval arms race. At first the hunt for an ally had been directed at Germany, leader of the Triple Alliance. But in August 1901 the Kaiser had mocked Britain's outstretched hand, offered by his uncle, Edward VII, the new King of England. In 1903 the royal hand was proffered again, this time to Paris—if the French were not too proud, after Fashoda, to grab it.

The chance came in mid-May, a week before the humanitarians' triumph in the Congo debate in the House of Commons. Edward VII made a state visit to Paris and delighted his hosts. The King was no diplomatist. (He had bungled his recent meeting with the Kaiser and by mistake handed over Lansdowne's private notes.) But he had always felt at home in France, putting money on French racehorses, tucking into gargantuan meals and losing his heart to French actresses. He captured Paris in his three-day state visit. The sour refrains of *"Vive Marchand!"* and *"Vive les Boers!"* changed to rapturous cries of *"Vive Edouard! Notre Bon Edouard!"*[15] When the state visit was returned by the French President in London in July, it was time for Lansdowne to get down to brass tacks with Delcassé. Would M. le Ministre be interested in a final settlement of the African account?

The bargaining began at the FO at 9.30 a.m. on 9 July. While President Loubet was preparing to review 15,000 troops at Aldershot, his Foreign Minister, Delcassé, the victim of Fashoda, was welcomed to Lansdowne's sumptuous room overlooking St James's Park. The two men grasped six colonial nettles, by far the most important of which were African nettles, Morocco and Egypt. The atmosphere was friendly. More surprisingly, progress was rapid. By lunchtime the two men had begun to discern the lines of a general settlement.

Apart from Ethiopia, Liberia, Tripoli and Cyrenaica, Morocco was the only independent African state to survive the Scramble. But the power of Abd-el-Haziz, the twenty-five-year-old Sultan of Morocco, was tottering. His downfall threatened the French colony of Algeria with trouble on its border—and also presented an interesting opportunity. "Give us a free hand in Morocco," said Delcassé. Lansdowne agreed, on condition that Britain was given a free hand in Egypt. At heart, the deal was as simple as that. The wrangling over the small print went on for months. By January 1904 there was stalemate. The British public would not tolerate a straight swap, Morocco for Egypt. After all, Egypt was already effectively a British protectorate, whereas the French still had to gain control of Morocco. Delcassé agreed; a straight swap would not work, but for the opposite reason. The English, he pointed out, had no formal share in the government of Morocco. In Egypt the French were partners in the Caisse and would be abandoning Napoleon's dream, sacred to every Frenchman. The answer was to throw in some French fishing rights off the coast of Newfoundland, and balance it with a border rectification in Nigeria. Delcassé resisted the temptation until the spring. By then a ferocious war, not in Africa but in the East, had threatened to involve Britain and France on opposite sides. If the *entente* was to be signed, it was now or never.

The war was between Russia, France's ally since 1892, and Japan, Britain's ally since 1901. At first it looked as though Japan, much the weaker (on paper) in ships and regiments, would ask Britain to send her own fleet to the rescue. But the Japanese army and navy were more competent, and the Russians less, than anyone had thought possible. The Japanese needed no allies. At the battle of Tsushima on 27 May 1905, the Japanese achieved the unthinkable against the unsinkable. The Russian navy, third most powerful in the world, was sent to the bottom and Manchuria snatched from the paws of the bear.

Hearing the approaching thunder over the eastern horizon, Britain and France kissed and made up, ending twenty years of squabbles in Africa. The *entente*—including a secret understanding to allow the French to take over most of Morocco—was signed on 8 April 1904. At the time it seemed a triumph of prudence, one of the few achievements of Balfour's government, now enfeebled by the resignation of Joe Chamberlain, who had in May 1903 split the Unionists by launching a campaign for tariff reform. After two years the *entente* with France led to an *entente* with Russia. Cromer at last got his free hand in Egypt and the Caisse was abolished.

But the FO had misunderstood the deal with France. The *entente* did not appear so friendly to Germany. It threatened her with encirclement. Delcassé had always grasped this. Indeed, it was one of the main attractions for Frenchmen who (following Gambetta's instructions) thought constantly of Armageddon, and the sacred pledge to liberate Alsace and Lorraine. The *entente* led smoothly down the slope to 1914.

* * *

It was on 4 June 1903, the year before the *entente* was signed, that the FO telegrams caught up with Roger Casement, the British Consul, staying with a missionary at Matadi, the rocky harbour connecting the navigable lower Congo with the new railway to Leopoldville. Casement found two of the telegrams in unintelligible code. But he had the cipher for the third, and it made his blood race. The FO commanded him (so he recorded in his diary) to "go to the interior" as soon as he could, to investigate Congo abuses. The Commons debate had proved a "terrible attack" on the Congo. Here was his chance. He would be Britain's special investigator—a public "avenger",[16] he called it. The next morning he started on the 200-mile train journey to Leopoldville.

Casement seemed somewhat innocent for a life in that seedy and brutal world hacked out by Bula Matari, the Breaker of Rocks. He was thirty-eight years old, with the arresting looks of a Spanish aristocrat—large poetic eyes contrasting with neatly-trimmed black beard. He wrote girlish poetry to express his feelings of alienation as an Irish Protestant from Northern Ireland, orphaned as a boy, and identifying with the oppressed Gaels. In the 1880s he had worked, like Morel, for the Elder Dempster Line, then knocked about the Congo, picking up jobs and going down with fever, giving Stanley a hand in 1884, enlisting with the Baptists, even taking ivory down to the coast on his own account. Sometimes he would disappear into the bush for weeks with only a stick for a weapon and only one Loanda and a couple of English bulldogs for company. In 1890, ten years before Conrad wrote *The Heart of Darkness,* he spent an instructive year in the Congo, and a fortnight with Casement was one of its pleasant features. Conrad found him "most intelligent and very sympathetic", with a "touch of the conquistadore" in him—and mysterious, too. "He could tell you things!" he wrote of Casement (as though as he were speaking of Marlow, the narrator of *The Heart of Darkness,* who was searching for a moral centre in Africa). "Things I have tried to forget, things I never did know."[17] But would Casement ever find the moral centre, in his own muddled search?

Casement was a slave to conflicting emotions and appetites. He was an ardent Irish nationalist yearning for social recognition in England; a hermit, thirsty for exotic pleasures, including the taste (recorded in his diary) for handsome sailors and muscular young Africans; a dispassionate investigator, hungry for the punishment of injustice.

Now, in 1903, after eleven years as a member of HM Consular Service in various foetid, fever-ridden African ports, Casement found these wild emotions converging as he took over the investigation of "the evils prevalent" in the Congo.

The main symptom, visible even in the lower Congo, was the growing depopulation of the country. Disease, especially sleeping sickness, was one of the causes. The other, he felt sure, was the system of forced labour imposed by the Free State. But he needed to get evidence that would stand up in the court of world opinion. He had already won the confidence of many individual missionaries, including members of the Baptist Missionary Society, whose committee in London was too frightened to co-operate with Morel. The missionaries knew the people and were the only independent witnesses of what they suffered; but they risked reprisals from the Congo government.

Fortunately, news of the debate in the British House of Commons in June 1903 followed him to the Congo and gave British subjects a new courage. Casement was determined to avoid being stifled by official channels. The American Baptists let him hire a small steam launch, the *Henry Reed,* and he stocked it with supplies—sugar, soup, custard and several cases of carrots. Under his own steam, he ascended 160 miles above Leopoldville and reached the edge of the rainforest, where the rubber zone began.

At Bolobo, a mission station which had once numbered 40,000 souls, Casement was told the population was now reduced to 1,000. There were reports of troops raiding villages nearby, to punish them for failing to pay the "food tax"—in other words, to do forced labour to provide food for the State. At Impoko he met witnesses to atrocities. A BMS missionary, Scrivener, took him to meet some Basingili men forced to work as blacksmiths who said they were refugees from persecution by State officials. Casement was shocked. At first, he would hardly credit the refugees' account of the way rubber was collected in the *Domaine de la Couronne,* a concessionary area under Leopold's direct control 100 miles to the south. When he asked why they had abandoned their homes, and all they possessed, to work like slaves with a neighbouring tribe, the men and their womenfolk shouted back: on account of the "rubber tax" levied by the government.

"How does the government impose the "tax"?"

"From our country each village had to take 20 loads of rubber. These loads were big; they were nearly as big as this . . . [He produced an empty basket which came nearly up to the handle of Casement's walking stick.] We had to take these loads in 4 times a month."

"How much pay do you get for this?"

[The entire audience]: "We got no pay. We got nothing . . . Our village got cloth and a little salt, but not the people who did the work . . . It used to take 10 days to get the 20 baskets of rubber—we were always in the forest to find the rubber vines, to go without food, and our women had to give up cultivating the fields and gardens. Then we starved. Wild beasts—the leopards—killed some of us while we were working away in the forest and others got lost or died from exposure or starvation and we begged the white men to leave us alone, saying we could get no more rubber, but the white men and their soldiers said: Go. You are only beasts yourselves. You are only Nyama [meat]. We tried, always going further into the forest, and when we failed and our rubber was short, the soldiers came to our towns and killed us. Many were shot, some had their ears cut off; others were tied up with ropes around their necks and bodies and taken away. The white men at the posts sometimes did not know of the bad things the soldiers did to us, but it was the white men who sent the soldiers to punish us for not bringing in enough rubber."

Another native took up the story:

"We said to the white man: "We are not enough people now to do what you want of us. Our country has not many people in it and the people are dying fast. We are killed by the work you make us do, by the stoppage of our plantations and the breaking up of our homes." The white man looked at us and said: "There are lots of white men in Mputu [Europe] . . . there must be a way, there must be many in the black man's country.""

An old man who lived nearby told Casement:

"We used to hunt elephants long ago and there were plenty in our forests, and we got much meat; but Bula Matari [the Congo State] killed the elephant hunters because they could not get rubber, and so we starved. We are sent out to get rubber, and when we come back with little rubber we are shot."

"Who shot you?"

"The white men sent their soldiers out to kill us."

"How do you know it was the white men sent the soldiers? It might only be the savage soldiers themselves?"

"No, no, sometimes we brought rubber into the white men's stations . . . when it was not enough the white men would put some of us in lines, one behind the other, and would shoot through all our bodies. Sometimes he would shoot us like that with his own hand; sometimes his soldiers would do it."[18]

Casement said he could hardly believe these tales told at Impoko, but later they were confirmed by one of the English missionaries, who visited the villages where the atrocities had occurred. Meanwhile, Casement steamed on upriver in the *Henry Reed*. At Lukokela he was taken by the local English missionary, the Reverend J. Whitehead, to meet more Basingili refugees. They had the same harrowing tale. "Poor frail folk seeking vexed mortality," Casement wrote poetically in his diary—incongruously close to a note about a temptingly well-endowed African boy. ("July 13. At State Beach photoed pier and Loanaga—about 9".")[19]

But the official dossier he kept was grim enough. Wherever he pulled in to the riverbank, the natives would flee in terror of "Bula Matari". Then, after the missionaries had reassured them, Casement was treated to stories of atrocities: children running into the bush as their mothers and sisters were shot down by the soldiers, and then perhaps eaten by cannibals; hundreds of families butchered, or burnt in their homes; village after village burnt and looted, the men taken off as slaves, the women and children hacked to death.

Most gruesome were the tales of severed hands. Soldiers collected them by the basketload, hacking them off their victims, dead or alive, to prove they had not wasted ammunition. One of the State officials admitted to Casement that this had been done "in the awful past". He claimed it no longer occurred. But the missionaries brought him much evidence to the contrary, and the natives assured him that the reign of terror continued.

As the *Henry Reed* steamed on into the sticky, claustrophobic heart of the rubber districts, Casement's official reports to the Foreign Office changed tone. At first it was the desolation that had shocked him. His tone was indignant but judicial:

In the lake district things were pretty bad . . . whole villages and districts I knew well and visited as flourishing communities in 1887 are today without a human being; others are reduced to a handful of sick or harassed creatures who say of the government: "Are the white men never going home; is this to last forever?"[20]

But by September the thought of the atrocities filled him with rage. On 6 September he was taken to see a boy of about sixteen, Epondo, whose right hand had been severed at the wrist—apparently by a soldier. Casement had seen enough. He set off for Stanley Pool and the coast, determined to return to London by the first boat. He must not lose control of himself. "Of all the shameful and infamous expedients", he wrote to the Foreign Office, "whereby man has preyed upon man . . . this vile thing [the rubber trade] dares to call itself commerce . . . ."[21]

The *Ambrose* landed him at Liverpool at 10:00 p.m. on 30 November, and he travelled that night by train to London. By 12 December, his eighty-four-page report exposing the evils of Leopold's government was typed, ready for what he called "the gang of stupidities" and "pifflers"[22] at the Foreign Office.

* * *

The Foreign Office officials found Casement's report surprisingly judicious. It detailed the abuses, but was terse and understated. Lansdowne congratulated him. It was "proof of the most painfully convincing kind".[23] But would the government find it politic to publish it? Already Leopold's lobby, led by Alfred Jones, was protesting at the damage it would do to British commercial interests.

Two days before finishing the report, Casement had at last made the acquaintance of Edmond Morel, the leader of the reformers. They met in a house in Chester Square lent by a friend. The meeting of these two outsiders proved a revelation to each of them. Casement found Morel "honest as the day".[24] Morel never forgot the impression of Casement's "long, lean, swarthy Van Dyck type of face, graven with power and . . . great gentleness". For hours Casement talked away in his soft, musical voice, telling "the story of a vile conspiracy against civilization, the difficulties he had had to overcome, the traps laid for him . . .". As the "monologue of horror" proceeded, Morel felt he could see those "hunted women clutching their children and flying panic-stricken to the bush; the blood flowing from those quivering black bodies as the hippopotamus-hide whip struck again and again; the savage soldiers rushing hither and thither, burning villages; the ghastly tally of severed hands".[25]

By February 1904 things looked hopeful for the reformers. At last one section of the British Baptists would back them openly: the Congo Bolobo Mission (though not the Baptist Missionary Society) threw its weight behind the movement. At the same time, Casement persuaded Morel that the campaign could not be left to Fox Bourne and Dilke. Morel—"Bulldog" Morel, Casement called him—must lead it himself. Morel duly founded the Congo Reform Association, backed by the money of Liverpool traders like John Holt.

In the same month Lansdowne decided to overrule the protests of Leopold's lobby and publish Casement's report—after judiciously removing most of the proper names. Casement was furious. Without the names of witnesses, his report would go off like a damp squib. In fact it made a deafening bang in the British press, a bang that was universally welcomed. Not since Stanley's day had the Congo captured such headlines. Morel was exultant. Casement—"Tiger" Casement, Morel called him—was every man's hero.

But at first Morel's dependence on Holt and the Liverpool traders seemed to have delivered him straight into the King's hands. Backed by his outraged Belgian subjects, Leopold planned his counterattack: a knee in Morel's and Casement's stomachs.

Neither France nor Germany had the slightest interest in convening a new conference on the Congo. France had sound economic reasons to be happy with the present arrangement; rubber gathering by concessionary companies using forced labour—the system borrowed from Leopold— was beginning to pay dividends in the French Congo. Germany maintained Bismarck's old policy of backing Leopold for fear he would hand over the Congo to France.

Anyway, Germany had more pressing troubles of her own in Africa. In January that year, 1904, there were reports of a great Herero revolt in southwest Africa which soon threatened to sweep the isolated German garrisons into the sea.

APPENDIX O
Photo of Barbara Mary Mill c. 1955

APPENDIX P

Photos of Guy Hospital: entrance and statue

GUY'S HOSPITAL—MAIN ENTRANCE

THOMAS GUY, FOUNDER OF GUY'S HOSPITAL
(Statue in the Quadrangle)

APPENDIX Q
"The Bard" letter

The Bard
By the Rev. A. G. MILL, Yakusu

As is well-known, the natives of Congo had no written language before the advent of the missionaries, but they sang their history every day in canoe songs and dance songs. A new era has arrived, and we want them now to write the history of the coming of the Gospel to their own land. Here is one of the first men to do it, and it was a very hard task to him. He would much rather have sung and danced over the exciting and wonderful parts of it than he would have sat down and written it as he has. This is more or less literally what he wrote to me in the native language:

HERE is the affair of the beginning of the work of God in Yalikina. It was long ago, when I was about fifteen, that I saw the white men, Grenfell and Stapleton, and the black woman Salamo, the mother of Neli, come in on the *Goodwill* to the beach of Yalikina, but that time they did not tell us about their work. Again they came, on the *Peace,* and looked at the bit of land where the B.M.S. now stands, before we knew that God's news was coming there. Once again they came, and the black engineer, Baluti Dawidi, called us children, and taught us to sing a hymn, showed us a picture, and preached to us about God, and taught us to read the signs i.u. and s.m. Then he went to Yakusu. We then had a visit for a few days from Botowafini and Waisangi, native teachers from the villages of Yangambi and Yaekela, who taught us some hymns and letters and then left before we knew enough.

Then after some months we saw the black engineer, Baluti Dawidi, and Kilongosi, the black teacher, arrive, who gathered us together and preached from a picture, and we heard a little. Up till then we had only heard by those who visited us, but the White men of Yakusu asked our Chief Bonjuma a few months later if we would have a teacher. All the village and the chief especially agreed heartily, then the B.M.S. teacher Bosa Mose was sent to us. We liked him very much, and so did the chief, but I don't know the date when he started, because at that time we were still blind.

"ABRAHAM." THE SON OF A CANNIBAL, he is now a shepherd of souls

Those who went to school were the generation following the patriarchs, and our uncles and our big brothers and our little brothers and we built the house of God immediately, and finished it quickly, and we had a big school of young men and young women who believe in it. Then we sang hymns, and read the laws about the things which God had forbidden His people to do, and we obeyed them carefully.

After Bosa Moses had been with us a long time, and his preaching had entered into our hearts, an elder called Lingomu and some others entered the enquirers' class. Mr. Millman came and approved of our work. Soon after the elder and two others were baptized, and since then many have passed through the school and many have been baptized.

Even before they were baptized some started to open a road into the forest tribe of the Esoos, to teach them, and in 1909 and 1914 and 1915 and 1916 we sent teachers there. These teachers have done a great work in teaching people the deeds of Jesus. They taught their scholars reading and writing and arithmetic, and praying and preaching, and many of the Kombe (nearer) district were baptized. They in their turn went to the Bondi and Wilo districts beyond. Thus because of Yalikina the word of God has spread in the Esoo tribe, and was like the seed of Abraham. Those of Yalikina begat Kombe, Kombe begat Bondi and Wilo, and Bondi and Wilo begat Yaoleo (the furthest district) and Yaoleo has begotten even others.

I am one of those who was taught by Bosa Moses, and was baptized 15/12/1907. Then on 15/6/1915, I went to work in the garden of God in a very thick place of the Esoo forest.

APPENDIX R

Historic letter from George Grenfell–1905

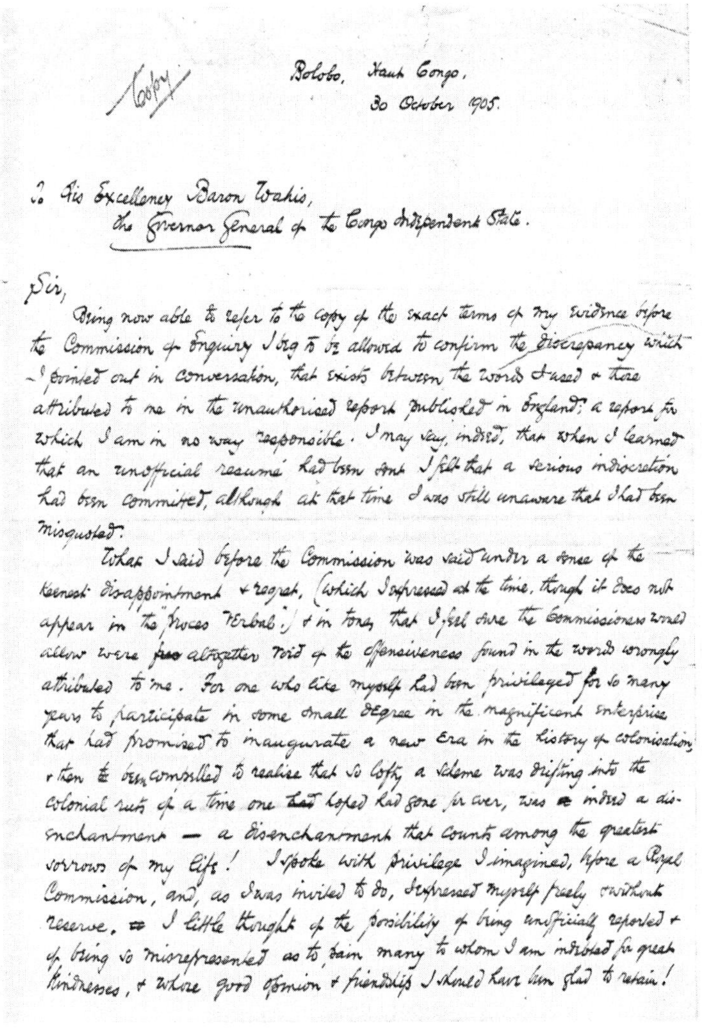

Copy

Bolobo, Haut Congo,
30 October 1905.

To His Excellency Baron Wahis,
the Governor General of the Congo Independent State.

Sir,

Being now able to refer to the copy of the exact terms of my evidence before the Commission of Enquiry I beg to be allowed to confirm the discrepancy which I pointed out in conversation, that exists between the words I used & those attributed to me in the unauthorised report published in England; a report for which I am in no way responsible. I may say, indeed, that when I learned that an unofficial resumé had been sent I felt that a serious indiscretion had been committed, although at that time I was still unaware that I had been misquoted.

What I said before the Commission was said under a sense of the keenest disappointment & regret, (which I expressed at the time, though it does not appear in the "Proces Verbal",) & in tones that I feel sure the Commissioners would allow were ~~free~~ altogether void of the offensiveness found in the words wrongly attributed to me. For one who like myself had been privileged for so many years to participate in some small degree in the magnificent enterprise that had promised to inaugurate a new Era in the history of colonisation, & then ~~to~~ been compelled to realise that so lofty a scheme was drifting into the colonial ruts of a time one ~~had~~ hoped had gone for ever, was ~~a~~ indeed a dis-enchantment — a disenchantment that counts among the greatest sorrows of my life! I spoke with privilege I imagined, before a Royal Commission, and, as I was invited to do, I expressed myself freely & without reserve, ~~&~~ I little thought of the possibility of being unofficially reported & of being so misrepresented as to pain many to whom I am indebted for great kindnesses, & whose good opinion & friendship I should have been glad to retain!

Under the circumstances I am exceedingly sorry I ventured to express myself at all on so delicate a matter as the decorations — it would have been far better had I continued to keep my own counsel as you said.

I would further beg to be allowed to say that the newspaper paragraphs of two months ago to the effect of my having authorised a missionary colleague to make statements on this topic on my behalf are not correct, & can only result from a mistake on the part of the newspaper reporter or of Mr Harris himself. In parting with Mr Harris on his way to England I assured him he had my sympathy in his attempts to make known the truth about the Congo, & I authorised him to say as much, but I certainly gave him no permission to go beyond this general expression. This voicing of my sympathy is my first public departure from the policy of non-intervention in the work of Congo reform, a policy which I have followed together with the Committee of our Society, in the belief that the Administration would, in due course, learn the truth, & that the needful reforms would as surely follow. I fear, however, (& I submit this with all respect,) that Your Excellency has not been informed as to the seriousness of the position, &, that Brussels is equally, if not more completely, in the dark; therefore, in urging that the truth should be made known I feel I am trying to serve the highest interests of the Colony, & of Belgium the mother country.

Assuring Your Excellency of the sincerity of my good wishes for the well being & prosperity of the Congo State, & of my desire that it should cast undimmed lustre upon the page of Belgian colonial history,

I have the honour to be,

Sir,

Your Excellency's my obedient,
humble servant,

George Grenfell.

Letter to Rev. Wilson, June 6, 1912

148 Stockwell Pk Rd
Brixton
London S.W.
19/12/10

Rev. C. E. Wilson B.A.

Dear Mr Wilson,

I have received a certificate of medical fitness from Dr Moorhead on condition that the deficiencies of my teeth be made up by a set of plates and that I be re-vaccinated. As soon as I am able to have these things attended to I will fill up and return form E. which has been sent me.

I am sorry to see however that he recommends my sphere of work to be India rather than Congo.

In view of the absence of constitutional disorder which I was led to believe was indicated at my examination I cannot see what serious barrier there may be to my going to Congo. I do trust this is not final. I should like to have a talk over the matter, with yourself with whom, I suppose, the decision rests. The possession of better health and the other advantages of India would not, in my opinion, make up for the loss of a life's aim and the opportunity of helping to reach the hitherto unreached tribes of Central Africa. Even if it meant the slight curtailment of the years of service I might hope to have I think I could do more for the Kingdom there, than during a longer period under Indian conditions. Concerning the matter of finances at Livingstone Coll. I have now received a promise from our

Principal that £25 could be paid by the Pastors Coll
toward the £50 required for the 6 months course
beginning on 9th Jan 1911. If you are now able
to confirm your kind offer to find the remainder of
this sum for me, I shall be glad to receive your
instructions and to make my application.

Regarding the matter of my sphere of work I
pray that guidance may be given and also light to
see the guidance and courage to follow it.

Yours sincerely
A. G. Mill

FINAL REPORT TO COMMITTEE ON CANDIDATE.

BAPTIST MISSIONARY SOCIETY,

19, FURNIVAL STREET, HOLBORN,

LONDON, E.C.

Dec. 16. 1900

MEDICAL DEPARTMENT.

Re Mr A G. Mill. Candidate for Congo.

This Candidate has been Carefully Examined by
D. Habershon who holds that no Candidate should
be accepted for the Congo who possesses any
flaw or weak point. Following out that doctrine
D. Habershon considers that the fact that Mr.
Mr Mill having had a nervous breakdown of a
few Months duration due to overwork in his
first College year is a flaw in his Case. Further
Mr Mill possesses a flat & sallow chest which
is always associated with diminution of resisting
power. The Medical opinion is therefore in favour
of sending Mr Mill to India, rather than to Congo.
Distinctly less athletic.

(Signed) H. Fletcher Moorshead
Medical Officer, B.M.S.

Date _____

FINAL REPORT TO COMMITTEE ON CANDIDATE.

BAPTIST MISSIONARY SOCIETY,

19, FURNIVAL STREET, HOLBORN,

LONDON, E.C.

July 3, 1911

MEDICAL DEPARTMENT.

Re Mr. A. G. Mill. Candidate for Congo

The Consulting Physician after a previous Examination endorses, without hesitancy, Mr. Mill's acceptance for Congo. He has decidedly improved in health during the past 6 months.

(Signed) R. Fletcher Moorshead

Medical Officer, B.M.S.

Date_____

APPENDIX S

Government registration card of Rev. A. G. Mill, 1919

APPENDIX T

Government registration card of
Rev. A. G. Mill, 1924

CONGO BELGE — BELGISCH-CONGO

Bureau d'immatriculation de — Inschrijvingsbureel van
Goma

INSCRIPTION AUX REGISTRES D'IMMATRICULATION
Inschrijving op het stamboek

Volume } Folio } N° _1464_
Deel } Folio } N°

Nom et prénoms du porteur : _Mill Alexander George_
Naam en voornamen van den drager :
Profession : _Missionaire_
Beroep :
Lieu de naissance : _Glasgow Ecosse_
Geboorteplaats :
Date de naissance : _20 Juillet 1885_
Geboorte datuum :
État-civil, (célibataire, marié, veuf, divorcé) : _Marié_
Burgerlijke stand, (ongehuwd, gehuwd, weduwenaar, gescheiden) :
Prénoms du père (en vie ou décédé) : _Frederick Décédé_
Voornamen van den vader (in leven of overleden) :
Nom et prénoms de la mère (en vie ou décédée) : _Goudie, Catherine Décédé_
Naam en voornamen van moeder (in leven of overleden) :
Nom de famille et prénoms du conjoint (même en cas de prédécès ou de divorce) : _Starte Ethel Ellen_
Naam en voornamen van den echtgenoot (zelfs in geval van voor-overlijden of van echtscheiding) :

Domicile : _Yakusu — Dis de Stanleyville_
Woonplaats :
Nationalité : _Britanique_
Nationaliteit :
Durée des séjours antérieurs au Congo Belge : _Un de 2 ans Deus de 4 ans._
Duur van de vroegere verblijven in Belgisch Congo :

Sceau du bureau qui délivre ce carnet
Zegel van het kantoor dat dit boekje aflevert

Date _29 Juin 1924_
Dagteeken

Signature de l'agent qui délivre le présent récépissé
Handteeken van den beambte afgevaardig ...

Résidences successives / Opeenvolgende woonplaatsen	Date de la déclaration / Dagteekening der verklaring	Inscription aux registres / Inschrijving op de registers			Signature de l'agent préposé à la tenue des registres / Handteeken van den beambte met het houden der registers belast
		Volume Deel	Folio	N° N°	
Yaonga	_14 Août 1924_	I	9	161	_Vuaubann_

397

APPENDIX U
THE CHRISTIAN COMMONWEALTH

ADVENTURES IN MUSIC FOR AFRICAN WORSHIP
By EPHRAIM AMU

I was born in West Africa, the son of a Christian father and mother who became Christians at their middle age. When I became a teacher in the Presbyterian Church of the Gold Coast and began to take a keen interest in the life of the Christians amongst whom I worked, I found that most of the illiterate Christians, who as pagans sang so lustily and happily, were almost silent in Christian worship. I determined to help them and began by regularly teaching them hymns on Sunday afternoons, but this was not much of a success.

When I came to try to discover why this should be I found that it was because the mode of singing taught by missionaries did not accord with the traditional African ways. I felt that what they needed was something purely African. In my spare time I went out into the villages to learn a number of songs from some outstanding pagan singers and wrote them down in tonic sol-fa notation. I carefully studied the poetry of the words and the rhythm of the music, and accordingly began to write simple songs with Christian words and taught them to the young people at the school in which I was teaching, as well as a band of Christian adults.

This so scandalized some of the elders of the Church that they took steps to suppress it. After unsuccessfully trying to make them understand my point of view, I was practically thrust out from the Church. They were scandalized because in their own minds these songs sounded very much like the pagan airs they claimed were wedded to obscene or pagan words.

The Achimota College, which had previously shown great interest in African music, took me on to its staff, and after a few years sent me to England to study Western music to enable me more fully to apply myself to the problem of the adaptation of African music to Christian worship along lines natural to the African himself.

In this article I shall discuss African songs in the Church according to the conclusions I have so far reached.

* * * *

When Christianity was introduced into Africa. European hymns were translated into a number of African languages and taught to the Christians. The first few Christians were all illiterate adults, and we have no idea what their hymn singing sounded like. But if we would get together a dozen Europeans picked at random and teach them to sing a typical African song carefully translated into English, French or German, I am certain the effect, as compared with genuine African singing, would give us some idea of what hymn singing by the early African Christians was like.

We might ask why did the Missionaries take this course? There appear to be two possible reasons, namely, first, that because of insufficient insight, African airs appeared to the Missionaries as unsuitable for Christian purposes; and, second, that the difference between African music and European music is so great that the study of African music, which is still no easy task for the professional European musician, was an almost impossible task for the Missionaries.

The following are some of the describable differences between African singing and European singing:

I. Time in music may either be duple or triple (quadruple time is only a form of duple time). Whereas a European song may have either one or the other of these two effects, an African song as a rule has these two effects alternating each other all through. The basic rhythm of African music is therefore a regular alternation of duple and triple effect. The bar of triple effect is of the same duration as that of duple effect.

II. Speech intonation is very closely observed in singing, e.g., *spoken:* Máwué náa mè, Máwúe teàa, mè àmè déké mé vlêè ò.
Sung:—
d¹ d¹ d¹ l t t s s
Mawue naa me Mawue teaa 'me
s s l l l s s
ame deke me vlee o

Any disregard of speech intonation is in the majority of cases likely to make the words suggest an entirely different meaning from what they were originally meant to convey.

No wonder, therefore, that the pupils of a mission school somewhere in East Africa could not help laughing in the middle of a hymn they were taught to sing in their own language just because the melody, disregarding

EPHRAIM AMU

actual speech intonation, made the words of a line to mean "Throw mud at God" instead of "Glory be to God."

III. (1) As a rule the words of one verse of a European hymn are entirely different from those of the other verses of the same hymn. This makes it extremely difficult to memorize any appreciable number of hymns, with the result that (a) in the schools a good deal of time is spent over memorizing hymns most of which are only to be forgotten later in life; (b) the use of hymn books has become a necessity, a fact which forbids the illiterate Christian (of which there are so many in Africa) to join in hymn singing at worship. Thus the illiterate convert who in his pagan days used to take hearty part in community singing is being penalized. It is worth remembering that the peoples all over Africa have hundreds and hundreds of "living" songs, none of which is written down, but are all sung from memory. But, we might ask, why cannot the African memorize the European hymns translated into his own language just as he does his own African songs? The answer to this question takes us to:

(2) The most important form of singing that obtains in Africa, namely, "solo and chorus" form. The soloist announces a song by singing it through whilst the chorus listen, quickly study the words and sort out for themselves (a) the soloist's part and (b) the main theme or the response which is the part of the chorus. The soloist then begins by singing his part and the chorus join by singing the response. The musical example on this page shows the "solo and chorus" form as follows:

Solo announcement: Mawue naa me, Mawue tea me, ame deke **meviê o.**
[God gives to man, God withholds from man, no man can acquire by physical force.]

Solo: (1) Agble nyo nyo be dede.

Chorus: Mawue naa me Mawue teea 'me ame deke mevlêe o.

[Prosperous farm. God gives to man, God withholds from man, no man can acquire by physical force.]

Solo: (2) Enuku nyo be xaxa.

Chorus: Mawue naa me, etc.

[Plenteous harvest. God gives to man, etc.]

Solo: (3) Asi nyonyo be dede.

Chorus: Mawue naa me, etc.

[The right wife. God gives to man, etc.]

The section marked A A in the music is that in which the soloist's improvisation comes in in this song. The melodic outline of each improvisation differs a little according as suggested by speech intonations of the words. Any intelligent singer who has a strong voice may, in course of community singing, assist the soloist by effectively improvising his own words. The soloist does not usually join the chorus in singing the response, this is all the time at his disposal to think out fresh words. It will be noticed in the music that the soloist begins a new verse just as the chorus are finishing their response, thereby making the two parts overlap. Any new song is learned by the method just described. The two necessary conditions which this form of singing demands are reasonable brevity and simplicity. Length and complexity are to be sought not in the form of singing but in rhythm. Brevity and simplicity make singing a real enjoyment and make individual self-expression not only possible but desirable.

IV. Singing in parts is natural with Africans, and whenever two or more persons sing together they will sing in parts. Singing in parts, therefore, is more the rule than exception. In the main it is two-part singing, the parts moving in parallel thirds intercepted here and there by a fourth or fifth (often parallel fourths and fifths). The interception of fourths and fifths is governed by the trend of the melody and words and comes spontaneously.

So much for the describable differences. What is indescribable is the spirit in which singers sing and the spontaneity of self-expression, both of which make for the ultimate effect of African singing. In view of the differences referred to, European hymn singing is to the African, be he literate or illiterate, rather dull. Dull because of its rhythm, dull because of the difficulty of memorizing the words, dull because certain conditions are incompatible with spontaneity.

* * * *

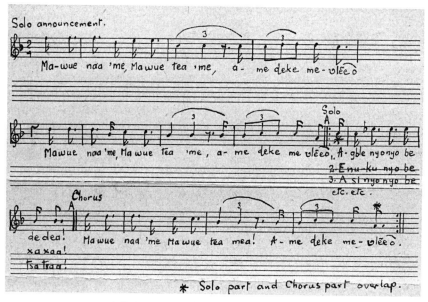

* Solo part and Chorus part overlap.

What then is to be done about hymn singing in Africa? To say that European hymn singing should be abandoned is to be unreasonable. Africans have learned not only to sing but to enjoy European hymns in spite of their dullness. There is no other occasion in England which gives me a greater inward joy and a stronger feeling of the brotherhood of man than a missionary meeting at which I join a crowd of Christian men and women in singing popular missionary hymns.

However, if music is to be made to play in the life of African Christians the part it plays in the life of Africans in general, then singing of African songs should be encouraged in the Church. There are some practical difficulties that cannot be overlooked. The literate Africans, for instance, have developed a strong liking for four-part singing and would not give it up, and in fact there is no need for giving it up. But how can African songs be harmonized in more than two parts without hybridizing? Whilst it is not easy to escape hybridizing, it is not impossible to steer clear of it. The right course to take in further development of African music requires a very careful study by those Africans who are specially interested in their country's music. It is a matter of experimenting in different ways. However, this much can be said: That there doesn't seem to be the need for inventing a different musical notation from the current Western musical notation; that the study of the principles of Western music is as absolute a necessity as is the careful study of African music; the right use of the principles of Western music in developing African music lies not in adoption but "adaptation"; and lastly, but most important of all, that in developing African music every effort should be made to retain its characteristic brevity and simplicity, both of which make for spontaneity of self-expression. This last point cannot be over-emphasized. For what would singing in Christian worship be worth if it is not the free outburst of the contents of our hearts before God?

APPENDIX V

Baptist Missionary Society,

Congo Secretariat.

Adresse Télégraphique:
ASIATIC, Kinshasa

B. M. S.

KINSHASA,

CONGO BELGE,

WEST CENTRAL AFRICA,

No. 211 PS.

————October 5, 1921.——— 19

Reply to

Object   To His Excellency
           The Governor General,
           B O M A.

Sir,

We understand that the sentence of death has been
passed on the so called "prophet" Simon Kimbangu.

We would humbly beg Your Excellency to consider
the possibility of an exercise of the clemency of His Majesty
King Albert on behalf of the condemned man, that the death
sentence may be changed for some other punishment.

With every expression of respect, and of confidence in your judgement,

We have the honour to be,

Sir,

Your Excellency's most obedient servants,

H. Ross-Phillips.

Représentant Légal de la Baptist
Missionary Society Corporation.

Joseph Clarke

Représentant Légal de la American
Baptist Foreign Mission Society.

APPENDIX W

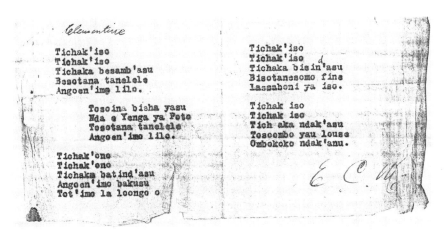

AUNT ETHEL WAS NOT GIVEN TO MUCH HILARITY, BUT DID HAVE A
HEALTHY SENSE OF HUMOR.
THIS IS HER AFRICAN ADAPTION OF THE TUNE "CLEMENTINE"